HISTORY BEGINS AT SUMER

SAMUEL NOAH KRAMER

CLARK RESEARCH PROFESSOR EMERITUS OF ASSYRIOLOGY
CURATOR EMERITUS OF THE TABLET COLLECTIONS
THE UNIVERSITY MUSEUM, UNIVERSITY OF PENNSYLVANIA

History Begins at Sumer

THIRTY-NINE FIRSTS IN MAN'S RECORDED HISTORY

Samuel Noah Kramer

upp

THE UNIVERSITY OF PENNSYLVANIA PRESS
PHILADELPHIA

HISTORY BEGINS AT SUMER
The Third Revised Edition

Cover photo: LYRE FROM UR (Courtesy of the University Museum, University of Pennsylvania).

Kramer, Samuel Noah, 1897-
  History begins at Sumer.
  Originally published under title: From the tablets of Sumer: Indian Hills, Colo. : Falcon's Wing Press, 1956.
  1. Sumerians. I. Title
DS72.K7   1981   935'.01   81-51144
ISBN 0-8122-7812-7 cloth   AACR2
ISBN 0-8122-1276-2 (pbk)

Printed in the United States of America

Preface to the Third Revised Edition

HISTORY BEGINS AT SUMER (Doubleday, Anchor Book) was published in 1959, more than twenty years ago. In the intervening decades a considerable number of new books, monographs, and articles relating to the Sumerians and their literature have been published by numerous cuneiformists the world over; the interested reader will find them itemized and listed in the annual bibliographies of the two scholarly journals: *Orientalia* (Rome) and *Archiv für Orientforschung* (Graz). A series of important contributions to Sumerian literary research have been made in more recent years by a group of younger scholars who, after years of study, completed their dissertations at various universities and especially at the University of Pennsylvania and its University Museum —these dissertations, consisting primarily of definitive editions of one or another of the Sumerian literary works, have proved to be basic and fundamental to Sumerological research.

Nor has this writer remained idle throughout these years. Between the years 1959-1980 I have published either alone, or jointly with other cuneiformists, more than sixty items relating to the Sumerians and their literature. Among these are twelve books ranging in content from specialized textual compendia to broad tentative syntheses. In the course of preparing these studies quite a number of significant new "Firsts" in man's recorded history came to light and I have selected twelve of the more important and timely of these for this third revised edition of *History Begins at Sumer*. I have also reexamined the twenty-seven "Firsts" in the first edition of the book in the light of the more significant and reliable investigations now available and the resulting *corrigenda* and *addenda* will be found at the end of this volume, together with a Glossary of names, epithets and other pertinent Sumerian words.

December 16, 1980   SAMUEL NOAH KRAMER

Preface to the First Edition

For the past twenty-six years I have been active in Sumerological research, particularly in the field of Sumerian literature. The ensuing studies have appeared primarily in the form of highly specialized books, monographs, and articles scattered in a number of scholarly journals. The present book brings together—for the layman, humanist, and scholar—some of the significant results embodied in those Sumerological researches and publications.

The book consists of twenty-five essays strung on a common thread: they all treat of "firsts" in man's recorded history. They are thus of no little significance for the history of ideas and the study of cultural origins. But this is only secondary and accidental, a by-product, as it were, of all Sumerological research. The main purpose of the essays is to present a cross section of the spiritual and cultural achievements of one of man's earliest and most creative civilizations. All the major fields of human endeavor are represented: government and politics, education and literature, philosophy and ethics, law and justice, even agriculture and medicine. The available evidence is sketched in what, it is hoped, is clear and unambiguous language. Above all, the ancient documents themselves are put before the reader either in full or in the form of essential excerpts, so that he can sample their mood and flavor as well as follow the main threads of the argument.

The greater part of the material gathered in this volume is seasoned with my "blood, toil, tears, and sweat"; hence the rather personal note throughout its pages. The text of most of the documents was first pieced together and translated by me, and in not a few cases I actually identified the tablets on which they are based and even prepared the hand copies of their inscriptions.

Sumerology, however, is but a branch of cuneiform studies, and these began more than a century ago. In the course of these years, scores of scholars have made innumerable contributions which the present-day cuneiformist utilizes and builds on, consciously and unconsciously. Most of these scholars are now long dead, and today's Sumerologist can do not more than bow his head in simple gratitude as he uses the results of his unnamed predecessors' labors. Soon his days, too, will come to an end, and his more fruitful findings will become part of the collective stream of cuneiform progress.

Among the more recent dead, there are three to whom I feel especially indebted: to the eminent French savant, François Thureau-Dangin, who dominated the cuneiform scene for half a century and who exemplified my ideal of a scholar—productive, lucid, aware of the significant, and ever prepared to admit ignorance rather than overtheorize; to Anton Deimel, the Vatican scholar with a keen sense of lexicographical order and organization, whose monumental *Schumerisches Lexikon* proved highly useful in spite of its numerous drawbacks; and to Edward Chiera, whose vision and diligence helped pave the way for my own researches in Sumerian literature.

Among the living cuneiformists whose work I have found most valuable, especially from the point of view of Sumerian lexicography, are Adam Falkenstein of Heidelberg, and Thorkild Jacobsen of the Oriental Institute of the University of Chicago. Their names and work will appear frequently in the text of this book. In the case of Jacobsen, moreover, a rather close collaboration has developed as a result of the tablet finds of the joint Oriental Institute-University Museum expedition to Nippur in the years 1948-1952. The stimulating and suggestive works of Benno Landsberger, one of the most creative minds in cuneiform studies, proved to be a constant source of information and guidance; his more recent works in particular are crowded treasure houses of cuneiform lexicography.

But it is to Arno Poebel, the leading Sumerologist of the past half century, that my researches owe the heaviest debt. In the early thirties, as a member of the Assyrian Dictionary Staff of the Oriental Institute, I sat at his feet and drank in his words. In those days, when Sumerology was practically an unknown discipline in America, Poebel, a master of Sumerological method, gave me generously of his time and knowledge.

Sumerology, as the reader may surmise, is not reckoned among the essential disciplines even in the largest American universities, and my chosen path was hardly paved with gold. The climb to a relatively stable and more or less comfortable professorial chair was marked by a constant financial struggle. The years 1937-42 were particularly critical for my scholarly career, and had it not been for a series of grants from the John Simon Guggenheim Memorial Foundation and the American Philosophical Society, it might well have come to a premature end. In recent years, the Bollingen Foundation has made it possible for me to secure at least a minimum of clerical and scientific help for my Sumerological researches, as well as to travel abroad in connection with them.

To the Department of Antiquities of the Republic of Turkey and to the Director of the Archaeological Museums in Istanbul, I am deeply grateful for generous cooperation. They made it possible for me to benefit from the use of the Sumerian literary tablets in the Museum of the Ancient Orient, whose two curators of the Tablet Collection—Muazzez Cig and Hatice Kizilyay—have been a constant source of very real help, particularly by copying several hundred fragments inscribed with portions of the Sumerian literary works.

Finally, I wish to express my heartfelt thanks to Mrs. Gertrude Silver, who helped prepare the typescript for this book.

SAMUEL NOAH KRAMER

Philadelphia, Pa.

Photographic Sources

The University Museum, University of Pennsylvania (Reuben Goldberg, photographer): Figures 1, 7, and 26; Plates 3, 4, 5, 6, 7, 9, 10, 12, 16, 18, 19, 21, 22, 23, 24, 25, 26, 27, 29, 30, 31, and 34; and for making the photographs of Plates 13, 14, and 15 from illustrations in *Découvertes en Chaldée* by Ernest de Souzec and Leon Heuzey.

Plates 32 and 33 are from the Photographic Department of the British Museum.

The Museum of Ancient Orient, Istanbul: Plates 8, 12, 17, and 20.

Antran Evan (staff photographer of the Iraqi Directorate of Antiquities, Baghdad: Plates 1 and 2.

Photographic Institute of the Friedrich Schiller University, Jena: Figure 27 and Plate 28.

Contents

CONTENTS

List of Illustrations

Line Drawings

Halftones

Introduction

nearly, approaching, almost

HE SUMEROLOGIST is one of the narrowest of specialists in the highly specialized academic halls of learning, a well-<u>nigh</u> perfect example of the man who "knows mostest about the leastest." He cuts his world down to that small part of it known as the Middle East, and limits his history to what happened before the days of Alexander the Great. He confines his researches to the written documents discovered in Mesopotamia, primarily clay tablets inscribed in the cuneiform script, and restricts his contributions to texts written in the Sumerian language. He writes and publishes articles and monographs bearing such stimulating titles as "The Be- and Bi-Prefix in the Times of the Early Princes of Lagash," "Lamentation over the Destruction of Ur," "Gilgamesh and Agga of Kish," "Enmerkar and the Lord of Aratta." After twenty to thirty years of these and similar world-shaking researches, he gets his reward: he is a Sumerologist. At least that is how it all happened to me.

Incredible as it may seem, however, this pinpoint historian, this <u>Toynbee</u> in reverse, has something of unusual interest (an "ace in the hole," as it were) to offer to the general reader. The Sumerologist, more than most other scholars and specialists, is in a position to satisfy man's universal quest for origins—for "firsts" in the history of civilization.

What, for example, were man's first recorded ethical ideals and religious ideas—his first political, social, and philosophical rationale? What did the first histories, myths, epics, and hymns sound like? How were the first legal contracts worded? Who was the first social reformer? When did the first tax reduction take

Joseph Toynbee (1889–1975) historian of the rise and fall of civilizations

place? Who was the first lawgiver? When did the first bicameral congress meet, and for what purpose? What were man's first schools like—their curriculum, faculty, and student body?

These and many similar "firsts" in man's recorded history are the Sumerologist's "meat." He can give the correct answer to many of the questions concerning cultural origins. Not, of course, because he is particularly profound or clairvoyant, unusually sagacious or erudite. Actually, the Sumerologist is a very limited fellow indeed, who rates "way down," even among the lowly academicians. Credit for the high number of cultural "firsts" goes not to the Sumerologist but to the Sumerians—that gifted and practical people who, as far as is known today, were the first to invent and develop a usable and effective system of writing.

One remarkable fact is that only a century ago nothing was known even of the existence of these Sumerians in ancient days. The archaeologists and scholars who, some hundred years ago, began excavating in that part of the Middle East known as Mesopotamia were looking not for Sumerians but for Assyrians and Babylonians. On these peoples and their civilizations they had considerable information from Greek and Hebrew sources, but of Sumer and the Sumerians they had no inkling. There was no recognizable trace either of the land or of its people in the entire literature available to the modern scholar. The very name Sumer had been erased from the mind and memory of man for more than two thousand years.

Yet today the Sumerians are one of the best-known peoples of the ancient Near East. We know what they looked like from their own statues and steles scattered throughout several of the more important museums in this country and abroad. Here, too, will be found an excellent representative cross section of their material culture—the columns and bricks with which they built their temples and palaces, their tools and weapons, pots and vases, harps and lyres, jewels and ornaments. Moreover, Sumerian clay tablets by the tens of thousands (literally), inscribed with their business, legal, and administrative documents, crowd the collections of these same museums, giving us much information about the social structure and administrative organization of the ancient Sumerians. Indeed—and this is where archaeology, because of its mute and static character, is usually least productive—we can even penetrate to a certain extent into their hearts and souls. We actually have a large number of Sumerian clay documents on which are inscribed the literary creations revealing Sumerian religion, ethics, and philosophy. And all this because the Sumerians were one of the very few peoples who not only probably invented a system of writing, but also developed it into a vital and effective instrument of communication.

It was probably toward the end of the *fourth* millennium B.C., about five thousand years ago, that the Sumerians, as a result of their economic and administrative needs, came upon the idea of writing on clay. Their first attempts were crude and pictographic; they could be used only for the simplest administrative notations. But in the centuries that followed, the Sumerian scribes and teachers gradually so modified and molded their system of writing that it completely lost its pictographic character and became a highly conventionalized and purely phonetic system of writing. In the second half of the third millennium B.C., the Sumerian writing technique had become sufficiently plastic and flexible to express without difficulty the most complicated historical and literary compositions. There is little doubt that sometime before the end of the third millennium B.C. the Sumerian men of letters actually wrote down—on clay tablets, prisms, and cylinders— many of their literary creations which until then had been current in oral form only. However, owing to archaeological accident, only a few literary documents from this earlier period have as yet been excavated, although this same period has yielded tens of thousands of economic and administrative tablets and hundreds of votive inscriptions.

It is not until we come to the first half of the *second* millennium B.C. that we find a group of several thousand tablets and fragments inscribed with the Sumerian literary works. The great majority of these were excavated between 1889 and 1900 at Nippur, an ancient Sumerian site not much more than a hundred miles from modern Baghdad. They are now located primarily in the University Museum of Philadelphia and the Museum of the Ancient Orient at Istanbul. Most of the other tablets and fragments were obtained from dealers rather than through excavations, and are now largely in the collections of the British Museum, the Louvre, the Berlin Museum, and Yale University. The documents range in size from large twelve-column tablets, inscribed with hundreds of compactly written lines of text, to tiny fragments containing no more than a few broken lines.

The literary compositions inscribed on these tablets and fragments run into the hundreds. They vary in length from hymns of less than fifty lines to myths of close to a thousand lines. From the point of view of form and content, they display a variety of types and genres which, considering their age, is both startling and revealing. In Sumer, a good millennium before the Hebrews wrote down their Bible and the Greeks their Iliad and Odyssey, we find a rich and mature literature consisting of myths and epic tales, hymns and lamentations, and numerous collections of proverbs, fables, and essays. It is not too unrealistic to predict that the recovery and restoration of this ancient and long-forgotten literature will turn out to be a major contribution of our century to the humanities.

Now, the accomplishment of this task is no simple matter. It will demand the concentrated efforts of numerous Sumerologists over a period of years—especially in view of the fact that most of the sun-baked clay tablets came out of the ground broken and fragmentary, so that only a small part of their original contents is preserved on each piece. Offsetting this disadvantage is the fact that the ancient Sumerian "professors" and their students prepared many copies of each literary work. The breaks and lacunae of one tablet or fragment can therefore frequently be restored from duplicating pieces, which may themselves be in a fragmentary condition. To take full advantage of these text-restoring duplications, however, it is necessary to have the source material available in published form. This frequently entails copying by hand hundreds and hundreds of minutely inscribed tablets and fragments—a tedious, wearisome, time-consuming task.

But let us take those rare instances where this particular hurdle no longer blocks the way—where the complete text of the Sumerian composition has been satisfactorily restored. All that remains in those instances is to translate the ancient document and get at its essential meaning, which is easier said than done. To be sure,

1. The Origin and Development of the Cuneiform System of Writing. A table showing the forms of eighteen representative signs from about 3000 B.C. to about 600 B.C.

the grammar of the long-dead Sumerian language is now fairly well known, as a result of the cumulative contributions of scholars over the past hundred years. But the vocabulary is something else again. In the matter of semantics, the uncomfortable Sumerologist finds himself time and again "chasing his own tail." Very often he can only guess the meaning of a word from the sense of the surrounding context, which itself may depend on the meaning of the word—a rather frustrating state of affairs. Nevertheless, in spite of textual difficulties and lexical perplexities, a number of reasonably trustworthy translations of the Sumerian literary works have appeared in recent years. Based on the contributions of various scholars, living and dead, the translations vividly illustrate the cumulative, cooperative, and international character of productive scholarship. The fact is that, in the decades following the excavations of the Sumerian literary tablets from Nippur, more than one scholar, realizing the value and importance of their contents for Oriental studies, examined and copied some of them. Among them were George Barton, Leon Legrain, Henry Lutz, and David Myhrman, all of whom contributed to this task.

Hugo Radau, the first to devote much time and energy to the Sumerian literary material, prepared careful and trustworthy copies of more than forty pieces in the University Museum at Philadelphia. Though the time was not ripe, he worked diligently on the translation and interpretation of the texts and made some progress in this direction. The well-known Anglo-American Orientalist, Stephen Langdon, picked up, in a sense, where Radau left off. He copied close to a hundred pieces from the Nippur collections of both the Istanbul Museum of the Ancient Orient and our own University Museum. Langdon had a tendency to copy too rapidly, and not a few errors crept into his work. Moreover, his attempted translations and interpretations have failed to stand the test of time. On the other hand, he did succeed in making available, in one form or another, a number of very important Sumerian literary texts that might otherwise have remained stored away in the museum cupboards. By his zest and enthusiasm he helped to make his fellow cuneiformists realize the significance of their contents.

At the same time the European museums were gradually making available the Sumerian literary tablets in their collections. As early as 1902, when Sumerology was still in its infancy, the British cuneiformist and historian L. W. King published sixteen excellently preserved tablets from the British Museum. Some ten years later, Heinrich Zimmern of Leipzig published two-hundred-odd copies of pieces in the Berlin Museum. In 1921, Cyril Gadd, then a Keeper in the British Museum, published copies of ten unusual pieces. In 1930, the late Henri de Genouillac, French excavator, made available ninety-eight copies of unusually well-preserved tablets which the Louvre had acquired. One of the outstanding contributors to the field of Sumerian literature and to Sumerological studies as a whole is Arno Poebel, the scholar who put Sumerology on a scientific basis with his publication of a detailed Sumerian grammar in 1923. In his monumental and invaluable *Historical and Grammatical Texts*, which contains superb copies of more than 150 tablets and fragments from the Nippur collection of the University Museum in Philadelphia, there are close to forty that are inscribed with parts of Sumerian literary works.

But it is the name of Edward Chiera, for many years a member of the faculty of the University of Pennsylvania, which is preeminent in the field of Sumerian literary research. He had a clearer idea than any of his predecessors of the scope and character of the Sumerian literary works. Aware of the fundamental need for copying and publishing the pertinent Nippur material in Istanbul and Philadelphia, he traveled to Istanbul in 1924 and copied some fifty pieces from the Nippur collection. A number of these were large and well-preserved tablets, and their contents gave scholars a fresh insight into Sumerian literary works. In the years that followed, he copied more than two hundred literary tablets and fragments from the Nippur collection of the University Museum. Thus he made available to his fellow cuneiformists more of these texts than all his predecessors put together. It is largely as a result of his patient and farsighted spadework that the true nature of Sumerian belles-lettres finally began to be appreciated.

My own interest in this highly specialized field of research stemmed directly from Edward Chiera's contributions, though I actually owe my Sumerological training to Arno Poebel, with whom I was privileged to work closely for a number of years in the early thirties. When Chiera was called to the Oriental Institute of the University of Chicago, as head of its Assyrian Dictionary project, he took with him his copies of the Nippur literary tablets, and the Oriental Institute undertook to publish them in two volumes. Upon Chiera's death in 1933, the editorial department of the Oriental Institute entrusted me with the preparation of these two volumes for posthumous (under Chiera's authorship) publication. It was in the course of carrying out this task that the significance of the Sumerian literary documents dawned on me, as well as the realization that all efforts to translate and interpret the documents would remain largely futile and barren until many more of the uncopied Nippur tablets and fragments in Istanbul and Philadelphia had been made available.

In the two decades that followed I have devoted most of my scientific efforts to the copying, piecing together, translation, and interpretation of the Sumerian literary compositions. In 1937 I traveled to Istanbul as a Guggenheim Fellow, and, with the full cooperation of the Turkish Directorate of Antiquities and of its authorized museum officials, I copied from the Nippur collection of its museum more than 170 tablets and fragments inscribed with portions of Sumerian literary works. These copies have now been published with a detailed introduction in Turkish and English. The succeeding years were spent largely at the University Museum in Philadelphia. Here, with the help of several generous grants from the American Philosophical Society, I studied and catalogued the hundreds of unpublished Sumerian literary documents, identifying the contents of most of them so that they could be attributed to one or another of the numerous Sumerian compositions, and I copied a number of them. In 1946 I traveled once again to Istanbul and copied another hundred-odd pieces, practically all inscribed with portions of myths and epic tales; these are now being prepared for publication. But this still left, as I knew only too well, hundreds of pieces in the Istanbul museum uncopied and unutilizable. It was for the purpose of continuing this task that I was awarded a Fulbright research professorship to Turkey for the academic year 1951-52. In this period, three of us—the ladies Hatice Kizilyay and Muazzez Cig (the Turkish curators of the Tablet Archives of the Istanbul Museum of the Ancient Orient) and I—copied close to 300 additional tablets and fragments.

In recent years, finally, a new stock of Sumerian literary pieces became available. In 1948, the Oriental Institute of the University of Chicago and the University Museum in Philadelphia pooled their financial resources and sent out a joint expedition to renew excavations at Nippur after a lapse of some fifty years. Not unexpectedly, this new expedition uncovered hundreds of new tablets and fragments, and these are being carefully studied by Thorkild Jacobsen of the Oriental Institute, one of the world's outstanding cuneiformists, and the present writer. It is already apparent that the newly discovered material will fill in many lacunae in Sumerian belles-lettres. There is good reason to hope that not a few Sumerian literary works will be made available in the next decade, and that these, too, will reveal numerous "firsts" in man's recorded history.

FROM THE TABLETS OF SUMER

THE FIRST SCHOOLS

THE SUMERIAN school was the direct outgrowth of the invention and development of the cuneiform system of writing, Sumer's most significant contribution to civilization. The first written documents were found in a Sumerian city named Erech. They consist of more than a thousand small pictographic clay tablets inscribed primarily with bits of economic and administrative memoranda. But among them are several which contain word lists intended for study and practice. That is, as early as 3000 B.C., some scribes were already thinking in terms of teaching and learning. Progress was slow in the centuries that followed. But by the middle of the third millennium, there must have been a number of schools throughout Sumer where writing was taught formally. In ancient Shuruppak, the home city of the Sumerian "Noah," there were excavated, in 1902-1903, a considerable number of school "textbooks" dating from about 2500 B.C.

However, it was in the last half of the third millennium that the Sumerian school system matured and flourished. From this period there have already been excavated tens of thousands of clay tablets, and there is little doubt that hundreds of thousands more lie buried in the ground, awaiting the future excavator. The vast majority are administrative in character; they cover every phase of Sumerian economic life. From them we learn that the number of scribes who practiced their craft throughout those years ran into the thousands. There were junior and "high" scribes, royal and temple scribes, scribes who were highly specialized for particular categories of administrative activities, and scribes

who became leading officials in government. There is every reason
to assume, therefore, that numerous scribal schools of considerable
size and importance flourished throughout the land.

But none of these earlier tablets deal directly with the Sumerian
school system, its organization, and its method of operation. For
this type of information we must go to the first half of the second
millennium B.C. From this later period there have been excavated
hundreds of practice tablets filled with all sorts of exercises actually prepared by the pupils themselves as part of their daily
school work. Their script ranges from the sorry scratches of the
first-grader to the elegantly written signs of the far-advanced
student about to become a "graduate." By inference, these ancient "copybooks" tell us not a little about the method of teaching current in the Sumerian school and about the nature of its
curriculum. Fortunately, the ancient Sumerian teachers themselves liked to write about school life, and several of their essays
on this subject have been recovered at least in part. From all
these sources we get a picture of the Sumerian school—its aims
and goals, its students and faculty, its curriculum and teaching
techniques. This is unique for so early a period in the history
of man.

The original goal of the Sumerian school was what we would
term "professional"—that is, it was first established for the purpose
of training the scribes required to satisfy the economic and administrative demands of the land, primarily those of the temple
and palace. This continued to be the major aim of the Sumerian
school throughout its existence. However, in the course of its
growth and development, and particularly as a result of the ever
widening curriculum, the school came to be the center of culture
and learning in Sumer. Within its walls flourished the scholar-
scientist, the man who studied whatever theological, botanical,
zoological, mineralogical, geographical, mathematical, grammatical, and linguistic knowledge was current in his day, and who in
some cases added to this knowledge.

Moreover, rather unlike present-day institutions of learning,
the Sumerian school was also the center of what might be termed
creative writing. It was here that the literary creations of the
past were studied and copied; here, too, new ones were com-

posed. While it is true that the majority of graduates from the
Sumerian schools became scribes in the service of the temple and
palace, and among the rich and powerful of the land, there were
some who devoted their lives to teaching and learning. Like the
university professor of today, many of these ancient scholars depended on their teaching salaries for their livelihood, and devoted themselves to research and writing in their spare time. The
Sumerian school, which probably began as a temple appendage,
became in time a secular institution; its curriculum, too, became
largely secular in character. The teachers were paid, apparently,
out of tuition fees collected from the students.

Education was neither universal nor compulsory. Most of the
students came from wealthy families; the poor could hardly afford the cost and time which a prolonged education demanded.
Until recently this was assumed *a priori* to be the state of affairs,
but in 1946 a German cuneiformist, Nikolaus Schneider, ingeni-
ously proved it from actual contemporary sources. In the thousands of published economic and administrative documents from
about 2000 B.C., some five hundred individuals listed themselves
as scribes, and for further identification many of them added the
name of their father and his occupation. Schneider compiled a
list of these data, and found that fathers of the scribes—that is, of
the school graduates—were governors, "city fathers," ambassa-
dors, temple administrators, military officers, sea captains, high
tax officials, priests of various sorts, managers, supervisors, fore-
men, scribes, archivists, and accountants. In short, the fathers
were the wealthier citizens of urban communities. Not a single
woman is listed as a scribe in these documents, and it is therefore
likely that the student body of the Sumerian school consisted of
males only.

Head of the Sumerian school was the *ummia*, "expert," "professor," who was also called "school father," while the pupil was
called "school son." The assistant professor was known as "big
brother," and some of his duties were to write the new tablets
for the pupils to copy, to examine the copies made by the pupils,
and to hear them recite their studies from memory. Other members of the faculty were "the man in charge of drawing" and
"the man in charge of Sumerian." There were also monitors in

charge of attendance and "a man in charge of the whip," who was presumably responsible for discipline. We know nothing of the relative rank of the school personnel, except that the headmaster was the "school father." Nor do we know anything about their sources of income. Probably they were paid by the "school father" from the tuition fees he received.

In regard to the curriculum of the Sumerian school, there is at our disposal a wealth of data from the schools themselves, which is indeed unique in the history of early man. In this case there is no need to depend on the statements made by the ancients or on inference from scattered bits of information. We actually have the written products of the schoolboys themselves, from the beginner's first attempts to the copies of the advanced student, whose work was so well prepared that it could hardly be distinguished from that of the professor himself. It is from these school products that we realize that the Sumerian school's curriculum consisted of two primary groups: the first may be described as semiscientific and scholarly; the second as literary and creative.

In considering the first, or semiscientific group, it is important to stress that the subjects did not stem out of what may be called the scientific urge—the search for truth for truth's sake. Rather, they grew and developed out of the main school aim: to teach the scribe how to write the Sumerian language. In order to satisfy this pedagogical need, the Sumerian scribal teachers devised a system of instruction which consisted primarily in linguistic classification—that is, they classified the Sumerian language into groups of related words and phrases and had the students memorize and copy them until they could reproduce them with ease. In the third millennium B.C., these "textbooks" became increasingly more complete, and gradually grew to be more or less stereotyped and standard for all the schools of Sumer. Among them we find long lists of names of trees and reeds; of all sorts of animals, including insects and birds; of countries, cities, and villages; of stones and minerals. These compilations reveal a considerable acquaintance with what might be termed botanical, zoological, geographical, and mineralogical lore—a fact that is only now beginning to be realized by historians of science.

Sumerian schoolmen also prepared various mathematical tables and many detailed mathematical problems together with their solutions. In the field of linguistics the study of Sumerian grammar was well represented among the school tablets. A number are inscribed with long lists of substantive complexes and verbal forms, indicating a highly sophisticated grammatical approach. Moreover, as a result of the gradual conquest of the Sumerians by the Semitic Akkadians in the last quarter of the third millennium B.C., the Sumerian professors prepared the oldest "dictionaries" known to man. The Semitic conquerors not only borrowed the Sumerian script but also treasured highly the Sumerian literary works, which they studied and imitated long after Sumerian had become extinct as a spoken language. Hence, there arose the pedagogical need for "dictionaries" in which Sumerian words and phrases were translated into the Akkadian language.

As for the literary and creative aspects of the Sumerian curriculum, it consisted primarily in studying, copying, and imitating the large and diversified group of literary compositions which must have originated and developed mainly in the latter half of the third millennium B.C. These ancient works, running into the hundreds, were almost all poetic in form, ranging in length from less than fifty lines to close to a thousand. Those recovered to date are chiefly of the following genres: myths and epic tales in the form of narrative poems celebrating the deeds and exploits of the Sumerian gods and heroes; hymns to gods and kings; lamentations bewailing the destruction of Sumerian cities; wisdom compositions including proverbs, fables, and essays. Of the several thousand literary tablets and fragments recovered from the ruins of Sumer, not a few are in the immature hand of the ancient Sumerian pupils themselves.

Little is known as yet of the teaching methods and techniques practiced in the Sumerian school. In the morning, upon his arrival in school, the student evidently studied the tablet which he had prepared the day before. Then the "big brother"—that is, the assistant professor—prepared a new tablet, which the student proceeded to copy and study. Both the "big brother" and the "school father" probably examined his copies to see if they were correct. No doubt memorizing played a very large role in the

students' work. The teachers and assistants must have supple-
mented, with considerable oral and explanatory material, the bare
lists, tables, and literary texts which the student copied and studied.
But these "lectures," which would have proved invaluable to
our understanding of Sumerian scientific, religious, and literary
thought, were in all probability never written down and hence
are lost to us forever.

One fact stands out: the Sumerian school had none of the
character of what we would call progressive education. In the
matter of discipline, there was no sparing of the rod. While
teachers probably encouraged their students, by means of praise
and commendation, to do good work, they depended primarily
on the cane for correcting the students' faults and inadequacies.
The student did not have an easy time of it. He attended school
daily from sunrise to sunset. He must have had some vacation in
the school year, but on this we have no information. He devoted
many years to his studies, staying in school from his early youth
to the day when he became a young man. It would be interesting
to know if, when, and to what extent the students were expected
to specialize in one study or another. But on this point, as indeed on many other points concerned with school activities, our
sources fail us.

What was the ancient Sumerian schoolhouse like? In several
Mesopotamian excavations, buildings have turned up which for
one reason or another were identified as possible schoolhouses—
one in Nippur, another in Sippar, and a third in Ur. But, except
for the fact that a large number of tablets were found in the
rooms, there seems little to distinguish them from ordinary house
rooms, and the identification may be erroneous. However, in the
winter of 1934-35, the French, who excavated ancient Mari far to
the west of Nippur, uncovered two rooms which definitely seem
to show physical features that might be characteristic of a school-
room, especially since they contained several rows of benches
made of baked brick, capable of seating one, two, or four people.
Strangely enough, no tablets were found in these rooms, and so
the identification must remain somewhat uncertain.

Just how did the students themselves feel about this system of education? For at least a partial answer, we turn, in Chapter 2, to a Sumerian essay on school life written almost four thousand years ago but only recently pieced together and translated. It is particularly informative on pupil-teacher relations and provides a unique "first" in the history of education.

THE FIRST CASE
OF "APPLE-POLISHING"

O NE OF THE most human documents ever exca-
vated in the Near East is a Sumerian essay dealing with the day-
to-day activities of a schoolboy. Composed by an anonymous
schoolteacher who lived about 2000 B.C., its simple, straightforward words reveal how little human nature has really changed
throughout the millenniums. In this ancient essay, a Sumerian
schoolboy, not unlike his modern counterpart, dreads being late
to school "lest his teacher cane him." On waking up, he urges
his mother to prepare his lunch hurriedly. In school, whenever he
misbehaves, he is caned by the teacher and his assistants; of this
we are quite sure, since the Sumerian sign for flogging consists
of "stick" and "flesh." As for the teacher, his pay seems to have
been as meager then as a teacher's pay is now; at least he was
only too happy to make a little extra from the parents to eke
out his earnings.

The composition, which was no doubt the creation of one of
the "professors" in the "tablet-house," begins with a direct question to the pupil: "Schoolboy, where did you go from earliest
days?" The boy answers: "I went to school." The author then
asks: "What did you do in school?" There follows the pupil's
reply, which takes up more than half the document and reads
in part: "I recited my tablet, ate my lunch, prepared my (new)
tablet, wrote it, finished it; then they assigned me my oral work,
and in the afternoon they assigned me my written work. When

school was dismissed, I went home, entered the house, and found my father sitting there. I told my father of my written work, then recited my tablet to him, and my father was delighted. . . . When I awoke early in the morning, I faced my mother and said to her: 'Give me my lunch, I want to go to school.' My mother gave me two 'rolls' and I set out; my mother gave me two 'rolls' and I went to school. In school the monitor in charge said to me 'Why are you late?' Afraid and with pounding heart, I entered before my teacher and made a respectful curtsy."

But curtsy or not, it seems to have been a bad day for this pupil. He had to take canings from the various members of the school staff for such indiscretions as talking, standing up, and walking out of the gate. Worst of all, the teacher said to him, "Your hand (copy) is not satisfactory," and caned him. This seems to have been too much for the lad, and he suggests to his father that it might be a good idea to invite the teacher home and mollify him with some presents—by all odds the first recorded case of "apple-polishing" in the history of man. The composition continues: "To that which the schoolboy said his father gave heed. The teacher was brought from school, and after entering the house he was seated in the seat of honor. The schoolboy attended and served him, and whatever he had learned of the art of tablet-writing he unfolded to his father."

The father then wined and dined the teacher, "dressed him in a new garment, gave him a gift, put a ring on his hand." Warmed by this generosity, the teacher reassures the aspiring scribe in poetic words, which read in part: "Young man, because you did not neglect my word, did not forsake it, may you reach the pinnacle of the scribal art, may you achieve it completely. . . . Of your brothers may you be their leader, of your friends may you be their chief, may you rank the highest of the schoolboys. . . . You have carried out well the school's activities, you have become a man of learning."

With these enthusiastic and optimistic words of the professor, the "school days" essay comes to an end. Little did he dream that his literary vignette on school life as he knew it would be resurrected and restored some four thousand years later by a twentieth-century professor in an American university. Fortunately it was a popular essay in ancient days, as can be seen from the fact that twenty-one copies, in various states of preservation, have come to light: thirteen are in the University Museum in Philadelphia; seven are in the Museum of the Ancient Orient in Istanbul, and one is in the Louvre in Paris.

The story of the gradual piecing together of the text is as follows: As early as 1909 the first bit of text from the "school days" document was copied and published by a young cuneiformist, Hugo Radau. It was an extract from the middle of the composition, and Radau had no way of knowing what it was all about. In the next twenty-five years, additional bits were published by the late famed Orientalists, Stephen Langdon, Edward Chiera, and Henri de Genouillac. But still there was not enough material on hand to gather the real significance of the text. In 1938, during a prolonged stay in Istanbul, I succeeded in identifying five more pieces belonging to our document. One of these was a fairly well-preserved four-column tablet which had originally contained the entire text of our composition. It enabled me to place the other pieces in their proper position. Since then, additional pieces in the University Museum have been identified, ranging in length from a well-preserved four-column tablet to small fragments containing no more than a few broken lines. As a result, except for a few broken signs, practically the entire text of the document was pieced together and restored.

But this was only the first hurdle in the scholarly process of making the contents of our ancient document available to the world at large. A trustworthy translation is every bit as important and far more difficult. Several portions of the document have been successfully translated by the Sumerologists Thorkild Jacobsen, of the Oriental Institute of the University of Chicago, and Adam Falkenstein, of the University of Heidelberg. These translations, together with a number of suggestions by Benno Landsberger, formerly of Leipzig and Ankara and now of the Oriental Institute of the University of Chicago, were utilized in the preparation of the first translation of the entire document. This was published in 1949 in the highly specialized *Journal of the American Oriental Society*. Needless to say, not a few of the Sumerian words and phrases in the ancient essay are still uncertain and obscure. No doubt some future professor will succeed in arriving at an exact rendering.

Though they may prefer not to admit it, it is not the professors and poets who run the world but the statesmen, politicians, and soldiers. And so our next "first," in Chapter 3, is about "power politics" and a Sumerian ruler of five thousand years ago who could manage "political incidents" successfully.

THE FIRST CASE OF
JUVENILE DELINQUENCY

IF JUVENILE DELINQUENCY is a serious problem in our day, it might be consoling to know that things were not too different in ancient days. Wayward, disobedient, and ungrateful children were the bane of their parents thousands of years ago as well as today. They roamed the streets and boulevards and loitered in the public squares, perhaps even in gangs, in spite of the fact that they were supervised by a monitor. They hated school and education and made their fathers sick to death with their everlasting gripes and complaints. All this we learn from the text of a Sumerian essay, which was only very recently pieced together. The seventeen clay tablets and fragments on which the essay has been found inscribed actually date back some 3,700 years; its original composition may go back several centuries earlier.

The composition which concerns a scribe and his perverse son, begins with an introduction consisting of a more or less friendly dialogue between father and son, in which the latter is admonished to go to school, work diligently, and report back without loitering in the streets. To make sure that the lad has paid close attention, the father has him repeat his words verbatim.

From here on the essay is a monolgue on the part of the father. It starts with a series of practical instructions to help make a man of his son; not to gad about in the streets and boulevards; to be humble before his monitor; to go to school and learn from the experience of man's early past. There follows a bitter rebuke to the wayward son, who, his father claims, has made him sick to death with his perennial fears and inhuman behavior. He, the father, is deeply disappointed at the son's ingratitude; he never made him work behind plow or ox, nor did he ever ask him to bring firewood, or support him as other fathers make their sons do. And yet his son turned out to be less of a man than the others.

Like many a disappointed parent of today, the father seems to be especially hurt that his son refuses to follow in his professional footsteps and become a scribe. He admonishes him to emulate his companions, friends, and brothers; to follow his own profession, the scribal art, in spite of the fact that it is the most difficult of all professions which the god of arts and crafts thought up and brought into being. It is most useful, the father argues, for the poetic transmission of man's experience. But in any case, he continues, it is decreed by Enlil, the king of all the gods, that a son should follow his father's profession.

After a final upbraiding for the son's pursuit of materialistic success rather than humanistic endeavor, the text becomes rather obscure; it seems to consist of brief, pithy sayings, intended perhaps to guide the son in true wisdom. In any case the essay closes on a happy note, with the father blessing his son and praying that he find favor in the eyes of his personal god, the moon-god Nanna and his wife, the goddess Ningal.

Here now is a quite literal, if tentative, translation of the more intelligible portions of the essay, omitting only here and there an obscure phrase or broken line.

The father begins by asking his son:

"Where did you go?"

"I did not go anywhere."

"If you did not go anywhere, why do you idle about? Go to school, stand before your 'school-father,' recite your assignment, open your schoolbag, write your tablet, let your 'big brother' write your new tablet for you. After you have finished your assignment and reported to your monitor, come to me, and do not wander about in the street. Come now, do you know what I said?"

"I know, I'll tell it to you."

"Come, now, repeat it to me."

"I'll repeat it to you."

"Tell it to me."

"Come on, tell it to me."

"You told me to go to school, recite my assignment, open my schoolbag, write my tablet, while my 'big brother' is to write my new tablet. After finishing my assignment, I am to proceed to my work and to come to you after I have reported to my monitor. That's what you told me."

The father now continues with a long monologue:

"Come now, be a man. Don't stand about in the public square, or wander about the boulevard. When walking in the street, don't look all around. Be humble and show fear before your monitor. When you show terror, the monitor will like you."

. . . . [About fifteen lines destroyed.]

"You who wander about in the public square, would you achieve success? Then seek out the first generations. Go to school, it will be of benefit to you. My son, seek out the first generations, inquire of them.

"Perverse one over whom I stand watch—I would not be a man did I not stand watch over my son—I spoke to my kin, compared its men, but found none like you among them.

"What I am about to relate to you turns the fool into a wise man, holds the snake as if by charms, and will not let you accept false phrases. Because my heart had been sated with weariness of you, I kept away from you and heeded not your fears and grumblings—no, I heeded not your fears and grumblings. Because of your clamorings, yes, because of your clamorings—I was angry with you—yes, I was angry with you. Because you do not look to your humanity, my heart was carried off as if by an evil wind. Your grumblings have put an end to me, you have brought me to the point of death.

"I, never in all my life did I make you carry reeds to the canebrake. The reed rushes which the young and the little carry, you, never in your life did you carry them. I never said to you 'Follow my caravans.' I never sent you to work, to plow my field. I never sent you to work to dig up my field. I never sent you to work as a laborer. 'Go, work and support me,' I never in my life said to you.

"Others like you support their parents by working. If you spoke to your kin, and appreciated them, you would emulate them. They provide 10 *gur* (72 bushels) barley each—even the young ones provided their fathers with 10 *gur* each. They multiplied barley for their father, maintained him in barley, oil, and wool. But you, you're a man when it comes to perverseness, but compared to them you are not a man at all. You certainly don't labor like them—they are the sons of fathers who make their sons labor, but me—I didn't make you work like them.

"Perverse one with whom I am furious—who is the man who can really be furious with his son—I spoke to my kin and found something hitherto unnoticed. The words which I shall relate to you, fear them and be on your guard because of them. Your partner, your yokemate—you failed to appreciate him; why do you not emulate him? Your friend, your companion—you failed to appreciate him; why do you not emulate him? Emulate your older brother. Emulate your younger brother. Among all mankind's craftsmen who dwell in the land, as many as Enki (the god of arts and crafts) called by name (brought into existence), no work as difficult as the scribal art did he call by name. For if not for song (poetry)—like the banks of the sea, the banks of the distant canals, is the heart of song distant—you wouldn't be listening to my counsel, and I wouldn't be repeating to you the wisdom of my father. It is in accordance with the fate decreed by Enlil for man that a son follows the work of his father.

"I, night and day am I tortured because of you. Night and day you waste in pleasures. You have accumulated much wealth, have expanded far and wide, have become fat, big, broad, powerful, and puffed. But your kin waits expectantly for your misfortune, and will rejoice at it because you looked not to your humanity."

(Here follows an obscure passage of 41 lines which seems to consist of proverbs and old saws; the essay then concludes with the father's poetic blessing.)

"From him who quarrels with you may Nanna, your god, save you,
From him who attacks you may Nanna, your god, save you,
May you find favor before your god,
May your humanity exalt you, neck and breast,
May you be the head of your city's sages,
May your city utter your name in favored places,
May your god call you by a good name,
May you find favor before your god Nanna,
May you be regarded with favor by the goddess Ningal."

But though they may prefer not to admit it, it is not the professors, poets, and humanists who run the world, but the statesmen, politicians, and soldiers. And so our next "first," in Chapter 4, is about "power politics," and a Sumerian ruler of five thousand years ago who could manage "political incidents" successfully.

THE FIRST "WAR OF NERVES"

HERE THE Sea of Marmara branches out into the gulf-like Golden Horn and the river-like Bosphorus, is situated a part of Istanbul known as Saray-burnu or "Palace-nose." Here, in the shelter of high and impenetrable walls, Mehmed II, the conqueror of Istanbul, built his palace and residence almost five hundred years ago. In the centuries that followed, sultan after sultan added afresh to this palace complex, building new kiosks and mosques, installing new fountains, laying out new gardens. In the well-paved courts and terraced gardens wandered the ladies of the harem and their attendants, the princes and their pages. Few were privileged to enter the palace grounds, and fewer still were permitted to witness its inner life.

But gone are the days of the sultans, and "Palace-nose" has taken on a different aspect. The high towered walls are largely broken down. The private gardens have been turned into public parks for the people of Istanbul to find shade and rest on hot summer days. As for the buildings themselves—the forbidden palaces and the secretive kiosks—most of them have become museums. Gone forever is the sultan's heavy hand. Turkey is a republic.

In a many-windowed room in one of these museums, the Museum of the Ancient Orient, I sit at a large rectangular table. On the wall facing me hangs a large photograph of the broad-faced, sad-eyed Ataturk, the beloved founder and hero of the new Turkish Republic. Much is still to be said and written about this remarkable man, in some ways one of the most significant political figures of our century. But it is not with modern "heroes" that I am concerned, no matter how epoch-making their achievements. I am a Sumerologist, and my business is with the long-forgotten "heroes" of the far-distant past.

On the table before me is a clay tablet written by a scribe who lived almost four thousand years ago. The script is cuneiform, or wedge-shaped; the language is Sumerian. The tablet is square in shape, nine by nine inches; it is therefore smaller in area than a standard sheet of typewriter paper. But the scribe who wrote this tablet divided it into twelve columns. By using a minute script, he succeeded in inscribing in this limited space more than six hundred lines of a Sumerian heroic poem. We may call it "Enmerkar and the Lord of Aratta." Though its characters and events go back almost five thousand years, they have a strangely familiar ring to our modern ears, for the poem records a political incident suggestive of the power-politics techniques of our own day and age.

Once upon a time, this poem tells us, many centuries before the scribe who wrote it was born, there lived a far-famed Sumerian hero named Enmerkar. He ruled over Erech, a city-state in southern Mesopotamia, between the Tigris and Euphrates Rivers. Far to the east of Erech, in Persia, lay Aratta, another city-state. It was separated from Erech by seven mountain ranges, and was perched so high on a mountain top that it was difficult to approach. Aratta was a prosperous town, rich in metal and stone—the very materials that were entirely lacking in the flat lowlands of Mesopotamia, where Enmerkar's city, Erech, was situated. No wonder, then, that Enmerkar cast longing and covetous eyes upon Aratta and its riches. Determined to make its people and ruler his subjects, he proceeded to unloose a "war of nerves" against the lord of Aratta and its inhabitants. He succeeded in breaking down their morale to the point where they gave up their independence and became the vassals of Erech.

All this is told in the leisurely, roundabout style characteristic of epic poetry the world over. Our poem begins with a preamble that sings the greatness of Erech and Kullab (a district within Erech or in its immediate neighborhood) from the very begin-

ning of time, and stresses its superiority over Aratta as a result
of the goddess Inanna's preference. The real action then begins
with the words "once upon a time."

The poet relates how Enmerkar, son of the sun-god Utu, having determined to make a vassal state of Aratta, implores his
sister, Inanna, the powerful Sumerian goddess of love and war,
to see to it that the people of Aratta bring gold, silver, lapis
lazuli, and precious stones, and build for him various shrines and
temples, particularly the *Abzu*-temple—that is, the "sea" temple
of Enki, the Sumerian water-god's main seat of worship in Eridu,
a city near the Persian Gulf.

Inanna, heeding Enmerkar's plea, advises him to seek out a

2. Enmerkar and the Lord of Aratta. Hand copy
from twelve-column tablet in Istanbul Museum of the
Ancient Orient.

suitable herald to cross the imposing mountains of Anshan (they separated Erech from Aratta) and assures him that the people of Aratta will submit to him and carry out the building operations he desires. Enmerkar selects his herald and sends him to the lord of Aratta with a message threatening to destroy and make desolate his city unless he and his people bring down silver and gold and build and decorate Enki's temple. To further impress the lord of Aratta, Enmerkar instructs his herald to repeat to him the "spell of Enki," which relates how the god Enki had put an end to man's "golden age" under Enlil's universal sway over the earth and its inhabitants.

The herald, after traversing seven mountains, arrives at Aratta, duly repeats his master's words to its lord, and asks for his answer. The latter, however, refuses to yield to Enmerkar, claiming that he is Inanna's protégé and that she had brought him to Aratta as its ruler. Thereupon the herald informs him that Inanna, who is now "Queen of Eanna" in Erech, has promised Enmerkar that Aratta would submit to him.

The lord of Aratta is stunned by this news. He composes an answer for the herald to take back to his king, in which he admonishes Enmerkar for resorting to arms and says that he prefers the "contest" (a fight between two selected champions). He goes on to say that, since Inanna has become his enemy, he is ready to submit to Enmerkar only if he will send him large quantities of grain. The herald returns to Erech posthaste and delivers the message to Enmerkar in the courtyard of the assembly hall.

Before making his next move, Enmerkar performs several acts, apparently ritualistic in character. First he takes counsel with Nidaba, the Sumerian goddess of wisdom. Then he has his beasts of burden loaded with grain. They are led to Aratta by the herald, who is to deliver to its lord a message eulogizing Enmerkar's scepter and commanding the lord to bring Enmerkar carnelian and lapis lazuli. On arrival, the herald piles up the grain in the courtyard and delivers his message. The people, delighted with the grain, are ready to present Enmerkar with the desired carnelian (nothing seems to be said of the lapis lazuli) and to have the "elders" build his "pure house" for him. But the hysterical lord of Aratta, after eulogizing his own scepter, insists, in words identical with those of Enmerkar, that the latter bring *him* carnelian and lapis lazuli.

On the herald's return to Erech, Enmerkar seems to consult the omens, in particular one involving a reed *sushima*, which he brings forth from "light to shade" and from "shade to light," until he finally cuts it down "after five years, after ten years had passed." He sends the herald forth once again to Aratta, this time merely placing the scepter in his hand without any accompanying message. The sight of the scepter seems to arouse terror in the lord of Aratta. He turns to his *shatammu*, and, after speaking bitterly of the plight of his city as a result of Inanna's displeasure, seems ready to yield to Enmerkar. Nevertheless, he once again issues a challenge to Enmerkar. This time he demands that Enmerkar select, as his representative, one of his "fighting men" to engage in single combat one of the lord of Aratta's "fighting men." Thus "the stronger will become known." The challenge, in riddlelike terms, asks that the selected retainer be neither black nor white, neither brown, yellow, nor dappled—all of which seems to make little sense when speaking of a man.

On the herald's arrival at Erech with this new challenge, Enmerkar bids him return to Aratta with a threefold message: (1) He (Enmerkar) accepts the lord of Aratta's challenge and is prepared to send one of his retainers to fight the lord of Aratta's representative to a decision. (2) He demands that the lord of Aratta heap up gold, silver, and precious stones for the goddess Inanna in Erech. (3) He once again threatens Aratta with total destruction unless its lord and people bring "stones of the mountain" to build and decorate for him the Eridu shrine.

In the first part of the message Enmerkar's words seem to clear up the lord of Aratta's riddlelike terms about the color of the retainer to be selected. Enmerkar substitutes the word "garment" for "fighting man." Presumably the color referred to garments worn by the combatants rather than to their bodies.

There follows a remarkable passage, which, if correctly interpreted, informs us that Enmerkar, the lord of Kullab, was, in the opinion of the poet, the first to write on clay tablets, and did so because his herald seemed "heavy of mouth" and unable to repeat the message (perhaps because of its length). The herald delivers the inscribed tablet to the lord of Aratta and awaits his answer. But help now seems to come to the lord of Aratta from an unexpected source. The Sumerian god of rain and storm, Ishkur, brings to Aratta wild-grown wheat and beans and heaps them up before the lord of Aratta. At the sight of the wheat the latter takes courage. His confidence regained, he informs Enmerkar's herald that Inanna had by no means abandoned Aratta and her house and bed in Aratta.

From here on the text becomes fragmentary and the context is

3. Enmerkar and the Lord of Aratta. Hand copy from twelve-column tablet in Istanbul Museum of the Ancient Orient.

difficult to follow, except for the statement that the people of Aratta did bring gold, silver, and lapis lazuli to Erech and heaped them up in the courtyard of Eanna for Inanna.

So ends the longest Sumerian epic tale as yet uncovered, the first of its kind in world literature. The text was restored from twenty tablets and fragments, of which the most important by far is the twelve-column tablet in the Istanbul Museum of the Ancient Orient, copied by me in 1946, and described in the foregoing paragraphs. The scientific edition of the poem for the specialist, consisting of the Sumerian text with translation and commentary, was published as a University Museum monograph in 1952. But even the nonspecialist will find this early example of heroic poetry of interest and merit. Following, therefore, is a literal translation of several of the better preserved passages in the first half of the poem which will serve to illustrate its particular mood, temper, and flavor. The passages include Enmerkar's plea to his patron deity Inanna; Inanna's advice; Enmerkar's instructions to his herald; the execution of these instructions by the herald; the lord of Aratta's indignant refusal; the herald's further argument that Inanna is now on Enmerkar's side and its distressing effect on the lord of Aratta. (Note that two, three, and four dots indicate the omission, for one reason or another, of one, two, and more than two words, respectively.)

> Once upon a time the lord chosen by Inanna in her holy heart,
> Chosen from the land Shuba by Inanna in her holy heart,
> Enmerkar, the son of Utu,
> To his sister, the queen of good . . . . ,
> To the holy Inanna makes a plea:
> "O my sister, Inanna; for Erech
> Let the people of Aratta fashion artfully gold and silver,
> Let them bring down pure lapis lazuli from the slab,
> Let them bring down precious stone and pure lapis lazuli;
> Of Erech, the holy land . . . . ,
> Of the house of Anshan where you stand,
> Let them build its . . . . ;
> Of the holy *gipar* where you have established your dwelling,
> May the people of Aratta fashion artfully its interior,
> I, I would offer prayers . . . . in its midst;
> Let Aratta submit to Erech,
> Let the people of Aratta,

Having brought down the stones of the mountains from their
 highland,
Build for me the great chapel, set up for me the great shrine,
Cause to appear for me the great shrine, the shrine of the gods,
Carry out for me my divine laws in Kullab,
Fashion for me the Abzu like a holy highland,
Purify for me Eridu like a mountain,
Cause to appear for me the holy chapel of the Abzu like a cavern;
I, when I utter the hymns from the Abzu,
When I bring the divine laws from Eridu,
When I make blossom the pure *en*-ship like a . . . ,
When I place the crown on my head in Erech, in Kullab,
May the . . of the great chapel be brought into the *gipar*,
May the . . of the *gipar* be brought into the great chapel,
May the people admire approvingly,
May Utu look on with joyful eye."

She who is . . . the delight of holy An, the queen who eyes the
 highland,
The mistress whose kohl is Amaushumgalanna,
Inanna, the queen of all the lands,
Says to Enmerkar, the son of Utu:
"Come, Enmerkar, instruction I would offer you, take my
 instruction,
A word I would speak to you, give ear to it!
Choose a word-wise herald from . . . ,
Let the great words of the word-wise Inanna be brought to him
 in . . ,
Let him ascend the . . mountains,
Let him descend the . . mountains,
Before the . . of Anshan,
Let him prostrate himself like a young singer,
Awed by the dread of the great mountains,
Let him wander about in the dust—
Aratta will submit to Erech;
The people of Aratta,
Having brought down the stones of the mountains from their
 land,
Will build for you the great chapel, set up for you the great
 shrine,
Cause to appear for you the great shrine, the shrine of the gods,
Carry out for you your divine laws in Kullab,
Fashion for you the Abzu like a holy highland,
Purify for you Eridu like a mountain,
Cause to appear for you the holy chapel of the Abzu like a
 cavern;

You, when you utter the hymns from the Abzu,
When you bring the divine laws from Eridu,
When you make blossom the pure *en*-ship like a . . . ,
When you place the crown on your head in Erech, in Kullab,
The . . of the great chapel will be brought into the *gipar*,
The . . of the *gipar* will be brought into the great chapel.
The people will admire approvingly,
Utu will look on with joyful eye;
The people of Aratta,
. . . . [Four lines omitted.]
Will bend the knee before you like highland sheep;
O holy 'breast' of the house, whose coming out is like the sun,
You are its beloved provider,
O . . . . Enmerkar, son of Utu, praise!"

The lord gave heed to the word of the holy Inanna,
Chose a word-wise herald from . . . ,
Brought to him the great words of the word-wise Inanna in . . :
"Ascend the . . mountains,
Descend the . . mountains,
Before the . . of Anshan,
Prostrate yourself like a young singer,
Awed by the dread of the great mountains,
Wander about in the dust—
O herald, speak unto the lord of Aratta and say unto him:
→'I will make the people of that city flee like the . . bird from
    its tree,
I will make them flee like a bird into its neighboring nest,
I will make it (Aratta) desolate like a place of . . . ,
I will make it hold dust like an utterly destroyed city,
Aratta, that habitation which Enki has cursed—
I will surely destroy the place, like a place which has been
    destroyed,
Inanna has risen up in arms behind it,
Has brought down the word, has turned it back,
Like the heaped-up dust, I will surely heap dust upon it;
Having made . . . gold in its ore,
Pressed . . silver in its dust,
Fashioned silver . . . ,
Fastened the crates on the mountain asses—
The . . . house of Sumer's junior Enlil,
Chosen by the lord Nudimmud in his holy heart,
Let the people of the highland of pure divine laws build for me,
Make it flower for me like the boxwood tree,
Light it up for me like Utu coming out of the *ganun*,

Adorn for me its thresholds.' "
. . . . [Twenty-seven lines omitted.]

The herald gave heed to the word of his king.
During the night he journeyed by the stars,
During the day he journeyed with Utu of heaven,
The great words of Inanna . . . . were brought unto him in . . ,
He ascends the . . mountains,
He descends the . . mountains,
Before the . . of Anshan,
He prostrated himself like a young singer,
Awed by the dread of the great mountains,
He wandered about in the dust;
Five mountains, six mountains, seven mountains he crossed,
Lifted his eyes, approached Aratta,
In the courtyard of Aratta he set a joyous foot,
Made known the exaltedness of his king,
Spoke reverently the word of his heart.

The herald says to the lord of Aratta:
"Your father, my king, has sent me to you,
The lord of Erech, the lord of Kullab, has sent me to you."
"Your king, what has he spoken, what has he said?"

"My king, this is what he has spoken, this is what he has said—
My king fit for the crown from his very birth,
The lord of Erech, the leading serpent of Sumer, who . . . like
    a . . ,
The ram full of princely might in the walled highland,
The shepherd who . . . . ,
Born of the faithful cow in the heart of the highland—
Enmerkar, the son of Utu, has sent me to you,
My king, this is what he says:
'I will make the people of his city flee like the . . bird from its tree,
I will make them flee like a bird into its neighboring nest,
I will make it desolate like a place of . . . ,
I will make it hold dust like an utterly destroyed city,
Aratta, that habitation which Enki has cursed—
I will surely destroy the place like a place which has been
    destroyed.
Inanna has risen up in arms behind it,
Has brought down the word, has turned it back,
Like the heaped-up dust, I will surely heap dust upon it;
Having made . . . gold in its ore,
Pressed . . silver in its dust,

Fashioned silver . . . ,
Fastened the crates on the mountain asses—
The . . . house of Sumer's junior Enlil,
Chosen by the lord Enki in his holy heart,
Let the people of the highland of the holy divine laws build
    for me,
Make it flower for me like the boxwood tree,
Light it up for me like Utu coming out of the *ganun*,
Adorn for me its thresholds.'
. . . . [Two lines omitted.]

"Command what I shall say concerning this matter,
And to the dedicated one who wears a long beard of lapis lazuli,
To him whose mighty cow . . s the land of pure divine laws.
To him whose seed came forth in the dust of Aratta,
To him who was fed milk in the fold of the faithful cow,
To him who was fit for lordship over Kullab, the land of all the
    great divine laws,
To Enmerkar, the son of Utu,
I will speak that word as a good word in the temple of Eanna;
In the *gipar* which bears fruit like a fresh . . plant,
I will deliver it to my king, the lord of Kullab."

After he had thus spoken to him,
"O herald, speak unto your king, the lord of Kullab, and say
    unto him:
'Me, the lord fit for the pure hand,
She who is the royal . . of heaven, the queen of heaven and
    earth,
The mistress of all the divine laws, the holy Inanna,
Has brought me to Aratta, the land of the holy divine laws,
Has made me close "the face of the highland" like a large door;
How then shall Aratta submit to Erech!
Aratta will not submit to Erech'—say unto him."

After he had thus spoken to him,
The herald answers the lord of Aratta:
"The great queen of heaven, who rides the fearful divine laws,
Who dwells in the mountains of the highland Shuba,
Who adorns the daises of the highland Shuba—
Because the lord, my king, who is her servant,
Made her the 'Queen of Eanna.'
'The lord of Aratta will submit'—
Thus said to him in the brickwork of Kullab."

Then was the lord depressed, deeply pained,

He had no answer, he kept seeking an answer,
At his own feet he cast a troubled eye, he finds an answer. . . .

The early rulers of Sumer, no matter how great their success
as conquerors, were not unbridled tyrants and absolute monarchs.
On all the more important questions of state, particularly those
involving war and peace, they consulted their more important
fellow citizens gathered in solemn assembly. One such crucial
"congress" took place at the very dawn of Sumerian history, some
five thousand years ago, although it is recorded in a heroic poem
composed in a much later day. This "first" in political history is
recorded in Chapter 5.

THE FIRST BICAMERAL CONGRESS

 M AN'S SOCIAL and spiritual development is often slow, devious, and hard to trace. The full-grown tree may well be separated from its original seed by thousands of miles and years. Take, for example, the way of life known as democracy and its fundamental institution, the political assembly. On the surface it seems to be practically a monopoly of our Western civilization and an outgrowth of recent centuries. Who could imagine that there were political congresses thousands and thousands of years ago, and in parts of the world rarely associated with democratic institutions? But the patient archaeologist digs deep and wide, and he never knows what he will come up with. As a result of the efforts of the "pick and spade" brigade, we can now read the record of a political assembly that took place some five thousand years ago in—of all places—the Near East.

The first political "congress" in man's recorded history met in solemn session about 3000 B.C. It consisted, not unlike our own congress, of two "houses": a "senate," or an assembly of elders; and a "lower house," or an assembly of arms-bearing male citizens. It was a "war congress," called together to take a stand on the momentous question of war and peace; it had to choose between what we would describe as "peace at any price" or war and independence. The "senate," with its conservative elders, declared for peace at all cost, but its decision was "vetoed" by the king, who then brought the matter before the "lower house." This body declared for war and freedom, and the king approved.

In what part of the world did the first "congress" known to

man meet? Not, as you might surmise, somewhere in the West, on the continent of Europe (the political assemblies in "democratic" Greece and republican Rome came much later). Our hoary congress met, surprising as it may seem, in that part of Asia now generally designated as the Near East, the traditional home of tyrants and despots, a part of the world where political assemblies were thought to be practically unknown. It was in the land known in ancient days as Sumer, situated north of the Persian Gulf between the Tigris and Euphrates Rivers, that the oldest known political assembly was convened. And when did this "congress" meet? In the third millennium B.C. In those days, this Near Eastern land Sumer (it corresponds roughly to the lower half of modern Iraq) was inhabited by a people who developed what was probably the highest civilization in the then known world.

Sumer, some four to five thousand years ago, boasted of many large cities centering about monumental and world-renowned public buildings. Its busy traders carried on an extensive commerce by land and sea with neighboring countries. Its more serious thinkers and intellectuals developed a system of religious thought which was accepted as gospel not only in Sumer but throughout much of the ancient Near East. Its gifted poets sang lovingly and fervently of their gods, heroes, and kings. To crown it all, the Sumerians gradually developed a system of writing by means of reed stylus on clay, which enabled man for the first time to make a detailed and permanent record of his deeds and thoughts, his hopes and desires, his judgments and beliefs. And so it is not surprising to find that in the field of politics, too, the Sumerians made important progress. Particularly, they took the first steps toward democratic government by curbing the power of the kings and recognizing the right of political assembly.

The political situation that brought about the convening of the oldest "congress" recorded in history may be described as follows: Like Greece of a much later day, Sumer, in the third millennium B.C., consisted of a number of city-states vying for supremacy over the land as a whole. One of the most important of these was Kish, which, according to Sumerian legendary lore, had received the "kingship" from heaven immediately after the "flood." But in time another city-state, Erech, which lay far to

the south of Kish, kept gaining in power and influence until it
seriously threatened Kish's supremacy in Sumer. The king of
Kish at last realized the danger and threatened the Erechites with
war unless they recognized him as their overlord. It was at this
crucial moment that Erech's two assemblies were convened—the
elders and the arms-bearing males—in order to decide which course
to follow, whether to submit to Kish and enjoy peace or to take
to arms and fight for independence.

The story of the struggle between Erech and Kish is told in the
form of a Sumerian epic poem whose chief characters are Agga,
the last ruler of the first dynasty of Kish, and Gilgamesh, the
king of Erech and "lord of Kullab." The poem begins with the
arrival in Erech of Agga's envoys bearing an ultimatum to its
king Gilgamesh. Before giving them his answer, Gilgamesh goes

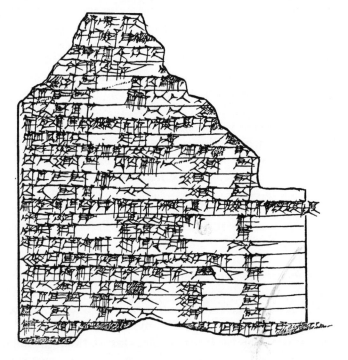

4. Gilgamesh and Agga. Hand copy of obverse of one of
eleven Nippur tablets and fragments utilized to restore
epic poem.

before "the convened assembly of the elders of his city" with an urgent plea not to submit to Kish but to take up arms and fight for victory. The "senators," however, are of a different mind; they would rather submit to Kish and enjoy peace. Their decision displeases Gilgamesh, who then goes before "the convened assembly of the men of his city" and repeats his plea. The men of this assembly decide to fight rather than submit to Kish. Gilgamesh is delighted, and seems confident of the results of the expected struggle. In a very short time—in the words of our poet, "It was not five days, it was not ten days"—Agga besieges Erech, and the Erechites are dumfounded. The meaning of the remainder of the poem is not too clear, but it seems that Gilgamesh in some way succeeds in gaining the friendship of Agga and in having the siege lifted without a fight.

Here, now, are the ancient Sumerian poet's actual words dealing with the Erech "congress"; the translation is quite literal, but omits a number of lines whose contents are still unintelligible.

The envoys of Agga, the son of Enmebaraggesi,
Proceeded from Kish to Gilgamesh in Erech.
The lord Gilgamesh before the elders of his city
Put the matter, seeks out the word:
"Let us not submit to the house of Kish, let us smite it with
weapons."

The convened assembly of the elders of his city
Answers Gilgamesh:
"Let us submit to the house of Kish, let us not smite it with
weapons."

Gilgamesh, the lord of Kullab,
Who performs heroic deeds for the goddess Inanna,
Took not the words of the elders of his city to heart.

A second time Gilgamesh, the lord of Kullab,
Before the fighting men of his city put the matter, seeks out the
word:
"Do not submit to the house of Kish, let us smite it with weapons."

The convened assembly of the fighting men of his city
Answers Gilgamesh:
"Do not submit to the house of Kish, let us smite it with weapons."

> Then Gilgamesh, the lord of Kullab,
> At the word of the fighting men of his city his heart rejoiced,
> his spirit brightened.

Our poet is all too brief; he merely mentions the Erech "congress" and its two assemblies, without giving any further details. What we would like to know, for example, is the size of the membership of each body, and just how the "congressmen" and "senators" were selected. Could each individual voice his opinion and be sure of a hearing? How was the final consensus of the body as a whole obtained? Did they have a device corresponding to the voting technique of our own day? Certainly there must have been a "speaker" in charge of the discussion who "spoke" for the assembly to the king. Then again, in spite of the poet's lofty language, we may rest assured that there was considerable "politicking" and "wire-pulling" among the old political "boys." The city-state of Erech was evidently split wide open into two opposing camps, a war party and a peace party. There was probably more than one behind-the-scenes conference of our own "smoke-filled room" type, before the leaders of each "house" announced the final and seemingly unanimous decisions.

But of all these ancient political bickerings and compromises we will probably never recover a trace. There is little likelihood that we will ever find any written historical records from the days of Agga and Gilgamesh, since, in their time, writing was either altogether unknown or had only just been invented and was still in its early picture stage. As for our epic poem, it must be borne in mind that it is inscribed on tablets written many centuries after the incidents it describes took place—probably more than a thousand years after the Erech "congress" had met and adjourned.

There are known, at present, eleven tablets and fragments inscribed with our political-assembly poem. Four of the eleven pieces were copied and published in the past four decades. But the significance of their contents for the history of political thought and practice was not realized until 1943, when Thorkild Jacobsen, of the Oriental Institute of the University of Chicago, published a study on *Primitive Democracy*. Since then it was my good fortune to identify and copy the remaining seven pieces in Istanbul and Philadelphia. As a result, the poem, consisting of 115 lines, is now complete. A scientific edition of its text, together with a newly revised translation, appeared in 1949 in the *American Journal of Archaeology*.

The two political events described here and in Chapter 3 took place about 3000 B.C. They are known to us not from contemporary historical documents but from epic poems written down at a much later date, and these poems contain only a kernel of historic truth. It is not until some six centuries later that we come upon a number of inscriptions recording and interpreting social and political events in a style which stamps them as man's first attempt at history-writing. One of these documents is described and analyzed in Chapter 6, after an introductory comment on the intellectual and psychological limitations of our first "historians." It is primarily concerned with a bitter and tragic civil war between two Sumerian city-states that ended in a temporary and uneasy stalemate, the only victors being death and destruction.

THE FIRST HISTORIAN

T HE SUMERIANS, it is safe to say, produced no historiography in the generally accepted sense of the word. Certainly no Sumerian man of letters wrote history as the modern historian conceives it, in terms of unfolding processes and underlying principles. Bound by his particular world view, the Sumerian thinker saw historical events as coming ready-made and "full-grown, full-blown" on the world scene, and not as the slow product of man's interaction with his environment. He believed, for example, that his own country, which he knew as a land of thriving cities and towns, villages and farms, and in which flourished a well-developed assortment of political, religious, and economic institutions and techniques, had always been more or less the same from the very beginning of days—that is, from the moment the gods had planned and decreed it to be so, following the creation of the universe. It probably never occurred even to the most learned of the Sumerian sages that Sumer had once been desolate marshland with but few scattered settlements, and had only gradually come to be what it was after many generations of struggle and toil marked by human will and determination, man-laid plans and experiments, and diverse discoveries and inventions.

The psychological techniques of definition and generalization, which the modern historian takes more or less for granted, seem to have been unknown to the Sumerian teacher and thinker, at least on the level of explicit formulation. Thus, in the linguistic field, we have quite a number of Sumerian grammatical lists that imply an awareness of numerous grammatical classifications, but nowhere do we find a single explicit grammatical definition or rule. In mathematics we find many tables, problems, and solutions, but no statement of general principles, axioms, and theorems. In what might be termed the "natural sciences," the Sumerian teachers compiled long lists of trees, plants, animals, and stones. The reason for the particular ordering of the objects listed is still obscure, but certainly it does not stem from a fundamental understanding of, or approach to, botanical, zoological, or mineralogical principles and laws. The Sumerians compiled numerous law codes, which no doubt contained, in their original complete state, hundreds of individual laws, but nowhere is there a statement of legal theory. In the field of history, the Sumerian temple and palace archivists noted and wrote down a varied assortment of significant events of a political, military, and religious character. But this did not lead to the writing of connected and meaningful history. Lacking the relatively recent discovery that history is a constantly changing process, and seemingly ignorant of the methodological tool of comprehensive generalization, the Sumerian man of letters could not possibly have done his history-writing in the modern sense of the word.

While it is not surprising that the Sumerian writers failed to produce the "modern" type of historiography, it does seem strange that even historical works of the kind current among the Hebrews and Greeks were unknown in Sumer. No Sumerian writer or scribe, as far as we know, ever made a conscious effort to write a cultural or political history of Sumer or any of its component states, let alone of the then known world. To be sure, Sumerian men of letters originated and developed a number of written literary genres—myths and epic tales, hymns and lamentations, proverbs and essays—and several of these, the epics and lamentations in particular, do utilize, at least to a very limited extent, what might be termed historical data. But the thought of preparing a connected history, prompted either by the love of learning or even by what we would term purposes of propaganda, never seemed to occur to the Sumerian teachers and writers. The documents that come closest to what might be termed history are the votive inscriptions on statues, steles, cones, cylinders, vases, and tablets. But the events recorded on them are merely a by-product of the urge to find favor with the gods. Moreover, these inscriptions usually record single contemporaneous events, in very brief form. Nevertheless, there are several among them which do refer back to earlier circumstances and events, and these reveal a sense of historical detail which—for that early date, about 2400 B.C.—is without parallel in world literature.

All our earliest "historians," as far as extant material goes, lived in Lagash, a city in southern Sumer that played a dominant political and military role for over a century, beginning about 2500 B.C. It was the seat of an active dynasty of rulers founded by Ur-Nanshe. The dynasty included Ur-Nanshe's conquering grandson, Eannatum, who succeeded for a brief period in making himself ruler of practically all Sumer; Eannatum's brother, Enannatum; and the latter's son, Entemena. It was not until the reign of Urukagina, the eighth ruler following Ur-Nanshe, that Lagash's star finally set. Urukagina was defeated by Lugalzaggisi of Umma, who was conquered in turn by the great Sargon of Akkad. It is the political history of this period, from the days of Ur-Nanshe to those of Urukagina, that is known to us from a varied group of contemporary records prepared by anonymous "historians" who, presumably as palace and temple archivists, had access to firsthand information on the events they described.

One of these documents is outstanding for its fullness of detail and clarity of meaning. It was prepared by one of the archivists of Entemena, the fifth in the line of Lagash rulers, starting with Ur-Nanshe. Its primary purpose was to record the restoration of the boundary ditch between Lagash and Umma, which had been destroyed in a struggle between the two cities. In order to set the event in its proper historical perspective, the archivist deemed it advisable to describe its political background. He recounted, ever so briefly to be sure, some of the important details in the struggle for power between Lagash and Umma from as far back as his written records reached—that is, from the days of Mesilim, the suzerain of Sumer and Akkad about 2600 B.C. In doing so, however, he did not use the straight factual form of narrative writing expected of the historian. Instead he strove to fit the historical events into the accepted framework of his theocratic world view, thus developing a rather unique literary style, which constantly interweaves the deeds of men and gods and often fails to distinguish between them. As a consequence, the actual historical incidents are not readily apparent from the text of the document, but must be painstakingly extracted and discriminately filled in with the help of relevant data obtained from other Sumerological sources. Cleared of its theological cloak and polytheistic phraseology, the document records the following series of political events in the history of Sumer (they can be verified in large part from other extant sources):

In the days when Mesilim was king of Kish, and at least the nominal suzerain of Sumer, there arose a border dispute between Lagash and Umma, two Sumerian city-states which evidently acknowledged Mesilim as their overlord. He proceeded to arbitrate the controversy by measuring off a boundary line between the two cities in accordance with what was given out to be an oracle of Sataran, a deity in charge of settling complaints, and he erected an inscribed stele to mark the spot and prevent future disputes.

However, the decision, which was presumably accepted by both parties, seemed to favor Lagash rather than Umma. Not long afterward Ush, an *ishakku* of Umma, violated the terms of the decision (the time is not stated, but there are indications that this violation took place not long before Ur-Nanshe founded his dynasty at Lagash). Ush ripped out Mesilim's stele to indicate that he was not bound by its terms, and then crossed the border and seized the northernmost territory belonging to Lagash, known as the Guedinna.

This land remained in the hands of the Ummaites until the days of Eannatum, the grandson of Ur-Nanshe, a military leader whose conquests had made him so powerful that he dared assume, at least for a brief period, the title "King of Kish," and thus claim the overlordship of all Sumer. It was this Eannatum, according to our document, who attacked and defeated the Ummaites; made a new border treaty with Enakalli, then the *ishakku* of Umma; dug a ditch in line with the new boundary which would help insure the fertility of the Guedinna; erected there for purposes of future record the old Mesilim stele, as well as several steles of his own; and constructed a number of buildings and shrines to several of the important Sumerian deities. To help minimize the possible source of future conflict between Umma and Lagash, he set aside a strip of fallow land on the Umma side of the boundary ditch, as a kind of "no-man's land." Finally, Eannatum, probably in an effort to alleviate the feelings of the Ummaites to some extent, since he was eager to expand his conquests in other directions, agreed to let them farm the fields lying in the Guedinna and even further south. But he granted this only under the condition that the Ummaites pay the Lagash rulers a share of the crops for the use of the land, thus assuring himself and his successors of a considerable revenue.

Thus far, Entemena's archivist dealt only with past events in the conflict between Umma and Lagash. He next turned to the most recent struggle between the cities, of which he was in all probability a contemporary witness—the battle between Ur-Lumma, the son of the unfortunate Enakalli, who had been compelled to agree to Eannatum's "shameful" terms, and Entemena, the son of Enannatum and nephew of Eannatum.

Despite Eannatum's mighty victory, it took the Ummaites only about a generation or so to recover their confidence, if not their former strength. Ur-Lumma repudiated the bitterly rankling agreement with Lagash, and refused to pay Enannatum the revenue imposed upon Umma. Moreover, he proceeded to "dry up" the boundary ditches; ripped out and put to fire both Mesilim's and Eannatum's steles with their irritating inscriptions; and destroyed the buildings and shrines which Eannatum had constructed along the boundary ditch to warn the Ummaites that they must not trespass on Lagash territory. He was now set to cross the border and enter the Guedinna. To assure himself of victory, he sought and obtained the military aid of the foreign ruler to the north of Sumer.

The two forces met in the Gana-ugigga of the Guedinna, not far south of the border. The Ummaites and their allies were under the command of Ur-Lumma himself, while the Lagashites were led by Entemena, since his father, Enannatum, must have been an old man at the time. The Lagashites were victorious. Ur-

Lumma fled, hotly pursued by Entemena, and many of his troops were waylaid and killed.

But Entemena's victory proved to be ephemeral. Upon Ur-Lumma's defeat and probable death, a new enemy appeared on the scene. This new enemy, whose name was Il, was the temple-head of a city named Zabalam, situated not far from Umma to the north. Il had evidently been shrewd enough to "wait it out" while Entemena and Ur-Lumma were struggling for a decision. But as soon as the battle was over, he attacked the victorious Entemena, met with initial success, and penetrated deep into Lagash territory. Although he was unable to hold on to his gains south of the Umma-Lagash border, he did succeed in making himself *ishakku* of Umma.

Il proceeded to show his contempt for the Lagash claims in almost the same manner as his predecessor. He deprived the boundary ditches of the water so essential to the irrigation of the nearby fields and farms, and refused to pay all but a fraction of the revenue imposed upon Umma by the old Eannatum treaty. And when Entemena sent envoys demanding an explanation for his unfriendly acts, Il answered by arrogantly claiming the entire Guedinna as his territory and domain.

The issue between Il and Entemena, however, was not decided by war. Instead, a compromise seems to have been forced upon them by a third party, probably the northern non-Sumerian ruler who claimed overlordship over Sumer as a whole. By and large, the decision seemed to favor Lagash, since the old Mesilim-Eannatum line was retained as the fixed boundary between Umma and Lagash. On the other hand, nothing is said of compensation by the Ummaites for the revenue which they had withheld. Nor do they seem to have been held responsible any longer for ensuring the water supply of the Guedinna. It was now up to the Lagashites themselves to see to the water supply.

The historical events marking the struggle for power between Lagash and Umma are by no means self-evident from a first study of the text of our document. Much of the history is derived from reading between the lines. The following literal translation of the inscription as a whole will help to show how this

was done, and at the same time give the reader some idea of the
unusual historiographic style developed by the Sumerian men of
letters:

Enlil (leading deity of the Sumerian pantheon), the king of all the
lands, the father of all the gods, marked off the boundary for Ningirsu
(the patron deity of Lagash), and Shara (the patron deity of Umma)
by his steadfast word, (and) Mesilim, the king of Kish, measured
it off in accordance with the word of Sataran, (and) erected a stele
there. (But) Ush, the *ishakku* of Umma, violated (both) the decree
(of the gods) and the word (given by man to man), ripped out its
(the boundary's) stele, and entered the plain of Lagash.

(Then) did Ningirsu, Enlil's foremost warrior, do battle with (the
men of) Umma in accordance with his (Enlil's) straightforward
word; by the word of Enlil he hurled the great net upon them, and
heaped up their skeleton (?) piles in the plain in their (various)
places. (As a result) Eannatum, the *ishakku* of Lagash, the uncle of
Entemena, the *ishakku* of Lagash, marked off the boundary with
Enakalli, the *ishakku* of Umma; led out its (the boundary's) ditch
from the Idnun (canal) to the Guedinna; inscribed (several) steles
along that ditch; restored Mesilim's stele to its (former) place; (but)
did not enter the plain of Umma. He (then) built there the Imdubba
of Ningirsu, the Namnunda-kigarra, (as well as) the shrine of Enlil,
the shrine of Ninhursag (the Sumerian "mother" goddess), the shrine
of Ningirsu, (and) the shrine of Utu (the sun-god).

(Moreover, following the boundary settlement) the Ummaites
could eat the barley of (the goddess) Nanshe (another patron deity
of Lagash) (and) the barley of Ningirsu to the amount of one *karu*
(for each Ummaite, and only) for interest; (also) he (Eannatum)
levied a tax on them, (and thus) brought in for himself (as revenue)
144,000 "large" *karu*.

Because this barley remained unpaid—(besides) Ur-Lumma, the
ishakku of Umma deprived the boundary ditch of Ningirsu (and)
the boundary ditch of Nanshe of water; ripped out its (the boundary ditch's) steles (and) put them to fire; destroyed the dedicated
(?) shrines of the gods which had been built in the Namnunda-
kigarra; obtained (the help of) the foreign lands; and (finally)
crossed the boundary ditch of Ningirsu—Enannatum fought with
him in the Gana-ugigga (where are) the fields and farms of Ningirsu,
(and) Entemena, Enannatum's beloved son, defeated him. Ur-Lumma
(then) fled, (while) he (Entemena) slew (the Ummaite forces) up
into Umma (itself); (moreover) his (Ur-Lumma's) elite force (consisting of) 60 soldiers he wiped out (?) on the bank of the Lumma-
girnunta canal. (As for) its (Umma's fighting) men, he (Entemena)
left their bodies in the plain (for the birds and beasts to devour)

and (then) heaped up their skeleton (?) piles in five (separate) places.

At that time (however) Il, the temple-head of Zabalam, ravaged (?) (the land) from Girsu to Umma. Il took to himself the *ishakku*-ship of Umma; deprived of water the boundary ditch of Ningirsu, the boundary ditch of Nanshe, the Imdubba of Ningirsu, that tract (of arable land) of the Girsu tracts which lies toward the Tigris, (and) the Namnunda-kigarra of Ninhursag; (and) paid (no more than) 3600 *karu* of the barley (due) Lagash. (And) when Entemena, the *ishakku* of Lagash, repeatedly sent (his) men to Il because of that (boundary) ditch, Il, the *ishakku* of Umma, the plunderer of fields and farms, the speaker of evil, said: "The boundary ditch of Ningirsu, (and) the boundary ditch of Nanshe are mine"; (indeed) he (even) said: "I shall exercise control from the Antasurra to the Dimgal-abzu temple." (However) Enlil and Ninhursag did not grant this to him.

Entemena, the *ishakku* of Lagash, whose name was pronounced by Ningirsu, made this (boundary) ditch from the Tigris to the Idnun in accordance with the straightforward word of Enlil, in accordance with the straightforward word of Ningirsu, (and) in accordance with the straightforward word of Nanshe, (and) restored it for his beloved king Ningirsu and for his beloved queen Nanshe (after) he had constructed of bricks the foundation of the Namnunda-kigarra. May Shulutula, the (personal) god of Entemena, the *ishakku* of Lagash, whom Enlil gave the scepter, whom Enki (the Sumerian god of wisdom) gave wisdom, whom Nanshe fixed upon (in her) heart, the great *ishakku* of Ningirsu, the man who had received the words of the gods, step forward (in prayer) for the life of Entemena before Ningirsu and Nanshe unto distant days.

The Ummaite who (at any future time) will cross the boundary ditch of Ningirsu (and) the boundary ditch of Nanshe in order to take to himself fields and farms by force, whether he be (really) an Ummaite or a foreigner—may Enlil destroy him; may Ningirsu, after hurling his great net on him, bring down on him his lofty hand (and) his lofty foot; may the people of his city, having risen in rebellion, strike him down in the midst of his city.

The text of this unique historical inscription has been found inscribed in practically identical language on two clay cylinders. One of these cylinders was found near Lagash in 1895, and was copied and translated by the late François Thureau-Dangin, a towering figure in cuneiform studies for almost half a century. The second cylinder is in the Yale Babylonian Collection. It was obtained from an antique dealer. Its text was published in

1920 by Nies and Keiser in their *Historical, Religious, and Economic Texts*. In 1926 a brilliant paper on the document, with a detailed study of its style and contents, was published by the eminent Sumerologist Arno Poebel. It is primarily on this work that my translation and analysis are based.

Fortunately for us, the ancient Sumerian "historians" wrote, in their votive inscriptions, not only of battles and wars but also of significant social and economic events. Chapter 7 tells about one of the most precious documents in the history of political evolution—a contemporary account of a social reform, including a rather enviable tax-reduction program that took place about thirty years after the death of Entemena of Lagash. This document uses the word "freedom" (*amargi*) for the first time in all history.

THE FIRST CASE OF TAX REDUCTION

T HE FIRST recorded social reform took place in the Sumerian city-state of Lagash in the twenty-fourth century B.C. It was directed against the abuses of "former days" practiced by an obnoxious and ubiquitous bureaucracy, such as the levying of high and multifarious taxes and the appropriation of property belonging to the temple. In fact, the Lagashites felt so victimized and oppressed that they threw off the old Ur-Nanshe dynasty and selected a ruler from another family altogether. It was this new *ishakku*, Urukagina by name, who restored law and order in the city and "established the freedom" of its citizens. All this is told in a document composed and written by the Urukagina archivists to commemorate the dedication of a new canal. To better understand and appreciate the contents of this unique inscription, here is a background sketch of some of the more significant social, economic, and political practices in a Sumerian city-state.

The state of Lagash, in the early third millennium B.C., consisted of a small group of prosperous towns, each clustering about a temple. Nominally the city of Lagash, like the other Sumerian city-states, was under the overlordship of the king of the entire land of Sumer. Actually its secular ruler was the *ishakku*, who ruled the city as the representative of the tutelary deity to whom, in accordance with the Sumerian world view, the city had been allotted after the creation. Just how the earlier *ishakku*'s came to power is uncertain; it may well be that they were selected by the freemen of the city, among whom the

temple administrators (*sanga*'s) played a leading political role.
In any case, the office became hereditary in time. The more ambitious and successful of the *ishakku*'s naturally tended to aug-
ment their power and wealth at the expense of the temple, and
this led at times to a struggle for power between temple and
palace.

By and large, the inhabitants of Lagash were farmers and cattle
breeders, boatmen and fishermen, merchants and craftsmen. Its
economy was mixed—partly socialistic and state-controlled, and
partly capitalistic and free. In theory, the soil belonged to the
city god, and therefore, presumably, to his temple, which held it
in trust for all the citizens. In actual practice, while the temple
corporation owned a good deal of land, which it rented out to
some of the people as sharecroppers, much of the soil was the
private property of the individual citizen. Even the poor owned
farms and gardens, houses and cattle. Moreover, because of Lagash's hot, rainless climate, the supervision of the irrigation proj-
ects and waterworks, which were essential to the life and welfare
of the entire community, necessarily had to be communally ad-
ministered. But in many other respects the economy was relatively free and unhampered. Riches and poverty, success and
failure, were, at least to some extent, the result of private enter-
prise and individual drive. The more industrious of the artisans
and craftsmen sold their handmade products in the free town
market. Traveling merchants carried on a thriving trade with
the surrounding states by land and sea, and it is not unlikely that
some of these merchants were private individuals rather than
temple representatives. The citizens of Lagash were conscious of
their civil rights and wary of any government action tending to
abridge their economic and personal freedom, which they cherished as a heritage essential to their way of life. It was this "freedom" that the Lagash citizens had lost, according to our ancient
reform document, in the days before Urukagina's reign. It was
restored by Urukagina when he came to power.

Of the events that led to the lawless and oppressive state of
affairs, there is not a hint in the document. But we may surmise
that it was the direct result of the political and economic forces
unloosed by the drive for power that characterized the ruling

dynasty founded by Ur-Nanshe about 2500 B.C. Inflated with grandiose ambitions for themselves and their state, some of these rulers resorted to "imperialistic" wars and bloody conquests. In a few cases they met with considerable success, and for a brief period one of them actually extended the sway of Lagash over Sumer as a whole, and even over several of the neighboring states. The earlier victories proved ephemeral, however, and in less than a century Lagash was reduced to its earlier boundaries and former status. By the time Urukagina came to power, Lagash had been so weakened that it was a ready prey for its unrelenting enemy to the north, the city-state of Umma.

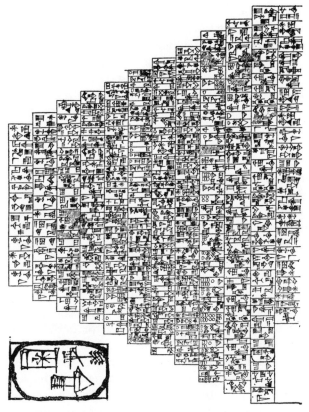

5. Social Reform and "Freedom." Copy of text inscribed on clay cone excavated by French at Tello, site of ancient Lagash.

It was during these cruel wars and their tragic aftermath that the citizens of Lagash found themselves deprived of their political and economic freedom. In order to raise armies and supply them with arms and equipment, the rulers found it necessary to infringe on the personal rights of the individual citizen, to tax his wealth and property to the limit, and to appropriate property belonging to the temple. Under the impact of war, these rulers met with little opposition. Once domestic controls were in the hands of the palace coterie, its members were most unwilling to relinquish them, even in peacetime, for the controls proved highly profitable. Indeed, our ancient bureaucrats devised a variety of sources of revenue and income, taxes and imposts, that might well be the envy of their modern counterparts.

But let the historian who lived in Lagash almost 4,500 years ago, and was therefore a contemporary of the events he reports, tell it more or less in his own words: The inspector of the boatmen seized the boats. The cattle inspector seized the large cattle, seized the small cattle. The fisheries inspector seized the fisheries. When a citizen of Lagash brought a wool-bearing sheep to the palace for shearing, he had to pay five shekels if the wool was white. If a man divorced his wife, the *ishakku* got five shekels, and his vizier got one shekel. If a perfumer made an oil preparation, the *ishakku* got five shekels, the vizier got one shekel, and the palace steward got another shekel. As for the temple and its property, the *ishakku* took it over as his own. To quote our ancient narrator literally: "The oxen of the gods plowed the *ishakku*'s onion patches; the onion and cucumber patches of the *ishakku* were located in the god's best fields." In addition, the more important temple officials, particularly the *sanga*'s, were deprived of many of their donkeys and oxen and of much of their grain.

Even death brought no relief from levies and taxes. When a dead man was brought to the cemetery for burial, a number of officials and parasites made it their business to be on hand to relieve the bereaved family of quantities of barley, bread, and beer, and various furnishings. From one end of the state to the other, our historian observes bitterly, "There were the tax collectors." No wonder the palace waxed fat and prosperous. Its lands and properties formed one vast, continuous, and unbroken estate. In the words of the Sumerian historian, "The houses of the *ishakku* and the fields of the *ishakku,* the houses of the palace harem and the fields of the palace harem, the houses of the palace nursery and the fields of the palace nursery crowded each other side to side."

At this low point in the political and social affairs of Lagash, our Sumerian historian tells us, a new and god-fearing ruler came to the fore, Urukagina by name, who restored justice and freedom to the long-suffering citizens. He removed the inspector of the boatmen from the boats. He removed the cattle inspector from the cattle, large and small. He removed the fisheries inspector from the fisheries. He removed the collector of the silver which had to be paid for the shearing of the white sheep. When a man divorced his wife, neither the *ishakku* nor his vizier got anything. When a perfumer made an oil preparation, neither the *ishakku,* nor the vizier, nor the palace steward got anything. When a dead man was brought to the cemetery for burial, the officials received considerably less of the dead man's goods than formerly, in some cases a good deal less than half. Temple property was now highly respected. From one end of the land to the other, our on-the-scene historian observes, "There was no tax collector." He, Urukagina, "established the freedom" of the citizens of Lagash.

But removing the ubiquitous revenue collectors and the parasitic officials was not Urukagina's only achievement. He also put a stop to the injustice and exploitation suffered by the poor at the hands of the rich. For example, "The house of a lowly man was next to the house of a 'big man,' and the 'big man' said to him, 'I want to buy it from you.' If, when he (the 'big man') was about to buy it from him, the lowly man said, 'pay me as much as I think fair,' and then he (the 'big man') did not buy it, that 'big man' must not 'take it out' on the lowly man."

Urukagina also cleared the city of usurers, thieves, and murderers. If, for instance, "a poor man's son laid out a fishing pond, no one would now steal its fish." No wealthy official dared trespass on the garden of a "poor man's mother," pluck the trees, and carry off their fruit, as had been their wont. Urukagina made a special covenant with Ningirsu, the god of Lagash, that he would not permit widows and orphans to be victimized by the "men of power."

How helpful and effective were these reforms in the struggle for power between Lagash and Umma? Unfortunately, they failed to bring about the expected strength and victory. Urukagina and his reforms were soon "gone with the wind." Like many another reformer, he seemed to have come "too late" with "too little." His reign lasted less than ten years, and he and his city were soon overthrown by Lugalzaggisi, the ambitious ruler of nearby Umma, who succeeded in making himself the king of Sumer and the surrounding lands, at least for a very brief period.

The Urukagina reforms and their social implications made a profound impression on our ancient "historians." The text of the documents has been found inscribed in four more or less varying versions on three clay cones and an oval-shaped plaque. All of them were excavated by the French at Lagash in 1878. They were copied and first translated by François Thureau-Dangin, the same painstaking cuneiformist who treated the historical document described in Chapter 6. However, the interpretation of the Urukagina reforms in the present volume is based on a still unpublished translation of the document prepared by Arno Poebel, the leading Sumerologist of our time.

Freedom under law, it should now be evident, was a way of life not unknown to the Sumerians of the third millennium b.c. Whether laws had already been written down and promulgated in the form of codes in Urukagina's day is still uncertain; at least no law codes from that period have as yet been recovered. But that proves little. For a long time the oldest law code known was one dating back to about 1750 b.c., but only recently three earlier codes have come to light. The oldest of these is the code of the Sumerian ruler Ur-Nammu; it dates from the end of the third millennium b.c. It was excavated in 1889-1900, but it was not until 1952 that it was identified and translated, and even then more or less by accident. For Ur-Nammu's law code, see Chapter 8.

THE FIRST "MOSES"

T HE MOST ANCIENT law code brought to light up till 1947 was that promulgated by Hammurabi, the far-famed Semitic king who began his rule about 1750 B.C. Written in the cuneiform script and in the Semitic language known as Babylonian, it contains close to three hundred laws sandwiched in between a boastful prologue and a curse-laden epilogue. The diorite stele on which the code is inscribed now stands solemn and impressive in the Louvre. From the point of view of fullness of legal detail and state of preservation, it is the most imposing ancient law document as yet uncovered—but not from the point of view of age and antiquity. In 1947 there came to light a law code promulgated by King Lipit-Ishtar, who preceded Hammurabi by more than one hundred and fifty years.

The Lipit-Ishtar code, as it is now generally called, is inscribed not on a stele but on a sun-baked clay tablet. It is written in the cuneiform script, but in the non-Semitic Sumerian language. The tablet was excavated shortly after the turn of the century, but for various reasons had remained unidentified and unpublished. As reconstructed and translated with my help by Francis Steele, formerly assistant curator in the University Museum, it is seen to contain a prologue, epilogue, and an unknown number of laws, of which thirty-seven are preserved wholly or in part.

But Lipit-Ishtar's claim to fame as the world's first lawgiver was short-lived. In 1948, Taha Baqir, the curator of the Iraq Museum in Baghdad, was digging in an obscure mound called Harmal, and he announced the discovery of two tablets inscribed with an older law code. Like the Hammurabi code, these tablets were written in the Semitic Babylonian language. They were studied and copied that very year by the well-known Yale cuneiformist Albrecht Goetze. In the brief prologue that precedes the laws (there is no epilogue), a king by the name of Bilalama is mentioned. He may have lived some seventy years before Lipit-Ishtar. It is this Semitic Bilalama code, therefore, which seemed to be entitled to priority honors until 1952, when I was privileged to copy and translate a tablet inscribed with part of a law code promulgated by a Sumerian king named Ur-Nammu. This ruler, who founded the now well-known Third Dynasty of Ur, began his reign, even according to lowest chronological estimates, about 2050 B.C., some three hundred years before the Babylonian King Hammurabi. The Ur-Nammu tablet is one of the hundreds of Sumerian literary tablets in the collection of the Museum of the Ancient Orient in Istanbul, where I spent the year 1951-52 as Fulbright Research Professor.

In all probability I would have missed the Ur-Nammu tablet altogether had it not been for an opportune letter from F. R. Kraus, now Professor of Cuneiform Studies at the University of Leiden in Holland. I had met Kraus a number of years before, during my earlier Sumerological researches in the Istanbul Museum of the Ancient Orient, where he was curator. Hearing that I was once again in Istanbul, he wrote me a letter of reminiscences and shop talk. His letter said that some years ago, in the course of his duties as curator in the Istanbul Museum, he had come upon two fragments of a tablet inscribed with Sumerian laws, had made a "join" of the two pieces, and had catalogued the resulting tablet as No. 3191 of the Nippur collection of the Museum. I might be interested in its contents, he added, and perhaps would want to copy it.

Since Sumerian law tablets are extremely rare, I had No. 3191 brought to my working table at once. There it lay, a sun-baked tablet, light brown in color, 20 by 10 centimeters in size. More than half of the writing was destroyed, and what was preserved seemed at first hopelessly unintelligible. But after several days of concentrated study, its contents began to become clear and take shape, and I realized with no little excitement that what I held in

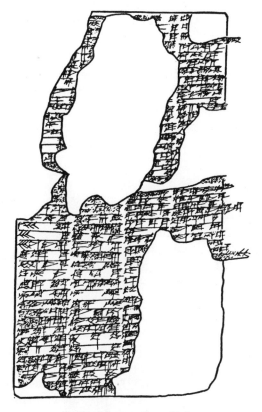

6. Ur-Nammu Law Code.
Hand copy of the Pro-
logue from tablet in Mu-
seum of the Ancient Ori-
ent.

my hand was a copy of the oldest law code as yet known to man.

The tablet was divided by the ancient scribe into eight columns, four on the obverse and four on the reverse. Each of the
columns contains about forty-five small ruled spaces, less than
half of which are legible. The obverse contains a long prologue
which is only partially intelligible, because of the numerous breaks
in the text. Briefly, it runs as follows:

After the world had been created, and after the fate of the

land Sumer and of the city Ur (the Biblical Ur of the Chaldees) had been decided, An and Enlil, the two leading deities of the Sumerian pantheon, appointed the moon-god Nanna as the King of Ur. One day, Ur-Nammu was selected by the god to rule over Sumer and Ur as his earthly representative. The new king's first acts had to do with the political and military safety of Ur and Sumer. In particular he found it necessary to do battle with the bordering city-state of Lagash, which was expanding at Ur's expense. He defeated and put to death its ruler, Namhani, and then, "with the power of Nanna, the king of the city," he reestablished Ur's former boundaries.

Now came the time to turn to internal affairs, and to institute social and moral reforms. He removed the "chiselers" and the grafters, or, as the code itself describes them, the "grabbers" of the citizens' oxen, sheep, and donkeys. He then established and regulated honest and unchangeable weights and measures. He saw to it that "the orphan did not fall a prey to the wealthy"; "the widow did not fall a prey to the powerful"; "the man of one shekel did not fall a prey to the man of one mina (sixty shekels)." Although the relevant passage is destroyed on the tablet, it was no doubt to ensure justice in the land and to promote the welfare of its citizens that he promulgated the laws which followed.

The laws themselves probably began on the reverse of the tablet. They are so badly damaged that the contents of only five of them can be restored with some degree of certainty. One of them seems to involve a trial by water ordeal; another seems to treat of the return of a slave to his master. But it is the other three laws, fragmentary and difficult as their contents are, that are of very special importance for the history of man's social and spiritual growth. For they show that, even before 2000 B.C., the law of "eye for eye" and "tooth for tooth"—still prevalent to a large extent in the Biblical laws of a much later day—had already given way to the far more humane approach in which a money fine was substituted as a punishment. Because of their historical significance, these three laws are here quoted in the original Sumerian, as transcribed into our alphabet, together with their literal translation:

tukum-bi	If
(*lu-lu-ra*	(a man to a man
gish- . . . -ta)	with a . . . -instrument)
. . . *-a-ni*	his . . .
gir in-kud	the foot has cut off,
10-gin-ku-babbar	10 silver shekels
i-la-e	he shall pay.
tukum-bi	If
lu-lu-ra	a man to a man
gish-tukul-ta	with a weapon
gir-pad-du	his bones
al-mu-ra-ni	of . . .
in-zi-ir	severed,
1-ma-na-ku-babbar	1 silver mina
i-la-e	he shall pay.
tukum-bi	If
lu-lu-ra	a man to a man
geshpu-ta	with a geshpu-instrument
ka- . . . in-kud	the nose (?) has cut off,
⅔-ma-na-ku-babbar	⅔ of a silver mina
i-la-e	he shall pay.

How long will Ur-Nammu retain his place as the world's first lawgiver? Perhaps not for long. There are indications that there were lawgivers in Sumer long before Ur-Nammu was born. Sooner or later, a lucky "digger" will come up with a copy of a law code preceding that of Ur-Nammu by a century or more.

Law and justice were key concepts in ancient Sumer, in both theory and practice, and Sumerian social and economic life was permeated by them. In the past century, archaeologists have uncovered thousands of clay tablets inscribed with all sorts of Sumerian legal documents—contracts, deeds, wills, promissory notes, receipts, and court decisions. In ancient Sumer the advanced student devoted much of his schooltime to the field of law, and he constantly practiced the writing of the highly specialized legal terminology, as well as of law codes and those court decisions which had taken on the force of legal precedents. The full text of one such court decision became available in 1950. This document, which records what might be termed "the case of the silent wife," is discussed in Chapter 9.

THE FIRST LEGAL PRECEDENT

A MURDER was committed in the land of Sumer in 1850 B.C. or thereabouts. Three men—a barber, a gardener, and one whose occupation is not known—killed a temple official by the name of Lu-Inanna. The murderers, for some unstated reason, then informed the victim's wife, Nin-dada, that her husband had been killed. Strangely enough, she kept their secret and did not notify the authorities.

But the arm of the law was long and sure, even in those days, at least in the highly civilized state of Sumer. The crime was brought to the attention of King Ur-Ninurta, in his capital city Isin, and he turned the case over for trial to the Citizens Assembly at Nippur, which acted as a court of justice.

In this assembly, nine men arose to prosecute the accused. They argued that not only the three actual murderers, but the wife as well, should be executed, presumably because she had remained silent after learning of the crime and could thus be considered an accessory after the fact.

Two men in the assembly then spoke up in defense of the woman. They pleaded that the woman had taken no part in the murder of her husband, and that she should therefore go unpunished.

The members of the assembly agreed with the defense. They argued that the woman was not unjustified in remaining silent, since it seemed that her husband had failed to support her. Their verdict concluded with the statement that "the punishment of those who actually killed should suffice." Accordingly, only the three men were condemned, by the Nippur assembly, to be executed.

The record of this murder trial was found inscribed in the Sumerian language on a clay tablet that was dug up in 1950 by a joint expedition of the Oriental Institute of the University of Chicago and the University Museum of the University of Pennsylvania. Thorkild Jacobsen and I studied and translated it. The translation of some of the Sumerian words and phrases on the tablet is still in doubt, but the essential meaning is reasonably assured. One corner of the newly found tablet is destroyed, but it was possible to fill in the missing lines from a small fragment of another copy of the same record dug up at Nippur by the earlier expedition of the University Museum. The fact that two copies of the same record have been found shows that the decision of the Nippur Assembly in the case of the "silent wife" was celebrated throughout the legal circles of Sumer as a memorable precedent, not unlike a decision of our own Supreme Court.

Nanna-sig, the son of Lu-Sin, Ku-Enlil, the son of Ku-Nanna, the barber, and Enlil-ennam, the slave of Adda-kalla, the gardener, killed Lu-Inanna, the son of Lugal-apindu, the *nishakku-official*.

After Lu-Inanna, the son of Lugal-apindu, had been put to death, they told Nin-dada, the daughter of Lu-Ninurta, the wife of Lu-Inanna, that her husband Lu-Inanna had been killed.

Nin-dada, the daughter of Lu-Ninurta, opened not her mouth, (her) lips remained sealed.

Their case was (then) brought to (the city) Isin before the king, (and) the King Ur-Ninurta ordered their case to be taken up in the Assembly of Nippur.

(There) Ur-gula, son of Lugal- . . , Dudu, the bird-hunter, Ali-ellati, the dependent, Buzu, the son of Lu-Sin, Eluti, the son of . . -Ea, Shesh-Kalla, the porter (?), Lugal-Kan, the gardener, Lugal-azida, the son of Sin-andul, (and) Shesh-kalla, the son of Shara- . . , faced (the Assembly) and said:

"They who have killed a man are not (worthy) of life. Those three males and that woman should be killed in front of the chair of Lu-Inanna, the son of Lugal-apindu, the *nishakku*-official."

(Then) Shu . . -lilum, the . . -official of Ninurta, (and) Ubar-Sin, the gardener, faced (the Assembly) and said:

"Granted that the husband of Nin-dada, the daughter of Lu-Ninurta, had been killed, (but) what had (?) the woman done (?) that she should be killed?"

(Then) the (members of the) Assembly of Nippur faced (them) and said:

"A woman whose husband did not support (?) her—granted that she knew her husband's enemies, and that (after) her husband had been killed she heard that her husband had been killed—why should she not remain silent (?) about (?) him? Is it she (?) who killed her husband? The punishment of those (?) who (actually) killed should suffice."

In accordance with the decision (?) of the Assembly of Nippur, Nanna-sig, the son of Lu-Sin, Ku-Enlil, the son of Ku-Nanna, the barber, and Enlil-ennam, the slave of Adda-kalla, the gardener, were handed over (to the executioner) to be killed.

(This is) a case taken up by the Assembly of Nippur.

After the translation had been made, it seemed relevant to compare the verdict with what the modern decision might have been in a similar situation. We therefore sent the translation to the late Owen J. Roberts, then dean of the Law School, University of Pennsylvania (he had been associate justice of the United States Supreme Court, 1930-45), and asked his opinion. His answer was of great interest, for in this legal case modern judges would have agreed with the Sumerian judges of long ago, and the verdict would have been the same. To quote Justice Roberts, "The wife would not be guilty as an accessory after the fact under our law. An accessory after the fact must not only know that the felony was committed, but must also receive, relieve, comfort, or assist the felon."

But law is not the only field in which significant Sumerian documents have recently come to light. In 1954 a medical document, inscribed with man's first pharmacopoeia, was described in a preliminary report including a translation of the more intelligible part of the document. To be sure, the physician was known in Sumer throughout the third millennium B.C. A physician by the name of Lulu practiced his profession in Ur, the Biblical Ur of the Chaldees, as early as 2700 B.C. or thereabouts. But all other medical texts from Mesopotamia published before 1954 were from the first millennium B.C., and these are often full of spells and incantations rather than real medical treatment. The newly translated tablet, on the other hand, dates back to the last quarter of the third millennium B.C., and the prescriptions inscribed on it do not contain a trace of magic and sorcery. This tablet, the oldest medical document, is discussed in Chapter 10.

THE FIRST PHARMACOPOEIA

A<small>N ANONYMOUS</small> Sumerian physician, who lived toward the end of the third millennium B.C., decided to collect and record, for his colleagues and students, his more valuable medical prescriptions. He prepared a tablet of moist clay, 3 ¾ by 6¼ inches in size, sharpened a reed stylus to a wedge-shaped end, and wrote down, in the cuneiform script of his day, more than a dozen of his favorite remedies. This clay document, the oldest medical "handbook" known to man, lay buried in the Nippur ruins for more than four thousand years, until it was excavated by an American expedition and brought to the University Museum in Philadelphia.

I first learned of the existence of the tablet from a publication by my predecessor in the University Museum, Dr. Leon Legrain, curator emeritus of the Babylonian Section. In an article in the 1940 *Bulletin* of the University Museum, under the title "Nippur Old Drugstore," he made a valiant attempt to translate part of its contents. But it was obvious that this was not a task for the cuneiformist alone. The phraseology of the inscription was highly technical and specialized, and the cooperation of a historian of science was needed, particularly one trained in the field of chemistry. After I had become curator of the tablet collections in the University Museum, I often went longingly to the cupboard where this "medical" tablet was kept and brought it to my desk for study. More than once I was tempted to make another effort at translating its contents. Fortunately I did not succumb. Again and again I returned it to its place and awaited the opportune moment.

One Saturday morning in the spring of 1953, a young man came into my office and introduced himself as Martin Levey, a Philadelphia chemist. A doctorate in the history of science had just been conferred on him, and he asked if I knew of any tablets in the Museum's collection that he could help with from the point of view of the history of science and technology. Here was my opportunity! Once again I took the tablet from its cupboard, but this time it did not go back until it was at least tentatively translated. For several weeks Levey and I worked on its contents. I restricted myself primarily to the reading of the Sumerian signs and the analysis of the grammatical construction. It was Martin Levey, with his understanding and knowledge of the chemical and technological processes of the ancients, who brought to life again the intelligible portions of man's first pharmacopoeia.

The Sumerian physician, we learn from this ancient document, went, as does his modern counterpart, to botanical, zoological, and mineralogical sources for his materia medica. His favorite minerals were sodium chloride (salt) and potassium nitrate (saltpeter). From the animal kingdom he utilized milk, snake skin, and turtle shell. But most of his medicinals came from the botanical world, from plants such as cassia, myrtle, asafoetida, and thyme, and from trees such as the willow, pear, fir, fig, and date. These simples were prepared from the seed, root, branch, bark, or gum, and must have been stored, as today, in either solid or powdered form.

The remedies prescribed by our physician were both salves and filtrates to be applied externally, and liquids to be taken internally. The usual instructions for compounding salves were to pulverize one or more simples, to infuse the powder with "kushumma" wine, and to spread both common tree oil and cedar oil over the mixture. For one prescription in which pulverized river clay was one of the simples, the powder was to be kneaded in water and honey, and "sea" oil instead of tree oil was to be spread over the mixture.

The filtrate prescriptions were more complicated and were followed by directions for treatment. Three of the prescriptions (the Sumerian text is reasonably certain) made use of the process of decoction. In order to extract the sought-for principles, the ingredients were boiled in water, and alkali and salts were added, probably to obtain a greater yield of total extract. To separate the organic materials, the aqueous solution was no doubt subjected to filtration, although this is not stated explicitly in any of the prescriptions. The ailing organ was then treated with the filtrate, either by sprinkling or washing. Following this, oil was rubbed on it, and then one or more additional simples were added.

As for those remedies which were to be taken internally, beer was usually the vehicle chosen to make them palatable to the patient. The several simples were ground to a powder and dissolved in beer for the sick man to drink. In one case, however, where milk as well as beer seems to have been used for infusion, an unidentified "river" (?) oil was the vehicle.

Even from this lone tablet—the only medical text as yet recovered from the third millennium B.C.—it is clear that Sumerian pharmacology had made considerable progress. The tablet reveals, though indirectly, a broad acquaintance with quite a number of rather elaborate chemical operations and procedures. For example, in several of the prescriptions the instructions were to "purify" the simples before pulverization, a step which must have required several chemical operations. For another example, the pulverized alkali used as a simple in one of the prescriptions is probably the alkali ash produced by the pit-burning of one of a number of plants of the Chenopodiaceae (most likely the *Salicornia fruticosa*), which are rich in soda. Soda ash derived in this manner was used in the seventh century B.C., and in the Middle Ages it was used for glassmaking. Chemically speaking, it is of interest that the two prescriptions on our tablet that called for alkali used it together with substances which contain a great deal of natural fat, thus producing a soap for external application.

Another substance prescribed by our Sumerian doctor which could have been obtained only with some chemical knowledge is potassium nitrate, or saltpeter. To judge from much later Assyrian times, it is not unlikely that the Sumerians inspected the surface drains in which nitrogenous waste products, such as urine, flowed, and removed for purification whatever crystalline formation was to be found. The problem of separating the components, which no doubt included sodium chloride and other salts of sodium and potassium, as well as degradation products of nitrogenous matter, was probably solved by the method of fractional crystallization. In India and Egypt there is still current the ancient procedure of mixing lime or old mortar with decomposing nitrogenous organic matter to form calcium nitrate, which is then lixiviated and boiled with wood ash containing potassium carbonate to yield niter on evaporation of the filtrate.

In one respect our ancient text is most disappointing. It fails to name the diseases for which the remedies were intended, and we are unable to check their therapeutic value. The remedies were probably of little value, since the Sumerian physician seems to have made no use of experiment and verification. The selection of many of the drugs no doubt reflected the long-standing confidence of the ancients in the odoriferous properties of plants. Some of the prescriptions had their good points—for example, the making of a detergent was of value. And such substances as salt and saltpeter were effective, the former as an antiseptic and the latter as an astringent.

These Sumerian prescriptions suffer from at least one other obvious omission: they fail to specify the quantities to be used in compounding the simples, as well as the dosage and frequency of application of the medicine. This may have been the result of "professional jealousy," and the Sumerian physician may have purposely concealed the quantitative details in order to protect his secrets from nonmedical groups or perhaps even from his colleagues. More probably, the quantitative details just did not loom important to the Sumerian prescription-writer, since they could be figured out more or less empirically in the course of actual preparation and use of the remedies.

It is interesting to note that the Sumerian physician who wrote our tablet did not resort to magic spells and incantations. Not one god or demon is mentioned anywhere throughout the text. This does not mean that the use of charms and exorcisms to cure the sick was unknown in Sumer in the third millennium B.C. Quite the contrary is true, as is obvious from the contents of some three-score small tablets inscribed with incantations and so designated by the authors of the inscriptions. Like the Babylonians of later days, the Sumerians attributed numerous diseases to the unwelcome presence of harmful demons in the sick man's body. Half a dozen such demons are actually named in a Sumerian hymn dedicated to the patron deity of the art of medicine, a goddess variously known as Bau, Ninisinna, and Gula, and described as "the great physician of the blackheaded people (the Sumerians)." However, the startling fact remains that our clay document, the oldest "page" of medical text as yet uncovered, is completely free from mystical and irrational elements.

The discovery of a medical tablet written toward the end of the third millennium B.C. was a surprise even to the cuneiformist, since it is in the field of agriculture rather than medicine that our first "handbook" might have been expected. Agriculture was the mainstay of the Sumerian economy, the primary source of its wealth and well-being. Farming methods and techniques were already highly developed before the third millennium B.C. But the only farmers' "handbook" that has as yet come to light dates from the early second millennium B.C. It is discussed in Chapter 11.

THE FIRST "FARMER'S ALMANAC"

A SMALL CLAY TABLET discovered by an American expedition in Iraq made possible the restoration of a document more than 3,500 years old that is of prime importance in the history of agriculture and its techniques. The 1949-50 expedition, sponsored jointly by the Oriental Institute of the University of Chicago and the University Museum of the University of Pennsylvania, excavated the 3- by 4½-inch inscription in the ancient Sumerian site Nippur. The tablet was in poor condition on its arrival. But after it had been baked, cleaned, and mended in the laboratory of the University Museum, practically its entire text became legible. Before the discovery at Nippur, eight other clay tablets and fragments inscribed with different parts of this agricultural "primer" were already known, but it was impossible to make a trustworthy restoration of the text as a whole until the new Nippur piece, with thirty-five lines from the middle of the composition, came to light.

The restored document, 108 lines in length, consists of a series of instructions addressed by a farmer to his son for the purpose of guiding him throughout his yearly agricultural activities, beginning with the inundation of the fields in May-June and ending with the cleaning and winnowing of the freshly harvested crops in the following April-May. Before the Nippur discovery, two similar farmer's "handbooks" were known from ancient days: Virgil's far-famed and highly poetic *Georgics* and Hesiod's *Work and Days*. The latter, which is by far the earlier of the two, was probably written in the eighth century B.C. On the other hand, the newly restored Sumerian clay document was actually inscribed about 1700 B.C., and thus antedates Hesiod's work by approximately a millennium.

The Sumerian farm "handbook" begins with the line, "In days of yore a farmer gave (these) instructions to his son." The directions that follow concern the more important chores and labors that a farmer must perform to ensure a successful crop. Since irrigation was essential for Sumer's parched soil, the in-

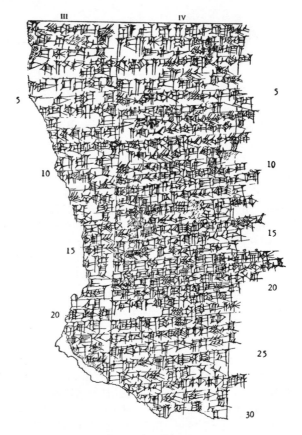

7. Farmer's Almanac. Hand copy (unpublished) of four-column tablet excavated in Nippur, 1949-50.

structions began with advice concerning irrigation works: Care must be taken that their water does not rise too high over the field; when the water subsides, the wet ground must be carefully guarded against trampling oxen and other prowlers; the field must then be cleared of weeds and stubble and fenced about.

The farmer was next counseled to have his household and hired help prepare in advance all the necessary tools, implements, baskets, and containers. He must see to it that he has an extra ox for the plow. Before beginning to plow, he should have the ground broken up twice by the mattock and once by the hoe. Where necessary the hammer must be used to pulverize the clods. He was counseled to stand over his laborers and see to it that they did not shirk their work.

The work of plowing and sowing was carried on simultaneously by means of a seeder—that is, a plow with an attachment that carried the seed from a container through a narrow funnel down to the furrow. The farmer was instructed to plow eight furrows to each strip of approximately twenty feet. He was told to see to it that the seed was placed at an even depth. In the words of the "handbook": "Keep an eye on the man who puts in the barley seed that he make the seed fall two fingers uniformly." If the seed failed to penetrate the earth properly, he must change the share, "the tongue of the plow." There were several kinds of furrows, according to the writer of the "handbook," who advised in particular: "Where you have plowed straight furrows, plow (now) diagonal furrows; where you have plowed diagonal furrows, plow (now) straight furrows." Following the sowing, the furrows had to be cleared of clods, so that the sprouting of the barley would not be impeded.

"On the day when the seed breaks through the ground," the Sumerian "handbook" continues, the farmer should say a prayer to Ninkilim, the goddess of field mice and vermin, lest these harm the growing grain; he should also scare away the birds. When the barley had grown sufficiently to fill the narrow bottoms of the furrows, he was to water it; and when it was dense enough to cover the field like the "mat in the middle of a boat," he was to water it a second time. A third time he was to water the "royal" grain. Should he then notice a reddening of the wet grain, it was the dread *samana*-disease that was endangering the crops. If the crop showed improvement, he was to water it a fourth time, and thus get an extra yield of 10 per cent.

When the time came for harvesting, the farmer was not to wait until the barley bent under its own weight, but was to cut it "in the day of its strength"; that is, just at the right moment. Three men worked as a team on the standing grain—a reaper, a binder, and a third whose duties are not clear.

The threshing which followed immediately upon the harvesting was done by means of a sledge drawn back and forth over the heaped-up grain stalks for a period of five days. The barley was then "opened" with an "opener," which was drawn by oxen. By this time, however, the grain had become unclean through contact with the ground. Therefore, following an appropriate prayer, the grain was winnowed with pitchforks, laid on sticks, and thus freed of dirt and dust.

The document closes with the statement that the agricultural rules laid down were not the farmer's own but those of the god Ninurta, the son and "true farmer" of the leading Sumerian deity, Enlil.

In order that the reader might taste the real flavor of the first farmer's handbook in man's recorded history, here is a literal

8. Plowing Scene. Reconstruction of plowing scene from a cylinder-seal impression on Nippur tablet in University Museum. Note seeder-plow.

translation of its first eighteen lines. The reader is asked to bear in mind that the renderings are in some cases tentative, since the text is full of obscure and perplexing technical terminology. The translation that follows (it will no doubt be considerably improved over the years as our knowledge of Sumerian language and culture grows) has been worked out *provisionally* by Benno Landsberger and Thorkild Jacobsen—cuneiformists of the Oriental Institute of the University of Chicago—and the present writer.

In days of yore a farmer gave (these) instructions to his son: When you are about to cultivate your field, take care to open the irrigation works (so that) their water does not rise too high in it (the field). When you have emptied it of water, watch the field's wet ground that it stays even; let no wandering ox trample it. Chase the prowlers and have it treated as settled land. Clear it with ten narrow axes (weighing no more than) ⅔ of a pound each. Its stubble (?) should be torn up by hand and tied in bundles; its narrow holes shall be gone over with a drag; and the four sides of the field shall be fenced about. While the field is burning (in the summer sun) let it be divided up into equal parts. Let your tools hum with activity (?). The yoke-bar should be made fast, your new whip should be fastened with nails, and the handle to which your old whip was fastened should be mended by the workers' children.

Not only cereal farms but also vegetable gardens and fruit groves were sources of Sumer's economic wealth. One of the more significant horticultural techniques practiced in Sumer from earliest days was shade-tree gardening—that is, the planting of broad shade trees to protect the garden plants from sun and wind. This we learn from a Sumerian poem that is presented in Chapter 12.

THE FIRST EXPERIMENT
IN SHADE-TREE GARDENING

As ANNUAL PROFESSOR of the American Schools of Oriental Research and representative of the University Museum, I traveled to Istanbul and Baghdad in 1946. In Istanbul I stayed some four months and copied more than a hundred tablets and fragments inscribed with Sumerian epics and myths. The majority of the copied pieces consisted of small and middle-sized fragments. But among them were a number of considerably longer tablets—for example, the twelve-column tablet inscribed with the "war of nerves" (see Chapter 4); the eight-column tablet inscribed with the disputation between summer and winter (see Chapter 18); and a six-column piece inscribed with a hitherto unknown myth which I have titled "Inanna and Shukallituda: The Gardener's Mortal Sin."

This last-mentioned document originally must have measured 6 by 7¼ inches, but now measures only 4¼ by 7 inches. The first and last columns are almost entirely destroyed, but the remaining four columns permit the restoration of some two hundred lines of text, of which more than half are complete. As the contents of the myth gradually became intelligible, it was obvious that not only was its plot unusual, but the poem was highly significant in two other respects. In the first place, it features an incident in which a deity, angered by the impious deed of a mortal, turns the water of an entire land into blood. The only parallel to this "blood-plague" motif in the entire range of ancient literature is the Biblical exodus story in which Jahweh turns the water of all Egypt into blood when Pharaoh refuses to send forth the enslaved Israelites to serve him. Secondly, the author of our ancient myth seems to explain the origin of shade-tree gardening, and thus reveals that the horticultural technique of planting shade trees in a garden or grove to protect the plants from wind and sun was known and practiced thousands of years ago. The plot of this myth runs as follows:

Once upon a time there lived a gardener by the name of Shukallituda, whose diligent efforts at gardening had met with nothing but failure. Although he had carefully watered his furrows and garden patches, the plants had withered away. The raging winds smote his face with the "dust of the mountains." All that he had carefully tended turned desolate. He thereupon lifted his eyes east and west to the starry heavens, studied the omens, observed and learned the divine laws. Having acquired new wisdom, he planted the (as yet unidentified) *sarbatu* tree in the garden, a tree whose broad shade lasts from sunrise to sunset. As a consequence of this horticultural experiment, Shukallituda's garden blossomed forth with all kinds of greens.

One day the goddess Inanna (the Sumerian counterpart of the Greek Aphrodite and the Roman Venus), after having traversed heaven and earth, lay down to rest her tired body not far from the garden of Shukallituda. He spied on her from the edge of his garden. Then he took advantage of her extreme weariness and cohabited with her. When morning came and the sun rose, Inanna looked about her in consternation and determined to ferret out, at all costs, the mortal who had so shamefully abused her. She therefore sent three plagues against Sumer: (1) She filled all the wells of the land with blood, so that all the palm groves and vineyards became saturated with blood. (2) She sent destructive winds and storms against the land. (3) The nature of the third plague is uncertain, since the relevant lines are too fragmentary.

Despite the three plagues, Inanna was unable to locate her defiler. After each plague Shukallituda went to his father's house and informed him of his danger. The father advised his son to direct his step to his brothers, the "blackheaded people" (the people of Sumer), and to stay close to the urban centers. Shukallituda followed this advice, and as a result Inanna did not find him. She realized bitterly that she was unable to avenge the outrage committed against her. She therefore decided to go to the city Eridu, to the house of Enki, the Sumerian god of wisdom, to seek his advice and help. Here the tablet breaks off, and the end of the story remains unknown.

The following is a tentative translation of one of the relevant and more intelligible portions of the poem:

> Shukallituda, ... ,
> When pouring water over the furrows,
> When digging wells by the patches, ... ,
> Stumbled over its roots, was cut up by them;
> The raging winds with whatever they carried,
> With the dust of the mountains, struck his face,
> At his . . face and . . hands,
> They blew it about, he knew not its . .
>
> He (thereupon) lifted his eyes toward the lands below,
>   Looked up at the stars in the east,
> Lifted his eyes toward the lands above,
>   Looked up at the stars in the west,
> Gazed at the auspicious inscribed heaven,
> From the inscribed heaven learned the omens,
> Saw there how to carry out the divine laws,
> Studied the decrees of the gods.
> In the garden, in five to ten unapproachable places,
> In those places he planted one tree as a protecting cover,
> The tree's protecting cover—the *sarbatu*-tree of wide shade—
> Its shade below, dawn,
> Noon, and dusk, did not turn away.
>
> One day my queen, after crossing heaven, crossing earth,
> Inanna, after crossing heaven, crossing earth,
> After crossing Elam and Shubur,
> After crossing . . . . ,
> The hierodule (Inanna) in her weariness approached (the garden),
>   fell fast asleep,
> Shukallituda saw her from the edge of his garden, ...
> Copulated with her, kissed her,
> Returned to the edge of his garden.
>
> Dawn broke, the sun rose,
> The woman looked about her in dread.
> Inanna looked about her in dread.

Then, the woman, because of her pudendum, what harm she did!
Inanna, because of her pudendum, what did she do!
All the wells of the land she filled with blood,
All the groves and gardens of the land she sated with blood,
The (male) slaves coming to gather firewood, drink nothing but
    blood,
The (female) slaves coming to fill up with water, fill up with
    nothing but blood,
"I must find him who copulated with me among all the lands,"
    she said.

But him who copulated with her she found not,
For the young man entered his father's house,
Shukallituda says to his father:
"Father, when pouring water over the furrows,
When digging wells by the patches, ... ,
I stumbled over its roots, was cut up by them;
The raging winds, with whatever they carried,
With the dust of the mountains, struck my face,
At my , . face and . . hands,
They blew it about, I knew not its . .

"I (thereupon) lifted my eyes toward the lands below,
    Looked up at the stars in the east,
Lifted my eyes toward the lands above,
    Looked up at the stars in the west,
Gazed at the auspicious inscribed heaven,
From the inscribed heaven learned the omens,
Saw there how to carry out the divine laws,
Studied the decrees of the gods.
In the garden, in five to ten unapproachable places,
In those places I planted one tree as a protecting cover.
The tree's protecting cover—the *sarbatu*-tree of wide shade—
Its shade below, dawn,
Noon, and dusk, did not turn away.

"One day my queen, after crossing heaven, crossing earth,
Inanna, after crossing heaven, crossing earth,
After crossing Elam and Shubur,
After crossing . . . . ,
The hierodule in her weariness approached (the garden), fell
    fast asleep;
I saw her from the edge of my garden,
Copulated with her, kissed her,
Returned to the edge of my garden.

"Dawn broke, the sun rose,

The woman looked about her in dread,
Inanna looked about her in dread.
Then, the woman, because of her pudendum, what harm she did!
Inanna, because of her pudendum, what did she do!
All the wells of the land she filled with blood,
All the groves and gardens of the land she sated with blood,
The (male) slaves coming to gather firewood, drink nothing but blood,
The (female) slaves coming to fill up with water, fill up with nothing but blood,
'I must find him who copulated with me,' she said."

But him who copulated with her she found not,
For his father answers the young man,
His father answers Shukallituda:
"Son, stay close to your brothers' cities,
Direct your step and go to your brothers, the blackheaded people,
The woman (Inanna) will not find you in the midst of the lands."
He (Shukallituda) stayed close to his brothers' cities,
Directed his step to his brothers, the blackheaded people,
The woman found him not in the midst of all the lands.

Then, the woman, because of her pudendum, what harm she did!
Inanna, because of her pudendum, what did she do! . . . .
(The poem continues with the second plague.)

We turn now from the material to the spiritual, from technology to philosophy. The Sumerians of the third millennium B.C., there is good reason to believe, evolved a number of metaphysical and theological concepts which, though never explicitly formulated, became more or less paradigmatic for the entire Near East, and even left their imprint on the Hebrew and Christian dogmas of later days. The more significant of their concepts are presented in Chapter 13, together with an analysis of the largely unformulated and unarticulated rational and logical inferences behind them. The chapter also shows how the Sumerian intellectual speculations and philosophical conclusions were isolated and adduced primarily from the Sumerian myths and epic tales, in spite of the fact that these resort to fantasy and imagination rather than reason and logic for their literary effect.

MAN'S FIRST COSMOGONY
AND COSMOLOGY

T HE SUMERIANS failed to develop a systematic philosophy in the accepted sense of the word. It never occurred to them to raise any questions concerning the fundamental nature of reality and knowledge, and they therefore evolved practically nothing corresponding to the philosophical subdivision which is commonly known today as epistemology. They did, however, speculate on the nature and, more particularly, the origin of the universe, and on its method of operation. There is good reason to infer that in the third millennium B.C. there emerged a group of Sumerian thinkers and teachers who, in their quest for satisfactory answers to some of the problems raised by their cosmic speculations, evolved a cosmology and theology carrying such high intellectual conviction that their doctrines became the basic creed and dogma of much of the ancient Near East.

These cosmological ideas and theological speculations are nowhere explicitly formulated in philosophical terms and systematic statements. Sumerian philosophers had failed to discover that all-important intellectual tool which we take for granted: the scientific method of definition and generalization, without which our present-day science would never have reached its prominence. To take even so relatively simple a principle as cause and effect, the Sumerian thinker, while fully aware of the innumerable concrete examples of its operation, never came upon the idea of formulating it as a general, all-pervading law. Almost all our information concerning Sumerian philosophy, theology, cos-

mology, and cosmogony, has to be ferreted out and pieced together from Sumerian literary works, particularly myths, epic
tales, and hymns.

What were some of the "scientific" data at their disposal, which
underpinned their assumptions and led to the narrowing down of
their philosophical speculations to theological certainties? In the
eyes of the Sumerian teachers and sages, the major components
of the universe were heaven and earth; indeed, their term for
universe was *an-ki*, a compound word meaning "heaven-earth."
The earth, they thought, was a flat disk; heaven, a hollow
space enclosed at top and bottom by a solid surface in the shape
of a vault. Just what this heavenly solid was thought to be is still
uncertain. To judge from the fact that the Sumerian term for
tin is "metal of heaven," it may have been tin. Between heaven
and earth they recognized a substance which they called *lil*, a
word whose approximate meaning is "wind" (air, breath, spirit);
its most significant characteristics seem to be movement and ex-
pansion, and it therefore corresponds roughly to our "atmosphere." The sun, moon, planets, and stars were taken to be made
of the same stuff as the atmosphere, but endowed, in addition,
with the quality of luminosity. Surrounding the "heaven-earth"
on all sides and at top and bottom was the boundless sea, in
which the universe somehow remained fixed and immovable.

From these basic assumptions concerning the structure of the
universe, which seemed to the Sumerian thinkers obvious and
indisputable facts, they evolved a cosmogony to fit. First, they
concluded, was the primeval sea; the indications are that they
looked upon the sea as a kind of "first cause" and "prime mover,"
and that they never asked themselves just what was prior to the
sea in time and space. In this primeval sea was somehow engendered the universe, the "heaven-earth," consisting of a vaulted
heaven superimposed over a flat earth and united with it. In
between, separating heaven from earth, was the moving and expanding "atmosphere." Out of this atmosphere were fashioned
the luminous bodies—the moon, sun, planets, and stars. Following
the separation of heaven and earth—and the creation of the light-
giving astral bodies—plant, animal, and human life came into
existence.

Who created this universe and kept it operating, day in day out, year in year out, throughout the ages? From as far back as our written records go, the Sumerian theologian assumed as axiomatic the existence of a pantheon consisting of a group of living beings, manlike in form but superhuman and immortal, who, though invisible to mortal eye, guide and control the cosmos in accordance with well-laid plans and duly prescribed laws. Each of these anthropomorphic but superhuman beings was deemed to be in charge of a particular component of the universe and to guide its activities in accordance with established rules and regulations. One or another of these beings had charge of the great realms of heaven and earth, sea and air; the major astral bodies, sun, moon, and planet; atmospheric forces such as wind, storm, and tempest; and, in the realm of the earth, natural entities such as river, mountain, and plain; cultural entities such as city and state, dike and ditch, field and farm; even implements such as the pickax, brickmold, and plow.

Behind this axiomatic assumption of the Sumerian theologians, no doubt, lay a logical inference, since they could hardly have seen any of these humanlike beings with their own eyes. They took their cue from human society as they knew it, and reasoned of course from the known to the unknown. They noted that lands and cities, palaces and temples, fields and farms—in short, all imaginable institutions and enterprises—are tended and supervised, guided and controlled, by living human beings, without whom lands and cities become desolate, temples and palaces crumble, fields and farms turn to desert and wilderness. Surely, therefore, the cosmos and all its manifold phenomena must also be tended and supervised, guided and controlled, by living beings in human form. But the cosmos being far larger than the sum total of human habitations, and its organization being far more complex, these living beings must obviously be far stronger and much more effective than ordinary humans. Above all, they must be immortal. Otherwise the cosmos would turn to chaos upon their death and the world would come to an end—alternatives which, for obvious reasons, did not recommend themselves to the Sumerian metaphysician. It was each of these invisible, anthropomorphic yet superhuman and immortal beings that the

Sumerian designated by his word *dingir*, which we translate by the word "god."

How did this divine pantheon function? In the first place, it seemed reasonable to the Sumerians to assume that the gods constituting the pantheon were not all of the same importance or rank. The god in charge of the pickax or brickmold could hardly be expected to compare with the god in charge of the sun. Nor could the god in charge of dikes and ditches be expected to equal in rank the god in charge of the earth as a whole. And, on analogy with the political organization of the human state, it was natural to assume that at the head of the pantheon was a god recognized by all the others as king and ruler. The Sumerian pantheon was therefore conceived as functioning as an assembly with a king at its head, its most important groups consisting of seven gods who "decree the fates" and fifty known as "the great gods." But a more significant division set up by the Sumerian theologians within their pantheon was that between creative and noncreative gods, a notion arrived at as a result of their cosmological views. According to these views, the basic components of the cosmos were heaven and earth, sea and atmosphere; every other cosmic phenomenon could exist only within one or another of these realms. Hence it seemed reasonable to infer that the four gods in control of heaven, earth, sea, and air were the creating gods, and that one or another of these four created every other cosmic entity in accordance with plans originating with them.

As for the creating technique attributed to these deities, Sumerian philosophers developed a doctrine which became dogma throughout the Near East—the doctrine of the creative power of the divine word. All that the creating deity had to do, according to this doctrine, was to lay his plans, utter the word, and pronounce the name. Probably this notion of the creative power of the divine word was the result of an analogical inference based on observation of human society. If a human king could achieve almost all he wanted by command—by no more than the words of his mouth—the immortal and superhuman deities in charge of the four realms of the universe could achieve much more. But perhaps this "easy" solution of the cosmological problems, in which thought and word alone are so important, is a reflection of the drive to escape into wish fulfillment characteristic of practically all humans in times of stress and misfortune.

Similarly, the Sumerian theologians arrived at what was for them a satisfying metaphysical inference to explain what keeps the cosmic entities and cultural phenomena, once created, operating continuously and harmoniously, without conflict and confusion. This is the concept designated by the Sumerian word *me*, whose exact meaning is still uncertain. In general it would seem to denote a set of rules and regulations assigned to each cosmic entity and cultural phenomenon for the purpose of keeping it operating forever in accordance with the plans laid down by the deities creating it. Here was another superficial, but evidently not altogether ineffective, answer to an insoluble cosmological problem, which merely hid the fundamental difficulties from view with a layer of largely meaningless words.

The Sumerian men of letters developed no literary genre comparable in any way to a systematic treatise of their philosophical, cosmological, and theological concepts. The modern scholar is compelled to "dig" out these concepts from the numerous myths recovered to date, wholly or in part. And this is no simple task, since the myth-makers and myth-writers must not be confused with the metaphysician and theologian. Psychologically and temperamentally they are poles apart, although often, no doubt, they were combined in one and the same person.

The mythographers were scribes and poets whose main concern was the glorification and exaltation of the gods and their deeds. Unlike the philosophers, they were not interested in discovering cosmological and theological truths. They accepted the current theological notions and practices without worrying about their origin and development. The aim of the myth-makers was to compose a narrative poem that would explain one or another of these notions and practices in a manner that would be appealing, inspiring, and entertaining. They were not concerned with proofs and arguments directed to the intellect. Their first interest was in telling a story that would appeal to the emotions. Their main literary tools, therefore, were not logic and reason, but imagination and fantasy. In telling their story, these poets did not hesitate to invent motives and incidents patterned on human action which could not possibly have any basis in reasonable and speculative thought. Nor did they hesitate to adopt legendary and folkloristic motifs that had nothing to do with rational cosmological inquiry and inference.

The failure to distinguish between the Sumerian mythographer and philosopher has confused some of the modern students of ancient Oriental thought, particularly those strongly affected by the current demands for "salvation" rather than "truth," and has led them into both underestimating and overestimating the minds of the ancients. On the one hand, they argued, the ancients were mentally incapable of thinking logically and intelligently on cosmic problems. On the other hand, they argued, the ancients were blessed with an intellectually "unspoiled" mythopoeic mind, which was naturally profound and intuitive and could therefore penetrate cosmic truths far more perceptively than the modern mind with its analytic and intellectual approach. For the most part, this is just stuff and nonsense. The more mature and reflective Sumerian thinker had the mental capacity of thinking logically and coherently on any problems, including those concerned with the origin and operation of the universe. His stumbling block was the lack of scientific data at his disposal. Furthermore, he lacked such fundamental intellectual tools as definition and generalization, and had practically no insight into the processes of growth and development, since the principle of evolution, which seems so obvious now, was entirely unknown to him.

No doubt, in some future day, with the continued accumulation of new data and the discovery of hitherto undreamed-of intellectual tools and perspectives, the limitations and shortcomings of the philosophers and scientists of our own day will become apparent. There is, however, this significant difference: modern thinking man is usually prepared to admit the relative character of his conclusions and is skeptical of all absolute answers. Not so the Sumerian thinker; he was convinced that his thoughts on the matter were absolutely correct and that he knew exactly how the universe was created and operated.

What evidence do we have of the Sumerian conception of the creation of the universe? Our major source is the introductory passage to a poem I have titled "Gilgamesh, Enkidu, and the Nether World." The plot of this poem is described in Chapter 23. What is of interest here is not the poem as a whole but its introduction, for the Sumerian poets usually began their myths or epic poems with a cosmological statement that had no direct bearing on the composition as a whole. Part of this introduction to "Gilgamesh, Enkidu, and the Nether World" consists of the following five lines:

> After heaven had been moved away from earth,
> After earth had been separated from heaven,
> After the name of man had been fixed,
> After (the heaven-god) An carried off the heaven,
> After (the air-god) Enlil carried off the earth . . . .

Upon having prepared the translation of these lines, I analyzed them and deduced that they contained the following cosmogonic concepts:

1. At one time heaven and earth were united.
2. Some of the gods existed before the separation of heaven and earth.
3. Upon the separation of heaven and earth, it was the heaven-god An who carried off heaven, but it was the air-god Enlil who carried off the earth.

Among the crucial points *not stated or implied* in this passage are the following:

1. Were heaven and earth conceived as created, and if so by whom?
2. What was the shape of heaven and earth as conceived by the Sumerians?
3. Who separated heaven from earth?

I hunted around among the available Sumerian texts and found the following answers to these three questions:

1. In a tablet, which gives a list of the Sumerian gods, the goddess Nammu, written with the pictograph for primeval "sea," is described as "the mother, who gave birth to heaven and

earth." Heaven and earth were therefore conceived by the
Sumerians as the created product of the primeval sea.

2. The myth "Cattle and Grain," which describes the birth in
heaven of the gods of cattle and grain, who were sent down
to earth to bring prosperity to mankind (see Chapter 14),
begins with the following two lines:

> On the mountain of heaven and earth
> An begot the Anunnaki.

3. A poem which describes the fashioning and dedication of the
pickax, the valuable agricultural implement, is introduced
with the following passage:

> The lord, in order to bring forth what was useful,
> The lord whose decisions are unalterable,
> Enlil, who brings up the seed of the "land" from the earth,
> Planned to move away heaven from earth,
> Planned to move away earth from heaven.

From the first line of "Cattle and Grain," it is not unreasonable to assume that heaven and earth united were conceived as a mountain whose base was the bottom of the earth and
whose peak was the top of the heaven. And the poem about the
pickax answers the question, Who separated heaven from earth?
It was the air-god Enlil.

After my hunt among available Sumerian texts had led to these
conclusions, it was possible to sum up the cosmogonic or creation
concepts evolved by the Sumerians. Their concepts explained the
origin of the universe as follows:

1. First was the primeval sea. Nothing is said of its origin or
birth, and it is not unlikely that the Sumerians conceived it
as having existed eternally.

2. The primeval sea engendered the cosmic mountain consisting of heaven and earth united.

3. Conceived as gods in human form, An (i.e., heaven) was the
male and Ki (i.e., earth) was the female. From their union
was begotten the air-god Enlil.

4. Enlil, the air-god, separated heaven from earth, and while his

father An carried off heaven, Enlil himself carried off the earth, his mother. The union of Enlil and his mother earth set the stage for the organization of the universe—the creation of man, animals, and plants, and the establishment of civilization.

For the origin and nature of the luminous bodies—moon, sun, planets, and stars—practically no direct explanation is given. But from the fact that, as far back as our written sources go, the Sumerians considered the moon-god, known by the two names Sin and Nanna, to be the son of the air-god Enlil, it is not unreasonable to infer that they thought of the moon as a bright, airlike body that was fashioned in some way from the atmosphere. And since the sun-god Utu and the Venus-goddess Inanna are always referred to in the texts as children of the moon-god, the probability is that these two luminous bodies were conceived as having been created from the moon after the latter had been fashioned from the atmosphere. This is also true of the remaining planets and the stars, which are described poetically as "the big ones who walk about (the moon) like wild oxen," and "the little ones who are scattered about (the moon) like grain."

Concerning the birth of the moon-god Sin, we have a charming and very human myth which seems to have been evolved to explain the begetting of the moon-god and of three deities who were doomed to spend their lives in the nether world instead of in the eastern sky where the more fortunate deities dwelt. My first attempt to piece together and translate this myth was published in *Sumerian Mythology* in 1944. However, the interpretation of the plot contained several serious errors of omission and commission. These were clarified and corrected by Thorkild Jacobsen in a careful and constructive review published in 1946 in Volume V of the *Journal of Near Eastern Studies*. Moreover, in 1952 the expedition to Nippur sponsored jointly by the Oriental Institute and the University Museum dug up a well-preserved tablet that fills in some of the gaps in the first part of the poem and clarifies it considerably. The plot of the myth, as revised in accordance with most of Jacobsen's suggestions and the contents of the newly discovered piece from Nippur, follows:

When man had not yet been created and the city of Nippur was inhabited by gods alone, "its young man" was the god Enlil; "its young maid" was the goddess Ninlil; and "its old woman" was Ninlil's mother Nunbarshegunu. One day the latter, having evidently set her mind and heart on Ninlil's marriage to Enlil, instructs her daughter thus:

> "In the pure stream, woman, bathe in the pure stream,
> Ninlil, walk along the bank of the stream Nunbirdu,
> The bright-eyed, the lord, the bright-eyed,
> The 'great mountain,' father Enlil, the bright-eyed, will see you,
> The shepherd . . . who decrees the fates, the bright-eyed,
>   will see you,
> Will forthwith embrace (?) you, kiss you."

Ninlil joyfully follows her mother's instructions:

> In the pure stream, the woman bathes, in the pure stream,
> Ninlil walks along the bank of the stream Nunbirdu,
> The bright-eyed, the lord, the bright-eyed,
> The "great mountain," father Enlil, the bright-eyed, saw her,
> The shepherd . . . who decrees the fates, the bright-eyed, saw
>   her.
>
> The lord speaks to her of intercourse (?), she is unwilling,
> Enlil speaks to her of intercourse (?), she is unwilling;
> "My vagina is too little, it knows not to copulate,
> My lips are too small, they know not to kiss" . . . .

Whereupon Enlil calls his vizier Nusku and tells him of his desire for the lovely Ninlil. Nusku brings up a boat, and Enlil rapes Ninlil while sailing on the stream, and impregnates her with the moon-god Sin. The gods are dismayed by this immoral deed, and, though Enlil is their king, they seize him and banish him from the city to the nether world.

The relevant passage, one of the few to shed some light on the organization of the pantheon and its method of operation, reads:

> Enlil walks about in the Kiur (Ninlil's private shrine),
> As Enlil walks about in the Kiur,

The great gods, the fifty of them,
The fate-decreeing gods, the seven of them,
Seize Enlil in the Kiur (saying):
"Enlil, immoral one, get you out of the city,
Nunamnir (an epithet of Enlil), immoral one, get you out of
　the city."

And so Enlil, in accordance with the fate decreed by the gods, departs in the direction of the Sumerian Hades. Ninlil, however, now big with child, refuses to remain behind and follows Enlil on his forced journey to the nether world. This disturbs Enlil, for it would mean that his son Sin, originally destined to be in charge of the largest luminous body, the moon, would have to dwell in the dark, gloomy nether world instead of in the sky. To circumvent this, he devises a rather complicated scheme. On the way to Hades from Nippur, the traveler meets up with three individuals, probably minor deities: the gatekeeper in charge of the gates, the "man of the nether world river," and the ferryman (the Sumerian "Charon" who ferries the dead across to Hades). What does Enlil do? He takes the form of each of these in turn (the first known example of divine metamorphosis) and impregnates Ninlil with three nether-world deities as substitutes for their older brother Sin, who is thus free to ascend to heaven.

Here, now, are several of the relevant passages (it should be stressed that the real meaning of a number of the lines is still far from clear, and that the significance of this part of the myth may ultimately be modified):

Enlil, in accordance with what was decreed for him,
Nunamnir, in accordance with what was decreed for him,
Enlil came, Ninlil followed,
Nunamnir came, Ninlil enters,
Enlil says to the man of the gate:

"Man of the gate, man of the lock,
Man of the bolt, man of the silver lock,
Your queen has come;
If she asks you about me,
Tell her not my whereabouts."

Ninlil says to the man of the gate:
"Man of the gate, man of the lock,

Man of the bolt, man of the silver lock,
Enlil, your lord, whence . . . ."

Enlil speaks up for the man of the gate:
"My lord did not . . the fairest, the fair,
Enlil did not . . the fairest, the fair,
He . . d in my anus, he . . d in my mouth;
My true distant heart . . . . ,
Thus has Enlil, the lord of all the lands, commanded me."

"Enlil is indeed your lord, but I am your lady."
"If you are my lady, let my hand touch your cheek (?)."
"The seed of your lord, the all-bright seed, is in my womb,
The seed of Sin, the all-bright seed, is in my womb."
"Let then my lord's seed go to the heaven above,
    Let my seed go to the earth below,
Let my seed in my lord's seed's stead go to the earth below."
Enlil, as [that is, impersonating] the man of the gate, lay with
    her in the bedchamber,
Copulated with her, kissed her,
Having copulated with her, kissed her,
He plants in her womb the seed of Meslamtaea . . .

Enlil then proceeds to the "nether-world river" (the Sumerian Styx), followed by Ninlil, and there exactly the same conversations take place between Enlil, the "man of the nether-world river," and Ninlil. Here Enlil, impersonating the "man of the river," impregnates Ninlil with the seed of the nether-world deity known as Ninazu. From there Enlil, followed by Ninlil, proceeds to where the Sumerian "Charon" is stationed. The scene is repeated a third time, and Enlil, impersonating the ferryman, impregnates Ninlil with the seed of a third deity (his name is destroyed, but he too is no doubt a god doomed to dwell in Hades). The myth then closes with a brief paean to Enlil as the lord of plenty and prosperity, whose word is unalterable.

This myth illustrates vividly the anthropomorphic character of the Sumerian gods. Even the most powerful and most knowing among them were regarded as human in form, thought, and deed. Like man, they planned and acted, ate and drank, married and raised families, supported large households, and were addicted to human passions and weaknesses. By and large, they preferred truth and justice to falsehood and oppression, but their motives are by no means clear, and man is often at a loss to understand them. They were thought to live on the "mountain of heaven and earth, the place where the sun rose," at least when their presence was not necessary in the particular cosmic entities over which they had charge. Just how they traveled from place to place is by no means certain. From available data we can infer that the moon-god traveled in a boat; the sun-god in a chariot or, according to another version, by foot; the storm-god on the clouds. But the Sumerian thinkers seem not to have troubled themselves too much with such realistic problems, and so we are not informed just how the gods were supposed to arrive at their various temples and shrines in Sumer, nor how they performed such human activities as eating and drinking. The priests presumably saw only the statues of the gods, which no doubt were tended and handled with great care. But just how the stone, wooden, and metal objects were to be regarded as having bone, muscle, and the breath of life was a question that never occurred to the Sumerian thinkers. Nor did they seem to be troubled by the inherent contradiction between immortality and anthropomorphism. Although the gods were believed to be immortal, they nevertheless had to have their sustenance; could become sick to the point of death; fought, wounded, and killed; and could themselves be wounded and killed.

No doubt Sumerian sages developed numerous theological notions in a futile attempt to resolve the inconsistencies and contradictions inherent in a polytheistic system of religion. But to judge from available material, they never wrote them down in systematic form, and we may therefore never learn much about them. In any case, it is hardly likely that they resolved many of the inconsistencies. What saved them from spiritual and intellectual frustration was no doubt the fact that many a question which according to our way of thinking should have troubled them, never came to their mind.

The Sumerians of the third millennium B.C. had hundreds of deities, at least by name. We know the names of many of them, not merely from lists compiled in the schools but also from lists of sacrifices on tablets which have been unearthed over the past century. We know others from such proper names as "X is a shepherd," "X has a great heart," "who is like X," "the servant of X," "the man of X," "the beloved X," "X has given me," and so on, X representing the name of a deity in each case. Many of these deities are secondary—that is, they are the wives and children and servants of the major deities thought up for them on the human pattern. Others are perhaps names and epithets of well-known deities who cannot at present be identified. But a large number of deities were actually worshiped throughout the year with sacrifices, adoration, and prayer. Of all these hundreds of deities, the four most important were the heaven-god, An; the air-god, Enlil; the water-god, Enki; and the great mother-goddess, Ninhursag. These four usually head the god-lists and are often listed as a group performing significant acts together. At divine meetings and banquets they took the seats of honor.

There is good reason to believe that An, the heaven-god, was at one time regarded by the Sumerians as the supreme ruler of the pantheon, although in our available sources, reaching to about 2500 B.C., it is the air-god, Enlil, who seems to have been the leader of the pantheon. The city-state in which An had his main seat of worship was called Uruk, or, as it is vocalized in the Bible, Erech, a city which played a preeminent political role in the history of Sumer. (At the site of Uruk, not long before the Second World War, a German expedition uncovered hundreds of small clay tablets, inscribed with semipictographic signs, which date from about 3000 B.C., not long after writing was first invented.) An continued to be worshiped in Sumer throughout the millenniums, but he lost much of his prominence. He became a rather shadowy figure in the pantheon and is rarely mentioned in the hymns and myths of later days, by which time most of his powers had been conferred upon the god Enlil.

By far the most important deity in the Sumerian pantheon, one who played a dominant role throughout in rite, myth, and prayer, was the air-god, Enlil. The events leading up to his general acceptance as a leading deity of the Sumerian pantheon are unknown, but from the earliest intelligible records Enlil is known as "the father of the gods," "the king of heaven and earth," "the king of all the lands." Kings and rulers boasted that it was Enlil who gave them the kingship of the land, who made the land prosperous for them, who gave them all the lands to conquer by their strength. It was Enlil who pronounced the king's name, gave him his scepter, and looked upon him with favorable eye.

From later myths and hymns we learn that Enlil was regarded as a beneficent deity who was responsible for the planning and creating of most productive features of the cosmos. He was the god who made the day come forth, who took pity on humans, who laid the plans that brought forth all seeds, plants, and trees from the earth. It was he who established plenty, abundance, and prosperity in the land. It was he who fashioned the pickax and the plow as the prototypes of the agricultural implements to be used by man.

I stress the beneficent features of Enlil's character in order to correct a misconception which has found its way into practically all handbooks and encyclopedias treating Sumerian religion and culture—namely, that Enlil was a violent and destructive storm deity whose word and deed nearly always brought nothing but evil. As not infrequently happens, this misunderstanding is due largely to an archaeological accident. Among the earliest Sumerian compositions published there was an unusually large number, proportionately, of the "lamentation" type in which Enlil had the unhappy duty of carrying out the destruction and misfortunes decreed by the gods for one reason or another. As a result he was stigmatized as a fierce and destructive deity by earlier scholars and even by later ones. Actually, when we analyze the hymns and myths, especially those which have been published since 1930, we find Enlil glorified as a friendly, fatherly deity who watches over the safety and well-being of all humans, particularly the inhabitants of Sumer.

One of the most important hymns to Enlil was pieced together in 1953 from a number of tablets and fragments. In 1951-52, while working in the Istanbul Museum of the Ancient Orient, I was fortunate enough to uncover the lower half of a four-column tablet whose upper half is in the University Museum in Philadelphia and had been published as early as 1919 by the late cuneiformist Stephen Langdon. And in 1952 the expedition to Nippur under the joint auspices of the Oriental Institute of the University

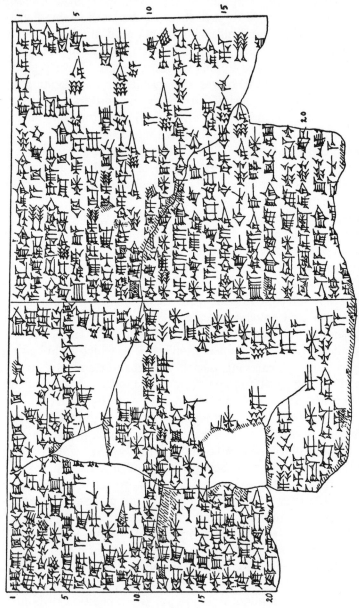

9. Hymn to Enlil. Reverse of lower half of four-column Nippur tablet in Istanbul Museum of the Ancient Orient.

of Chicago and the University Museum uncovered another large fragment of the hymn. The text is still incomplete, and its translation is no simple matter. It begins with a paean to Enlil himself, particularly as a god who punishes evildoers; continues with a glorification of his great temple in Nippur known as the Ekur; and closes with a poetic summary of civilization's debt to him. The following are some of the more intelligible passages of the 170-line hymn:

> Enlil, whose command is far-reaching, whose word is holy,
> The lord whose pronouncement is unchangeable, who forever
> decrees destinies,
> Whose lifted eye scans the lands,
> Whose lifted light searches the heart of all the lands,
> Enlil who sits broadly on the white dais, on the lofty dais,
> Who perfects the decrees of power, lordship, and princeship,
> The earth-gods bow down in fear before him,
> The heaven-gods humble themselves before him . . . . .
>
> The city (Nippur), its appearance is fearsome and awesome, ... ,
> The unrighteous, the evil, the oppressor,
> The . . . , the informer,
> The arrogant, the agreement-violator,
> He does not tolerate their evil in the city,
> The great net . . . . ,
> He does not let the wicked and evildoer escape its meshes.
>
> Nippur—the shrine where dwells the father, the "great mountain,"
> The dais of plenty, the Ekur which rises . . . ,
> The high mountain, the pure place . . . ,
> Its prince, the "great mountain," Father Enlil,
> Has established his seat on the dais of the Ekur, lofty shrine;
> The temple—its divine laws like heaven cannot be overturned,
> Its pure rites, like the earth cannot be shattered,
> Its divine laws are like the divine laws of the abyss, none can
> look upon them,
> Its "heart" like a distant shrine, unknown like heaven's zenith . . . . ,
> Its words are prayers,
> Its utterances are supplication . . . . ,
> Its ritual is precious,
> Its feasts flow with fat and milk, are rich with abundance,
> Its storehouses bring happiness and rejoicing, ... ,
> Enlil's house, it is a mountain of plenty . . . . .

The Ekur, the lapis-lazuli house, the lofty dwelling place, awe-
   inspiring,
Its awe and dread are next to heaven,
Its shadow is spread over all the lands
Its loftiness reaches heaven's heart,
All the lords and princes conduct thither their holy gifts, offerings,
Utter there prayer, supplication, and petition.

Enlil, the shepherd upon whom you gaze (favorably),
Whom you have called and made high in the land, ... ,
Who prostrates the foreign lands wherever he steps forth,
Soothing libations from everywhere,
Sacrifices from heavy booty,
Has brought; in the storehouse,
In the lofty courtyards he has directed his offerings;
Enlil, the worthy shepherd, ever on the move,
Of the leading herdsman of all who have breath (the king),
Brought into being his princeship,
Placed the holy crown on his head . . . . .

Heaven—he is its princely one; earth—he is its great one,
The Anunnaki—he is their exalted god;
When, in his awesomeness, he decrees the fates,
No god dare look on him.
Only to his exalted vizier, the chamberlain Nusku,
The command, the word of his heart,
Did he make known, did he inform,
Did he commission to execute his all-embracing orders,
Did he entrust all the holy rules, all the holy laws.

Without Enlil, the great mountain,
No cities would be built, no settlements founded,
No stalls would be built, no sheepfolds established,
No king would be raised, no high priest born,
No *mah*-priest, no high-priestess would be chosen by sheep-omen,
Workers would have neither controller nor supervisor, ... ,
The rivers—their floodwaters would not bring overflow,
The fish of the sea would lay no eggs in the canebrake,
The birds of heaven would not build nests on the wide earth,
In heaven the drifting clouds would not yield their moisture,
Plants and herbs, the glory of the plain, would fail to grow,
In field and meadow the rich grain would fail to flower,
The trees planted in the mountain-forest would not yield their
   fruit . . . . .

The third of the Sumerian leading deities was Enki, the god in charge of the abyss, or, as the Sumerian word for it reads, the *abzu*. Enki was the god of wisdom, and it was primarily he who organized the earth, in accordance with the decisions of Enlil, who made only general plans. The actual details and execution were left to Enki, the resourceful, skillful, hardy, and wise. For example, in a myth that may be titled "Enki and the World Order: The Organization of the Earth and Its Cultural Processes," an account is given of Enki's creative activities in instituting the natural and cultural phenomena essential to civilization. This myth, the contents of which I sketched for the first time in *Sumerian Mythology* (pages 59-62), also serves as a vivid illustration of the Sumerians' relatively superficial notions about nature and its mysteries. Nowhere is there an attempt to get at the fundamental origins, either of the natural or cultural processes. Instead they are ascribed to Enki's creative efforts, in words approximating the statement "Enki did it." Where the creative technique is mentioned at all, it consists of the god's word and command, nothing more.

The first one hundred lines (approximately) of the poem "Enki and the World Order" are too fragmentary for a reconstruction of their contents. When the poem becomes intelligible, Enki is decreeing the fate of Sumer:

"O Sumer, great land, of the lands of the universe,
Filled with steadfast light, dispensing from sunrise to sunset the divine laws to (all) the people,
Your divine laws are exalted laws, unreachable,
Your heart is profound, unfathomable,
The true learning which you bring . . . , like heaven is untouchable,
The king to whom you give birth is adorned with the everlasting diadem,
The lord to whom you give birth sets ever crown on head,
Your lord is an honored lord; with An, the king, he sits on the heavenly dais,
Your king is the great mountain, the father Enlil, ... ,
The Anunnaki, the great gods,
In your midst have taken up their dwelling place,
In your large groves they consume (their) food.
O house of Sumer, may your stables be many, may your cows multiply,

> May your sheepfolds be many, may your sheep be
>   myriad, ... ,
> May your steadfast temples lift hand to heaven,
> May the Anunnaki decree the fates in your midst."

Enki then goes to Ur (probably the capital of Sumer at the time this poem was composed) and blesses it.

> To Ur, the shrine, he came,
> Enki, king of the abyss, decrees the fate:
> "O City, well-supplied, washed by much water, firm-standing ox,
> Dais of abundance of the land, knees opened, green like the
>   mountain,
> *Hashur*-forest, wide of shade, heroic beyond . . ,
> May your perfected divine laws be well directed,
> The great mountain, Enlil, in heaven and earth has uttered your
>   exalted name;
> City whose fates have been decreed by Enki,
> Shrine Ur, may you rise heaven high."

Enki then comes to Meluhha, the "black mountain" (it can probably be identified with Ethiopia). Remarkably enough, Enki is almost as favorably disposed to this land as to Sumer itself. He blesses its trees and reeds, its oxen and birds, its silver and gold, its bronze and copper, its human beings.

From Meluhha, Enki goes to the Tigris and Euphrates Rivers. He fills them with sparkling water and places the god Enbilulu in charge. Enki then fills the rivers with fishes and makes a deity described as the "son of Kesh" responsible for them. He next turns to the sea (Persian Gulf), sets up its rules, and appoints the goddess Sirara in charge.

Enki now calls to the winds and appoints over them the god Ishkur, who rides the thundering storms. Next, Enki directs the plow and yoke, fields and vegetation:

> The plow and the yoke he directed,
> The great prince Enki . . . . ,
> Opened the holy furrows,
> Made grain grow in the perennial field,
> The lord, the jewel and ornament of the plain,
> Fitted out on its strength, Enlil's farmer,
> Enkimdu, the god of the canals and ditches,
> Enki placed in their charge.

> The lord called to the perennial field, caused it to produce
>   *gunu*-grain,
> Enki made it bring forth abundantly its small and large beans,
> The . . . . grains he heaped up for the granary,
> Enki added granary to granary,
> With Enlil he multiplied abundance for the people; . . . . ,
> The lady who . . , the source of strength of the land, the
>   steadfast support of the blackheaded people,
> Ashnan, strength of all things,
> Enki placed in charge.

Enki now turns to the pickax and the brickmold, and appoints the brick-god Kabta in charge. He then directs the building implement *gugun*, lays foundations, and builds houses, and places them under the charge of Mushdamma, the "great builder of Enlil." He then fills the plain with plant and animal life, and places Sumugan, "King of the Mountain," in control. Finally Enki builds stables and sheepfolds, fills them with milk and cream, and puts them in the care of the shepherd-god Dumuzi. (The rest of the text is destroyed, and there is no way of knowing how the poem ends.)

Fourth among the creating deities was the mother-goddess Ninhursag, also known as Ninmah ("the exalted lady"). In an earlier day, this goddess was of even higher rank, and her name often preceded that of Enki in the god-lists of one type or another. There is reason to believe that her name had originally been Ki ("Earth"), and that she was taken to be the consort of An ("Heaven"), and that they were the parents of all the gods. She was also known as Nintu ("the lady who gave birth"). All the early Sumerian rulers liked to describe themselves as "nourished by the trustworthy milk of Ninhursag." She was regarded as the mother of all living things, the mother-goddess. In one myth involving this goddess, she plays an important role in the creation of man (see Chapter 14), and in another myth she starts a chain of divine births which lead up to a "forbidden fruit" motif (see Chapter 19).

Finally we come to the *me*'s, the divine laws, rules, and regulations which, according to the Sumerian philosophers, governed the universe from the days of its creation and kept it operating. In this case we have considerable direct evidence, particularly in

bring reasoning or discourse into or to a certain form

regard to the *me*'s governing man and his culture. One of the ancient Sumerian poets, in composing or <u>redacting</u> one of his myths, found it desirable to list all these cultural *me*'s. He therefore divided civilization as he knew it into over one hundred elements. Only sixty-odd of these elements are at present intelligible, and some are only bare words which, because of lack of context, give but a hint of their real significance. But enough remains to show the character and import of this first recorded attempt at culture analysis, resulting in a considerable list of what are now generally termed "culture traits and complexes." These consist of various institutions, priestly offices, ritualistic paraphernalia, mental and emotional attitudes, and sundry beliefs and dogmas.

Here are the more intelligible portions of the list in the exact order given by the ancient Sumerian writer himself: (1) lordship; (2) godship; (3) the exalted and enduring crown; (4) the throne of kingship; (5) the exalted scepter; (6) the royal insignia; (7) the exalted shrine; (8) shepherdship; (9) kingship; (10) lasting ladyship; (11) "divine lady" (the priestly office); (12) *ishib* (the priestly office); (13) *lumah* (the priestly office); (14) *gutug* (the priestly office); (15) truth; (16) descent into the nether world; (17) ascent from the nether world; (18) *kurgarru* (the eunuch); (19) *girbadara* (the eunuch); (20) *sagursag* (the eunuch); (21) the (battle) standard; (22) the flood; (23) weapons (?); (24) sexual intercourse; (25) prostitution; (26) law (?); (27) libel (?); (28) art; (29) the cult chamber; (30) "hierodule of heaven"; (31) *gusilim* (the musical instrument); (32) music; (33) eldership; (34) heroship; (35) power; (36) enmity; (37) straightforwardness; (38) the destruction of cities; (39) lamentation; (40) rejoicing of the heart; (41) falsehood; (42) the rebel land; (43) goodness; (44) justice; (45) art of woodworking; (46) art of metal working; (47) scribeship; (48) craft of the smith; (49) craft of the leatherworker; (50) craft of the builder; (51) craft of the basket weaver; (52) wisdom; (53) attention; (54) holy purification; (55) fear; (56) terror; (57) strife; (58) peace; (59) weariness; (60) victory; (61) counsel; (62) the troubled heart; (63) judgment; (64) decision; (65) *lilis* (the musical instrument); (66) *ub* (the musical instrument); (67) *mesi* (the musical instrument); (68) *ala* (the musical instrument).

We owe the preservation of this bit of ancient anthropological lore to the fact that it was utilized in the plot of a Sumerian myth involving the popular Sumerian goddess Inanna. The list of more than one hundred cultural elements is repeated *four* times in the story, and hence, in spite of the numerous breaks in the text, can be reconstructed in large part. As early as 1911, a fragment belonging to this myth (it is in the University Museum) was published by David W. Myhrman. Three years later, Arno Poebel published another Philadelphia tablet inscribed with part of the composition—a large, well-preserved six-column tablet whose upper left corner was broken off. This broken corner piece I was fortunate enough to uncover in 1937, in the Museum of the Ancient Orient at Istanbul. Although a large part of the myth had been copied and published by 1914, no translation had been attempted, since the story seemed to make no connected sense and to lack intelligent motivation. The small piece that I located and copied in Istanbul supplied the missing clue, and as a result this charming tale of the all-too-human Sumerian gods was sketched and analyzed for the first time in *Sumerian Mythology* (pages 64-68).

Inanna, Queen of Heaven, the tutelary goddess of Erech, is anxious to increase the welfare and prosperity of her city, to make it the center of Sumerian civilization, and thus to exalt her name and fame. She therefore decides to go to Eridu, the ancient seat of Sumerian culture, where Enki, the Lord of Wisdom, "who knows the very heart of the gods," dwells in his watery abyss, the Abzu. Enki has under his charge all the divine laws that are fundamental to civilization, and if she can obtain them, by fair means or foul, and bring them to her city, Erech, its glory and her own will be unsurpassed. As she approaches the Abzu of Eridu, Enki, no doubt taken in by her charm, calls his messenger Isimud, whom he addresses as follows:

> "Come, my messenger Isimud, give ear to my instructions,
> A word I shall say to you, take my word.
> The maid, all alone, has directed her step to the Abzu,

> Inanna, all alone, has directed her step to the Abzu,
> Have the maid enter the Abzu of Eridu,
> Have Inanna enter the Abzu of Eridu,
> Give her to eat barley cake with butter,
> Pour for her cold water that freshens the heart,
> Give her to drink beer in the 'face of the lion'
> At the holy table, the Table of Heaven,
> Speak to Inanna words of greeting."

Isimud does exactly as bidden by his master, and Inanna and Enki sit down to feast and banquet. After their hearts have become happy with drink, Enki exclaims:

> "By the name of my power, by the name of my power,
> To holy Inanna, my daughter, I shall present the divine laws."

He thereupon presents, several at a time, the more than one hundred divine laws that are the basis of the culture pattern of civilization. Inanna is only too happy to accept the gifts offered her by the drunken Enki. She takes them and loads them on her Boat of Heaven, and makes off for Erech with her precious cargo. But after the effects of the banquet have worn off, Enki notices that the *me*'s are gone from their usual place. He turns to Isimud, who informs him that he, Enki himself, presented them to his daughter Inanna. Enki bitterly rues his munificence and decides to prevent the Boat of Heaven from reaching Erech at all costs. He therefore dispatches his messenger Isimud, together with a group of sea monsters, to follow Inanna and her boat to the first of the seven stopping stations that are situated between the Abzu of Eridu and Erech. Here the sea monsters are to seize the Boat of Heaven from Inanna, but Inanna herself must be permitted to continue her journey to Erech afoot.

The passage covering Enki's instructions to Isimud and Isimud's conversation with Inanna, who reproaches her father for expecting his gift to be returned, is, in its way, a poetic gem. It runs as follows:

> The prince calls his messenger Isimud,
> Enki gives the word to the Good Name of Heaven.
> "O my messenger Isimud, my Good Name of Heaven."

"O my king, here I stand, forever is praise."
"The Boat of Heaven, where now has it arrived?"
"At the wharf Idal it has arrived."
"Go and let the sea monsters seize it from her."

Isimud does as bidden, overtakes the Boat of Heaven, and says
to Inanna:

"O my queen, your father has sent me to you,
O Inanna, your father has sent me to you,
Your father, exalted is his speech,
Enki, exalted is his utterance,
His great words are not to go unheeded."

Holy Inanna answers him:
"My father, what has he spoken to you, what has he said to you?
His great words that are not to go unheeded, what, pray,
    are they?"

"My king has spoken to me,
Enki has said to me:
'Let Inanna go to Erech,
But you, bring me back the Boat of Heaven to Eridu.'"

Holy Inanna says to the messenger Isimud:
"My father, why, pray, has he changed his word to me?
Why has he broken his righteous word to me?
Why has he defiled his great words to me?
My father has spoken to me falsely, has spoken to me falsely,
Falsely has he sworn by the name of his power, by the name of
    the Abzu."

Barely had she uttered these words,
The sea monsters seized the Boat of Heaven.
Inanna says to her messenger Ninshubur:
"Come, my true messenger of Inanna,
My messenger of favorable words,
My carrier of true word,
Whose hand never falters, whose foot never falters,
Save the Boat of Heaven and Inanna's presented divine laws."

This Ninshubur does. But Enki is persistent. He sends Isimud,
accompanied by various sea monsters, to seize the Boat of Heaven
at each of the seven stopping points between Eridu and Erech.
And each time Ninshubur comes to Inanna's rescue. Finally
Inanna and her boat arrive safe and sound at Erech, where, amidst

jubilation and feasting on the part of the delighted inhabitants, she unloads the divine laws one at a time.

The Sumerian thinkers did not formulate a system of philosophy, nor did they evolve an explicit system of moral laws and principles. They produced no formal treatises on ethics. What we do know about Sumerian ethics and morals has to be searched out in various Sumerian literary works. Chapter 14 analyzes some of the Sumerian ethical ideas, together with relevant evidence.

THE FIRST MORAL IDEALS

S
UMERIAN THINKERS, in line with their world view, had no exaggerated confidence in man and his destiny. They were firmly convinced that man was fashioned of clay and created for one purpose only: to serve the gods by supplying them with food, drink, and shelter, so that they might have full leisure for their divine activities. Life, they believed, is beset with uncertainty and haunted by insecurity, since man does not know beforehand the destiny decreed for him by the unpredictable gods. When he dies, his emasculated spirit descends to the dark, dreary nether world, where life is but a dismal and wretched reflection of earthly life.

One fundamental moral problem, a favorite with Western philosophers, never troubled the Sumerian thinkers at all—namely, the delicate problem of free will. Convinced beyond all need for argument that man was created by the gods solely for their benefit and pleasure, the thinkers accepted man's dependent status just as they accepted the divine decision that death is man's lot and that only the gods are immortal. To the gods was attributed all credit for the high moral qualities and ethical virtues that the Sumerians had no doubt evolved gradually and painfully from their social and cultural experiences. It was the gods who planned; man only followed divine orders.

The Sumerians, according to their own records, cherished goodness and truth, law and order, justice and freedom, righteousness and straightforwardness, mercy and compassion. And they abhorred evil and falsehood, lawlessness and disorder, injustice and oppression, sinfulness and perversity, cruelty and pitilessness. Kings and rulers constantly boasted of the fact that they had established law and order in the land; protected the weak from the strong, the poor from the rich; and wiped out evil and violence. In the unique document analyzed in Chapter 7, the Lagashite ruler Urukagina, who lived in the twenty-fourth century B.C., proudly recorded that he restored justice and freedom to the long-suffering citizens, did away with ubiquitous and oppressive officials, put a stop to injustice and exploitation, and protected the widow and the orphan. Less than four centuries later, Ur-Nammu, founder of the Third Dynasty of Ur, promulgated his law code (see Chapter 8), which lists in its prologue some of his ethical achievements: he did away with a number of prevalent bureaucratic abuses, regulated weights and measures to ensure honesty in the market place, and saw to it that the widow, the orphan, and the poor were protected from ill-treatment and abuse. Some two centuries later, Lipit-Ishtar of Isin promulgated a new law code, in which he boasted that he was especially selected by the great gods An and Enlil for "the princeship of the land in order to establish justice in the lands, to banish complaints, to turn back enmity and rebellion by force of arms, and to bring well-being to the Sumerians and Akkadians." The hymns of a number of Sumerian rulers abound in similar claims of high ethical and moral conduct.

The gods, too, according to the Sumerian sages, preferred the ethical and moral to the unethical and immoral, and practically all the major deities of the Sumerian pantheon are extolled in Sumerian hymns as lovers of the good and the just, of truth and righteousness. Indeed, there were several deities who had the supervision of the moral order as their main function—the sun-god Utu, for example. Another deity, a Lagashite goddess by the name of Nanshe, is also sporadically mentioned in the texts as devoted to truth, justice, and mercy. But it is only now that we are beginning to get some idea of the significant role played by this goddess in the sphere of man's ethical and moral conduct. In 1951 a Sumerian hymn consisting of about 250 lines was pieced together from 19 tablets and fragments excavated in Nippur, and this hymn contains some of the most explicit ethical

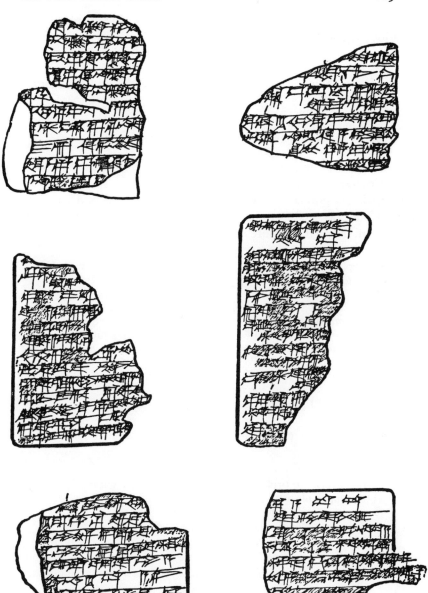

10. Social Justice. Unpublished fragments, in Istanbul Museum, inscribed with parts of Nanshe hymn.

and moral statements yet found in Sumerian documents. It describes the goddess Nanshe as follows:

> Who knows the orphan, who knows the widow,
> Knows the oppression of man over man, is the orphan's mother,
> Nanshe, who cares for the widow,
> Who seeks out (?) justice (?) for the poorest (?).
> The queen brings the refugee to her lap,
> Finds shelter for the weak.

In a passage whose meaning is still largely obscure, Nanshe is pictured as judging mankind on New Year's day. By her side are Nidaba, the goddess of writing and accounts, and Nidaba's husband Haia, as well as numerous witnesses. The evil human types who suffer her displeasure are described as follows:

> (People) who walking in *transgression* reached out with high
>   hand, ... ,
> Who transgress the established norms, violate contracts,
> Who looked with favor on the places of evil, ... ,
> Who *substituted* a small weight for a large weight,
> Who *substituted* a small measure for a large measure, ... ,
> Who having eaten (something not belonging to him) did not
>   say "I have eaten it."
> Who having drunk, did not say "I have drunk it," . . . . ,
> Who said "I would eat that which is forbidden."
> Who said "I would drink that which is forbidden."

Nanshe's social conscience is further revealed in lines which read:

> To comfort the orphan, to make disappear the widow,
> To set up a place of destruction for the mighty,
> To *turn over* the mighty to the weak, ... ,
> Nanshe searches the heart of the people.

Although the leading gods were assumed to be moral in their conduct, the fact remains that in the world view of the Sumerians these were the very gods who, in the process of establishing civilization, also planned evil and falsehood, violence and oppression—in short, all the immoral modes of human conduct. For example, the list of *me*'s—the rules and regulations devised by the gods to make the cosmos run smoothly and effectively—included not only rules concerning "truth," "peace," "goodness," "justice," but also rules concerning "falsehood," "strife," "lamentation," "fear." Why did the gods find it necessary to plan and create sin and evil, suffering and misfortune? (One Sumerian pessimist could say, "Never has a sinless child been born to his mother.") To judge from our available material, the Sumerian sages, if they asked the question at all, were prepared to admit their ignorance in this respect; the will of the gods and their motives were at times inscrutable. The proper course for a Sumerian "Job" to pursue was not to argue and complain in the face of seemingly unjustifiable misfortune, but to plead and wail, to lament, and to confess his inevitable sins and failings.

But would the gods give heed to him, a lone and not very effective mortal, even if he prostrated and humbled himself in heartfelt prayer? Probably not, it seemed to the Sumerian teachers. As they saw it, gods were like the mortal rulers the world over, and no doubt had more important things to attend to. And so, as in the case of kings, man must have an intermediary to intercede in his behalf, one whom the gods would be willing to hear and favor. The Sumerian thinkers therefore evolved the notion of a personal god, a kind of good angel to each particular individual and family head—his divine father who had begot him, as it were. It was to *him*, to his personal deity, that the individual sufferer bared his heart in prayer and supplication, and it was through him that he found his salvation.

The Sumerian ethical concepts and ideals were dominated by the dogma that man was fashioned of clay to serve the gods. The pertinent evidence comes primarily from two myths. One is devoted entirely to the creation of man. The other consists largely of a disputation between two minor deities, but contains an introduction which gives a detailed statement of the purpose for which man was created.

The composition narrating the creation of man has been found inscribed on two duplicating tablets: one is a Nippur tablet in the University Museum; the other is in the Louvre, which acquired it from an antique dealer. The Louvre tablet and the greater part of the University Museum tablet had been copied

and published by 1934, yet the contents remained largely unintelligible, primarily owing to the fact that the University Museum
tablet, which is better preserved than the Louvre fragment, arrived in Philadelphia, some four or five decades ago, broken into
four parts. By 1919 two of the pieces had already been recognized and joined; these were copied and published by Stephen
Langdon. In 1934 Edward Chiera published the third piece, but
he failed to recognize that it joined the two pieces published
by Langdon in 1919. I realized this fact a decade or so later
while trying to piece together the text of the myth for my
Sumerian Mythology. At that time I identified in the University
Museum tablet collection the fourth—and still unpublished—
fragment of the tablet, which actually joins the three published
pieces. It was now possible for the first time to arrange the
contents of the myth in their proper order and to prepare at
least a tentative interpretation of the myth, although the text
was still difficult, obscure, and far from complete (see *Sumerian
Mythology*, pages 68-72).

The poem begins with what may be a description of the difficulties of the gods in procuring their bread, especially after the
female deities had come into being. The gods complain, but
Enki, the water-god—as the Sumerian god of wisdom he might
have been expected to come to their aid—is lying asleep in the
deep and fails to hear them. Thereupon his mother, the primeval
sea, "the mother who gave birth to all the gods," brings the tears
of the gods before Enki, saying:

> "O my son, rise from your bed, from your . . . work what is wise,
> Fashion servants of the gods, may they produce their
>   doubles (?)."

Enki gives the matter thought, leads forth the host of "good
and princely fashioners," and says to his mother, Nammu, the
primeval sea:

> "O my mother, the creature whose name you uttered, it exists,
>   Bind upon it the image (?) of the gods;
> Mix the heart of the clay that is over the abyss,
> The good and princely fashioners will thicken the clay,

> You, do you bring the limbs into existence;
> Ninmah (the earth-mother goddess) will work above you,
> The goddesses (of birth) . . . . will stand by you at your fashioning;
> O my mother, decree its (the newborn's) fate,
>   Ninmah will bind upon it the image (?) of the gods,
> It is man . . . . ."

Here the poem turns from the creation of man as a whole to the creation of certain imperfect human types in an attempt to explain the existence of these abnormal beings. It tells of a feast arranged by Enki for the gods, no doubt to commemorate man's creation. At this feast, Enki and Ninmah drink much wine and become somewhat exuberant. Thereupon Ninmah takes some of the clay that is over the abyss and fashions six different types of abnormal individuals, and Enki decrees their fate and gives them bread to eat. The character of only the last two imperfect types —the barren woman and the sexless creature—is intelligible. The lines read:

> The . . . she (Ninmah) made into a woman who cannot give
>   birth.
> Enki, upon seeing the woman who cannot give birth,
> Decreed her fate, destined her to be stationed in the "woman
>   house."
> The . . . she (Ninmah) made into one who has no male organ,
>   who has no female organ.
> Enki, upon seeing him who has no male organ, who has no
>   female organ,
> To stand before the king, decreed as his fate.

After Ninmah has created these six types of man, Enki decides to do some creating of his own. The way in which he goes about it is not clear, but, whatever it is that he does, the resulting creature is a failure; it is weak and feeble in body and spirit. Enki, anxious that Ninmah help this forlorn creature, addresses her as follows:

> "Of him whom your hand has fashioned, I have decreed the fate,
>   Have given him bread to eat;
> Do you decree the fate of him whom my hand has fashioned,
>   Do you give him bread to eat."

Ninmah tries to be good to the creature, but to no avail. She talks to him, but he fails to answer. She gives him bread to eat, but he does not reach out for it. He can neither sit nor stand, nor bend his knees. A long conversation between Enki and Ninmah then follows. (The tablets are so badly broken at this point that it is impossible to make out the sense.) Finally Ninmah seems to utter a curse against Enki because of the sick, lifeless creature he has produced—a curse which Enki seems to accept as his due.

The second myth significant for the Sumerian conception of the creation of man, which may be titled "Cattle and Grain," represents a variation of the disputation genre of compositions, which was very popular with Sumerian writers. The protagonists of the myth are the cattle-god Lahar and his sister, the grain-goddess Ashnan. These two, according to the myth, were created in the creation chamber of the gods in order that the Anunnaki, the children of the heaven-god An, might have food to eat and clothes to wear. But the Anunnaki were unable to make effective use of cattle and grain until man was created. All this is told in an introductory passage which reads:

> After on the mountain of heaven and earth,
> An (the heaven-god) had caused the Anunnaki (his followers) to
> be born,
> Because the name Ashnan (the grain-goddess) had not been
> born, had not been fashioned,
> Because Uttu (the goddess of clothing) had not been fashioned,
> Because to Uttu no temenos had been set up,
> There was no ewe, no lamb was dropped,
> There was no goat, no kid was dropped,
> The ewe did not give birth to its two lambs,
> The goat did not give birth to its three kids.
>
> Because the name of Ashnan, the wise, and Lahar (the
> cattle-god),
> The Anunnaki, the great gods, did not know,
> The *shesh*-grain of thirty days did not exist,
> The *shesh*-grain of forty days did not exist,
> The small grains, the grain of the mountain, the grain of the
> pure living creatures did not exist.
>
> Because Uttu had not been born, because the crown (of
> vegetation?) had not been raised,

Because the lord . . . had not been born,
Because Sumugan, the god of the plain, had not come forth,
Like mankind when first created,
They (the Anunnaki) knew not the eating of bread,
Knew not the dressing of garments,
Ate plants with their mouth like sheep,
Drank water from the ditch.

In those days, in the creation chamber of the gods,
In their house Duku, Lahar and Ashnan were fashioned;
The produce of Lahar and Ashnan,
The Anunnaki of the Duku eat, but remain unsated;
In their pure sheepfolds *shum*-milk, the good,
The Anunnaki of the Duku drink, but remain unsated;
For the sake of their pure sheepfolds, the good,
Man was given breath.

The passage following the introduction describes the descent of Lahar and Ashnan from heaven to earth, and the cultural benefits which they bestow on mankind:

In those days Enki says to Enlil:
"Father Enlil, Lahar and Ashnan,
They who have been created in the Duku,
Let us cause them to descend from the Duku."

At the pure word of Enki and Enlil,
Lahar and Ashnan descended from the Duku.
For Lahar they (Enlil and Enki) set up the sheepfold,
Plants and herbs in abundance they present to him;
For Ashnan they establish a house,
Plow and yoke they present to her.

Lahar standing in his sheepfold,
A shepherd increasing the bounty of the sheepfold is he;
Ashnan standing among the crops,
A maid kindly and bountiful is she.

Abundance which comes from heaven,
Lahar and Ashnan caused to appear (on earth),
In the assembly they brought abundance,
In the land they brought the breath of life,
The laws of the gods they direct,
The contents of the warehouses they multiply,
The storehouses they fill full.

In the house of the poor, hugging the dust,

Entering they bring abundance;
The pair of them, wherever they stand,
Bring heavy increase into the house;
The place where they stand they sate, the place where they sit
   they supply,
They made good the heart of An and Enlil.

But then Lahar and Ashnan drink much wine, and so they begin to quarrel in the farms and fields. In the arguments that ensue, each deity extolls his achievements and belittles those of his opponent. Finally Enlil and Enki intervene and declare Ashnan the victor.

The Sumerian sages believed and taught the doctrine that man's misfortunes are the result of his sins and misdeeds, and that no man is without guilt. They argued that there are no cases of unjust and undeserving human suffering; it is always man who is to blame, not the gods. In moments of adversity more than one sufferer must have been tempted to challenge the fairness and justice of the gods. It was, perhaps, in an effort to forestall such resentment against the gods and to ward off disillusionment with the divine order, that one of the Sumerian sages composed the edifying essay presented in Chapter 15, which contains the earliest known example of the "Job" motif.

THE FIRST "JOB"

A PAPER I read before the Society of Biblical Literature on December 29, 1954, was titled "Man and His God: A Sumerian Version of the Job Motif." It was based on a Sumerian poetic essay consisting of about 135 lines. The text of the essay was pieced together from six clay tablets and fragments excavated by the first University of Pennsylvania expedition to Nippur, about a hundred miles south of modern Baghdad in Iraq. Four of the six pieces are now in the University Museum in Philadelphia, and two are in the Museum of the Ancient Orient in Istanbul.

Up to the date of my lecture, only two of the six pieces, both from the University Museum, had been published, and the text of the poem had therefore remained largely unknown and unintelligible. While in Istanbul in 1951-52 as Fulbright Research Professor, I recognized and copied the two pieces belonging to the poem in the Museum of the Ancient Orient. Upon my return to Philadelphia, I identified the two additional fragments in the University Museum with the help of Edmund Gordon, a research assistant in the Mesopotamian Section of the museum. While we were going over my translation of the poem for final publication, it dawned upon us that the two Istanbul fragments join two of the four Philadelphia pieces—that is, they actually belong to the very same tablets but had become detached either in very ancient days or in the course of the excavations, and had been brought separately to the two far-flung museums on the Marmara and the Schuylkill. Fortunately I was able to verify these long-distance "joins" in 1954 on a visit to Istanbul as a Bollingen Fellow.

The new identifications and the "joins" across the ocean made it possible for me to piece together and translate the larger part of the text of the poem. It then became obvious that here was the first written essay on human suffering and submission, the theme made famous in world literature and religious thought by the Biblical Book of Job. The Sumerian poem in no way compares with the latter in breadth of scope, depth of understanding, and beauty of expression. Its major significance lies in the fact that it represents man's first recorded attempt to deal with the age-old yet very modern problem of human suffering. All the tablets and fragments on which our Sumerian essay is inscribed date back to more than a thousand years before the compilation of the Book of Job.

The main thesis of our poet is that in cases of suffering and adversity, no matter how seemingly unjustified, the victim has but one valid and effective recourse, and that is to glorify his god continually, and keep wailing and lamenting before him until he turns a favorable ear to his prayers. The god concerned is the sufferer's "personal" god; that is, the deity who, in accordance with the accepted Sumerian credo, acted as the man's representative and intercessor in the assembly of the gods. To prove his point, our poet does not resort to philosophical speculation and theological argumentation; instead, with characteristic Sumerian practicality, he cites a case. Here is a man, unnamed to be sure, who had been wealthy, wise and righteous, or at least seemingly so, and blessed with both friends and kin. One day sickness and suffering overwhelmed him. Did he defy the divine order and blaspheme? Not at all! He came humbly before his god, with tears and lamentation, and poured out his heart in prayer and supplication. As a result, his god was highly pleased and moved to compassion; he gave heed to his prayer, delivered him from his misfortunes, and turned his suffering to joy.

Structurally, the poem may be tentatively divided into four sections. First comes a brief introductory exhortation that man should praise and exalt his god and soothe him with lamentations.

The poet then introduces the unnamed individual who, upon being smitten with sickness and misfortune, addresses his god with tears and prayers. There follows the sufferer's petition, which constitutes the major part of the poem. It begins with a description of the ill-treatment accorded him by his fellow men —friend and foe alike; continues with a lament against his bitter fate, including a rhetorical request to his kin and to the professional singers to do likewise; and concludes with a confession of guilt and a direct plea for relief and deliverance. Finally comes the "happy ending," in which the poet informs us that the man's prayer did not go unheeded, and that his god accepted the entreaties and delivered him from his afflictions. All of this leads to a further glorification of his god.

To illustrate the mood and temper of the poem, some of its more intelligible passages are quoted here. The reader must constantly bear in mind that Sumerian is still not fully understood, and that in time some of the translations will be modified and improved. Here is part of the sufferer's petition in his own words:

"I am a man, a discerning one, yet who respects me prospers not,
My righteous word has been turned into a lie,
The man of deceit has covered me with the Southwind, I am forced to serve him,
Who respects me not has shamed me before you.

"You have doled out to me suffering ever anew,
I entered the house, heavy is the spirit,
I, the man, went out to the streets, oppressed is the heart,
With me, the valiant, my righteous shepherd has become angry, has looked upon me inimically.

"My herdsman has sought out evil forces against me who am not his enemy,
My companion says not a true word to me,
My friend gives the lie to my righteous word,
The man of deceit has conspired against me,
And you, my god, do not thwart him. . . .

"I, the wise, why am I bound to the ignorant youths?
I, the discerning, why am I counted among the ignorant?
Food is all about, yet my food is hunger,

On the day shares were allotted to all, my allotted share was
  suffering.

"My god, (I would stand) before you,
Would speak to you, . . . , my word is a groan,
I would tell you about it, would bemoan the bitterness of my path,
(Would bewail) the confusion of . . . .

"Lo, let not my mother who bore me cease my lament before
  you.
Let not my sister utter the happy song and chant.
Let her utter tearfully my misfortunes before you,
Let my wife voice mournfully my suffering,
Let the expert singer bemoan my bitter fate.

"My god, the day shines bright over the land, for me the day
  is black.
The bright day, the good day has . . like the . . .
Tears, lament, anguish, and depression are lodged within me,
Suffering overwhelms me like one chosen for nothing but tears,
Evil fate holds me in its hand, carries off my breath of life,
Malignant sickness bathes my body. . . .

"My god, you who are my father who begot me, lift up my face.
Like an innocent cow, in pity . . . the groan,
How long will you neglect me, leave me unprotected?
Like an ox, ... ,
How long will you leave me unguided?

"They say—valiant sages—a word righteous and straightforward:
'Never has a sinless child been born to its mother,
. . . . a sinless youth has not existed from of old.' "

So much for the man's prayer and supplication. The "happy
ending" reads as follows:

The man—his god harkened to his bitter tears and weeping,
The young man—his lamentation and wailing soothed the heart
  of his god.
The righteous words, the pure words uttered by him, his god
  accepted.
The words which the man prayerfully confessed,
Pleased the . . . . , the flesh of his god, and his god withdrew
  his hand from the evil word,
. . which oppresses the heart, ... he embraces,
The encompassing sickness-demon, which had spread wide its
  wings, he swept away.

The (disease) which had smitten him like a . . . , he dissipated,
The evil fate which had been decreed for him in accordance
    with his sentence, he turned aside,
He turned the man's suffering into joy,
Set by him the kindly genii as a watch and guardian,
Gave him . . angels with gracious mien.

We now turn from the sublime to the mundane, from Sunday's preaching to Monday's practice, from poetic prayers to prosaic proverbs. It is in its proverbs that a people gives itself away, as it were, for proverbs reveal the characteristic attitudes, the basic drives, and the inner motives behind man's day-to-day actions, which the more poetic literary works tend to cloak and disguise. Sumerian proverbs by the hundreds are now in the process of restoration and translation, primarily through the efforts of Edmund Gordon, and some are presented in Chapter 16.

THE FIRST PROVERBS AND SAYINGS

T HE HEBREW Book of Proverbs was long believed to be the oldest collection of maxims and sayings in man's recorded history. With the discovery and unraveling of the ancient Egyptian civilization, in the past century and a half, collections of Egyptian proverbs and precepts were uncovered which antedate the Biblical Book of Proverbs by many years. But these are by no means the oldest of man's recorded aphorisms and adages. The Sumerian proverb collections antedate most, if not all, of the known Egyptian compilations by several centuries.

Until about two decades ago, almost no Sumerian unilingual proverbs were known. A small number of bilingual sayings, written in Sumerian with Akkadian translations, had been published, and these were practically all inscribed on tablets dating from the first millennium B.C. In 1934, however, Edward Chiera published several proverb tablets and fragments from the University Museum's Nippur collection, which were inscribed in the eighteenth century B.C. They indicated that the Sumerian men of letters must have compiled quite a number of collections of proverbs and sayings. Since 1937 I have devoted much time to this literary genre, identifying a large number of proverb pieces in the Istanbul Museum of the Ancient Orient and the University Museum in Philadelphia, and actually copying a number of them in both museums. But it was not until 1951-52, during my stay in Turkey as a Fulbright Research Professor, that I succeeded in copying practically all the Istanbul material, consisting of more than eighty tablets and fragments.

On my return to Philadelphia and the University Museum, with its hundreds of proverb fragments, it became evident that, because there was so much to do on Sumerian literature in general, I would not have the time to concentrate on this huge collection of proverb material. I therefore turned over my Istanbul copies and other pertinent data to Edmund Gordon, research assistant in the University Museum. After months of devoted effort, Gordon found that more than a dozen Sumerian collections, each containing scores and even hundreds of proverbs, could be pieced together and restored from the available material. He has already prepared a definitive edition of two such collections and pieced together some three hundred practically complete proverbs, many of which were unknown. Some of his material is utilized in this chapter. The reader should bear in mind, however, that proverbs are particularly difficult to translate because of their laconic language, and that future study may show that some of the sayings here quoted miss the meaning, wholly or in part. *brief - concise*

One of the significant characteristics of proverbs in general is the universal relevance of their content. If you ever begin to doubt the brotherhood of man and the common humanity of all peoples and races, turn to their sayings and maxims, their precepts and adages. More than any other literary products, they pierce the crust of cultural contrasts and environmental differences, and lay bare the fundamental nature of all men, no matter where and when they live. The Sumerian proverbs were compiled and written down more than thirty-five hundred years ago, and many had no doubt been repeated by word of mouth for centuries before they were put in written form. They concern a people that differs from us in language and physical environment, in manners and customs, in politics, economics, and religion, and yet the basic character revealed by the Sumerian proverbs is remarkably like our own. We have little difficulty in recognizing in them reflections of our own drives and attitudes, foibles and weaknesses, confusions and dilemmas.

For example, we find there the whiner, who attributes all his failures to fate and keeps complaining, "I was born on an ill-fated day."

Then there are the perpetual explainers who parade their transparent excuses in spite of the clearest evidence to the contrary. Of them, the ancients said:

> Can one conceive without intercourse,
> Can one get fat without eating!

What the Sumerians thought of their misfits is shown in their saying:

> You are put in water, the water becomes foul,
> You are put in a garden, the fruit begins to rot.

As in our own times, confusion and hesitation in economic matters beset not a few. Our ancients put it this way:

> We are doomed to die, let us spend;
> We will live long, let us save.

And in another way:

> The early barley will thrive—how do we know?
> The late barley will thrive—how do we know?

Sumer had, of course, its perennial poor with their troubles, and these are rather nicely summed up in the contrasting lines:

> The poor man is better dead than alive;
> If he has bread, he has no salt,
> If he has salt, he has no bread,
> If he has meat, he has no lamb,
> If he has a lamb, he has no meat.

The poor man frequently had to dig into his savings. As the Sumerian proverb-writer puts it, "The poor man nibbles away at his silver." When his savings gave out, he had to borrow from the ancient counterparts of our own loan sharks. Hence the saying: "The poor man borrows and worries." This is the Sumerian equivalent of our own: "Money borrowed is soon sorrowed."

No doubt the poor as a whole were submissive. There is nothing to indicate that the Sumerian poor consciously rebelled against the rich ruling classes. Nevertheless, their proverb, "Not all the households of the poor are equally submissive," if the translation is correct, does indicate a certain degree of class consciousness.

Suggestive of Ecclesiastes 5:12, "The sleep of a labouring man is sweet," and particularly of the Talmudic "Who multiplies possessions multiplies worry," is this Sumerian proverb:

> Who possesses much silver may be happy,
> Who possesses much barley, may be happy,
> But who has nothing at all, can sleep.

Occasionally the poor man realized that he was a failure not through a fault of his own but because he had tied up with the wrong associates:

> I am a thoroughbred steed,
> But I am hitched to a mule
> And must draw a cart,
> And carry reeds and stubble.

Of the poor artisan who, ironically enough, could not afford to have the very things he made, the Sumerian said: "The valet always wears dirty clothes."

Clothes, incidentally, were highly appreciated by the Sumerians, for they said, "Everybody takes to the well-dressed man."

In any case there were some valets who evidently succeeded in getting a formal education, to judge from the saying, "He is a valet who has actually studied Sumerian."

Evidently not all ancient scribes, any more than all their modern counterparts, the stenographers, were perfect at taking dictation. Hence the Sumerian saying:

> A scribe whose hand moves in accordance with the mouth
>   (that is, the dictated word),
> He is indeed a scribe!

The Sumerians even had their quota of scribes who could not spell properly, as is implied in this rhetorical question:

A scribe who does not know Sumerian,
What kind of scribe is he!

The so-called weaker sex is well represented in Sumerian sayings, and not always to its advantage. To be sure, the "golddigger" seems to have been unknown in Sumer, but Sumerians had their share of practical virgins. As one marriageable young lady who had grown weary of waiting for the ideal match, and decided to stop picking and choosing, said:

Who is well established, who is wind,
For whom shall I hold my love?

Marriage among the Sumerians was no light burden. They put it in a negative way:

Who has not supported a wife or child,
His nose has not borne a leash (the allusion is to the nose leash of
   prisoners).

The Sumerian husband felt himself frequently neglected, as shown in the saying:

My wife is in church (literally "the outdoor shrine"),
My mother is down by the river (probably attending some
   religious rite),
And here am I starving of hunger.

As for the restless, discontented wife who just did not know what was wrong with her, even in those ancient days the doctor was her refuge. At least so we might gather, if the translation is correct, from the saying:

A restless woman in the house
Adds ache to pain.

No wonder, then, that the Sumerian male at times regretted his marriage, as is evident from the proverb:

For his pleasure: marriage.
On his thinking it over: divorce.

No wonder the bride and groom entered into marriage in quite different spirits, to judge from these terse words:

A joyful heart: the bride.
A sorrowful heart: the groom.

As for the mother-in-law, she seems to have been far less difficult than her modern counterpart; at least, no Sumerian mother-in-law stories have as yet come to light. In ancient Sumer it was the daughter-in-law who had an unenviable reputation. This seems evident from a Sumerian epigram on what is good and bad for a man, which reads:

The desert canteen is a man's life,
The shoe is a man's eye,
The wife is a man's future,
The son is a man's refuge,
The daughter is a man's salvation,
The daughter-in-law is a man's devil.

Friendship was highly valued by the Sumerians. But, as with ourselves, "blood was thicker than water." As they put it:

Friendship lasts a day,
Kinship endures forever.

Interestingly enough from the point of view of comparative culture, the dog was by no means considered a "man's best friend" by the Sumerians. Rather, he was thought of as essentially disloyal to man, to judge from such sayings as these:

The ox plows,
The dog spoils the deep furrows.

It is a dog that does not know its home.

The smith's dog could not overturn the anvil;
He (therefore) overturned the waterpot instead.

If the Sumerian's attitude toward the dog seems a bit strange to us, here are several psychological insights which are practically identical with our own, though expressed in different words: "The boatman is a man of belligerence" compares with our "A sailor will fight at the drop of a hat."

The Sumerian saying,

> He did not yet catch the fox,
> Yet he is making a neck-stock for it,

is the equivalent of our "Don't count your chickens before they are hatched."

Finally,

> Upon my escaping from the wild-ox,
> The wild cow confronted me,

is just another way of saying: "Out of the frying pan, into the fire."

The need for diligence has, no doubt, been preached in all places and at all times. But even "Poor Richard" could hardly have put it better than the Sumerian who said:

> Hand and hand, a man's house is built;
> Stomach and stomach, a man's house is destroyed.

At least some Sumerians tried hard to "keep up with the Joneses." For them, this rather drastic warning was coined:

> Who builds like a lord, lives like a slave;
> Who builds like a slave, lives like a lord.

With respect to war and peace, our ancients found themselves in the same dilemma that confronts us. On the one hand, preparedness seems to be necessary for self-preservation, or, as they put it:

> The state weak in armaments—
> The enemy will not be driven from its gates.

On the other hand, the futility of war and its tit-for-tat character are only too obvious:

You go and carry off the enemy's land;
The enemy comes and carries off your land.

But war or peace, the thing to do is to "keep your eye on the ball" and not be fooled by appearances. The Sumerian put it in words which are not untimely:

You can have a lord, you can have a king,
But the man to fear is the tax collector!

The Sumerian men of letters included in their numerous proverb collections not only sayings of all kinds, such as maxims, truisms, adages, bywords, and paradoxes, but fables as well. These approach quite closely the cassical "Aesopic" fable in that they consist of a short introductory passage in narrative form, followed by a brief quoted speech serving as a punch line. Occasionally there is even a protracted dialogue between the characters. Chapter 17 will cite numerous examples of these early "Aesopica" from translations prepared by Dr. Edmund Gordon in the past year or two.

THE FIRST ANIMAL FABLES

A MONG THE Greeks and Romans, the invention of the literary genre of animal fables was ascribed to Aesop, who lived in Asia Minor during the sixth century B.C. Today, however, it is well known that at least some of the fables attributed to Aesop were already in existence long before Aesop. In any case the animal fable of the "Aesopic" type is found in Sumer more than a millennium before Aesop was born.

Animals, as might well have been expected, played a large role in Sumerian wisdom literature. In the past several years Gordon has pieced together and translated a total of 295 proverbs and fables relating to some 64 different species of animal life: mammals, birds, and members of the so-called lower classes of animal life down to insects. The order of frequency of the various animals in these texts, if we may judge from the extant material, is in itself not uninstructive. The *dog* comes first, being referred to in some 83 proverbs and fables. Next come *domestic cattle*, and then the *donkey*. Then the *fox*, followed by the *pig*, and only then the *domestic sheep*. Next in prominence come the *lion* and *wild ox* (that is, the now extinct *Bos primigenius*), followed by the *domestic goat* and the *wolf*, and so on. Here now are Gordon's tentative translations of some of the better preserved and more intelligible Sumerian fables, starting with the dog and ending with the monkey.

The greediness of the dog is illustrated by these two brief fables:

1. The donkey was swimming in the river, and the dog held tightly onto him, saying: "When is he going to climb out, and be eaten."

2. The dog went to a banquet, but when he looked at the bones there, he went away, saying: "Where I am going now, I shall get more to eat than this."

On the other hand, one of the finest expressions of mother love is voiced in a dog fable which reads:

Thus speaks the bitch with pride: Whether I have fawn-colored (puppies) or whether I have brindled ones, I love my young.

In the case of the wolf, it was his predatory nature that was foremost in the minds of the Sumerians, to judge from the better-preserved fables in which he appears. In one fable, which unfortunately has two short breaks in the text, a pack of ten wolves have attacked some sheep, but one of the wolves manages to play a deceitful trick on the others with a shrewd bit of sophistry, thus:

Nine wolves and a tenth one slaughtered some sheep.
The tenth one was greedy and did not (*one or two words broken*)
. . . When he had treacherously (*one or two words broken*) . . . he said: "I will divide them for you! There are nine of you, and so one sheep will be your joint share. Therefore I, being one, shall take nine. This shall be my share."

The wild animal whose character seems to be *most* clearly delineated is the fox. In the Sumerian proverbs, the fox is an animal full of conceit, who constantly exhibits—in both his actions and speech—a tendency to exaggerate his own role in the world. But, being at the same time a coward, he is frequently not equal to the task of living up to his bravado. For example:

The fox trod upon the hoof of the wild ox, saying: "Didn't it hurt?"
Or:
The fox could not build his own house, and so he went to the house of his friend as a conqueror!
Or:
The fox had a stick with him (and said): "Whom shall I hit?"
He carried a legal document with him (and said): "What can I challenge?"
Or:
The fox gnashes its teeth, but its head is trembling!

Here are two of the longest fables about the fox, which further illustrate his cowardice and conceit. Both are rather complex and seem to leave us hanging in mid-air at the end, but by and large their meaning and implications are clear:

The fox says to his wife:
"Come! Let us crush the city of Uruk with our teeth, as though it were a leek! Let us strap the city of Kullab upon our feet as though it were a sandal!" But when they had not even come within a distance of 600 *gar* (about two miles) from the city, the dogs began to howl at them from within the city: "Geme-Tummal, Geme-Tummal! (presumably the name of the fox's wife) Go home! Get along now!" they howled menacingly from within the city.

And we can assume that the fox and his wife turned on their heels, and did exactly that.

The other Sumerian fable uses a motif which later occurs in Aesop, not in connection with the fox, but in the fable of "The Rats and the Weasels." It reads as follows:

The fox requested the horns of a wild ox from the god Enlil (and so) the horns of a wild ox were attached to him. But then the wind and rain were stirred up, and he could not enter his burrow. Toward the end of the night, when the cold north wind and storm clouds and rain had showered (?) down upon him, he said: "As soon as it gets light . . . (*unfortunately the text breaks off here, and we can only guess that the fox begged that the horns be removed*).

Thus, the fox of the Sumerians seems to have little in common with the clever and sly beast that he is in much of the later European folklore, although in a number of ways he is very much akin to the fox in several of Aesop's fables, including the "Sour Grapes" fable. It should also be noted that two Sumerian fables exist—both of them unfortunately in a poor state of preservation—in which the fox appears with the raven or the crow, a combination which occurs also in the later fables of Aesop.

The bear is represented by only two Sumerian fables, in one of which there seems to be an allusion to his annual hibernation.

While very little can be said about the bear, there is a good bit of information to be gleaned from the proverbs about the mongoose. The mongoose was kept as a domestic animal in ancient Mesopotamia, as it is in modern Iraq, for the purpose of killing rats. To the Sumerians, the mongoose seems to have been noted for its directness in attacking its prey, in contrast to the cat's patient and apparently deliberate manner before pouncing upon its quarry. Thus they said:

A cat—for its thoughts;
A mongoose—for its actions!

On the other hand, the food-stealing and alcohol-filching habits of the mongoose seem to have been regarded with a sort of bitter tolerance:

If there is any food around, the mongoose consumes it;
If it leaves any food for *me*, a stranger comes and consumes it!

In one proverb, however, a pet mongoose was regarded by its owner as a source of amusement, because of its "poor taste":

My mongoose, which eats only spoiled food, will not climb up after beer and ghee!

The hyena may be alluded to in one proverb, but even in this case the meaning of the allusion is uncertain.

As for the cat, it occurs but rarely in Sumerian literature, and there are two references in the proverbs. One was just cited above in connection with the mongoose. In the other, a cow who follows a basket carrier around is compared to the cat.

The lion, according to the proverbs and fables, was at home in a type of terrain overgrown with trees and reeds, which can be referred to as "the bush," although at least two fables, which are either badly broken or obscure, locate him in the open steppe country. While the "bush" provided the lion with a protective cover, men had to protect themselves from him by learning his habits. Thus:

O lion, the dense "bush" is your ally!
And:
In the "bush," the lion does not eat up the man who knows him!

The latter proverb sounds at least superficially like the motif of "Androcles and the Lion."

Another fable, which is badly broken, tells of a lion who had fallen into a trap, and a fox. In a number of fables, the lion's natural role as predatory beast par excellence is played up, his prey there being sheep, goats, and the "bush"-pig; thus:

When the lion came to the sheepfold, the dog was wearing a leash of spun wool!

And:

The lion had caught a "bush"-pig and proceeded to bite him, saying: "Up until now, your flesh has not filled my mouth, but your squeals have created a din in my ears!"

But the lion is not always the victor, for he can even be outwitted by the flattery of the "helpless she-goat." Here we have one of the longer Sumerian fables, which most closely resembles those of Aesop:

The lion had caught a helpless she-goat. "Let me go, (and) I will give you a sheep, one of my companions!" (said the she-goat). "If I am to let you go, (first) tell me your name!" (said the lion). The she-goat (then) answered the lion: "Do you not know my name? My name is 'You-are-clever'!" (And so,) when the lion came to the sheepfold, he roared out: "Now that I have arrived at the sheepfold, I will release you!" She (then) answered him from the other side (of the fence [?]), saying: "So you have released me! Were you (really so) clever? Instead of (giving you) the sheep (which I promised you), even I shall not stay here!"

There is one Sumerian fable concerned with the elephant. It presents the beast as a boaster, who must be "taken down a peg" by one of the smallest of birds, the wren:

The elephant boasted (?) about himself, saying: "There is nothing like me in existence! Do not (*the text is broken at the end of this line, but we might expect some such phrase as* "Do not compare yourself to me!) . . . !" The wren (then) answered him, saying: "But I, too, in my own small way, was created just as you were!"

The donkey, as is well known, served as the chief beast of burden and draught animal in ancient Mesopotamia, and the Sumerians good-humoredly represented him as the same slow-moving, and frequently foolish, creature that he is in European literature of a later date. His main objective in life seems to be to act contrary to the wishes of his master; for example:

One must drive him (by force) into a plague-stricken city like a pack ass!

Or:

The donkey eats its own bedding!

Or:

"Your helpless donkey has no more speed left! O Enlil, your help-less man has no more strength left!"

Or:

My donkey was not destined to run quickly, he was destined to bray!

Or:

The donkey lowered its face, and its owner patted it on the nose, saying:

"We must get up and away from here! Quickly now! Come on!"

At times the donkey even threw off his burden, and was berated for it:

The donkey, after he had thrown off his packs, said: "The woes of the past are still plentiful in my ears!"

And on occasion the donkey might run away, and not return to its master. The runaway donkey provides an interesting simile in two proverbs:

Like a runaway donkey, my tongue does not turn around and come back!

And:

My youthful vigor has quit my thighs like a runaway donkey.

There are also allusions to certain unpleasant physical traits of the donkey, as for example:

Were there a donkey without a stench, he would be a donkey without a groom!

Finally, there is a proverb which gives us an interesting bit of sociological information, since this proverb which reads:

I will not marry a wife who is only three years old as the donkey does!

apparently indicates disapproval of child marriage.

As for the horse, one Sumerian fable has now quite unexpectedly thrown some new light on the early history of the horse's domestication, for it provides us with what is clearly the earliest reference to horseback riding now known. To be sure, the tablets on which this proverb is inscribed date from about 1700 B.C. But since this fable is found both on a large tablet from the city of Nippur, as well as on a roughly contemporaneous school tablet from the city of Ur, one may deduce a considerably older date for the actual original composition of the fable to allow time, not only for its diffusion, but also for its inclusion within one of the standard proverb collections. It is not unlikely therefore that the horse was already being used for riding in Mesopotamia by about 2000 B.C., even though the next oldest allusion to horseback riding now known is some three centuries later. The fable reads:

The horse, after he had thrown off his rider, said: "If my burden is always to be this, I shall become weak!"

Another proverb seems to refer to the sweating of the horse:

You sweat like a horse; it is what you have been drinking!

which is essentially our colloquial English phrase "He sweats like a horse."

There is only one extant proverb about the hybrid mule, and that proverb, interestingly enough, actually alludes to the animal's parentage! It reads:

O mule, will your *sire* recognize you, or will your *dam* recognize you?

The pig, interestingly enough was for the Sumerians one of the most "kosher" of animals, since the animal most frequently mentioned in the proverbs as being slaughtered for food is actually the pig! For example:

The fatted pig is about to be slaughtered, and so he says: "It was the food which I ate!"

Or:

He was at the end of his means (?), and so he slaughtered his pig!

Or:

The pork butcher slaughters the pig, saying: "Must you squeal? This is the road which your sire and your grand-sire traveled, and now you are going on it too! (And yet) you are squealing!"

As yet no Sumerian fables concerned with the monkey have come to light. But we have one proverb, and a related mock letter from a monkey to his mother, and these both indicate that the monkey was used for entertainment in the Sumerian music halls, and that he was treated rather shabbily. The proverb reads:

All of Eridu is prosperous, but the monkey of the Great Music Hall sits in the garbage heap!

The related letter goes as follows:

> To Lusalusa, my "mother," speak!
> Thus says Mr. Monkey:
> "Ur is the delightful city of the god Nanna,
> Eridu is the prosperous city of the god Enki;
> But here am I, sitting behind the doors of the Great Music Hall,
> I must eat garbage; may I not die from it!
> I don't even get a taste of bread; I don't even get a taste of beer.
> Send me a special courier—Urgent!"

It would seem, therefore, that a monkey belonging to the Great Music Hall at Eridu, the prosperous lake-port city of southeastern Sumer, went unfed and was forced to seek his own food in the garbage heaps of the city. For some reason, the poor animal's predicament became proverbial; and, as seems probable, eventually one of the scribes with a bent for satire expanded the proverb into a mock letter addressed to the monkey's "mother," whose name Lusalusa may possibly be intended to mean "Aping Man." The "letter," in view of the fact that at least four copies have come down to us, seems to have become a minor literary classic, while the original proverb itself found its way into one of the proverb collections.

Compilations of proverbs and fables constitute only one category of Sumerian wisdom literature. The Sumerian men of letters also developed the didactic essay, which may consist of a collection of precepts or instructions such as the "Farmer's Almanac" (Chapter 11) or may be devoted to a description of life in school (Chapter 2). But there was one type of wisdom composition that was a particular favorite with Sumerian writers: the disputation, a battle of words utilizing the rivalry motif. It consists primarily of a dispute between two rivals, each of whom may personify a season, animal, plant, metal, stone, or, as in the highly abbreviated Biblical Cain-Abel story, an occupation. The subject of the first literary debates in history is discussed in Chapter 18.

THE FIRST LITERARY DEBATES

S UMERIAN TEACHERS and men of letters were not —and indeed could not be—systematic philosophers and profound thinkers. But they were keen observers of nature and the immediate world about them. The long lists of plants, animals, metals, and stones which the professors compiled for pedagogic purposes (see Chapter 1) imply a careful study of at least the more obvious characteristics of natural substances and living organisms. Too, the Sumerian forerunners of our modern cultural anthropologists consciously set about analyzing civilization as they knew it, and divided it into more than one hundred institutions, occupations, crafts, attitudes, and modes of action.

One of the obvious features in the world about us is the natural clustering into pairs of certain seasons, animals, plants, metals, and implements; so much so that the mere mention of the one immediately brings the other to mind. In the agricultural milieu typified by Sumerian society, such pairs were, for example, summer and winter, cattle and grain, bird and fish, tree and reed, silver and bronze, pickax and plow, shepherd and farmer. To some degree and in certain respects, each of the pair was the opposite of the other; their common feature was the significant and useful role they played in man's life. The question that naturally comes to mind is, Which was *more useful* for man? This particular problem of evaluation struck a sympathetic chord among Sumerian schoolmen, and the more creative among them devised a literary genre devoted especially to it—the debate or disputation. Its major component is the argument between two protagonists, which goes back and forth several times, and in its course each of the rivals "talks up" his own importance and "talks down" that of his opponent. All this is written in poetic form, since the Sumerian men of letters were the direct heirs and descendants of the illiterate minstrels of much earlier days, and poetry came to them more naturally than prose. The composition was rounded out formally with an appropriate mythological introduction, which usually told of the creation of the protagonists, and with a suitable ending in which the dispute was settled by the decision of one or more of the leading deities of the Sumerian pantheon.

We now have the text, wholly or in part, of seven such literary debates, but only three of these have been more or less adequately studied to date. One is the debate between cattle and grain sketched in considerable detail in Chapter 14. The second may be titled "Summer and Winter: Enlil Chooses the Farmer-God." It is one of the longest of the group, and once the text has been pieced together from all available material, it will probably prove to be one of the most informing from the point of view of ancient agricultural practice. Its contents may be tentatively sketched as follows:

Enlil, the air-god, has set his mind on bringing forth all sorts of trees and grain, and on establishing abundance and prosperity in the land. For this purpose, two cultural beings, the brothers Emesh (Summer) and Enten (Winter) are created, and Enlil assigns to each his specific duties. The following lines tell how these duties were executed:

> Enten made the ewe give birth to the lamb, the goat give birth to the kid,
> Cow and calf to multiply, cream and milk to increase,
> In the plain he made rejoice the heart of the wild goat, sheep, and donkey,
> The birds of heaven—in the wide earth he made them set up their nests,
> The fish of the sea—in the canebrake he made them lay their eggs,
> In the palm grove and vineyard he made honey and wine abound,
> The trees, wherever planted, he caused to bear fruit,
> The gardens he decked out in green, made their plants luxuriant,
> Made grain increase in the furrows,

Like Ashnan (the grain goddess), the kindly maid, he made it come forth sturdily.

Emesh brought into being the trees and fields, made wide the stalls and the sheepfolds,
In the farms he multiplied produce, bedecked the earth . . . . ,
Caused the abundant harvest to be brought into the houses, the granaries to be heaped high,
Cities and habitations to be founded, houses to be built in the land,
Temples to rise mountain-high.

Their mission accomplished, the two brothers decide to go to

11. Hand copy of two left columns of obverse of text for "Summer and Winter."

Nippur to the "house of life," and bring thank-offerings to their father Enlil. Emesh brings sundry wild and domestic animals, birds, and plants as his gift, while Enten chooses precious metals and stones, trees, and fish as his offering. But right at the door of the "house of life," the jealous Enten starts a quarrel with his brother. The arguments go back and forth between them, and finally Emesh challenges Enten's claim to the position of "farmer of the gods." And so they betake themselves to Enlil's great temple, the *Ekur*, and each states his case. Enten complains to Enlil:

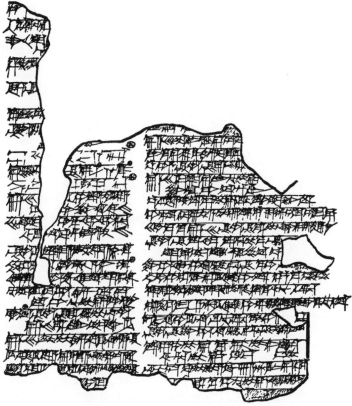

12. Hand copy of two right columns of obverse of text for "Summer and Winter."

"Father Enlil, you have given me charge of the canals, I brought
　　the water of abundance,
Farm I made touch farm, heaped high the granaries,
I made grain increase in the furrows,
Like Ashnan, the kindly maid, I made it come forth sturdily,
Now Emesh, the . . . . , who has no understanding for fields,
Has jostled my . . . arm and . . shoulder,
At the king's palace. . . ."

Emesh's version of the quarrel, which begins with several flat-
tering phrases cunningly directed to win Enlil's favor, is brief
but (as yet) unintelligible. Then Enlil answers Emesh and Enten:

"The life-producing waters of all the lands—Enten is in charge
　　of them,
Farmer of the gods—he produces everything,
Emesh, my son, how do you compare yourself with your brother
　　Enten!"
The exalted word of Enlil, with meaning profound,
Whose verdict is unalterable—who dares transgress it!

Emesh bent the knee before Enten, offered him a prayer,
Into his house he brought nectar, wine, and beer,
They sate themselves with heart-cheering nectar, wine, and beer,
Emesh presents Enten with gold, silver, and lapis lazuli,
In brotherhood and companionship, they pour joyous
　　libations . . . .

In the dispute between Emesh and Enten,
Enten, the faithful farmer of the gods, having proved himself
　　the victor over Emesh,
. . . . Father Enlil, praise!

The third of the disputation compositions may be titled, "The
Wooing of Inanna." In formal structure it actually differs from
the others of this genre. It is built up more like a playlet, with
a number of characters, each having his say in his proper place,
and there is therefore no mythological introduction. Moreover,
the main body of the poem does not take the form of an argument, but rather consists of a long uninterrupted speech by one
of the characters, who, feeling rejected and frustrated, is impelled
to enumerate his superior qualities. To be sure, at a later moment this character actually goes looking for a quarrel with his

rival, but the latter proves to be a peaceful, cautious type who would rather appease than fight.

There are four characters in this poem: the goddess Inanna; her brother, the sun-god Utu; the shepherd-god Dumuzi; and the farmer-god Enkimdu. Its contents may be summarized as follows: After a brief (but largely fragmentary) introduction, Utu addresses his sister and urges her to become the wife of the shepherd Dumuzi.

> Her brother, the hero, the warrior, Utu
> Says to the pure Inanna:
> "O my sister, let the shepherd marry you,
> O maid Inanna, why are you unwilling?
> His cream is good, his milk is good,
> The shepherd, everything his hand touches is bright,
> O Inanna, let the shepherd Dumuzi marry you,
> O you who are bedecked with jewels, why are you unwilling?
> His good cream he will eat with you,
> O protector of the king, why are you unwilling?"

Inanna's answer is a flat refusal; she is determined to marry the farmer Enkimdu.

> "Me the shepherd shall not marry,
> In his new garment he shall not drape me,
> His fine wool shall not cover me,
> Me, the maid, the farmer shall marry,
> The farmer who makes plants grow abundantly,
> The farmer who makes grain grow abundantly. . ."

After several fragmentary lines of uncertain meaning, the text continues with a long address by the shepherd, which is probably directed to Inanna. In it he details his superior qualities as compared with the farmer.

> "The farmer more than I, the farmer more than I, the farmer
>   what has he more than I?
> Enkimdu, the man of dike, ditch, and plow,
> More than I, the farmer, what has he more than I?
> Should he give me his black garment,
> I would give him, the farmer, my black ewe for it,
> Should he give me his white garment,

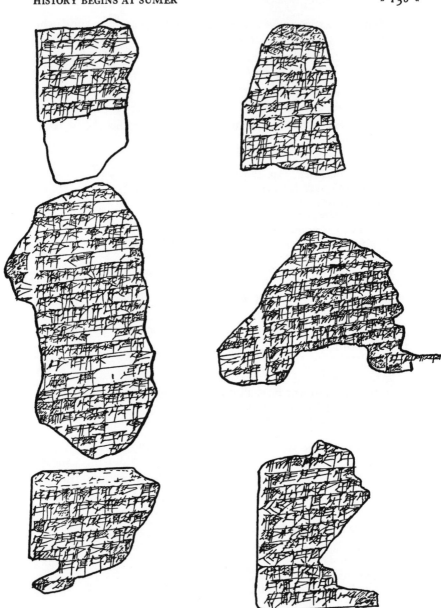

13. "Bird-fish" and "Tree-reed." Unpublished hand copies of fragments, in Museum of Ancient Orient, inscribed with debates between bird and fish, and tree and reed.

I would give him, the farmer, my white ewe for it,
Should he pour me his prime beer,
I would pour him, the farmer, my yellow milk for it,
Should he pour me his good beer,
I would pour him, the farmer, my *kisim*-milk for it,
Should he pour me his seductive beer,
I would pour him, the farmer, my . . -milk for it,
Should he pour me his diluted beer,
I would pour him, the farmer, my plant-milk for it,
Should he give me his good portions,
I would give him, the farmer, my *itirda*-milk,
Should he give me his good bread,
I would give him, the farmer, my honey-cheese for it,
Should he give me his small beans,
I would give him, the farmer, my small cheeses for them;
After I shall have eaten, shall have drunk,
I would leave for him the extra cream,
I would leave for him the extra milk;
More than I, the farmer, what has he more than I?"

We then find the shepherd rejoicing on the riverbank, perhaps because his argument had convinced Inanna and induced
her to change her mind. There he meets Enkimdu and starts a
quarrel with him.

He rejoiced, he rejoiced on the riverbank loam, he rejoiced,
On the riverbank, the shepherd on the riverbank rejoiced,
The shepherd, moreover, led the sheep on the riverbank.
To the shepherd walking to and fro on the riverbank,
To him who is a shepherd, the farmer approached,
The farmer Enkimdu approached.
Dumuzi . . . the farmer, the king of dike and ditch,
In his plain, the shepherd in his plain starts a quarrel with him,
The shepherd Dumuzi in his plain starts a quarrel with him.

But Enkimdu refuses to quarrel, and agrees to allow Dumuzi's
flocks to pasture anywhere in his territory.

"I against you, shepherd, against you, shepherd, I against you
Why shall I strive?
Let your sheep eat the grass of the riverbank,
In my cultivated lands let your sheep walk about,
In the bright fields of Erech let them eat grain,
Let your kids and lambs drink the water of my *Unun* (canal)."

Dumuzi, thus appeased, invites the farmer to his wedding as one of his friends.

> "As for me who am a shepherd, at my marriage,
> Farmer, may you be counted as my friend,
> Farmer Enkimdu, as my friend, farmer, as my friend,
> May you be counted as my friend."

Whereupon Enkimdu offers to bring him and Inanna several selected farm products as a wedding gift:

> "I will bring you wheat, I will bring you beans,
> I will bring you lentils . . . . ,
> You, maid, whatever is . . for you,
> Maid, Inanna, I would bring you . . . . ."

The poet then ends the composition with these conventional literary notations:

> In the dispute which took place between the shepherd and the
>   farmer,
> O maid Inanna, your praise is good.
> It is a *balbale* (poem).

The reader of these pages has no doubt caught the faint sounds of more than one Biblical echo. The primeval sea, separation of heaven and earth, fashioning of man from clay, ethics, laws and law codes, suffering and submission, Cain-Abel-like disputes—all are reminiscent, at least to some small extent, of Old Testament themes and motifs. We now turn to a Sumerian poem revolving about a paradise myth that brings to mind several passages in the Book of Genesis. To be sure, this is a divine, not a human, paradise. And in it are no Adam and Eve to succumb to temptation. But the myth does have several motifs parallel to the Biblical paradise story, and it is barely possible that it provides a rather surprising explanation for the origin and background of the "rib" episode.

THE FIRST BIBLICAL PARALLELS

ARCHAEOLOGICAL discoveries made in Egypt and in the Near East in the past hundred years have opened our eyes to a spiritual and cultural heritage undreamed of by earlier generations. What with the unearthing of civilizations buried deep in dirt and dust, the deciphering of languages dead for millenniums, and the recovery of literatures long lost and forgotten, our historical horizon has been widened by several millenniums. One of the major achievements of all this archaeological activity in "Bible lands" is that a bright and revealing light has been shed on the background and origin of the Bible itself. We can now see that this greatest of literary classics did not come upon the scene full-blown, like an artificial flower in a vacuum; its roots reach deep into the distant past and spread wide across the surrounding lands. Both in form and content, the Biblical books bear no little resemblance to the literatures created by earlier civilizations in the Near East. To say this is not to detract in any way from the significance of the Biblical writings, or from the genius of the Hebrew men of letters who composed them. Indeed, one can only marvel at what has been well termed "the Hebrew miracle," which transformed the static motifs and conventionalized patterns of their predecessors into what is perhaps the most vibrant and dynamic literary creation known to man.

The literature created by the Sumerians left its deep impress on the Hebrews, and one of the thrilling aspects of reconstructing and translating Sumerian belles-lettres consists in tracing resemblances and parallels between Sumerian and Biblical literary motifs. To be sure, the Sumerians could not have influenced the Hebrews directly, for they had ceased to exist long before the Hebrew people came into existence. But there is little doubt that the Sumerians had deeply influenced the Canaanites, who preceded the Hebrews in the land that later came to be known as Palestine, and their neighbors, such as the Assyrians, Babylonians, Hittites, Hurrians, and Arameans. A good illustration of Sumerian-Hebrew parallels is provided by the myth "Enki and Ninhursag." Its text was published in 1915, but its contents remained largely unintelligible until 1945, when I published a detailed edition of the text as *Supplementary Study No. 1 of the Bulletin of the American Schools of Oriental Research*. The poem consists of 278 lines inscribed on a six-column tablet now in the University Museum, with a small duplicate in the Louvre identified by Edward Chiera. Briefly sketched, the plot of this Sumerian paradise myth, which treats of gods rather than humans, runs thus:

Dilmun is a land that is "pure," "clean," and "bright"—a "land of the living," which knows neither sickness nor death. What is lacking, however, is the fresh water so essential to animal and plant life. The great Sumerian water-god Enki therefore orders Utu, the sun-god, to fill it with fresh water brought up from the earth. Dilmun is thus turned into a divine garden, green with fruit-laden fields and meadows. In this paradise of the gods eight plants are made to sprout by Ninhursag, the great mother-goddess of the Sumerians (probably originally Mother Earth). She succeeds in bringing these plants into being only after an intricate process involving three generations of goddesses, all begotten by the water-god and born—so the poem repeatedly underlines—without the slightest pain or travail. But perhaps because Enki wanted to taste them, his messenger, the two-faced god Isimud, plucks these precious plants one by one, and gives them to his master Enki, who proceeds to eat them each in turn. Whereupon the angered Ninhursag pronounces upon him the curse of death. Evidently to make sure that she will not change her mind and relent, she disappears from among the gods.

Enki's health begins to fail; eight of his organs become sick. As Enki is sinking fast, the great gods sit in the dust. Enlil, the air-god, the king of the Sumerian gods, seems unable to cope with the situation. Then the fox speaks up. If properly rewarded, he says to Enlil, he will bring Ninhursag back. As good as his word, the fox succeeds in some way (the relevant passage is unfortunately destroyed) in having the mother-goddess return to the gods and heal the dying water-god. She seats him by her side, and after inquiring which eight organs of his body ache him, she brings into existence eight corresponding healing deities, and Enki is brought back to life and health.

How does all this compare with the Biblical paradise story? First, there is some reason to believe that the very idea of a divine paradise, a garden of the gods, is of Sumerian origin. The Sumerian paradise was located, according to our poem, in the land of Dilmun, a land that was probably situated in south-western Persia. It is in this same Dilmun that, later, the Babylonians, the Semitic people who conquered the Sumerians, located their "land of the living," the home of their immortals. There is good indication that the Biblical paradise, which is described as a garden planted *eastward* in Eden, from whose waters flow the four world rivers including the Tigris and Euphrates, may have been originally identical with Dilmun, the Sumerian paradise-land.

Again, the passage in our poem describing the watering of Dilmun by the sun-god with fresh water brought up from the earth, is suggestive of the Biblical, "But there went up a mist from the earth, and watered the whole face of the ground" (Genesis 2:6). The birth of the goddesses without pain or travail illuminates the background of the curse against Eve that it shall be her lot to conceive and bear children in sorrow. And Enki's eating of the eight plants and the curse uttered against him for this misdeed calls to mind the eating of the fruit of the tree of knowledge by Adam and Eve, and the curse pronounced against each of them for this sinful action.

But perhaps the most interesting result of our comparative analysis is the explanation provided by the Sumerian poem for one of the most puzzling motifs in the Biblical paradise story— the famous passage describing the fashioning of Eve, "the mother of all living," from the rib of Adam. Why a rib? Why did the

Hebrew storyteller find it more fitting to choose a rib rather than any of the other organs of the body for the fashioning of the woman whose name, Eve, according to the Biblical notion, means approximately "she who makes live"? The reason becomes clear if we assume that a Sumerian literary background, such as that represented by the Dilmun poem, underlies the Biblical paradise tale. In the Sumerian poem, one of Enki's sick organs is the rib. The Sumerian word for "rib" is *ti* (pronounced *tee*). The goddess created for the healing of Enki's rib is called Nin-ti, "the lady of the rib." But the Sumerian word *ti* also means "to make live." The name Nin-ti may therefore mean "the lady who makes live," as well as "the lady of the rib." In Sumerian literature, therefore, "the lady of the rib" came to be identified with "the lady who makes live" through what may be termed a play on words. It was this, one of the most ancient of literary puns, which was carried over and perpetuated in the Biblical paradise story, although here, of course, it loses its validity, since the Hebrew word for "rib" and that for "who makes live" have nothing in common.

I came upon this possible Sumerian background for the explanation of the Biblical "rib" story quite independently in 1945, but it had already been suggested thirty years earlier by the eminent French cuneiformist Père Scheil, as the American Orientalist William Albright, who edited my publication, pointed out to me—which makes it all the more likely to be true.

To illustrate the mood and temper of the Sumerian poem, I shall quote several pertinent and characteristic extracts. Thus Dilmun, as a land of immortality where there is neither sickness nor death, is described in an obliquely phrased passage as follows:

> In Dilmun the raven utters no cry,
> The *ittidu*-bird utters not the cry of the *ittidu*-bird,
> The lion kills not,
> The wolf snatches not the lamb,
> Unknown is the kid-devouring wild dog,
> Unknown is the grain-devouring . . ,
> Unknown is the widow,
> The bird on high . .s not his . . ,
> The dove droops not the head,

The sick-eyed says not "I am sick-eyed,"
The sick-headed says not "I am sick-headed,"
Its (Dilmun's) old woman says not "I am an old woman,"
Its old man says not "I am an old man,"
Unbathed is the maid, no sparkling water is poured in the city,
Who crosses the river (of death?) utters no . . ,
The wailing priests walk not round about him,
The singer utters no wail,
By the side of the city he utters no lament.

The passage concerned with the painless and effortless birth of the goddesses after only nine days, instead of nine months, of bearing, reads in part as follows:

The goddess Ninmu came out to the riverbank,
Enki in the marshlands looks about, looks about,
He says to his messenger Isimud:
"Shall I not kiss the young one, the fair?
Shall I not kiss Ninmu, the fair?"

His messenger Isimud answers:
"Kiss the young one, the fair,
Kiss Ninmu, the fair,
For my king I shall blow up a mighty wind."

Alone he set his foot in the boat,
A second time he set there . . . . ,
He embraced her, he kissed her,
Enki poured the seed into the womb,
She took the seed into the womb, the seed of Enki,
One day being her one month,
Two days being her two months,
Nine days being her nine months, the months of "womanhood,"
Like . . -cream, like . . -cream, like good, princely cream,
Ninmu, like . . -cream, like . . -cream, like good, princely cream,
Gave birth to the goddess Ninkurra.

The eating of the eight plants is told in a passage revealing a typical Sumerian repetition pattern:

Enki in the marshlands looks about, looks about,
He says to his messenger Isimud:
"Of their plants their fate I would decree, their 'heart' I
    would know;
What, pray, is this (plant)? What, pray, is this (plant)?"

His messenger Isimud answers:
"My king, the tree-plant," he says to him;
He cuts it down for him, he (Enki) eats it.

"My king, the honey-plant," he says to him;
He plucks it for him, he eats it.

"My king, the roadweed (?)-plant," he says to him;
He cuts it down for him, he eats it.

"My king, the water-plant," he says to him;
He plucks it for him, he eats it.

"My king, the thorn-plant," he says to him;
He cuts it down for him, he eats it.

"My king, the caper-plant," he says to him;
He plucks it for him, he eats it.

"My king, the . . -plant," he says to him;
He cuts it down for him, he eats it.

"My king, the cassia-plant," he says to him;
He plucks it for him, he eats it.

Of the plants, Enki decreed their fate, knew(?) their heart.
Thereupon Ninhursag cursed the name of Enki:
"Until he is dead I shall not look upon him with the eye of life."

Ninhursag now disappears, but the fox in some way succeeds in bringing her back. Whereupon she proceeds to heal Enki's eight sick organs, including the rib, through the birth of eight deities, thus:

Ninhursag seated Enki by her pudendum,
"My brother, what hurts you?"
"My . . hurts me."
"To the god Abu I have given birth for you."

"My brother, what hurts you?"
"My jaw hurts me."
"To the god Nintulla I have given birth for you."

"My brother, what hurts you?"
"My tooth hurts me."
"To the goddess Ninsutu I have given birth for you."

"My brother, what hurts you?"
"My mouth hurts me."

"To the goddess Ninkasi I have given birth for you."

"My brother, what hurts you?"
"My . . hurts me."
"To the goddess Nazi I have given birth for you."

"My brother, what hurts you?"
"My arm hurts me."
"To the goddess Azimua I have given birth for you."

"My brother, what hurts you?"
"My rib hurts me."
"To the goddess Ninti (that is, 'lady of the rib' or 'lady who makes live') I have given birth for you."

"My brother, what hurts you?"
"My . . hurts me."
"To the god Enshag I have given birth for you."

Paradise, according to the Sumerian theologians, was for the immortal gods, and for them alone, not for mortal man. One mortal, however, and only one, according to the Sumerian myth-makers, did succeed in gaining admittance to this divine paradise. This brings us to the Sumerian "Noah" and the deluge myth, the closest and most striking Biblical parallel as yet uncovered in cuneiform literature.

HE FIRST "NOAH"

T HAT THE Biblical deluge story is not original with the Hebrew redactors of the Bible has been known from the time of the discovery and deciphering of the eleventh tablet of the Babylonian "Epic of Gilgamesh" by the British Museum's George Smith. The Babylonian deluge myth itself, however, is of Sumerian origin. In 1914 Arno Poebel published a fragment consisting of the lower third of a six-column Sumerian tablet in the Nippur collection of the University Museum, the contents of which are devoted in large part to the story of the flood. This fragment still remains unique and unduplicated, and although scholars have been "all eyes and ears" for new deluge tablets, not a single additional fragment has turned up in any museum, private collection, or excavation. The piece published by Poebel is still our only source, and the translation prepared by him is still basic and standard.

The contents of this lone tablet are noteworthy not only for the flood episode, although that is its main theme, but also for the passages preceding and introducing the deluge story. Badly broken as the text is, these passages are nevertheless of significance for Sumerian cosmogony and cosmology. They include a number of revealing statements concerning the creation of man, the origin of kingship, and the existence of at least five antediluvian cities. Here, then, is practically the entire extant text of the myth with all its tantalizing obscurities and uncertainties. It provides an apt example of what the cuneiformist is up against, and of the surprises the future holds in store for him.

Since it is the lower third of the tablet that is preserved, we start right off with a break of some 37 lines, and there is no way of knowing just how the myth began. We then find a deity addressing other deities, probably stating that he will save mankind from destruction and that as a result man will build the cities and temples of the gods. Following the address are three lines which are difficult to relate to the context; they seem to describe the actions performed by the deity to make his words effective. Then come four lines concerned with the creation of man, animals, and plants. This entire passage reads:

"My mankind, in its destruction I will . . ,
To Nintu I will return the . . . of my creatures,
I will return the people to their settlements,
Of the cities, they will build their places of the divine laws,
I will make restful their shade,
Of our houses, they will lay their bricks in pure places,
The places of our decisions they will found in pure places."

He directed the pure fire-quenching water,
Perfected the rites and the exalted divine laws,
On the earth he . . . d, placed the . . . there.

After An, Enlil, Enki, and Ninhursag
Had fashioned the blackheaded people,
Vegetation luxuriated from the earth,
Animals, four-legged (creatures) of the plain, were brought artfully into existence.

There follows another break of about 37 lines, after which we learn that kingship was lowered from heaven and that five cities were founded:

After the . . . of kingship had been lowered from heaven,
After the exalted tiara and the throne of kingship had been lowered from heaven,
He perfected the rites and the exalted divine laws . . . . ,
Founded the five cities in . . . pure places,
Called their names, apportioned them as cult centers.

The first of these cities, Eridu, he gave to Nudimmud, the leader,
The second, Badtibira, he gave to . . ,
The third, Larak, he gave to Endurbilhursag,

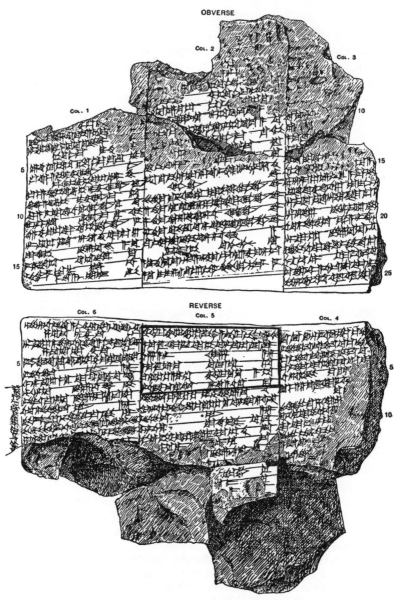

14. The Flood, the Ark, and the Sumerian Noah. Arno Poebel's hand copy of "flood" tablet, in University Museum, remains only document of this myth.

The fourth, Sippar, he gave to the hero Utu,
The fifth, Shuruppak, he gave to Sud.

When he had called the names of these cities, apportioned them
    as cult centers,
He brought . . . . ,
Established the cleaning of the small rivers as . . . . ."

A break of about 37 lines follows next; these must have dealt
largely with the decision of the gods to bring the flood and
destroy mankind. When the text becomes intelligible again, we
find some of the gods dissatisfied and unhappy over the cruel
decision. We are then introduced to Ziusudra, the counterpart
of the Biblical Noah. He is described as a pious, god-fearing
king, who is constantly on the lookout for divine revelations in
dreams or incantations. Ziusudra seems to station himself by a
wall, where he hears the voice of a deity informing him of the
decision taken by the assembly of the gods to send a flood and
"to destroy the seed of mankind." The longest passage reads:

The flood . . . .
. . . .
Thus was treated . . . . .
Then did Nintu weep like a . . . ,
The pure Inanna set up a lament for its people,
Enki took counsel with himself,
An, Enlil, Enki, and Ninhursag . . . . ,
The gods of heaven and earth uttered the name of An and Enlil.

Then did Ziusudra, the king, the *pashishu* of . . . . ,
Build a giant . . . . ;
Humbly, obedient, reverently he . . . . ,
Attending daily, constantly he . . . . ,
Bringing forth all kinds of dreams, he . . . . ,
Uttering the name of heaven and earth, he . . . . .
. . . . the gods a wall . . . . ,
Ziusudra, standing at its side, listened.

"Stand by the wall at my left side . . . . ,
By the wall I will say a word to you, take my word,
Give ear to my instructions:
By our . . a flood will sweep over the cult centers;
To destroy the seed of mankind . . . . ,
Is the decision, the word of the assembly of the gods.

By the word commanded by An and Enlil . . . . .
Its kingship, its rule (will be put to an end)."

The text must have continued with detailed instructions to
Ziusudra to build a giant boat and thus save himself from destruction. But this is missing, since there is another break of
about 40 lines at this point. When the text becomes intelligible
once again, we find that the flood in all its violence had already
come upon the "land" and raged there for seven days and nights.
Then the sun-god Utu comes forth again, bringing his precious
light everywhere, and Ziusudra prostrates himself before him and
offers sacrifices. The lines read:

All the windstorms, exceedingly powerful, attacked as one,
At the same time, the flood sweeps over the cult centers.

After, for seven days and seven nights,
The flood had swept over the land,
And the huge boat had been tossed about by the windstorms on
    the great waters,
Utu came forth, who sheds light on heaven and earth,
Ziusudra opened a window on the huge boat,
The hero Utu brought his rays into the giant boat.

Ziusudra, the king,
Prostrated himself before Utu,
The king kills an ox, slaughters a sheep.

Here, again, there follows a break of about 39 lines. The last
extant lines of our text describe the deification of Ziusudra.
After he had prostrated himself before An and Enlil, he was
given "life like a god" and breath eternal, and translated to
Dilmun, "the place where the sun rises." Thus:

An and Enlil uttered "breath of heaven," "breath of earth," by
    their . . it stretched itself,
Vegetation, coming up out of the earth, rises up.

Ziusudra, the king,
Prostrated himself before An and Enlil.
An and Enlil cherished Ziusudra,
Life like a god they give him:
Breath eternal like a god they bring down for him.

Then, Ziusudra the king,
The preserver of the name of vegetation and of the seed of
mankind,
In the land of crossing, the land of Dilmun, the place where the
sun rises, they caused to dwell.

The remainder of the tablet, containing about 39 lines of the
text, is destroyed, and so we know nothing of what may have
happened to the transfigured Ziusudra in the home of the immortals.

From Paradise we now turn to Hades, from the "great above"
to the "great below," or, as the Sumerians themselves described
it, "the land of no return." To this dark, dread land of the dead
a restive and unruly goddess descends to satisfy her unbounded
ambitions. The story of this "descent to the nether world," told
in Chapter 21, is one of the best preserved Sumerian myths thus
far uncovered. It provides a rare parallel to one of the most
significant New Testament motifs.

THE FIRST TALE
OF RESURRECTION

THE SUMERIAN word for the Greek *Hades* and the Hebrew *Sheol* is *Kur*, which originally meant "mountain" and later came to mean "foreign land" because the mountainous countries bordering Sumer were a constant menace to its people. Cosmically considered, Kur is the empty space between the earth's crust and the primeval sea, and to it went all the shades of the dead. To reach it, a "man-devouring river" had to be crossed on a boat conducted by a special "man of the boat"— the Sumerian counterpart of the river Styx and the boatman Charon.

Though the nether world is the abode of the dead, "life" in it has its "lively" side. Isaiah 14:9-11, for example, describes the stirring of Sheol and the shades of former kings and chiefs at the approach of a king to Babylon. In the University Museum there is a tablet published by Stephen Langdon in 1919, inscribed with a poem which actually describes some of the experiences of a Sumerian king in the nether world. The extant part of the tablet runs as follows:

After his death, the great king Ur-Nammu comes to Kur. He first presents gifts and offerings to the seven underworld deities —to each in his own palace. He then brings gifts to two other deities, one of whom is the scribe of the nether world, to make sure of their support. Finally he arrives at the special spot which the priestly officials of Kur have prepared as his habitation.

Here he is greeted by certain of the dead and made to feel at home. The dead hero Gilgamesh, who has become "the judge of the nether world," initiates him into the rules and regulations that govern the infernal regions. But after "seven days," after "ten days," had passed, the "wail of Sumer" reaches him. The walls of Ur which he had left unfinished, his newly built palace which he had left unpurified, his wife whom he could no longer press to his bosom, his child whom he could no longer fondle on his knee—all these disturb his peace in the nether world, and he sets up a long and bitter lament.

The shades of the dead could on special occasions be "raised" to the earth temporarily. The First Book of Samuel (Chapter 28) tells of the calling up of the shade of the prophet from Sheol at the insistence of King Saul. This is paralleled in the Sumerian poem "Gilgamesh, Enkidu, and the Nether World" (see Chapter 23) which tells of the ascent of the shade of Enkidu from Kur to the waiting embrace of his master Gilgamesh, and reports the ensuing conversation between them.

Although Kur might be assumed to have been for mortals only, quite a number of supposedly immortal deities were found there. We even have the myths explaining the presence of several deities in the nether world.

According to the poem "The Begetting of the Moon-God" (see Chapter 14), Enlil, the leading deity of the Sumerian pantheon, is banished from Nippur to the nether world by the other gods because he raped the goddess Ninlil. On the way he begets three underworld deities (two of them at least are well known from other sources). But it is in the case of the shepherd-god Dumuzi, the most renowned of the "dead" gods, that we can follow in considerable detail the events leading to his downfall, in a myth which primarily concerns his wife, the goddess Inanna, a high favorite with Sumerian myth-makers.

The goddess of love, whatever her name among ancient peoples, sparked the imagination of men throughout the ages. Venus to the Romans, Aphrodite to the Greeks, Ishtar to the Babylonians, had minstrels and poets singing of their deeds and misdeeds. The Sumerians worshiped the goddess of love under the name of Inanna, "queen of heaven." Her husband was the shepherd-god

Dumuzi, the Biblical Tammuz, the weeping for whose death was denounced as an abomination by the prophet Ezekiel as late as the second half of the first millennium B.C. His wooing and winning of Inanna is told in two versions. One, involving a rival, the farmer-god Enkimdu, was sketched in Chapter 18. In the other, Dumuzi is the sole suitor for Inanna's hand. According to this story, the shepherd Dumuzi comes to Inanna's house, milk and cream dripping from his hands and sides, and clamors for admittance. After consultation with her mother, Inanna bathes and anoints herself, puts on her queenly robes, adorns herself with precious stones, and opens the door for her groom-to-be. They embrace and probably cohabit, and he then carries her off to the "city of his god."

Little did Dumuzi dream, however, that the marriage which he so passionately desired would end in his own perdition and that he would be dragged down to hell. He failed to reckon with a woman's overwhelming ambition. This is told in "Inanna's Descent to the Nether World," a myth noteworthy for its resurrection motif. The plots runs as follows:

Though already mistress of heaven, the "Great Above," as her name indicates, Inanna longs for still greater power and sets her goal to rule the infernal regions, the "Great Below," as well. She therefore decides to descend to the nether world to see what can be done. Having collected all the appropriate divine laws and having adorned herself with her queenly robes and jewels, she is ready to enter the "land of no return."

The queen of the nether world is her older sister and bitter enemy, Ereshkigal, Sumerian goddess of death and gloom. Fearing, not without reason, lest her sister put her to death in the domain she rules, Inanna instructs her vizier Ninshubur, who is always at her beck and call, that if after three days she has failed to return, he is to set up a lament for her by the ruins, in the assembly hall of the gods. He is then to go to Nippur, the city of Enlil, the leading god of the Sumerian pantheon, and plead with him to save her and not let her be put to death in the nether world. If Enlil refuses, Ninshubur is to go to Ur, the city of the moon-god Nanna, and repeat his plea. If Nanna, too, refuses, he is to go to Eridu, the city of Enki, the god of wisdom, who "knows the food of life," who "knows the water of life," and he will surely come to her rescue.

Inanna then descends to the nether world and approaches Ereshkigal's temple of lapis lazuli. At the gate she is met by the chief gatekeeper, who demands to know who she is and why she has come. Inanna concocts a false excuse for her visit, and the gatekeeper, on instructions from his mistress, leads her through the seven gates of the nether world. As she passes through one gate after another, her garments and jewels are removed piece by piece in spite of her protests. Finally, after entering the last gate, she is brought stark naked and on bended knees before Ereshkigal and the Anunnaki, the seven dreaded judges of the nether world. They fasten upon her their eyes of death, and she is turned into a corpse, which is then hung from a stake.

Three days and three nights pass. On the fourth day, Ninshubur, seeing that his mistress has not returned, proceeds to make the rounds of the gods in accordance with her instructions. As Inanna had surmised, both Enlil and Nanna refuse all help. Enki, however, devises a plan to restore her to life. He fashions the *kurgarru* and the *kalaturru*, two sexless creatures, and entrusts to them the "food of life" and the "water of life," with instructions to proceed to the nether world and sprinkle this "food" and "water" on Inanna's impaled corpse. This they do, and Inanna revives.

Though Inanna is once again alive, her troubles are far from over, for it was an unbroken rule of the "land of no return" that no one who entered its gates might return to the world above unless he produced a substitute to take his place in the nether world. Inanna is no exception to the rule. She is indeed permitted to reascend to the earth, but is accompanied by a number of heartless demons with instructions to bring her back to the lower regions if she fails to provide another deity to take her place. Surrounded by these ghoulish constables, Inanna first proceeds to visit the two Sumerian cities Umma and Bad-tibira. The protecting gods of these cities, Shara and Latarak, terrified at the sight of the unearthly arrivals, clothe themselves in sackcloth and grovel in the dust before Inanna. Inanna seems to be gratified by their humility, and when the demons threaten to carry them off to the nether world she restrains the demons and thus saves the lives of the two gods.

Inanna and the demons, continuing their journey, arrive at the Sumerian city of Kullab. The guardian deity of this city is the shepherd-god Dumuzi, and since he is her husband, it is not surprising to find him refusing to wear sackcloth and grovel in the dust before his spouse. He dresses up instead in festive array and sits loftily upon his throne. Enraged, Inanna looks down upon him with "the eye of death" and hands him over to the eager and unmerciful demons to be carried off to the nether world. Dumuzi turns pale and weeps. He lifts his hands to the sky and pleads with the sun-god Utu, who is Inanna's brother and therefore his own brother-in-law. Dumuzi begs Utu to help him escape the clutches of the demons by changing his hand into the hand of a snake, and his foot into the foot of a snake.

Here, unfortunately, right in the middle of Dumuzi's prayer to Utu, our tablets come to an end. But since Dumuzi is well known from various sources as an underworld deity, the likelihood is that his plea to Utu was not heeded and that he was actually carried off to the nether world.

Here is the myth in the words of the ancient poet himself (a number of repetitious passages are omitted):

> From the "great above" she set her mind toward the "great below,"
> The goddess, from the "great above" she set her mind toward the "great below,"
> Inanna, from the "great above" she set her mind toward the "great below."
>
> My lady abandoned heaven, abandoned earth,
> 　　To the nether world she descended,
> Inanna abandoned heaven, abandoned earth,
> 　　To the nether world she descended,
> Abandoned lordship, abandoned ladyship,
> 　　To the nether world she descended.
>
> The seven divine laws she fastened at the side,
> Gathered all the divine laws, placed them in her hand,
> All the laws she set up at her waiting foot,
> The *shugurra*, the crown of the plain, she put upon her head,
> Locks of hair she fixed upon her forehead,

The measuring rod and line of lapis lazuli she gripped in her hand,
Small lapis lazuli stones she tied about her neck,
Twin *nunuz*-stones she fastened to her breast,
A gold ring she gripped in her hand,
The breastplate "Come, man, come" she bound about her breast,
With the *pala*-garment of ladyship she covered her body,
The ointment "Let him come, let him come" she daubed on her
    eyes.

Inanna walked toward the nether world,
Her vizier Ninshubur walked at her side,
The pure Inanna says to Ninshubur:
"O you who are my constant support,
My vizier of favorable words,
My knight of true words,
I am now descending to the nether world.

"When I shall have come to the nether world,
Set up a lament for me as (is done) by ruins,
In the assembly shrine beat the drum for me,
In the house of the gods wander about for me,
Lower your eyes for me, lower your mouth for me, . . . ,
Like a pauper in a single garment dress for me,
To the Ekur, the house of Enlil, all alone direct thy step.

"Upon entering the Ekur, the house of Enlil,
Weep before Enlil:
'O father Enlil, let not your daughter be put to death in the
    nether world,
Let not your good metal be covered with the dust of the
    nether world,
Let not your good lapis lazuli be broken up into the stone of the
    stoneworker,
Let not your boxwood be cut up into the wood of the
    woodworker,
Let not the maid Inanna be put to death in the nether world.'
If Enlil stands not by you in this matter, go to Ur.

"In Ur upon entering the . . -house of the land,
The Ekishnugal, the house of Nanna,
Weep before Nanna:
'O Father Nanna, let not your daughter . . . . ' (Five lines
    repeated.)
If Nanna stands not by you in this matter, go to Eridu.

"In Eridu upon entering the house of Enki,
Weep before Enki:
'O Father Enki, let not your daughter . . . . ' (Five lines
    repeated.)

Father Enki, the lord of wisdom,
Who knows the 'food of life,' who knows the 'water of life,'
He will surely bring me back to life."

Inanna walked toward the nether world,
To her messenger Ninshubur she says:
"Go, Ninshubur,
The word which I have commanded you do not neglect."

When Inanna had arrived at the palace, the lapis-lazuli mountain,
At the door of the nether world she acted boldly,
In the palace of the nether world she spoke boldly,
"Open the house, gatekeeper, open the house,
Open the house, Neti, open the house, all alone I would enter."

Neti, the chief gatekeeper of the nether world,
Answers the pure Inanna:
"Who, pray, are you?"

"I am the queen of heaven, the place where the sun rises."

"If you are the queen of heaven, the place where the sun rises,
Why, pray, have you come to the land of no return?
On the road whose traveler returns not, how has your heart
    led you?"

The pure Inanna answers him:
"My elder sister Ereshkigal,
Because her husband, the lord Gugalanna, had been killed,
To witness the funeral rites,
. . . . ; so be it."

Neti, the chief gatekeeper of the nether world,
Answers the pure Inanna:
"Stay, Inanna, to my queen let me speak,
To my queen Ereshkigal let me speak, . . . let me speak."

Neti, the chief gatekeeper of the nether world,
Enters the house of his queen Ereshkigal and says to her:
"O my queen, it is a maid who like a god . . . . , ... ,
The seven divine laws . . . . " (The entire third stanza is
    here repeated.)

Then Ereshkigal bit her thigh, was filled with wrath,
Says to Neti, her chief gatekeeper:
"Come, Neti, chief gatekeeper of the nether world,
The word which I command you, neglect not.
Of the seven gates of the nether world, lift their bolts,

Of its one palace Ganzir, the 'face' of the nether world, press
   open its doors.
Upon her entering,
Bowed low, let her be brought naked before me."

Neti, the chief gatekeeper of the nether world,
Heeded the word of his queen.
Of the seven gates of the nether world, he lifted their bolts,
Of its one palace Ganzir, the "face" of the nether world, he
   pressed open its doors.
To the pure Inanna he says:
"Come, Inanna, enter."

Upon her entering,
The *shugurra*, "the crown of the plain" of her head, was removed.
"What, pray, is this?"
"Be silent, Inanna, the laws of the nether world are perfect,
O, Inanna, do not deprecate the rites of the nether world."

Upon her entering the second gate,
The measuring rod and line of lapis lazuli was removed.
"What, pray, is this?"
"Be silent, Inanna, the laws of the nether world are perfect,
O Inanna, do not deprecate the rites of the nether world."

Upon her entering the third gate,
The small lapis-lazuli stones of her neck were removed.
    (Inanna's question and the gatekeeper's answer are repeated
      here, and in the following parallel passages.)

Upon her entering the fourth gate,
The twin *nunuz*-stones of her breast were removed.

Upon her entering the fifth gate,
The gold ring of her hand was removed.

Upon her entering the sixth gate,
The breastplate "Come, man, come" of her breast was removed.

Upon her entering the seventh gate,
The *pala*-garment of ladyship of her body was removed.
Bowed low, she was brought naked before her.

The pure Ereshkigal seated herself upon her throne,
The Anunnaki, the seven judges, pronounced judgment before
   her,
She fastened her eye upon her, the eye of death,
Spoke the word against her, the word of wrath,
Uttered the cry against her, the cry of guilt,

The sick woman was turned into a corpse,
The corpse was hung from a nail.

After three days and three nights had passed,
Her vizier Ninshubur,
Her vizier of favorable words,
Her knight of true words,
Set up a lament for her as (is done) by ruins,
Beat the drum for her in the assembly shrine,
Wandered about for her in the house of the gods,
Lowered his eyes for her, lowered his mouth for her, ... ,
Like a pauper in a single garment dressed for her,
To the Ekur, the house of Enlil, all alone he directed his step.

Upon his entering the Ekur, the house of Enlil,
Before Enlil he weeps:
"O father Enlil, let not your daughter be put to death in the
    nether world,
Let not your good metal be covered with the dust of the nether
    world,
Let not your good lapis lazuli be broken up into the stone of the
    stoneworker,
Let not your boxwood be cut up into the wood of the
    woodworker,
Let not the maid Inanna be put to death in the nether world."

. . . .
Father Enlil stood not by him in this matter, he went to Ur.

In Ur upon his entering the . . -house of the land,
The Ekishnugal, the house of Nanna,
Before Nanna he weeps:
"O Father Nanna, let not your daughter . . . . " (Five lines
    repeated.)

. . . .
Father Nanna stood not by him in this matter, he went to Eridu.

In Eridu upon his entering the house of Enki,
Before Enki he weeps:
"O Father Enki, let not your daughter . . . . " (Five lines
    repeated.)

Father Enki answers Ninshubur:
"What now has happened to my daughter! I am troubled,
What now has happened to Inanna! I am troubled,
What now has happened to the queen of all the lands! I am
    troubled,
What now has happened to the hierodule of heaven! I am
    troubled."

He brought forth dirt from his fingernail and fashioned the
 kurgarru,
He brought forth dirt from the red-painted fingernail and
 fashioned the *kalaturru,*
To the *kurgarru* he gave the 'food of life,'
To the *kalaturru* he gave the 'water of life,'
Father Enki says to the *kalaturru* and *kurgarru*:

". . . .

Only the last part of Enki's speech is preserved. It reads:

"They (the nether world gods) will offer you the water of the
 river, do not accept it,
They will offer you the grain of the field, do not accept it,
'Give us the corpse hung from the nail,' say to her (Ereshkigal),
One of you sprinkle upon her the 'food of life,' the other the
 'water of life,'
Then will Inanna arise."

The *kurgarru* and *kalaturru* carry out Enki's instruction, but
only the last part of this passage is preserved. It reads:

They offer them the water of the river, they accept it not,
They offer them the grain of the field, they accept it not,
"Give us the corpse hung from the nail," they said to her.

The pure Ereshkigal answers the *kalaturru* and *kurgarru*:
"The corpse, it is your queen's."

"The corpse, though it is our queen's, give to us," they said to her.

They give them the corpse hung from the nail,
One sprinkled upon her the "food of life," the other, the
 "water of life."
Inanna arose.

Inanna is about to ascend from the nether world,
The Anunnaki seized her (saying):
"Who of those who have descended to the nether world ever
 ascends unharmed from the nether world!
If Inanna would ascend from the nether world,
Let her give someone as her substitute."

Inanna ascends from the nether world,
The small demons like *shukur*-reeds,

The large demons like *dubban*-reeds,
Held on to her side.
Who was in front of her, though not a vizier, held a scepter
   in his hand,
Who was at her side, though not a knight, had a weapon
   fastened about the loin.
They who accompanied her,
They who accompanied Inanna,
Were beings who know not food, who know not water,
Eat not sprinkled flour,
Drink not libated water,
Take away the wife from the man's lap,
Take away the child from the nursemaid's breast.

Inanna proceeds to the two Sumerian cities Umma and Badtibira, whose two deities prostrate themselves before her and
are thus saved from the clutches of the demons. Then she arrives
at the city Kullab, whose tutelary deity is Dumuzi. The poem
continues:

Dumuzi put on a noble robe, he sat high on (his) seat.
The demons seized him by his thighs . . . . ,
The seven (demons) rush at him as at the side of a sick man,
The shepherds play not the flute and pipe before him.

She (Inanna) fastened the eye upon him, the eye of death,
Spoke the word against him, the word of wrath,
Uttered the cry against him, the cry of guilt:
"As for him, carry him off."
The pure Inanna gave the shepherd Dumuzi into their hands.

They who accompanied him,
They who accompanied Dumuzi,
Were beings who know not food, know not water,
Eat not sprinkled flour,
Drink not libated water,
Sate not with pleasure the wife's lap,
Kiss not the well-fed children,
Take away the man's son from his knee,
Carry off the daughter-in-law from the house of the
   father-in-law.

Dumuzi wept, his face turned green,
Toward heaven to (the sun-god) Utu he lifted his hand:
"O Utu, you are my wife's brother, I am your sister's husband,
I am one who brings cream to your mother's house,

I am one who brings milk to Ningal's house,
Turn my hand into the hand of a snake,
Turn my foot into the foot of a snake,
Let me escape my demons, let them not seize me."

The reconstruction and translation of "Inanna's Descent to the Nether World" has been a slow and gradual process, in which a number of scholars played an active role. It began in 1914, when Arno Poebel first published three small pieces belonging to this myth in the University Museum at Philadelphia. In the same year, the late Stephen Langdon published two pieces which he had uncovered in the Museum of the Ancient Orient at Istanbul. One of these was the upper half of a large four-column tablet which proved to be of major importance for the reconstruction of the text of the myth. Edward Chiera uncovered three additional pieces in the University Museum. These were published in his two posthumous volumes consisting of copies of Sumerian literary texts. I prepared these volumes for publication for the Oriental Institute in 1934.

By 1934 we had eight pieces, all more or less fragmentary, dealing with the myth. Nevertheless, the contents remained obscure, for the breaks in the tablets were so numerous and came at such crucial points in the story that an intelligent reconstruction of the extant parts of the myth remained impossible. It was a fortunate and remarkable discovery of Chiera's that saved the situation. He identified in the University Museum at Philadelphia the *lower* half of the same four-column tablet whose *upper* half had been found and copied by Langdon years before in the Museum of the Ancient Orient at Istanbul. The tablet had evidently been broken before or during the excavation, and the two halves had become separated. One had been retained in Istanbul, and the other had come to Philadelphia. Chiera died before he was in a position to utilize its contents.

It was Chiera's recognition of the lower half of the "Inanna's Descent" tablet that enabled me to publish the first edition of the myth in 1937 in the *Revue d'Assyriologie*, for, when the lower was joined to the upper half, the combined text furnished an excellent framework in which all the other extant fragments

could be properly arranged. There were still numerous gaps and
breaks in the text which made its translation and interpretation
no easy matter, and the meaning of several significant passages in
the story remained obscure. In 1937, while working in the Istanbul Museum of the Ancient Orient as a Guggenheim Fellow, I
was fortunate enough to discover in Istanbul three additional
pieces belonging to the myth, and upon returning to the United
States in 1939 I located another large piece in the University
Museum at Philadelphia and yet another in 1940. These five
fragments helped to fill in some of the most serious <u>lacunae</u> in
the first reconstruction and translation, and it was now possible
to prepare a considerably fuller edition of the text. This appeared in the *Proceedings of the American Philosophical Society*
in 1942.

But matters did not rest there. Some time afterward, I was
privileged to examine and help identify the hundred-odd Sumerian literary tablets in the Yale Babylonian Collection, which contains one of the most important tablet collections in the world. In
the course of this work, I came upon an excellently preserved
tablet, already identified by Edward Chiera as early as 1924 in
a note which had escaped my attention, inscribed with ninety-
two lines of text. The last thirty lines contain an entirely new
passage which carries on the story from where it had broken off
in previously known texts.

This new material turned out to have an unexpected significance. It cleared up a misconception concerning the god Dumuzi
which students of Mesopotamian mythology and religion had
held for more than half a century. Almost ever since the Semitic
version of our myth, commonly known as "Ishtar's Descent to
the Nether World," was first published, and long before its
Sumerian counterpart came to be known to any extent, it had
been generally supposed that the god Dumuzi was carried off to
the nether world, for some unknown reason, *before* Inanna's
descent. It had been assumed that Inanna descended to the lower
regions in order to free her husband Dumuzi and bring him back
to earth. The new Yale text, however, proved these assumptions
to be groundless. Inanna did not save her husband Dumuzi from
the nether world. Rather, it was she who, angered by his con-

temptuous attitude, actually handed him over to the demons to be carried off to the land of no return. The addition of the Yale tablet (Ferris Stephens, Curator of the Yale Babylonian Collection, prepared an excellent copy) made it necessary to publish a third edition of the myth. This up-to-date revision, which includes many constructive suggestions by my Sumerological colleagues Adam Falkenstein, Benno Landsberger, and Thorkild Jacobsen, was published in 1951 in Volume V of the *Journal of Cuneiform Studies.*

In the first part of the present chapter, the word Kur was explained as the cosmic space separating the earth's crust from the violent primeval sea (the Biblical Tehom) below. But Kur also seems to have stood for a monstrous dragon who held Tehom's destructive waters in check. The slaying of dragons by gods and heroes, a favorite motif in Sumerian mythology, is discussed in Chapter 22.

THE FIRST "ST. GEORGE"

T HE DRAGON-SLAYING motif is a high favorite with the mythographers of almost all peoples and ages. In Greece especially, where tales involving gods and heroes were legion, there was hardly a hero who did not slay his dragon. Perhaps Heracles and Perseus are the best-known of the Greek killers of monsters. With the rise of Christianity, the heroic feat was transferred to the saints; witness the story of St. George and the Dragon, and its ubiquitous parallels. The names and the details vary from place to place and story to story. But what is the original source of the incidents? Since the dragon-slaying theme was an important motif in the Sumerian mythology of the third millennium B.C., it is reasonable to assume that many a thread in the texture of the Greek and early Christian dragon tales winds back to Sumerian sources.

At present we have at least three versions of the dragon-slaying motif as it was current in Sumer more than thirty-five hundred years ago. In two of these versions the heroes are deities—the water-god Enki, the closest Sumerian counterpart of the Greek Poseidon, and Ninurta, the god in charge of the South Wind. The third version introduces a mortal dragon-killer—the hero Gilgamesh—who may well be the original "St. George."

In the myth involving Enki, it is the monster Kur who seems to be the villain of the piece. The struggle probably took place not long after the separation of heaven and earth, and (if the fragmentary lines are correctly interpreted) Kur's wrongdoing consisted in the abducting of a sky-goddess, which calls to mind the Greek story of the rape of Persephone. Unfortunately we have only a dozen laconic lines from which to reconstruct the story, for none of the tablets on which the details of the myth were inscribed have as yet been excavated. The story is told in a brief passage which is part of the prologue to the epic tale "Gilgamesh, Enkidu, and the Nether World." The passage comes immediately after the "creation" lines. The contents are as follows:

After heaven and earth had been separated, An, the heaven-god, carried off heaven, while Enlil, the air-god, carried off the earth. It was then that the foul deed was committed. The goddess Ereshkigal was probably carried off violently as the prize of the Kur (it is not stated who committed the deed, but it is not unlikely that it was the Kur itself). Thereupon Enki set out in a boat to the Kur. His purpose is not stated but it was probably to avenge the abduction of the goddess Ereshkigal. The Kur fought savagely with all kinds of stones, and it attacked Enki's boat, front and rear, with the primeval waters which it controlled. Here the brief prologue passage ends, since the author of "Gilgamesh, Enkidu, and the Nether World" was not interested in the dragon story primarily, but was anxious to proceed with his Gilgamesh tale. And so we are left in the dark concerning the outcome of the battle. There is little doubt, however, that Enki was victorious. And it is not unlikely that the myth was invented for the purpose of explaining why, in historical times, Enki, like the Greek Poseidon, was conceived as a sea-god and why his temple in Eridu was designated as the Abzu, a Sumerian word for "sea."

Here, in full, is the prologue passage from which this particular dragon-slaying myth is adduced:

> After An had carried off the heaven,
> After Enlil had carried off the earth,
> After Ereshkigal had been carried off to Kur as its prize,
>
> After he had set sail, after he had set sail,
> After the father had set sail against Kur,
> After Enki had set sail against Kur,
> Against the king, the small ones it (Kur)hurled;
> Against Enki, the large ones it hurled.

> Its small ones, stones of the hand,
> Its large ones, stones of "dancing" reeds,
> The keel of the boat of Enki
> In battle, like the attacking storm, overwhelm.
>
> Against the king, the water at the head of the boat
> Like a wolf devours,
> Against Enki, the water at the rear of the boat
> Like a lion strikes down.

The second version of the dragon-slaying motif forms part of a poem of more than six hundred lines, which may be titled "The Deeds and Exploits of the God Ninurta." Its contents are reconstructed from several scores of tablets and fragments, many of which are still unpublished.

The villain of the piece is not Kur but Asag, the demon of sickness and disease, whose abode is in the Kur—that is, the nether world. The hero is Ninurta, the god of the South Wind, who was regarded as the son of Enlil, the air-god. Following a hymnal introduction, the poem begins the story with an address to Ninurta by Sharur, his personified weapon. For some unstated reason the Sharur has set his mind against the Asag-demon, and therefore his address is full of phrases extolling the heroic qualities and deeds of Ninurta, whom he urges to attack and destroy the monster. Ninurta sets out to do as bidden. At first he seems to have met more than his match, and he "flees like a bird." However, the Sharur addresses him once again with reassuring words. Ninurta now attacks the Asag fiercely with all the weapons at his command, and the demon is destroyed.

With the destruction of the Asag, a serious calamity overtakes Sumer. The primeval waters of the Kur rise to the surface, and as a result of their violence no fresh waters can reach the fields and gardens. The gods of Sumer who "carried its pickax and basket"—that is, who had charge of irrigating Sumer and preparing it for cultivation—are desperate. The Tigris does not rise; it has no "good" water in its channel.

> Famine was severe, nothing was produced,
> At the small rivers, there was no "washing of the hands,"
> The waters rose not high.

The fields were not watered,
 There was no digging of (irrigation) ditches.
In all the lands there was no vegetation,
 Only weeds grew.

Thereupon the lord put his lofty mind to it.
Ninurta, the son of Enlil, brought great things into being.

Ninurta sets up stones over the Kur, heaping them like a great wall in front of Sumer. These stones hold back the "mighty waters," and as a result the waters of the Kur no longer rise to (the surface of the) earth. As for the waters which have already flooded the land, Ninurta gathers them and leads them into the Tigris, which is now in a position to water the fields with its overflow. In the language of the poet:

What had been scattered, he gathered,
What of the Kur had been scattered,
He guided and hurled into the Tigris,
The high waters it pours over the fields.
Behold, now, everything on earth,
Rejoiced afar at Ninurta, the king of the land.
The fields produced abundant grain,
The vineyard and orchard bore their fruit,
(The harvest) was heaped up in granaries and hills,
The Lord made mourning to disappear from the land,
He made happy the spirit of the gods.

Hearing of her son's great and heroic deeds, his mother, Ninmah, is filled with compassion for him; she becomes so restless that she is unable to sleep in her bedchamber. She therefore addresses Ninurta from afar with a prayer for permission to visit him and gaze upon him. He looks at her with the "eye of life," saying:

"O lady, because you would come to the Kur,
O Ninmah, because for my sake you would enter the inimical land,
Because you have no fear of the terror of the battle
 surrounding me,
Therefore, of the hill which I, the hero, have heaped up,
Let its name be Hursag (Mountain) and you be its queen."

Ninurta then blesses the Hursag that it may produce all kinds of herbs; wine and honey; various kinds of trees; gold, silver, and bronze; cattle, sheep, and all "four-legged creatures." Following this blessing, he turns to the stones, cursing those which had been his enemies in his battle with the Asag-demon, and blessing those which had been his friends. This passage, in style and tone, brings to mind the blessing and cursing of Jacob's sons in the Book of Genesis. The poem then closes with a long hymnal passage in exaltation of Ninurta.

In the third version of the dragon-slaying tales, a man, not a god, is the protagonist. He is Gilgamesh, the most renowned of all Sumerian heroes. The monster whom he kills is Huwawa, the guardian of the "Land of the Living," particularly its holy cedars. The story is told in a poem which I have titled "Gilgamesh and the Land of the Living," pieced together from fourteen tablets and fragments, and last published in 1950 in *Ancient Near Eastern Texts* (edited by James Pritchard). As yet only the first 174 lines of the poem have been recovered. Even so, the poem is recognizable as a literary creation which must have had a profound emotional and aesthetic appeal to its highly credulous Sumerian audience. Its motivating theme, man's anxiety about death and its sublimation in the notion of an immortal name, has a universal significance that lends it high poetic value. Its plot structure reveals a careful and imaginative selection of such details as are essential to its predominantly poignant mood. Stylistically, the poet obtains a fitting rhythmic effect by his skillful use of varied patterns of repetition and parallelism. All in all, this poem is one of the finest Sumerian literary works as yet uncovered. Its contents may be summarized as follows:

The "lord" Gilgamesh, realizing that, like all mortals, he must die sooner or later, is determined at least to "raise up a name" for himself before he meets his destined end. He therefore sets his heart on journeying to the far-distant "Land of the Living," with the probable intention of felling its cedars and bringing them to Erech. He informs his loyal servant and constant companion, Enkidu, of his proposed undertaking. Enkidu advises him first to acquaint the sun-god Utu with his plan, for it is Utu who has charge of the cedar land.

Acting on this advice, Gilgamesh brings offerings to Utu and

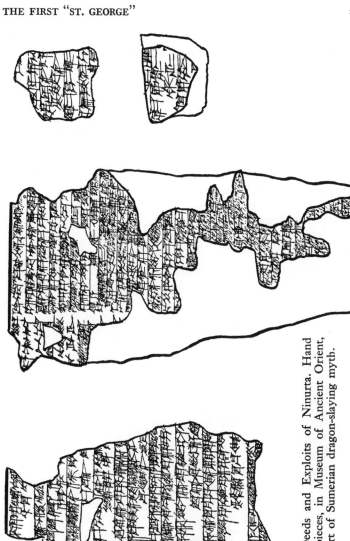

15. & 16. The Deeds and Exploits of Ninurta. Hand copies of three pieces, in Museum of Ancient Orient, inscribed with part of Sumerian dragon-slaying myth.

pleads for his support of the contemplated journey to the "Land of the Living." At first Utu seems skeptical of Gilgamesh's qualifications, but Gilgamesh repeats his plea in more persuasive language. Utu takes pity on him and decides to help him—probably by immobilizing the seven vicious demons personifying the destructive weather phenomena that might menace Gilgamesh in his journey across the mountains between Erech and the "Land of the Living." Overjoyed, Gilgamesh gathers fifty volunteers from Erech—unattached men who have neither "house" nor "mother" and who are ready to follow him in whatever he does. After he has had weapons of bronze and wood prepared for himself and his companions, they cross the seven mountains with the help of Utu.

Just what happens immediately after the crossing of the last of the seven mountains is not clear, since the relevant passage is poorly preserved. When the text becomes intelligible again, we find that Gilgamesh has fallen into a heavy sleep from which he is awakened only after considerable time and effort. Thoroughly aroused by this delay, he swears by his mother Ninsun and his

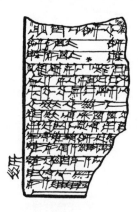

17. Gilgamesh and the Land of the Living. Hand copy of two unpublished Nippur fragments in Museum of Ancient Orient.

father Lugalbanda that he will enter the "Land of the Living" and will brook no interference from either man or god. Enkidu pleads with him to turn back, for the guardian of the cedars is the fearful monster Huwawa, whose destructive attack none may withstand. But Gilgamesh will have none of this caution. Convinced that with Enkidu's help no harm can befall either of them, he bids his servant to put away fear and go forward with him.

The monster Huwawa, spying them from his cedar house, makes frantic but apparently vain efforts to drive off Gilgamesh and his adventurous band. Following a break of some lines, we learn that Gilgamesh, after cutting down seven trees, has probably come to Huwawa's inner chamber. Strangely enough, at the very first, and seemingly very light, attack by Gilgamesh, Hu-

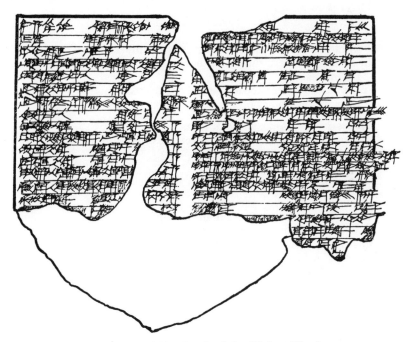

18. Gilgamesh and the Land of the Living. Hand copy of obverse of unpublished four-column Nippur tablet, in Museum of Ancient Orient, inscribed with a variant version of dragon-slaying motif.

wawa is overcome with fright. He utters a prayer to the sun-god Utu, and adjures Gilgamesh not to kill him. Gilgamesh would like to act the generous victor, and, in riddle-like phrases, suggests to Enkidu that Huwawa be set free. But Enkidu is fearful of the consequences and advises against such unwise action. Following Huwawa's indignant criticism of Enkidu's ungenerous attitude, our two heroes cut off Huwawa's neck. They then seem to bring his corpse before Enlil and Ninlil. But what follows is altogether uncertain, for after several fragmentary lines, the available material comes to an end.

Here is the literal translation of the more intelligible portions of the poem:

> The lord, toward the Land of the Living set his mind,
> The lord, Gilgamesh, toward the Land of the Living set his mind,
> He says to his servant Enkidu:
> "O Enkidu, not (yet) have brick and stamp brought forth the fated end,
> I would enter the 'land,' I would set up my name,
> In its places where the names have been raised up, I would raise up my name,
> In its places where the names have not been raised up, I would raise up the names of the gods."
>
> His servant Enkidu answers him:
> "O my master, if you would enter the 'land,' inform Utu,
> Inform Utu, the hero Utu—
> The 'land,' it is Utu's charge,
> The land of the cut-down cedar, it is the hero Utu's charge—inform Utu."
>
> Gilgamesh laid his hands on an all-white kid,
> A brown kid, an offering, he pressed to his breast,
> In his hand he placed the silver staff of his . . . ,
> He says to Utu of heaven:
> "O Utu, I would enter the 'land,' be my ally,
> I would enter the land of the cut-down cedar, be my ally."
>
> Utu of heaven answers him:
> "True you are . . . , but what are you to the 'land'?"
>
> "O Utu, a word I would speak to you, to my word your ear,
> I would have it reach you, give ear to it.
> In my city man dies, oppressed is the heart,
> Man perishes, heavy is the heart,

I peered over the wall,
Saw the dead bodies . . . floating in the river;
As for me, I too will be served thus; verily 'tis so.
Man, the tallest, cannot reach to heaven,
Man, the widest, cannot cover the earth.
Not (yet) have brick and stamp brought forth the fated end,
I would enter the 'land,' I would set up my name,
In its places where the names have been raised up, I would raise
  up my name,
In its places where the names have not been raised up, I would
  raise up the names of the gods."

Utu accepted his tears as an offering,
Like a man of mercy, he showed him mercy,
The seven heroes, the sons of one mother, ... ,
He brings into the mountain caves.

Who felled the cedar, acted joyfully,
The lord Gilgamesh acted joyfully,
In his city, as one man, he . . . . ,
As two companions, he . . . . ,
"Who has a house, to his house! Who has a mother, to his
  mother!
Let single males who would do as I (do), fifty, stand at my side."

Who had a house, to his house; who had a mother, to his mother,
Single males who would do as he (did), fifty, stood at his side.

To the house of the smiths he directed his step,
The . . , the . . -ax, his "Might of Heroism" he caused to be cast
  there.
To the . . garden of the plain he directed his step,
The . . -tree, the willow, the apple-tree, the box-tree, the . . -tree
  he felled there.
The "sons" of his city who accompanied him placed them in
  their hands.

The next fifteen lines are fragmentary, but we learn that
Gilgamesh, after crossing the seven mountains, has fallen asleep,
and someone is waking him, thus:

He touches him, he rises not,
He speaks to him, he answers not.
"Who are lying, who are lying,
O Gilgamesh, lord, son of Kullab, how long will you lie?
The 'land' has become dark, the shadows have spread over it,
Dusk has brought forth its light,

Utu has gone with lifted head to the bosom of his mother, Ningal,
O Gilgamesh, how long will you lie?
Let not the sons of your city who have accompanied you,
Stand waiting for you at the foot of the mountain,
Let not your mother who gave birth to you be driven off to the
    'square' of the city."

He gave heed,
With his "word of heroism" he covered himself like a garment,
His garment of thirty shekels which he carried in his hand he
    wrapped about his breast,
Like a bull he stood on the "great earth,"
He put his mouth to the ground, his teeth shook.
"By the life of Ninsun, my mother who gave birth to me, of pure
    Lugalbanda, my father,
May I become as one who sits to be wondered at on the knee of
    Ninsun, my mother who gave birth to me."
A second time moreover he says to him:
"By the life of Ninsun, my mother who gave birth to me,
    of pure Lugalbanda, my father,
Until I will have killed that 'man,' if he be a man, until I will
    have killed him, if he be a god,
My step directed to the 'land,' I shall not direct to the city."

The faithful servant pleaded, . . d life,
He answers his master:
"O my master, you who have not seen that 'man,' are not
    terror-stricken,
I who have seen that 'man' am terror-stricken.
The warrior, his teeth are the teeth of a dragon,
His face is the face of a lion,
His . . is the onrushing floodwater,
From his forehead which devours trees and reeds, none escape.
O my master, journey you to the 'land,' I will journey to the city,
I will tell your mother of your glory, let her shout,
I will tell her of your ensuing death, let her shed bitter tears."

"For me another will not die, the loaded boat will not sink,
The three-ply cloth will not be cut,
The . . . will not be overwhelmed,
House and hut, fire will not destroy.
Do you help me (and) I will help you, what can happen
    to us? . . . .
Come, let us go forward, we will cast eyes upon him,
If we go forward,
(And) there be fear, there be fear, turn it back,
There be terror, there be terror, turn it back,
In your . . . , come, let us go forward."

When they had not yet come within a distance of 1200 feet,
Huwawa . . d his cedar house,
Fastened his eye upon him, the eye of death,
Nodded his head to him, shook his head at him, ...
He (Gilgamesh) himself uprooted the first tree,
The "sons" of his city who accompanied him
Cut down its crown, bundle it,
Lay it at the foot of the mountain.
After he himself had finished off the seventh, he approached his
    chamber,
Turned upon the "snake of the wine-quay" in his wall,
Like one pressing a kiss he slapped his cheek.

Huwawa, (his) teeth shook, . . . his hand trembled,
"I would say a word to you . . . ,
(O Utu), a mother who gave birth to me I know not, a father
    who reared me I know not,
In the 'land' you gave birth to me, you raised me."
He adjured Gilgamesh by the life of heaven, life of earth, life
    of the nether world,
Took him by the hand, brought him to . . . .

Then did the heart of Gilgamesh take pity on the . . . ,
He says to his servant Enkidu:
"O Enkidu, let the caught bird go (back) to its place,
Let the caught man return to the bosom of his mother."

Enkidu answers Gilgamesh:
"The tallest who has not judgment,
Namtar (demon of death) will devour, Namtar who knows no
    distinctions.
If the caught bird goes (back) to its place,
If the caught man returns to the bosom of his mother,
You will not return to the city of the mother who gave birth
    to you."

Huwawa says to Enkidu:
"Against me, O Enkidu, you have spoken evil to him,
O hired man . . . . you have spoken evil to him."

When he had thus spoken,
They cut off his neck;
Placed upon him . . . . ,
Brought him before Enlil and Ninlil . . . .

Gilgamesh is the most celebrated of all Sumerian heroes and a
favorite with ancient poets and minstrels. However, modern

Orientalists first came to know of him and his heroic exploits not from Sumerian but from Semitic sources. He is the protagonist in the Babylonian epic now generally admitted to be the most significant literary creation of the whole of ancient Mesopotamia. But a comparative analysis of this Babylonian epic and its Sumerian forerunners shows that the Babylonian authors and redactors utilized, modified, and molded Sumerian epics for their own purposes. In Chapter 23 an effort is made to distinguish the Sumerian warp from the Semitic woof.

THE FIRST CASE
OF LITERARY BORROWING

G EORGE SMITH, an Englishman who had been studying the thousands of clay tablets and fragments brought to the British Museum from the mounds covering ancient Nineveh, read a paper, on December 3, 1862, before the then recently organized Society of Biblical Archaeology. His paper proved to be a milestone for Biblical studies, particularly in their comparative aspects.

In this paper Smith announced that, on one of the clay tablets dug up from the long-buried library of King Ashurbanipal, who reigned in the seventh century B.C., he had discovered and deciphered a version of the deluge myth which showed marked resemblances to the flood story in the Book of Genesis. The announcement caused no small sensation in scholarly circles and even aroused the enthusiasm of the general public the world over. The *Daily Telegraph*, a London newspaper of the period, immediately volunteered funds for a new expedition to Nineveh. George Smith himself undertook the excavations, but his health and temperament were unsuited to the Near East. He died in the field at the early age of thirty-six.

Not long after he had announced the discovery of the Babylonian flood story, Smith realized, on further study of the tablets and fragments from the Ashurbanipal library, that this deluge myth formed but a small part of a long poem, and that the ancient Babylonians themselves referred to it as the "Gilgamesh

Cycle." According to the ancient scribes, it consisted of twelve songs or cantos of about three hundred lines each. Each canto was inscribed on a separate tablet in the Ashurbanipal library. The deluge story formed the major part of the eleventh tablet.

Since the days of George Smith, numerous new pieces of this Semitic "Gilgamesh Cycle," or "Epic of Gilgamesh" as it is now generally called, have been excavated in Iraq. Some of these were inscribed in the Old Babylonian period—that is, as early as the seventeenth or eighteenth century B.C. Ancient translations of parts of the poem into Hurrian, as well as the Indo-European Hittite language, have been found on clay tablets excavated in Asia Minor, from the second half of the second millennium B.C. It is thus evident that the Babylonian "Epic of Gilgamesh" was studied, translated, and imitated in ancient times all over the Near East. Today about half of its approximately 3,500 lines of text have been recovered. A superb edition of practically all the available material was published in 1930 by another Englishman, the late archaeologist and humanist R. Campbell Thompson. Since then two new and more up-to-date English translations have appeared: Alexander Heidel's *The Gilgamesh Epic and Old Testament Parallels* and Ephraim Speiser's in *Ancient Near Eastern Texts* (edited by James Pritchard).

There is good reason for this popularity, both ancient and modern, for, from the point of view of human interest and dramatic impact, the "Epic of Gilgamesh" is unique in Babylonian literature. In most Babylonian literary works, it is the gods who hold the center of the stage—gods who tend to represent abstractions rather than personalities, personified intellectualizations rather than profound spiritual forces. Even in Babylonian tales where the protagonists seem to be mortal men, the role they play is mechanical, impersonal, and lacking in dramatic impact. The characters are bloodless, colorless creatures whose puppet-like movements serve the purpose of the highly stylized etiological myth.

The situation is different in the "Epic of Gilgamesh." In this poem it is man who holds the center of the stage—the man Gilgamesh, who loves and hates, weeps and rejoices, strives and wearies, hopes and despairs. True, the gods are not absent; indeed, Gilgamesh himself, in the mythological patter and pattern of the times, is two-thirds divine and one-third mortal. But it is Gilgamesh as man who dominates the action of the poem. The gods and their activities serve only as background and setting for the dramatic episodes in the hero's life. What gives these episodes lasting significance and universal appeal is their *human* quality. They revolve about forces and problems common to man everywhere through the ages—the need for friendship, the instinct for loyalty, the impelling urge for fame and name, the love of adventure and achievement, the all-absorbing fear of death, and the all-compelling longing for immortality. It is the varied interplay of these emotional and spiritual drives in man that constitutes the drama of the "Epic of Gilgamesh"—drama which transcends the confines of time and space. Little wonder that the influence of this poem on ancient epic literatures was as wide as it was deep. Even the reader of today is moved by the universal sweep of its action, the elemental power of its tragedy.

The poem begins with a short introductory passage in praise of Gilgamesh and his city, Erech. We then read that Gilgamesh, the king of Erech, is a restless hero, unrivaled and undisciplined, who tyrannizes over the dwellers of his city. Especially oppressive are his demands for the satisfaction of his Rabelaisian sex appetite. The Erechites cry out in anguish to the gods, who, realizing that Gilgamesh acts the tyrant and bully because he has still to find his match among his fellow humans, direct the great mother-goddess Aruru to put an end to the intolerable situation. She proceeds to fashion from clay the powerful Enkidu, who, naked and long-haired, and innocent of all human relations, spends his days and nights with the wild beasts of the plains. It is Enkidu, more brute than man, who is to subdue Gilgamesh's arrogance and discipline his spirit. First, however, Enkidu must be "humanized," a process which turns out to be largely woman's task. An Erechite courtesan arouses and satisfies his sex instincts. As a result he loses in physical stature and brute strength but gains in mental and spiritual stature. This sex experience makes

Enkidu wise, and the wild beasts no longer recognize him as their own. Patiently the courtesan guides him in the civilized arts of eating, drinking, and dressing.

The humanized Enkidu is now ready to meet Gilgamesh, whose arrogant and tyrannical spirit he is destined to subdue. Gilgamesh has already learned in his dreams of the coming of Enkidu. Eager to display his unrivaled position in Erech, he arranges a nocturnal orgy and invites Enkidu to attend. Enkidu, however, is repelled by Gilgamesh's sexual cravings, and blocks his way in an effort to prevent him from entering the house appointed for the unseemly gathering. Thereupon the two titans join in combat—Gilgamesh, the sophisticated townsman, and Enkidu, the simple plainsman. Enkidu seems to be getting the better of his rival, when (for some unstated reason) Gilgamesh's wrath leaves him, and the two kiss and embrace. Out of this bitter struggle is born the friendship of the two heroes—a friendship destined to become proverbial in world lore as loyal and lasting, and rich in heroic achievement.

But Enkidu is not happy in Erech. Its gay, sensuous life is making a weakling of him. And so Gilgamesh reveals to his friend his adventurous plan to journey to the far-distant cedar forest, kill its fearful guardian, the mighty Huwawa, fell the cedar tree, and "destroy all that is evil from the land." Enkidu, who in his early savage days had wandered freely through the cedar forest, warns Gilgamesh of the mortal danger of the undertaking. But Gilgamesh only mocks his fears; it is enduring fame and name that he longs for, not a prolonged but unheroic existence. He confers with the elders of Erech, obtains the approval of the sun-god Shamash, the patron of all travelers, and has the craftsmen of Erech cast gigantic weapons for himself and Enkidu. Thus prepared, they set out on their adventure. After a long, wearisome journey, they arrive at the dazzlingly beautiful cedar forest, kill Huwawa, and fell the cedar.

Adventure leads to adventure. Upon their return to Erech, Ishtar, the goddess of love and lust, becomes infatuated with the well-formed Gilgamesh. With the promise of many rich favors, she tries to induce Gilgamesh to satisfy her desires. But Gilgamesh is no longer the undisciplined tyrant of former days.

Well aware of her promiscuity and faithlessness, he mocks at her offer and spurns it. Thereupon Ishtar, bitterly disappointed and deeply offended, tries to persuade Anu, the heaven-god, to send the Bull of Heaven against Erech to destroy Gilgamesh and his city. Anu at first refuses, but when Ishtar threatens to bring up the dead from the nether world, he is forced to consent. The Bull of Heaven descends and begins to lay waste the city of Erech, slaughtering its warriors by the hundreds. Gilgamesh and Enkidu together take up the struggle against the beast, and in a mighty concerted effort succeed in killing him.

The two heroes have now reached the pinnacle of their career, and the city of Erech rings out with the song of their exalted deeds. But inexorable fate brings a sudden and cruel end to their happiness. Because of his part in killing Huwawa and the Bull of Heaven, Enkidu is sentenced to an early death by the gods. After a twelve-day illness, Enkidu breathes his last, while his friend Gilgamesh looks on helplessly, stunned with grief. His anguished spirit is now obsessed with one doubly bitter thought: Enkidu is dead, and sooner or later he will meet the same fate. He finds little comfort in the fame and glory of his past heroic deeds. It is tangible, physical immortality which his tormented spirit now craves. He must seek and find the secret of eternal life.

As Gilgamesh well knew, there was but one individual in history who had succeeded in obtaining immortality—Utanapishtim, the wise and pious king of ancient Shuruppak, one of the five royal cities that had existed before the flood. (The mound which covers this city was excavated by German and American expeditions, and a large group of tablets from the first half of of the third millennium were discovered.)

Gilgamesh decides to make his way at all costs to the distant dwelling place of Utanapishtim. Perhaps that immortalized hero would reveal his precious secret. He wanders long and far, over mountain and plain, ever exposed to wild beasts and famine. He crosses the primeval sea and "the waters of death." Finally, weary and emaciated, his hair long and shaggy, his filthy body covered with raw animal hides, the once-proud ruler of Erech stands before Utanapishtim, eager to learn the mystery of eternal life.

But Utanapishtim's words are far from encouraging. The king

of Shuruppak narrates at great length the story of the destructive deluge that the gods had once brought against the earth in order to exterminate all living creatures. He, too, would surely have perished, had it not been for the sheltering boat he had built on the advice of the great Ea, the god of wisdom. As for the gift of eternal life, it was the gods who willed its bestowal upon him; where, however, was the god who willed Gilgamesh's immortality? Despairing of his fate, Gilgamesh is ready to return empty-handed to Erech, when a ray of hope appears. Utanapishtim, at the urging of his wife, reveals to Gilgamesh the whereabouts of the plant of eternal youth that lies at the bottom of the sea. Gilgamesh dives to the bottom, brings up the plant, and proceeds joyfully to Erech. But the gods willed otherwise. While Gilgamesh goes bathing in a well, a snake carries off the plant. Weary and bitterly disappointed, the hero returns to Erech, to find what comfort he can in its enduring walls.

So much for the contents of the first eleven tablets of the Babylonian "Epic of Gilgamesh." (The so-called twelfth tablet, which actually does not belong to the epic at all, is treated at the end of the present chapter.) As to the date of the composition of the poem, a comparison of the text of the Old Babylonian version with that of the much later Assyrian, shows that the poem was current, in substantially the form in which we know it, as early as the first half of the second millennium B.C. As to its origins, even a superficial examination, restricted mainly to onomastic considerations, shows that much of its contents must go back to Sumerian rather than Semitic sources, in spite of the antiquity of the Babylonian poem. The names of the two protagonists, Gilgamesh and Enkidu, are in all likelihood of Sumerian origin. The parents of Gilgamesh bear the Sumerian names Lugalbanda and Ninsun. The goddess Aruru, who fashioned Enkidu, is the all-important Sumerian mother-goddess more commonly known under the names Ninmah, Ninhursag, and Nintu (see Chapter 14). The Sumerian god An, who fashioned the Bull of Heaven for the vengeful Ishtar, was taken over in Babylonian as Anu. It is the Sumerian god Enlil who decreed Enkidu's death. In the deluge episode, it is the Sumerian gods who played the predominant roles.

But there is no need to rely on logical deduction alone for the conclusion that much of the "Epic of Gilgamesh" is of Sumerian origin. We actually have the Sumerian forerunners of several of the episodes narrated in the poem. From 1911 to 1935, twenty-six Sumerian tablets and fragments inscribed with Gilgamesh poems were published by such well-known cuneiformists as Radau, Zimmern, Poebel, Langdon, Chiera, De Genouillac, Gadd, and Fish. Fourteen of these texts came from the hand of Edward Chiera alone. Since 1935 I have identified in Istanbul and Philadelphia more than sixty additional Gilgamesh pieces and have copied a goodly portion of them.

Thus we now have a relatively large group of Sumerian Gilgamesh texts. A comparative analysis of their contents with those of the "Epic of Gilgamesh" will reveal in what manner and to what extent the creators of the Babylonian epic utilized Sumerian sources. However, the problem of the Sumerian origin of the "Epic of Gilgamesh" is not as simple as it may seem at first glance, and unless the underlying complexities are clearly grasped, they could lead to the wrong solution. Therefore it is advisable to restate the problem in the form of an outline of questions:

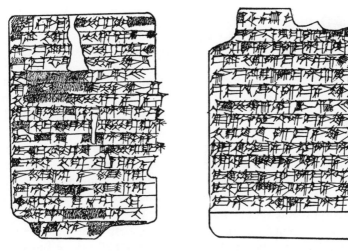

19. Nether-World Taboos. Hand copy of unpublished tablet, in University Museum, inscribed with extract of epic tale "Gilgamesh, Enkidu, and the Nether World," which helped to clarify plot.

1. Is there a Sumerian original for the "Epic of Gilgamesh" as a whole? That is, can we expect to find a Sumerian poem which, in spite of differences in form and content, so closely resembles the Babylonian epic that it can be readily recognized and accepted as its Sumerian precursor?

2. If it becomes clear from the material on hand that there is no Sumerian original for the Babylonian epic as a whole, and that only some of its episodes go back to Sumerian prototypes, are we in a position to identify these episodes with reasonable certainty?

3. In the case of those episodes for which no Sumerian version is as yet available, are we justified in assuming a Semitic origin, or is there reason to believe that these, too, go back to Sumerian sources?

With these questions in mind, we are ready to make a comparative analysis of the contents of the relevant available Sumerian material. This material consists of six poems which may be titled as follows:

"Gilgamesh and the Land of the Living"
"Gilgamesh and the Bull of Heaven"
"The Deluge"
"The Death of Gilgamesh"
"Gilgamesh and Agga of Kish"
"Gilgamesh, Enkidu, and the Nether World"

It should be understood that the text of most of these poems is still fragmentary and that the translation is often difficult and uncertain even where the text is complete. Nevertheless, the available Sumerian material does provide sufficient data to answer with certainty Nos. 1 and 2 in our outline of questions. And while the question in No. 3 cannot be answered with equal certainty, we can arrive at some reasonably safe conclusions.

Before the three questions can be answered, it is necessary to examine the contents of each of the six poems:

1. The contents of the poem "Gilgamesh and the Land of the Living" were sketched in Chapter 22. This tale is obviously the counterpart of the cedar-forest episode of the Babylonian "Epic of Gilgamesh." But when the two versions are put side

by side for a comparison, they are found to have only the bare skeleton of the story in common. In both versions Gilgamesh decides to journey to the cedar forest; he is accompanied by Enkidu; he seeks and obtains the protection of the sun-god; they arrive at their destination; the cedar is felled; Huwawa is killed. But the two versions vary greatly in detail, arrangement, and emphasis. For example, in the Sumerian poem, Gilgamesh is accompanied not only by Enkidu but also by a party of fifty Erechites, while in the Babylonian version he is accompanied by Enkidu alone. Again, in the Sumerian poem, no reference is made to the council of elders of the city of Erech, which plays so prominent a role in the Semitic version.

2. The Sumerian poem "Gilgamesh and the Bull of Heaven" is still unpublished. Its contents, poorly preserved as they are, may be sketched as follows: After a lacuna of some twenty lines, the poem continues with an address to Gilgamesh by the goddess Inanna (the Sumerian counterpart of the Babylonian Ishtar), in which she describes the gifts and favors she is prepared to shower upon him. It is reasonable to assume that the preceding missing portion of the text contained Inanna's love proposals. Another break in the text follows, which must have contained Gilgamesh's rejection of Inanna's offers. When the text becomes intelligible once again, we find Inanna before An, the heaven-god, asking to be presented with the Bull of Heaven. An at first refuses, but Inanna threatens to take up the matter with all the great gods of the universe. Terrified, An grants her request. Inanna then sends the Bull of Heaven down against Erech, and it ravages the city. From here on, the available text, which concludes with an address by Enkidu to Gilgamesh, becomes unintelligible. The end of the poem, which probably described Gilgamesh's victorious struggle with the Bull of Heaven, is missing altogether.

When the contents of this Sumerian poem are compared with those of its Babylonian counterpart in the "Epic of Gilgamesh," they show a close and unmistakable resemblance in the broad outlines of the plot. In both poems Inanna (Ishtar) offers her love and tempting gifts to Gilgamesh; the offer is rejected; with the unwilling consent of An (Anu), the Bull of Heaven is sent to attack Erech; the beast ravages the city, but is finally killed. As for the details, the two versions vary almost beyond the point of recognition. The gifts offered by Inanna (Ishtar) to tempt Gilgamesh are quite different in the two versions. Gilgamesh's rejection speech, which, in the Babylonian epic, consists of 56 lines and is filled with learned allusions to Babylonian mythology and proverbs, is much briefer in the Sumerian version. The conversations between Inanna (Ishtar) and An (Anu) bear little similarity in the two versions. Nor is there any reason to doubt that the concluding details of the Sumerian poem, when these are recovered, will have but little in common with those of the Babylonian epic.

3. The Sumerian poem known as "The Deluge" is described in Chapter 20, which gives a translation of the poem's entire flood-episode passage. The flood episode also constitutes the major part of the eleventh tablet of the Babylonian "Epic of Gilgamesh." The fact that the Sumerian account of the flood is not in any way connected with the Sumerian Gilgamesh tales provides us with a clue for determining some of the procedures employed in ancient literary borrowing.

The Sumerian flood episode is part of a poem devoted primarily to the myth of the immortalization of Ziusudra, and this myth was artfully utilized by the Babylonian poets for their own purposes. Thus, when the weary Gilgamesh comes before Utanapishtim (the Babylonian Ziusudra) and questions him concerning the secret of eternal life, the Babylonian poets did not let him answer briefly and to the point; instead, they took advantage of this opening to insert their version of the deluge myth. The first (the creation) part of the Sumerian myth, they omitted altogether as unnecessary to their theme. They retained only the deluge episode ending with Ziusudra's immortalization. And by making Utanapishtim (Ziusudra) the narrator, and putting the narration into the first person instead of the third, they changed the Sumerian form, in which the narrator was a nameless poet.

In addition we find variation in details. Ziusudra is described as a pious, humble, god-fearing king, but Utanapishtim is not thus described. On the other hand, the Babylonian version is much more lavish with details concerning the building of the boat, and the nature and violence of the flood. In the Sumerian myth the flood lasts seven days and seven nights; in the Babylonian version it lasts six days and seven nights. Finally, the sending of the birds to test the degree of water abatement is found only in the Babylonian epic.

4. The text of the poem designated tentatively as "The Death of Gilgamesh," is still quite fragmentary (see *Ancient Near Eastern Texts*, pages 50-52). From its meager extant portions, only the following contents are recognizable: Gilgamesh still seems to be on his quest for immortality. He is informed, however, that eternal life is impossible to obtain. Kingship, prominence, heroism in battle—all these have been decreed for him, but not immortality. Fragmentary as it is, the available text of our poem shows an indubitable source relationship to the portions of the ninth, tenth, and eleventh tablets of the "Epic of Gilgamesh." These tablets contain Gilgamesh's plea for eternal life, and the rejoinder that it is death, not immortality, which is man's fate. As for the Sumerian description of the death of Gilgamesh, strangely enough it has no counterpart in the extant versions of the Babylonian "Epic of Gilgamesh."

5. There is no trace of the Sumerian poem "Gilgamesh and Agga" (see Chapter 5) in the Babylonian epic. This is one of the shortest of all Sumerian epic tales; it consists of no more than 115 lines of text. Nevertheless, it is of significance from several points of view. In the first place, its plot deals with humans only; unlike other Sumerian epic tales, it introduces no mythological motifs involving the Sumerian deities. Secondly, it is of considerable historical importance, for it provides a number of hitherto unknown facts concerning the early struggles of the Sumerian city-states. Finally, it is of special significance for the history of political thought and practice, since it reveals the existence of what were to some extent democratic institutions as early as 3000 B.C. Perhaps these are the very factors which induced the Babylonian redactors to omit this epic tale altogether from the "Epic of Gilgamesh." The Sumerian tale lacks those superhuman qualities and supernatural heroics so characteristic of epic poetry.

6. For comments on Babylonian borrowings from the Sumer-

ian poem "Gilgamesh, Enkidu, and the Nether World," see the end of the present chapter.

This brings to an end the comparative analysis of the contents of the relevant Sumerian Gilgamesh material at our disposal, and it is now possible to answer the questions formulated earlier.

1. Is there a Sumerian original of the Babylonian "Epic of Gilgamesh" as a single organic unit? Obviously not. The Sumerian poems vary considerably in length, and they consist of individual, disconnected tales. The plot sequence of the Babylonian epic, in which the several episodes are modified and connected to form a reasonably integrated whole, is a Babylonian innovation and achievement.

2. Are we in a position to identify those episodes in the Babylonian epic which go back to Sumerian prototypes? Yes, at least to some extent. The cedar-forest episode (Tablets III-V of the epic); the "Bull of Heaven" (Tablet VI); portions of the "quest for immortality" episode (Tablets IX, X, XI); the "deluge" story (Tablet XI)—all have their Sumerian counterparts. The Babylonian versions, however, are no slavish reproductions of their Sumerian originals. It is only the broad outlines of the plot that they have in common.

3. But what of those portions of the "Epic of Gilgamesh" for which no Sumerian prototypes have been found? These include the introduction at the beginning of the epic; the series of incidents culminating in the forging of the bond of friendship between Gilgamesh and Enkidu (Tablets I and II); the death and burial of Enkidu (Tablets VII, VIII). Are these of Babylonian origin, or do they, too, go back to Sumerian sources? The answer to these questions must be hypothetical. Nevertheless, an analysis of this Babylonian material in the light of extant Sumerian epics and myths permits a number of suggestive, if tentative, conclusions.

First, there is the introductory passage of the Babylonian epic. After portraying the hero as an all-seeing, all-knowing wanderer who had built the walls of Erech, the poet continues with a rhapsodic description of these walls, largely in the form of a rhetorical address to the reader. In none of the known Sumerian epic material do we find a parallel stylistic feature. We may therefore conclude that the introduction to the epic was a Babylonian innovation.

The chain of events leading to the friendship between the two heroes, which follows the introduction and constitutes the major part of Tablets I and II of the Babylonian epic, consists of the following episodes: the tyranny of Gilgamesh; the creation of Enkidu; the "fall" of Enkidu; the dreams of Gilgamesh; the civilizing of Enkidu; the struggle between the heroes. These incidents form a well-knit plot progression, culminating in the friendship of the two heroes. In all probability, this friendship motif was then utilized by the poet to help motivate the journey to the cedar forest. No such motivation is to be found in the Sumerian version of the journey to the cedar forest, and we may assume that we will find no Sumerian counterpart of the chain of incidents as linked in the Babylonian epic. It would not surprise us, however, to find Sumerian prototypes for several of the individual incidents comprising the plot chain, although these prototypes need not always consist of Gilgamesh tales. The mythological motifs in the episodes concerned with the creation of Enkidu, the dreams of Gilgamesh, and the struggle between the heroes, certainly reflect Sumerian sources. As for the "fall" and civilizing of Enkidu, the criteria for a reasonably safe conclusion are lacking at the moment, and we must leave undecided the interesting question whether the concept that sex experience is responsible for man's wisdom is of Semitic or Sumerian origin.

Finally, the story of the death of Enkidu and his burial is in all likelihood of Babylonian rather than Sumerian origin. According to the Sumerian poem "Gilgamesh, Enkidu, and the Nether World," Enkidu did not die at all in the ordinary sense of the word but was seized and held fast by Kur, a dragon-like demon in charge of the nether world, after he had knowingly broken the taboos of the nether world. The incident of the death of Enkidu was invented by the Babylonian authors of the "Epic of Gilgamesh" in order to motivate dramatically Gilgamesh's quest for immortality, which climaxes the poem.

To sum up: Of the various episodes comprising the "Epic of Gilgamesh," several go back to Sumerian prototypes actually involving the hero Gilgamesh. Even in those episodes which lack Sumerian counterparts, most of the individual motifs reflect Sumerian mythic and epic sources. In no case, however, did the Babylonian poets slavishly copy the Sumerian material. They so modified its content and molded its form, in accordance with their own temper and heritage, that only the bare nucleus of the Sumerian original remains recognizable. As for the plot structure of the epic as a whole—the forceful and fateful episodic drama of the restless, adventurous hero and his inevitable disillusionment—it is definitely a Babylonian, rather than Sumerian, development and achievement. In a very deep sense, therefore, the "Epic of Gilgamesh" may be truly described as a Semitic creation.

But it is only the first eleven tablets of the "Epic of Gilgamesh" which can be described as a Semitic literary creation (in spite of obvious borrowings from Sumerian sources). Tablet XII (the last tablet of the epic) is nothing more than a practically verbatim translation into the Semitic Akkadian—also known as Babylonian or Assyrian—of the second half of a Sumerian poem. The Babylonian scribes tacked this on to the first eleven tablets in total disregard of the sense and continuity of the epic as a whole.

It had long been suspected that the twelfth tablet was nothing more than an appendage to the first eleven tablets, which constitute a reasonably well-integrated unit, but the proof was not available until the text of the Sumerian poem "Gilgamesh, Enkidu, and the Nether World" was pieced together and translated. However, as early as 1930, in connection with his publication of a Sumerian tablet from Ur inscribed with part of the poem, C. J. Gadd, formerly of the British Museum, recognized the close relationship between its contents and those of the twelfth tablet of the Semitic epic.

The full text of the poem "Gilgamesh, Enkidu, and the Nether World" is still unpublished. (See "Gilgamesh and the *Huluppu-Tree*," *Assyriological Study No. 8* of the Oriental Institute of the University of Chicago; and *Sumerian Mythology*, pages 30 ff.) Here is a brief sketch:

The poem begins with an introduction of twenty-seven lines, the contents of which have nothing to do with the story itself. The first thirteen lines of this passage contain some of the basic data for the analysis of the Sumerian concepts of the creation of the universe (see Chapter 13), while the remaining fourteen lines describe the struggle between Enki and Kur (see Chapter 22). Then follows the story:

Once upon a time a *huluppu*-tree (perhaps a willow), planted on the bank of the Euphrates and nurtured by its waters, was violently attacked by the South Wind and flooded by the waters of the Euphrates. The goddess Inanna, walking by, took the tree in her hand and brought it to her city, Erech, where she planted it in her holy garden. There she tended it most carefully, for she planned that when the tree had grown big she would make of its wood a chair for herself and a couch.

Years passed. The tree matured and grew big. But Inanna found herself unable to cut it down, for at its base the snake who "knows no charm" had built its nest; in its crown, the *Imdugud*-bird had placed its young; in its middle, Lilith had built her house. And so Inanna, the lighthearted and ever joyful maid, shed bitter tears.

As dawn broke, and her brother, the sun-god Utu, came forth from his sleeping chamber, Inanna tearfully repeated to him all that had befallen her *huluppu*-tree. Thereupon Gilgamesh, who presumably heard her plaint, chivalrously came to her aid. He donned his armour, weighing fifty minas; and with his ax of the road, seven talents and seven minas in weight, he slew the snake who "knows no charm" at the base of the tree. Seeing this, the *Imdugud*-bird fled with its young to the mountain, while Lilith tore down her house and fled to the desolate places. Gilgamesh and the men of Erech who accompanied him then cut down the tree, and gave it to Inanna for her chair and couch.

What did Inanna do? From the base of the tree she fashioned a *pukku* (perhaps a drum); and from its crown, a *mikku* (drumstick). There follows a passage of twelve lines describing Gilgamesh's activity in Erech with this *pukku* and *mikku*, or "drum" and "drumstick." Despite the fact that the text is in perfect condition, it is still impossible to penetrate its meaning. It is probable that it describes certain tyrannical acts which brought woe to the inhabitants of Erech. When the story becomes intelligible once again, it continues with the statement that "because of the outcry of the young maidens," the *pukku* and the *mikku* fell into the nether world. Gilgamesh put in his hand and his foot to retrieve them, but was unable to reach them. He then seated himself at the gate of the nether world and lamented:

"O my *pukku*, O my *mikku*,
My *pukku* with lustiness irresistible,
My *mikku* with dance—rhythm unrivaled,
My *pukku* which was with me formerly in the house of the
    carpenter—
The wife of the carpenter was with me then like the mother
    who gave birth to me,
The daughter of the carpenter was with me then like my
    younger sister—
My *pukku*, who will bring it up from the nether world,
My *mikku*, who will bring it up from the 'face' of the nether
    world?"

Gilgamesh's servant Enkidu thereupon volunteered to descend to the nether world and bring them up for him, saying:

"O my master, why do you cry, why is your heart sick?
Your *pukku*, lo, I will now bring it up from the nether world,
Your *mikku*, I will bring it up from the 'face' of the nether
    world."

Hearing his servant's generous offer, Gilgamesh warned him of a number of nether-world taboos which he must guard against. The passage runs as follows:

Gilgamesh says to Enkidu:
"If now you will descend to the nether world,
A word I speak to you, take my word,
Instruction I offer you, take my instruction.
Do not put on clean clothes,
Lest like an enemy the (nether world) stewards will come forth,

Do not anoint yourself with the good oil of the *bur*-vessel,
Lest at its smell they will crowd about you.

"Do not throw the throw-stick in the nether world,
Lest they who were struck by the throw-stick will surround you,
Do not carry a staff in your hand,
Lest the shades will flutter all about you.

"Do not put sandals on your feet,
In the nether world make no cry;
Kiss not your beloved wife,
Strike not your hated wife,
Kiss not your beloved son,
Strike not your hated son,
Lest the outcry of Kur will seize you,
(The outcry) for her who is lying, for her who is lying,
To the mother of Ninazu who is lying,
Whose holy body no garment covers,
Whose holy breast no cloth wraps."

The mother of Ninazu in these lines may refer to the goddess Ninlil, who, according to the myth concerning the birth of the moon-god Sin (see Chapter 13), accompanied the god Enlil to the nether world.

Enkidu did not heed the instructions of his master, but committed those very acts against which Gilgamesh had warned him. And so he was seized by Kur and was unable to ascend again to the earth. Thereupon Gilgamesh proceeded to Nippur and wept before Enlil:

"O Father Enlil, my *pukku* fell into the nether world,
My *mikku* fell into the 'face' of the nether world,
I sent Enkidu to bring them up, Kur has seized him.
Namtar (the demon of death) has not seized him, Asag (the demon of disease) has not seized him,
Kur has seized him.
Nergal's ambusher (that is Death), who spares no one, has not seized him,
Kur has seized him.
In battle, the place of manliness, he has not fallen,
Kur has seized him."

But Enlil refused to stand by Gilgamesh, who then proceeded to Eridu and repeated his plea before Enki. The latter

ordered the sun-god Utu to open a hole in the nether world
and to allow the shade of Enkidu to ascend to the earth. Utu
did as bidden, and the shade of Enkidu appeared before Gilgamesh. Master and servant embraced, and Gilgamesh ques-
tioned Enkidu about what he saw in the nether world. The first
seven questions concern the treatment in the nether world of
those who were fathers of from one to seven sons. The remaining
text of the poem is poorly preserved, but we have parts of the
Gilgamesh-Enkidu colloquy concerning the treatment, in the
nether world, of the palace servant, of the birth-giving woman,
of him who falls in battle, of him whose shade has no one to
care for it, and of him whose body lies unburied in the plain.

It is the second half of the poem which the Babylonian scribes
translated practically verbatim and appended to the "Epic of
Gilgamesh" as its twelfth tablet. For the modern scholar this
was no mean boon, since, with the aid of the Sumerian version,
it was possible to restore numerous broken words, phrases, and
whole lines in the Akkadian text, and thus to clarify, at long
last, the contents of the twelfth tablet, which had remained unintelligible in spite of the efforts of a number of distinguished
cuneiformists.

Gilgamesh was not the only Sumerian hero. His two predecessors, Enmerkar and Lugalbanda, were also favorites with
Sumerian poets. As a matter of fact, the Sumerians, to judge from
their epic literature, had developed a so-called Heroic Age. This
Heroic Age, together with its significance for the early history
of Sumer and Mesopotamia, is discussed in Chapter 24.

1. The Temple at Tell Harmal.

2. The Ziggurat at Aqar Quf.

3. Nippur Scribal Quarter—New Excavations. Ruins of houses on "Tablet Hill" unearthed during joint Oriental Institute-University Museum expedition, 1948-52.

4. Schooldays: The Teacher's Blessing. Obverse (CBS 6094) of four-column tablet, in University Museum, inscribed with essay on school life. Note signature of writer below double line on left column.

5. This is the reverse of Schooldays, plate 4.

4.

5.

6. Juvenile Delinquency. Obverse of a small tablet in the University
Museum Tablet Collection.

7.

8.

9.

7. A Sumerian of about 2500 B.C. Limestone statuette excavated by the University of Pennsylvania in the temple at Khafaje.

8. *Dudu*. A Sumerian scribe of (ca.) 2350 B.C. who lived in Lagash. Statue is now in Iraq Museum in Baghdad.

9. A Bearded Priest. Statuette excavated at Khafaje by a University of Pennsylvania expedition. It is now in the University Museum.

10. Enlil Myth. Clay cylinder inscribed with myth written about 2400 B.C., now in the University Museum.

11. A "Botany-Zoology Textbook." Reverse of tablet excavated in ruins of Tell Harmal on outskirts of Baghdad. Iraq Museum, Baghdad.

12. Enmerkar and the Lord of Aratta: The Istanbul tablet. Obverse of twelve-column Nippur Tablet in Istanbul Museum of the Ancient Orient.

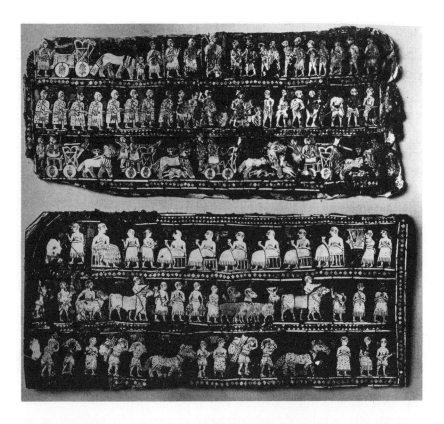

13. War and Peace: The "Standard" from Ur depicting scenes of
Sumerian king in battle and celebrating victory. British Museum,
London.

14. **Ur-Nanshe, King of Lagash.** This limestone plaque, now in the Louvre, depicts ruler of Lagash dynasty surrounded by his children and courtiers, and sitting and drinking at a feast.

15. Stele of the Vultures. War scenes depicting Eannatum,
conquering hero of Lagash dynasty, leading Lagashites to battle;
inscription records his victory over Ummaites and treaty of
peace forced upon them. Louvre, Paris.

16. Aesopica. Reverse of a tablet in the University Museum inscribed with animal proverbs and fables.

17. Ur-Nammu Law
Code: The Laws.
Reverse of Istanbul
tablet.

18. Ur-Nammu: The First "Moses." Part of stele excavated in Ur, now
in University Museum.

19. Man's Oldest Prescriptions. Reverse of "medical" tablet from Nippur in University Museum.

20. Inanna and Shukalletuda: The Gardener's Mortal Sin. Reverse of six-column tablet in Istanbul Museum of the Ancient Orient inscribed with myth noted for its "blood-plague" motif.

21. Separation of Heaven and Earth. Nippur tablet, in
University Museum, inscribed with part of poem,
"Gilgamesh, Enkidu, and the Nether World."

22. Cultural Anthropology. Reverse of six-column tablet inscribed with myth about Inanna and Enki. University Museum.

23/24. Creation of Man. Obverse of same Nippur tablet, in University Museum, before and after "joining."

25. Proverbs: The "Fate" Collection. Nine-column
Nippur tablet, in University Museum, inscribed in the
main with proverbs about fate and various animals.

26. Sumerian Original of the Twelfth
Tablet of the Babylonian Epic of
Gilgamesh. Reverse of unpublished six-
column Nippur tablet, in University
Museum, inscribed with epic tale
"Gilgamesh, Enkidu, and the Nether
World."

27. Sacred (?) Cows. Mosaic dairy frieze
unearthed at Al-Ubaid near Ur, dating from
about 2500 B.C.

26.

27.

28. Map of Nippur. Photograph of original tablet. See also
Appendix A. Hilprecht Collection.

30. Shulgi, the Ideal King. Fragment
from a large tablet in the University
Museum inscribed with a Shulgi hymn
in which he portrays himself as sage,
sportsman, diviner, diplomat, patron of
the arts, and happy provider of all
that is good for Sumer and its people.

29. Perverse Students. Reverse of a tablet from the University Museum inscribed with the concluding section of a dispute between two students.

30.

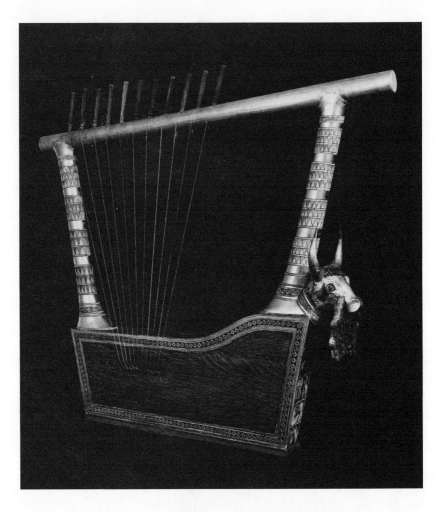

31. Lyre from Ur of the Chaldees. A reconstruction of a lyre
excavated by Leonard Woolley in the royal cemetery at Ur. It is part
of the University Museum's collection and has just recently been rebuilt.

32. Death and Resurrection.
Obverse of a tablet from Ur,
excavated by Leonard Woolley
and now in the British Museum.
This tablet provides the
concluding episode to Inanna's
Descent to the Nether World.

33. Right edge of tablet 32.

34. U-a a-u-a. Obverse of the "lullaby" tablet excavated at Nippur and now in the University Museum.

MAN'S FIRST HEROIC AGE

Historians now generally realize (and this is largely to the credit of the English scholar H. Munro Chadwick) that the so-called Heroic Ages, which are come upon from time to time and from place to place in the history of civilization, represent not mere literary imagination but very real and significant social phenomena. Thus, to take only three of the better-known examples, there is the Greek Heroic Age, which flourished on the mainland of Greece toward the very end of the second millennium B.C.; the Heroic Age of India, which probably dates only a century or so later than that of Greece; and the Teutonic Heroic Age, which dominated much of northern Europe from the fourth to the sixth centuries A.D. All three of these Heroic Ages reveal a marked resemblance in social structure, governmental organization, religious concepts, and aesthetic expression. It is obvious that they owe their origin and being to similar social, political, and psychic factors.

The Sumerian heroic narrative poems sketched in this and the foregoing chapters constitute an epic literature which introduces a new Heroic Age to world history and literature—the Sumerian Heroic Age. Although it probably had its *floruit* no later than the first quarter of the third millennium B.C., and thus precedes by more than 1,500 years even the oldest of the three Indo-European Heroic Ages (that of the Greeks), its culture pattern is remarkably close to the culture pattern typical of the long-known Heroic Ages.

The Greek, Indian, and Teutonic Heroic Ages, as Chadwick

concludes from relevant literary records, are essentially barbaric periods which show a number of salient characteristics in common. The political unit consists of a petty kingdom ruled by a king or prince who obtains and holds his rule through military prowess. His mainstay in power consists of the comitatus, a retinue of armed loyal followers who are prepared to do his bidding without question, no matter how foolhardy and dangerous the undertaking. There may be an assembly, but it is convened at the ruler's pleasure and serves only in an advisory and confirmatory capacity. The ruling kings and princes of the separate principalities carry on among themselves a lively, and at times friendly and even intimate, intercourse. They thus tend to develop into what may be termed an international aristocratic caste whose thoughts and acts have little in common with those of their subjects.

On the religious side, the three Indo-European Heroic Ages are characterized by a worship of anthropomorphic deities, which to a large extent seem to be recognized throughout the various states and principalities. These gods form organized communities in a chosen locality, though, in addition, each god has a special abode of his own. There are few traces of a chthonic or spirit cult. At death the soul travels to some distant locality that is regarded as a universal home and is not reserved for members of any particular community. Some of the heroes are conceived as springing from the gods, but there is no trace of heroic worship or hero cults. All these features common to the Heroic Ages of Greece, India, and Northern Europe, are shared by the Heroic Age of Sumer.

But the parallelism extends even further. Indeed, it is particularly apparent on the aesthetic plane, especially in literature. One of the notable achievements of all four of these Heroic Ages was the creation of heroic narrative tales—in *poetic form*—that were to be spoken or sung. They reflect and illuminate the spirit of the age and its temper. Impelled by the thirst for fame and name so characteristic of the ruling caste during a Heroic Age, the bards and minstrels attached to the court were moved to improvise narrative poems or lays celebrating the adventures and achievements of kings and princes. These epic lays, with the primary object of providing entertainment at the frequent courtly banquets and feasts, were probably recited to the accompaniment of the harp or lyre.

None of these early heroic lays have come down to us in their original form, since they were composed when writing was either altogether unknown or, if known, of little concern to the illiterate minstrel. The written epics of the Greek, Indian, and Teutonic Heroic Ages date from much later days, and consist of highly complex literary redactions in which only a selected number of the earlier lays are imbedded, and these in a highly

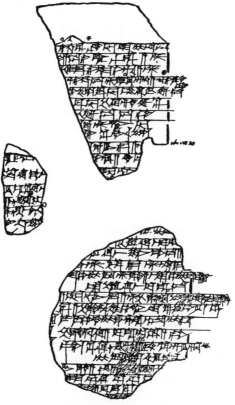

20. Enmerkar and Ensukushsiranna. Hand copy of two unpublished fragments in Istanbul Museum of Ancient Orient.

modified and expanded form. In Sumer, there is good reason to believe, some of the early heroic lays were first inscribed on clay five to six hundred years following the close of the Heroic Age, and then only after they had undergone considerable transformation at the hands of priests and scribes. However, it should be carefully noted that the copies of the Sumerian epic texts which we have at present date almost entirely from the first half of the second millennium B.C.

The written epics of the three Indo-European Heroic Ages show a number of striking similarities in form and content. In the first place, all the poems are concerned primarily with individuals. It is the deeds and exploits of the individual hero that are the prime concern of the poet, not the fate or glory of the state or community. Moreover, while there is little doubt that some of the adventures celebrated in the poems have a historical basis, the poet does not hesitate to introduce unhistorical motifs and conventions, such as exaggerated notions of the hero's powers, ominous dreams, and the presence of divine beings. Stylistically, the epic poems abound in static epithets, lengthy repetitions, and recurrent formulas, and in descriptions that tend to be over-leisurely and unusually detailed. Particularly noteworthy is the fact that all the epics devote considerable space to speeches.

In all these respects, the pattern of Sumerian heroic poetry is similar to the pattern of Greek, Indian, and Teutonic epic material. Since it is hardly likely that a literary genre so individual in style and technique as narrative poetry was created and developed independently, at different time intervals, in Sumer, Greece, India, and Northern Europe, and since the narrative poetry of the Sumerians is by all odds the oldest of the four, it seems reasonable to conclude that in Sumer may be found the origin of epic poetry.

To be sure, there are a number of outstanding differences between the Sumerian epic material and that of the Greeks, Indians, and Teutons. For example, the Sumerian epic poems consist of individual, disconnected tales of varying length, each of which is restricted to a single episode. There is no attempt to articulate and integrate these episodes into a larger unit. As shown in Chapter 23, this was first achieved by the Babylonian poets, who borrowed, modified, and molded the relatively brief and episodic Sumerian tales—particularly in their "Epic of Gilgamesh"—with the view of fashioning an epic of considerable length and complexity. There is relatively little characterization and psychological penetration in the Sumerian material. The heroes tend to be broad types, more or less undifferentiated, rather than highly personalized individuals. Moreover, the incidents and plot motifs are related in a rather static and conventionalized style; there is little of that plastic, expressive movement which characterizes such poems as Homer's *Iliad* and *Odyssey*. Another interesting difference: Mortal women play hardly any role in Sumerian epic literature, while they have a very prominent part in Indo-European epic literature. Finally, in the matter of technique, the Sumerian poet gets his rhythmic effects primarily from variations in the repetition patterns. He makes no use whatever of the meters or uniform line so characteristic of Indo-European epics.

Let us turn now to the contents of the extant Sumerian epic poems. At present we can identify nine epic tales varying in length from one hundred to more than six hundred lines. Two of these revolve about the hero Enmerkar; two revolve about the hero Lugalbanda (in one of these Enmerkar, too, plays a considerable role); and five revolve about the most famous of the three heroes, Gilgamesh. All three are known from the Sumerian king list, a historical document which, like our epic material, has been found inscribed on tablets dating from the first half of the second millennium B.C. The list was probably composed in the last quarter of the third millennium B.C. In the king list, these three heroes are stated to be the second, third, and fifth rulers of the first dynasty of Erech, which, according to the Sumerian sages, followed the first dynasty of Kish, which in turn followed immediately upon the flood. The contents of one of the Enmerkar tales and of all five Gilgamesh poems have been discussed in Chapters 4, 5, 22 and 23. This leaves only three tales—one of Enmerkar and two of Lugalbanda—to complete the sketch of the extant Sumerian epic literature.

The second Enmerkar tale, like the tale treated in Chapter 4, is concerned with the submission of a lord of Aratta to Enmerkar.

However, in this poem it is not Enmerkar who makes the first demands on his rival, the lord of Aratta. It is, rather, the lord of Aratta himself who first issues the challenge that leads to his own discomfiture. Throughout the second Enmerkar poem, the lord of Aratta is referred to by his actual name, Ensukush-siranna, and it is therefore not certain whether he is identical with the lord of Aratta who remains unnamed in the first Enmerkar poem. As for the available contents of this second Enmerkar tale, until 1952 only approximately one hundred well-preserved lines, at the beginning of the poem, and some twenty-five well-preserved lines toward the end, were identifiable. But in the 1951-52 excavations of Nippur under the joint auspices of the Oriental Institute and the University Museum, two excellently preserved tablets, which fill in much of the missing text, were unearthed. As a result, the plot can now be tentatively reconstructed as follows:

In the days when Ennamibaragga-Utu was (perhaps) king of Sumer as a whole, Ensukushsiranna, the lord of Aratta, whose vizier had the name Ansiggaria, issued a challenge via a herald to Enmerkar, the lord of Erech, whose vizier was Namenna-duma. The gist of the message was that Enmerkar should recognize Ensukushsiranna as his overlord, and that the goddess Inanna should be brought to Aratta.

Enmerkar is contemptuous of the challenge and, in a long address in which he depicts himself as the favorite of the gods, declares that Inanna will remain in Erech and demands that Ensukushsiranna should be his vassal. Thereupon Ensukushsiranna gathers in the members of his council and asks them what to do. They seem to advise him to submit, but he refuses indignantly. Then the *mashmash*-priest of Aratta, probably Urgirnunna by name, comes to his aid, and boasts (unfortunately it is uncertain from the text just who the speaker is) that he will cross "the river of Erech," subdue all the lands "above and below, from the sea to the cedar mountain," and return with heavily laden boats (sic!) to Aratta. Ensukushsiranna is delighted, and gives him five minas of gold and five minas of silver, as well as the necessary supplies.

When the *mashmash* reaches Erech (the poem does not state

how he got there) he steps up to the holy stable and sheepfold
of the goddess Nidaba and induces her cow and goat to withhold
their cream and milk from her dining halls. The flavor of the
passage may be felt from the following tentative rendering:

He (the *mashmash*) speaks with the cow, converses with her
  like a human,
"Cow, who eats your cream, who drinks your milk?"

"Nidaba eats my cream,
Nidaba drinks my milk,
My milk and cheese . . . . ,
Is placed as fitting in the large (dining) halls, the halls of Nidaba.
I would bring my cream . . from the holy stable,
I would bring my milk . . from the sheepfold,
The steadfast cow, Nidaba, Enlil's foremost child. . . . ."

"Cow, . . your cream to your . . , . . your milk to your. . . . ."

The cow . . d her cream to her . . , . . d her milk to her. . , ...

(These lines are then repeated for the goat.)

As a result of this withholding act on the part of Nidaba's cow
and goat, the stables and sheepfolds of Erech are laid waste. The
shepherds mourn and wail while their helpers take to the road.
Thereupon Nidaba's two shepherds, Mashgula and Uredinna,
"sons born of one mother," intervene and, probably on the
advice of the sun-god Utu (the relevant passage is poorly preserved), they succeed in outwitting the *mashmash* with the help
of Mother Sagburru. The passage follows:

The two of them (Mashgula and Uredinna) threw the prince
  into the river,
The *mashmash* brought forth the great *suhur-fish* out of the water,
Mother Sagburru brought forth the . . -bird out of the water,
The . . -bird snatched the *suhur*-fish, brought him to the
  mountain.

A second time they threw the prince into the river,
The *mashmash* brought forth a ewe and its lamb out of the water,
Mother Sagburru brought forth the wolf out of the water,
The wolf snatched the ewe and its lamb, brought them to the
  wide plain.

A third time they threw the prince into the river,
The *mashmash* brought forth a cow and its calf out of the water,
Mother Sagburru brought forth the lion out of the water,
The lion snatched the cow and its calf, brought them to the
    canebrake.

A fourth time they threw the prince into the river,
The *mashmash* brought forth the wild sheep out of the water,
Mother Sagburru brought forth the mountain leopard out of
    the water,
The mountain leopard snatched the wild sheep, brought him to
    the mountain.

A fifth time they threw the prince into the river,
The *mashmash* brought forth the young gazelle out of the water,
Mother Sagburru brought forth the *gug*-beast out of the water,
The *gug*-beast snatched the young gazelle, brought him to the
    forests.

Having thus been outwitted again and again, the *mashmash*'s
"face turns black, his counsel is dissipated." When Mother Sagburru begins to taunt him for his stupidity, he pleads with her
to let him return to Aratta in peace, and promises to sing her
praises there. But Sagburru will have none of this. Instead she
kills him and throws his dead body into the Euphrates.

When Ensukushsiranna hears of what has happened to the
mashmash, he hurriedly sends a messenger to Enmerkar and
completely capitulates:

"You are the beloved of Inanna, you alone are exalted,
Inanna has truly chosen you for her holy lap;
From the lower (lands) to the upper (lands) you are their
    lord, I am second to you,
From (the moment of) conception, I was not your equal, you
    are the 'big brother,'
I cannot compare with you ever."

The poem ends with lines characteristic of a "disputation"
composition (see Chapter 18):

"In the dispute between Enmerkar and Ensukushsiranna,
After (?) victory of Enmerkar over Ensukushsiranna; O Nidaba,
    praise."

We turn now to the epic tales in which the hero Lugalbanda plays the leading role. The first, which may be titled "Lugalbanda and Enmerkar," is a poem of more than four hundred lines, the majority of which are excellently preserved. In spite of the relatively few breaks in the text, the sense of many passages is far from clear, and the following sketch of the intelligible parts of its contents, based on repeated efforts to get at the meaning of the poem, must still be considered highly tentative.

The hero Lugalbanda, who seems to find himself against his will in the far-distant land of Zabu, is eager to get back to his city, Erech. He is determined to first win the friendship of the *Imdugud*-bird who decrees the fates and utters the word which none may transgress. While the *Imdugud*-bird is away, therefore, he goes to his nest and presents his young with fat, honey, and bread, paints their faces, and places the *shugurra* crown upon their heads. The *Imdugud*-bird, upon returning to his nest, is most gratified with this godlike treatment of his young, and proclaims himself ready to bestow friendship and favor upon whatever god or man has done this gracious deed.

Lugalbanda steps up to receive his reward, and the *Imdugud*-bird, in a eulogistic passage replete with blessings, bids him go, head high, to his city. Upon Lugalbanda's request, he decrees for him a favorable journey, and adds some pertinent advice which he is to repeat to no one, not even his closest followers. The *Imdugud*-bird reenters his nest, while Lugalbanda returns to his friends and tells them of his imminent journey. They try to dissuade him, for it is a journey from which none return, since it involves the crossing of high mountains and of the dreaded river of Kur. However, Lugalbanda is adamant, and the outcome is the successful journey to Erech.

In Erech, Lugalbanda's lord and liege, Enmerkar, son of the sun-god Utu, is in great distress. For many years past, the Semitic Martu had been ravaging both Sumer and Akkad. Now they were laying siege to Erech itself. Enmerkar finds that he must get through a call for help to his sister, the goddess Inanna of Aratta. But he can find no one to undertake the dangerous journey to Aratta to deliver his message. Whereupon Lugalbanda steps up to his king and bravely volunteers for the task. Upon

Enmerkar's insistence on secrecy, he swears he will make the journey alone, unaccompanied by his followers. After receiving from Enmerkar the exact words of his message to Inanna of Aratta, Lugalbanda hastens to his friends and followers and informs them of his imminent journey. They try to dissuade him, but to no avail. He takes up his weapons, crosses the seven mountains that reach from one end of Anshan to the other, and finally arrives with joyful step at his destination.

There in Aratta, Lugalbanda is given a warm welcome by Inanna. On her asking what brought him all alone from Erech

21. Lugalbanda and Enmerkar: Istanbul. Hand copy of unpublished Nippur fragment in Museum of Ancient Orient, inscribed with part of epic tale.

to Aratta, he repeats verbatim Enmerkar's message and call for help. Inanna's answer, which marks the end of the poem, is obscure. It seems to involve a river and its unusual fish, which Enmerkar is to catch; also certain water vessels that he is to fashion; and finally, workers of metal and stone whom he is to settle in his city. But just how all this will remove the threat of the Martu from Sumer and Akkad, or lift the siege from Erech, is far from clear.

The second Lugalbanda tale, which may tentatively be titled "Lugalbanda and Mount Hurrum," probably runs well over four hundred lines. At present, however, with both the beginning and end of the poem missing, we can account only for some three hundred and fifty lines of text, of which about half are in excellent condition. The available contents, as far as they can be reconstructed from the fragmentary and difficult text, may be sketched as follows:

In the course of a journey from Erech to the far-distant Aratta, Lugalbanda and his followers arrive at Mount Hurrum. There Lugalbanda falls ill. His companions, believing that he is soon to die, decide to proceed without him. They plan to pick up his dead body on their return from Aratta, and to carry it back to Erech. To take care of his immediate wants, however, they leave with him a considerable quantity of food, water, and strong drink, and his weapons. Alone, ill, and forsaken, Lugalbanda utters a prayer to the sun-god Utu, who sees to it that his health is restored by means of the "food of life" and the "water of life."

Upon regaining his health, Lugalbanda wanders alone over the highland steppe, living by hunting its wild life and gathering its uncultivated plants. Once, having fallen asleep, he dreams that he is commanded, perhaps by the sun-god Utu, to take up his weapons, hunt and kill a wild ox, and present its fat to the rising Utu; also to slaughter a kid and pour out its blood in a ditch and its fat on the plain. Upon awaking, Lugalbanda does exactly as he was bidden. In addition he prepares food and strong drink for An, Enlil, Enki, and Ninhursag—the four leading deities of the Sumerian pantheon. The approximately last hundred lines of the extant text seem to contain a eulogy of seven heavenly lights which help Nanna the moon-god, Utu the sun-god, and Inanna the Venus-goddess, to illuminate the cosmos.

So much for our survey of extant Sumerian epic literature and the Heroic Age which it reveals. Let us turn now to a historical question which has troubled Near Eastern archaeologists and scholars for decades, and has come to be known as "The Sumerian Problem." It revolves about the arrival of the Sumerians in Mesopotamia. The question is, Were the Sumerians the first people to settle in Lower Mesopotamia, or were they preceded by some other ethnic group or groups? On the surface, there seems to be little connection between this problem and the Sumerian Heroic Age. However, the discovery of the existence of the Sumerian Heroic Age proves to be highly significant for the resolution of the "Sumerian Problem." It even permits a reinterpretation of the earliest history of Mesopotamia that is possibly closer to the truth than any earlier interpretation. But the "Sumerian Problem," which has served to divide Near Eastern archaeologists into two diametrically opposed camps, needs to be stated here in brief:

As a result of the excavation of the prehistoric levels of a number of sites in the past several decades, the earliest culture phase of Lower Mesopotamia is divided, by general agreement, in accordance with a number of pertinent archaeological criteria, into two distinct periods: the Obeid period, the remains of which are found everywhere immediately above virgin soil; and the Uruk period, the remains of which overlie those of the Obeid period. Moreover, the Uruk period is subdivided into two major stages, an earlier and a later one. It is in the later stage of the Uruk period that we find the introduction of the cylinder seal as well as the first inscribed tablets. And since, according to present indications, the language represented on these tablets, in spite of the largely pictographic character of the signs, seems to be Sumerian, most archaeologists agree that the Sumerians must already have been in Lower Mesopotamia during the later stage of the Uruk period.

It is with respect to the earlier Uruk period, and the still earlier Obeid period, that we find a very serious conflict of views. From analysis of the material remains of these earlier periods, one group of archaeologists concludes that while the remains of the earlier stage differ considerably from those of the later stage of the Uruk period, and of the periods which follow, the earlier remains can nevertheless be recognized as the prototypes of the later remains. And since the later remains are admittedly Sumerian, the earliest remains must also be attributed to the Sumerians. Hence, this group concludes, the Sumerians were the first settlers in Mesopotamia. Another group of archaeologists, after analyzing practically the same archaeological data, arrives at an exactly opposite conclusion. This group claims that while the remains of the earliest periods do show certain similarities to those of the later and admittedly Sumerian periods, the differences between them are significant enough to indicate a major ethnic break between the later stage of the Uruk period and the preceding stages; and since the later stage is Sumerian, the earlier stages must be attributed to a pre-Sumerian culture in Lower Mesopotamia. Hence, says this group, the Sumerians were not the first settlers in that region.

The solution of the "Sumerian Problem" has reached more or less of an impasse. The mere piling up of more archaeological material from new excavations will do little to resolve the deadlock, for the evidence provided by the new finds will no doubt be interpreted in line with one or the other school of thought. What is needed is new evidence based on data differing in essence and kind from the necessarily ambiguous material remains utilized hitherto.

This is why the Sumerian epic poems, and the Heroic Age which they reveal, are so important. They provide new and significant criteria of a purely literary and historical character. To be sure, the proof is by no means obvious and direct; there are no explicit statements in the ancient texts concerning the first arrival of the Sumerians in Mesopotamia. It is adduced and deduced from a study of the cultural pattern and historical background of the Sumerian Heroic Age as compared with the long-known Heroic Ages of the Greek, Indian, and Teutonic peoples.

There are two factors that are primarily responsible for the characteristic features of Greek, Indian, and Teutonic Heroic Ages (here again, Chadwick's studies are fundamental), the second factor being by far the more significant: (1) These Heroic Ages coincide with a period of national migrations, a *Völkerwanderungszeit*. (2) These peoples—that is, the Achaeans, the Aryans, and the Teutons—while still on a relatively primitive and tribal level, had come in contact with a civilized power in the process of disintegration. Particularly as mercenaries in the military service of this power during its struggle for survival, they absorbed the military technique and, to a superficial extent, some of the cultural accomplishments of their far more civilized neighbors. It is when they finally break through the frontiers of this civilized empire and carve out kingdoms and principalities for themselves within its territory, amassing considerable wealth in the process, that they develop that rather adolescent and barbaric cultural stage known as a Heroic Age.

The Heroic Age whose historical antecedents are best known —the Teutonic Heroic Age—coincided with a period of national migrations. But more significantly, for a number of centuries preceding their Heroic Age, the relatively primitive Teutonic peoples had come in contact with the far more civilized but ever weakening Roman Empire, and had been subjected to its cultural influences, particularly as hostages in its court and as mercenaries in its armies. By the fifth and sixth centuries A.D., these Teutonic peoples had succeeded in occupying most of the territories which had formerly been part of the Roman Empire, and these are the two centuries that mark the *floruit* of the Teutonic Heroic Age.

If we assume that the factors responsible for the origin and development of the Sumerian Heroic Age were analogous to those responsible for the origin and development of the Greek, Indian, and Teutonic Heroic Ages—and there seems to be no reason to assume otherwise—we may conclude that the Sumerian Heroic Age must have coincided with a period of national migrations. More important, the occupation of Lower Mesopotamia by the Sumerians, which gave birth to their Heroic Age, must have marked the culminating stage in a historical process that had begun several centuries earlier, when Lower Mesopotamia was still part of a power whose state of civilization was far more advanced than the civilization of the Sumerians, who were settled somewhere along its outer fringes. It is from this more civilized power that the relatively primitive Sumerians—no doubt largely as mercenaries in that power's military employ—had absorbed some of the essentials of its military technique as well as some of its cultural attainments. Finally, the Sumerians succeeded in breaking through the frontiers of this power, occupying a considerable portion of its territory and amassing considerable wealth in the process. It is this period which marks the *floruit* of the Sumerian Heroic Age.

As a result of determining the existence of a Sumerian Heroic Age, we seem justified in drawing the conclusion that the Sumerians were *not* the first settlers in Lower Mesopotamia, but that they must have been preceded by a civilized power of some magnitude, one that was culturally far more advanced than were the Sumerians. What is generally spoken of as "Sumerian" civilization—a civilization that played a predominant role in the Ancient Near East, and whose influence persisted long after the Sumerians had ceased to exist as a political entity—must be looked upon as the product of some five or six centuries of cultural activity *following* the immature and barbaric Sumerian Heroic Age, and resulted no doubt from a constructive application of the Sumerian genius to the material and spiritual heritage of the pre-Sumerian civilization in Southern Mesopotamia.

With this fresh insight into the cultural morphology of early Lower Mesopotamia, we can now attempt to reconstruct the major outlines of its history. This reconstruction, though tentative and hypothetical, should prove of considerable value for the interpretation and integration of the relevant archaeological material already unearthed in Southern Mesopotamia, and the material still to be unearthed. From the days of the first settlements to those of the great Akkadian king Sargon, who may be said to mark the beginning of the end of Sumerian political domination in the land, the history of Lower Mesopotamia may be divided into two major periods: the pre-Sumerian (which might be more meaningfully named the Irano-Semitic), and the Sumerian.

The pre-Sumerian period began as a peasant-village culture. As is now generally assumed, it was introduced into Lower Meso-

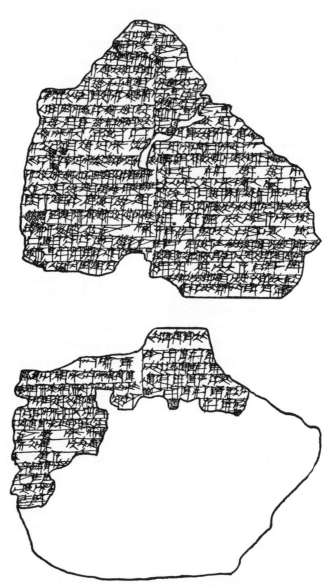

22. Lugalbanda and Enmerkar: Philadelphia. Hand
copy of unpublished Nippur fragment, in University Museum, joins large tablet published in 1934.

potamia by immigrants from southwestern Iran noted for their specialized type of painted pottery. Not long after the establishment of the first settlement by the Iranian immigrants, the Semites probably infiltrated into Southern Mesopotamia, both as peaceful immigrants and as warlike conquerors. As a result of the fusion of these two ethnic groups—the Iranians from the East and the Semites from the West—and the cross-fertilization of their cultures, there came into being the first civilized *urban* state in Lower Mesopotamia. Like the later Sumerian civilization, it consisted of a group of city-states between which there was continual strife for supremacy over the land as a whole. But now and again through the centuries, relative unity and stability were no doubt achieved, at least for brief intervals. At such times the Mesopotamian power, in which the Semitic element was no doubt predominant, must have succeeded in extending its influence over many of the surrounding districts, and developed what may well have been the first empire in the Near East, probably the first empire in the history of civilization.

Part of the territory which this empire came to dominate, both culturally and politically, no doubt consisted of the more westerly parts of the Iranian plateau, including the country later known as Elam. It was in the course of these political activities and their accompanying military campaigns, that the Mesopotamian state first came in conflict with the Sumerians. This primitive and probably nomadic people, who may have erupted from either Transcaucasia or Transcaspia, was pressing upon the districts of western Iran, and these had to be defended at all costs, since they served as buffer states between the Mesopotamian empire and the barbarians beyond.

In their first encounters, there is little doubt that the Mesopotamian forces, with their superior military technique, were more than a match for the Sumerian hordes. But in the long run, it was the mobile primitive Sumerians who had the advantage over their more civilized, sedentary adversary. Over the years, as captive hostages in Mesopotamian cities, and as mercenaries in the Mesopotamian armies, the Sumerian warriors learned what they most needed of the military techniques of their captors. And as the Mesopotamian power weakened and tottered, the Sumerians poured through the buffer states of western Iran and invaded Lower Mesopotamia itself, where they took over as masters and conquerors.

To summarize, the pre-Sumerian period in Mesopotamia began as a peasant-village culture, introduced by the Iranians from the East. It passed through an intermediate stage of immigration and invasion by the Semites from the West. It culminated in an urban, and probably predominantly Semitic, civilization whose political rule was brought to an end by the invading Sumerian hordes.

Turning now from the pre-Sumerian, or Irano-Semitic, period in the earlier history of Lower Mesopotamia, to the following Sumerian period, we find the latter to consist of three cultural stages: the preliterate, the proto-literate, and the early-literate. The first, or preliterate, stage of the Sumerian period began with an era of stagnation and regression following the collapse of the earlier and more advanced Irano-Semitic civilization, and the incursion of the Sumerian barbaric war bands into Lower Mesopotamia. During these centuries, which culminated in the Sumerian Heroic Age, it was the culturally immature and psychologically unstable Sumerian war lords, with their highly individualistic and predatory dispositions, who held sway over the sacked cities and burnt villages of the first vanquished Mesopotamian empire. These Sumerian invaders were themselves far from secure in their new Mesopotamian habitat, for it seems that not long after they had made themselves masters in the land, new nomadic hordes from the western desert—Semitic tribes known as the Martu, "who know not grain"—poured into Lower Mesopotamia. As late as the days of Enmerkar and Lugalbanda—that is, at the peak of the Sumerian Heroic Age—the struggle between these desert barbarians and the but recently "citified" Sumerians was still raging. Under these circumstances it is hardly likely that the times immediately following the arrival of the Sumerian hordes were conducive to economic and technological progress or to creative efforts in the fields of art and architecture. Only in the literary field may we assume a marked creative activity—on the part of the court minstrels, who were moved to compose epic lays for the entertainment of their lords and masters.

It is when we come to the second, or proto-literate, stage of the Sumerian period that we find the Sumerians firmly planted and deeply rooted in their new land. It was probably in this cultural phase that the name Sumer first came to be applied to Lower Mesopotamia. By this time the more stable elements of the ruling caste—particularly the court and temple administrators and intellectuals—were coming to the fore. There was a strong movement for law and order in the land, and an awakening of community spirit and patriotic pride. Moreover, the unusually fruitful fusion, both ethnic and cultural, of the Sumerian conquerors with the vanquished but more civilized native population, brought about a creative spurt that was fraught with significance not alone for Sumer but for Western Asia as a whole.

It was during this cultural stage that architecture was developed to a new high level. This was also the time that probably witnessed the invention of writing, an event which proved to be the decisive factor in molding the Near East into a cultural unit in spite of its diverse and polyglot ethnic elements. The Sumerian system of writing, in its later conventionalized form, was borrowed by practically all the cultured peoples of Western Asia. As a result, the study of the Sumerian language and literature became a major discipline in the narrowly restricted, but highly influential, literate circles of the ancient Near East. It was this leaven of Sumerian achievement on the intellectual and spiritual plane that raised the Near Eastern ethos to a new high point in the early history of civilization. (Note that Sumerian achievements were actually the product of at least three ethnic groups—the proto-Iranian, the Semitic, and the Sumerian.)

The last, or early-literate, cultural stage of the Sumerian period witnessed the further development of those material and spiritual achievements which mainly originated in the preceding, and more creative, proto-literate stage—particularly in the matter of writing. The largely pictographic and ideographic script of the preceding era was molded and modified over the years into a thoroughly conventionalized and purely phonetic system of writing. By the end of this period it could be utilized for even the more complex historical compositions.

It was probably during this early-literate stage, or perhaps

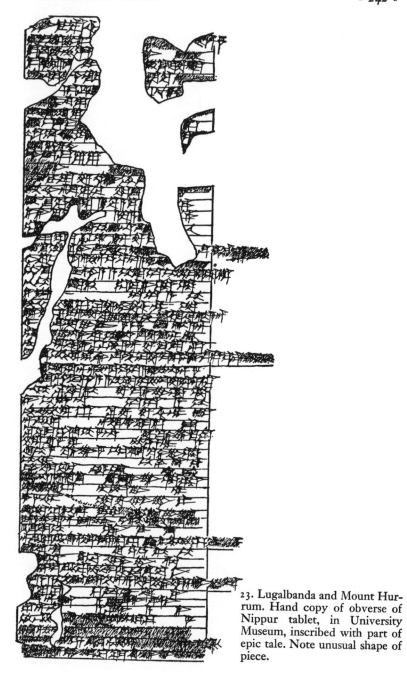

23. Lugalbanda and Mount Hurrum. Hand copy of obverse of
Nippur tablet, in University
Museum, inscribed with part of
epic tale. Note unusual shape of
piece.

even toward the end of the preceding proto-literate phase, that strong Sumerian dynasties first came into being. In spite of the constant strife between city and city for the hegemony over Sumer, some of them did succeed, if only for brief intervals, in extending the political boundaries of Sumer considerably beyond Lower Mesopotamia itself. Thus there came into being what might be termed the second—and this time predominantly Sumerian—empire in the history of the Near East. Finally the Sumerian empire, like its presumed Semitic predecessor, weakened and crumbled. As a result of continued infiltration into the land, the Semitic Akkadians became ever more powerful, until, with the reign of Sargon, which may be said to mark the beginning of the Sumero-Akkadian period, the Sumerian period comes to a close.

In conclusion, it may prove of value to attempt to assign specific dates to the cultural stages described in the foregoing reconstruction of the earliest history of Lower Mesopotamia, particularly since of late a predisposition to a "high" chronology (an understandable archaeological weakness) is again manifesting itself.

Let us start with the well-known Hammurabi, a key figure in Mesopotamian history and chronology. Several decades ago, the beginning of his reign was dated as early as the twentieth century B.C. It is now generally agreed that this was far too early, and that 1750 B.C. would be a more likely date. In fact, even this date may prove too high by four to five decades. The interval between the beginning of Hammurabi's reign and that of Sargon the Great of Akkad, the key Mesopotamian ruler, which not long ago was taken to be some seven centuries, turns out to be only about five and a half centuries. Sargon's rule, therefore, began about 2300 B.C. If now, judging in part from the development of the cuneiform system of writing, we attribute some four centuries to the early-literate stage of the Sumerian period, its beginning would reach back to approximately 2700 B.C. The preceding proto-literate stage probably did not last longer than two centuries, and the barbaric Sumerian Heroic Age which it followed may therefore be assigned to the first century of the third millennium B.C. As for the first arrival of the conquering but primitive Sumerians in Lower Mesopotamia, this must have taken place in the last quarter of the fourth millennium B.C. If we further attribute some five to six centuries to the Irano-Semitic civilization, the first settlements in Lower Mesopotamia may have taken place in the first quarter of the fourth millennium B.C.

Unlike narrative and hymnal poetry, the lyric is rather rare in Sumerian literature—particularly the love lyric. To date, only two love poems have been recovered among hundreds and thousands of Sumerian tablets. These two poems, as is apparent from the translations in Chapter 25, are not love poems in the secular sense. Both are probably rhapsodic songs of love uttered by a royal bride to her king. They call to mind the Biblical "Song of Songs."

THE FIRST LOVE SONG

WHILE WORKING in the Istanbul Museum of the Ancient Orient as Fulbright Research Professor—it was toward the end of 1951—I came upon a little tablet with the museum number 2461. For weeks I had been studying, more or less cursorily, drawerful after drawerful of still uncopied and unpublished Sumerian literary tablets, in order to identify each piece and, if possible, assign it to the composition to which it belonged. All this was spadework preparatory to the selection, for copying, of those pieces which were most significant—since it was clear that there would be no time that year to copy all of them. The little tablet numbered 2461 was lying in one of the drawers, surrounded by a number of other pieces.

When I first laid eyes on it, its most attractive feature was its state of preservation. I soon realized that I was reading a poem, divided into a number of stanzas, which celebrated beauty and love, a joyous bride and a king named Shu-Sin (who ruled over the land of Sumer close to four thousand years ago). As I read it again and yet again, there was no mistaking its content. What I held in my hand was one of the oldest love songs written down by the hand of man.

It soon became clear that this was not a secular poem, not a song of love between just "a man and a maid." It involved a king and his selected bride, and was no doubt intended to be recited in the course of the most hallowed of ancient rites, the rite of the "sacred marriage." Once a year, according to Sumerian belief, it was the sacred duty of the ruler to marry a priestess and votary of Inanna, the goddess of love and procreation, in order to ensure fertility to the soil and fecundity to the womb. The time-honored ceremony was celebrated on New Year's day and was preceded by feasts and banquets accompanied by music, song, and dance. The poem inscribed on the little Istanbul clay tablet was in all probability recited by the chosen bride of King Shu-Sin in the course of one of these New Year celebrations.

The poem was copied by Muazzez Cig, one of the Turkish curators of the Istanbul tablet collection. An edition of the poem consisting of copy, text, transliteration, translation, and commentary was published jointly with Cig in the *Belleten* of the Turkish Historical Commission, Volume 16 (pages 345 ff.). Here is a tentative translation:

> Bridegroom, dear to my heart,
> Goodly is your beauty, honeysweet,
> Lion, dear to my heart,
> Goodly is your beauty, honeysweet.
>
> You have captivated me, let me stand tremblingly before you,
> Bridegroom, I would be taken by you to the bedchamber,
> You have captivated me, let me stand tremblingly before you,
> Lion, I would be taken by you to the bedchamber.
>
> Bridegroom, let me caress you,
> My precious caress is more savory than honey,
> In the bedchamber, honey filled,
> Let us enjoy your goodly beauty,
> Lion, let me caress you,
> My precious caress is more savory than honey.
>
> Bridegroom, you have taken your pleasure of me,
> Tell my mother, she will give you delicacies,
> My father, he will give you gifts.
>
> Your spirit, I know where to cheer your spirit,
> Bridegroom, sleep in our house until dawn,
> Your heart, I know where to gladden your heart,
> Lion, sleep in our house until dawn.
>
> You, because you love me,
> Give me pray of your caresses,
> My lord god, my lord protector,
> My Shu-Sin who gladdens Enlil's heart,
> Give me pray of your caresses.

Your place goodly as honey, pray lay (your) hand on it,
Bring (your) hand over it like a *gishban*-garment,
Cup (your) hand over it like a *gishban-sikin*-garment,

It is a *balbale*-song of Inanna.

The only other known Sumerian love song is also inscribed on an Istanbul tablet. Although it was published by Edward Chiera in 1924, it was not translated until 1947, when Adam Falkenstein's excellent and detailed edition of the text appeared in *Die Welt des Orients* (pages 43-50). This poem, too, consists of the loving words of an unnamed votary to her king, but its structure is not too clear and its meaning is obscure in spots. It seems to consist of six strophes: two of four lines each, one of six lines, two more of four lines, and one of six lines. The logical relationship between the various strophes is not too clear. The first strophe sings of the birth of Shu-Sin, while the second seems to consist of exclamatory lines exalting Shu-Sin, his mother Abisimti, and his wife Kubatum. In the third and longer strophe,

24. Love Poem. Hand copy of obverse and reverse of Istanbul tablet inscribed with love poem to King Shu-Sin reminiscent of Biblical "Song of Songs."

the poetess tells of the gifts presented her by the king as a reward for her joyous *allari*-songs. Of the last three strophes, the first and third consist of exclamatory lines exalting the king, while the second sings temptingly of the poetess' own charms. Here is the tentative translation of the entire poem:

> She gave birth to him who is pure, she gave birth to him who
>   is pure,
> The queen gave birth to him who is pure,
> Abisimti gave birth to him who is pure,
> The queen gave birth to him who is pure.
>
> O my (queen) who is favored of limb,
> O my (queen) who is . . d of head, my queen Kubatum,
> O my (lord) who is . . d of hair, my lord Shu-Sin,
> O my (lord) who is . . d of word, my son of Shulgi!
>
> Because I uttered it, because I uttered it, the lord gave me a gift,
> Because I uttered the *allari*-song, the lord gave me a gift,
> A pendant of gold, a seal of lapis lazuli, the lord gave me as a gift,
> A ring of gold, a ring of silver, the lord gave me as a gift,
> Lord, your gift is brimful of . . , lift your face unto me,
> Shu-Sin, your gift is brimful of . . , lift your face unto me.
>
> . . . . lord . . . . lord . . . . ,
> . . . . like a weapon . . . . ,
> The city lifts its hand like a dragon, my lord Shu-Sin,
> It lies at your feet like a lion-cub, son of Shulgi.
>
> My god, of the wine-maid, sweet is her drink,
> Like her drink sweet is her vulva, sweet is her drink,
> Like her lips sweet is her vulva, sweet is her drink,
> Sweet is her mixed drink, her drink.
>
> My Shu-Sin who favored me,
> O my (Shu-Sin) who favored me, who fondled me,
> My Shu-Sin who favored me,
> My beloved of Enlil, (my) Shu-Sin,
> My king, the god of his land!
>
> It is a *balbale* of Bau.

The Sumerian poems and essays that are analyzed in the present volume represent only a small fraction of the available Sumerian literary remains—not to mention the innumerable tablets still underground. By the first half of the second millennium B.C. a large number of Sumerian literary works of all types were current in Sumerian schools. They were inscribed on clay tablets, prisms, and cylinders of assorted sizes and shapes, which had to be handled, stored, and cared for. *A priori* it seemed reasonable to suppose that some of the Sumerian faculty personnel would find it convenient to list the names of groups of literary works for purposes of reference and filing. In 1942 two such book lists were identified. One is in the Louvre, and the other in the University Museum. These, the first "library catalogues," are discussed in Chapter 26.

THE FIRST LIBRARY CATALOGUE

T HE UNIVERSITY MUSEUM has a tablet catalogued as No. 29-15-166. It is an ancient Sumerian "book list." It is small, only 2½ inches in length by 1½ inches in width, and in practically perfect condition. The scribe, by dividing each side into two columns, and by using a minute script, succeeded in cataloguing the titles of sixty-two literary works on this small tablet. The first forty titles he divided into groups of ten by ruling a dividing line between numbers 10 and 11, 20 and 21, 30 and 31, 40 and 41. The remaining twenty-two he separated into two groups, the first consisting of nine titles and the second of thirteen. At least twenty-four of the titles which this scribe listed in his catalogue can be identified as belonging to compositions for which we now have the texts themselves, in full or in large part. We may have considerable portions of the texts of many more of the listed works. But since the title of a Sumerian composition consisted of part—and usually the *first* part—of its first line, there is no way of identifying the titles of those poems or essays in which the first lines were broken away or seriously damaged.

The recognition of the contents of the little tablet in the University Museum as a "book list" did not come about simply and at first glance. When I first took the little tablet from its place in the cupboard to study it, I had no inkling of the true nature of its contents. Blithely assuming that it was but another Sumerian poem, I tried to translate it as a connected text. To be sure, I was troubled by the extreme brevity of the individual lines, and by the inexplicable division of the text into various groupings by means of ruled lines. But the thought that it was a "book list" would probably never have entered my mind, had I not grown familiar with the initial lines of a number of the Sumerian literary works in my efforts, over the years, to piece together their available texts. As I read and reread, again and again, the individual phrases on the little tablet, the similarity between them and the first lines of a number of the poems and essays struck me as unusual. From there on it was relatively simple, and a detailed comparison led to the conclusion that the lines inscribed on the tiny document contained not a connected text, but a disjointed list of titles of a number of Sumerian literary works.

Once the contents of the catalogue tablet had been recognized and deciphered, it seemed advisable to look through all the Sumerian material published by the various museums during the past decades to see if a similar document, the nature of its contents unrecognized, had already been published. Sure enough, in searching through the Louvre publication *Textes Religieux Sumériens*, I found that the Louvre tablet AO 5393, described as a hymn by its copyist, the French scholar Henri de Genouillac, is really a catalogue corresponding in large part to our University Museum tablet. Indeed, to judge from the script, it may have been written by the very same scribe. The Louvre tablet is also divided into four columns. It catalogues sixty-eight titles, six more than the University Museum tablet. Forty-three of the titles are identical on the two tablets, although the order frequently varies. The Louvre tablet therefore has twenty-five tablets that are not in the University Museum tablet, while the latter has nineteen titles that are not in the former. Altogether, the two catalogues list the titles of eighty-seven literary compositions. Among the twenty-five listed only on the Louvre tablet, eight titles are of compositions whose texts we now have in large part. This brings the total identifiable compositions to thirty-two.

As for the principles which guided the scribe in the arrangement of his catalogue, these are by no means clear. In the first place, since the forty-three titles common to both catalogues differ considerably in the order of their arrangement, it is obvious that the guiding principles were not identical for the two catalogues. *A priori* one might have expected the nature of the contents of the compositions to have been the determining criterion. Actually, this is rarely the case. The only very convincing example of arrangement according to content is that of the last thirteen titles of the University Museum tablet, which are all "wisdom" compositions. Interestingly enough, none of these are found on the Louvre tablet.

At present we are ignorant of the practical purposes which the catalogue was intended to serve and can only guess at the actual factors that impelled the scribe to a particular choice. To mention some of the more obvious possibilities, he may have written the titles as he "packed" the literary tablets in a jar, or as he "unpacked" them, or perhaps as he arranged them on the shelves of the library room of the "tablet house." In any case, the size of the tablet may have played a considerable role in the order of selection. Until additional data comes to light, the problem of the catalogue arrangement must remain obscure.

For purposes of illustration, here is a list of those titles in the two documents which can be identified with the poems and essays discussed throughout this book:

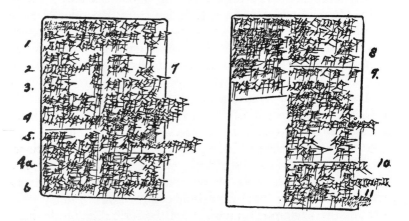

25. "Library Catalogue." Compositions treated in this book. In this hand copy of "Catalogue," numbers refer to literary works discussed in present volume.

1. *Ene nigdue* ("The Lord, That Which Is Appropriate"), listed as No. 3 in the University Museum tablet (and probably also in the Louvre document, which is broken at this point), begins the myth "The Creation of the Pickax," the first lines of which were utilized for deducing the Sumerian concepts of the creation of the universe (see Chapter 13).

2. *Enlil Sudushe* ("Enlil Far-reaching"), listed as No. 5 in both documents, begins the Enlil hymn quoted in large part in Chapter 13.

3. *Uria* ("The Days of Creation"), listed as No. 7 in both catalogues, begins the epic tale "Gilgamesh, Enkidu, and the Nether World" (see Chapter 23). The title *Uria* appears two more times in the catalogues, which indicates that the cataloguer must have had two additional works beginning with this phrase. Nevertheless, he did not seem to feel it necessary to distinguish between these three identical titles.

4. *Ene kurlutilashe* ("The Lord toward the Land of the Living"), listed as No. 10 in both catalogues, begins the dragon-slaying tale "Gilgamesh and the Land of the Living" (see Chapter 22).

5. *Lukingia Ag* ("The Heralds of Ag(ga)"), listed as No. 11 in the University Museum tablet but omitted in the Louvre piece, begins the politically significant epic tale, "Gilgamesh and Agga" (see Chapter 5). The Sumerian title stops with the syllable *Ag*, although this is only the first part of the name.

6. *Hursag ankibida* ("On the Mountain of Heaven and Earth"), listed as No. 17 in the University Museum tablet but omitted in the Louvre document, begins the disputation "Cattle and Grain" (see Chapter 14), which is important for the Sumerian ideas concerning the creation of man.

7. *Uru nanam* ("Lo, the City"), listed as No. 22 in the University Museum tablet but omitted in the Louvre piece, begins the *Nanshe* hymn (see Chapter 14), which is important for the history of Sumerian ethics and morals.

8. *Lugalbanda* ("Lugalbanda"), listed as No. 39 in the University Museum tablet but omitted in the Louvre piece, begins the epic tale "Lugalbanda and Enmerkar" (see Chapter 24).

9. *Angalta kigalshe* ("From the Great Above to the Great Be-

low"), listed as No. 41 in the University Museum document but as No. 34 in the Louvre tablet, begins the myth "Inanna's Descent to the Nether World" (see Chapter 21).

10. *Mesheam iduden* ("Where Did You Go?"), listed as No. 50 in the University Museum tablet but omitted in the Louvre document, is the end of the first line of the "schooldays" composition discussed in Chapter 2. The entire first line of this essay reads *Dumu edubba uulam meshe iduden* ("School-boy, where did you go from earliest days?"). But the ancient scribe chose the last rather than the first part of this line for his catalogue, perhaps because there were a number of essays beginning with the word *Dumu edubba* ("Schoolboy"), and he wished to distinguish between them.

11. *Uul engarra* ("In Days of Yore the Farmer"), listed as No. 53 in the University Museum tablet but omitted in the Louvre piece, begins the essay containing the instructions of a farmer to his son, and described as the first "Farmer's Almanac" in Chapter 11.

12. *Lugale u melambi nirgal*, listed as No. 18 in the Louvre tablet but omitted in the University Museum document, begins the dragon-slaying myth "The Deeds and Exploits of the God Ninurta" (see Chapter 22).

13. *Lulu nammah dingire* ("Man, the Exaltedness of the Gods"), listed as No. 46 in the Louvre piece and omitted in the University Museum tablet, begins the poetic essay on human suffering and submission discussed in Chapter 15.

The Sumerians held out no comforting hopes for man and his future. To be sure, they longed for security and at least three of the four freedoms that we espouse today—freedom from fear, want, and war. But it never occurred to them to project these longings and wishes into the future. Instead, they thought of them in retrospect and relegated them to the long-gone past. The first recorded ideas concerning a Golden Age are presented in Chapter 27.

MAN'S FIRST GOLDEN AGE

I N CLASSICAL mythology, the Golden Age is represented as an age of perfect happiness, when men lived without
toil or strife. In Sumerian literature, we have, preserved for us
on a tablet, man's first conception of the Golden Age. The
Sumerian view of the Golden Age is found in the epic tale
"Enmerkar and the Land of Aratta" (see Chapter 4). In this
tale there is a passage of twenty-one lines that describes a once-
upon-a-time state of peace and security, and ends with man's
fall from this blissful state. Here is the passage:

> Once upon a time, there was no snake, there was no scorpion,
> There was no hyena, there was no lion,
> There was no wild dog, no wolf,
> There was no fear, no terror,
> Man had no rival.
>
> Once upon a time, the lands Shubur and Hamazi,
> Many (?)-tongued Sumer, the great land of princeships'
> divine laws,
> Uri, the land having all that is appropriate,
> The land Martu, resting in security,
> The whole universe, the people in unison (?),
> To Enlil in one tongue gave praise.
>
> (But) then, the father-lord, the father-prince, the father-king,
> Enki, the father-lord, the father-prince, the father-king,
> The irate (?) father-lord, the irate (?) father-prince, the
> irate (?) father-king,
> . . . . abundance . . . .
> . . . . (5 lines destroyed)
> . . man . . . .

The first eleven lines, which are excellently preserved, describe those happy "long ago" days when man, fearless and unrivaled, lived in a world of peace and plenty, and all the peoples of the universe worshiped the same deity, Enlil. Indeed, if "in one tongue" is to be taken literally, and not as a figurative expression for a phrase such as "with one heart," the words would indicate that the Sumerians, like the Hebrews of later times, believed in the existence of a universal speech prior to the period of the confusion of languages.

As for the ten lines that constitute the next part of the passage, they are so fragmentary that we can only guess at their content. To judge from the context, it seems safe to surmise that Enki, displeased with, or jealous of, the sway of Enlil, took some action to disrupt it, and thus put an end to man's Golden Age by bringing about conflicts and wars among the peoples of the world. Perhaps (on the assumption that lines 10 and 11 are to be taken literally), Enki even brought about a confusion of languages. If so, we may have here the first inkling of a Sumerian parallel to the Biblical "Tower of Babel" story (Genesis 11:1-9), except that the Sumerians attributed man's fall to the jealousy between the gods while the Hebrews believed it resulted from Elohim's jealousy of man's ambition to be like a god.

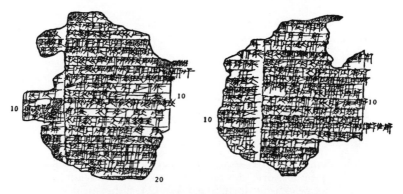

26. Man's "Golden Age." Hand copy of obverse and reverse of Nippur fragment, in University Museum, inscribed with part of epic tale, "Enmerkar and the Lord of Aratta."

The poet of the Golden Age passage designated it as the "Spell of Enki." Enmerkar, the lord of Erech and a favorite of the god Enki—so runs the story—is determined to make a vassal state of the mineral-rich Aratta. He therefore sends a herald to the lord of Aratta with a message threatening Aratta's destruction unless he and his people bring down precious metal and stone, and build and decorate Enki's temple, the Abzu. It was to further impress the lord of Aratta that Enki instructed the herald to repeat the "Spell of Enki," which relates how Enki

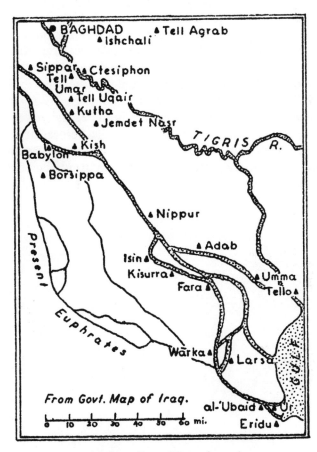

27. Ancient Sites. Map of southern Iraq locating important excavated sites.

had put an end to Enlil's sway over the earth and its inhabitants.

Besides shedding light on the Sumerian ideas of man's blissful past, the passage of twenty-one lines is of importance for another reason: It gives some idea of the size and geography of the physical world known to the Sumerians. To judge from lines 6 to 9, the poet conceived of the universe as four major land divisions. His own country, Sumer, formed the southern boundary of this universe and consisted (roughly estimated) of the territory between the Tigris and Euphrates Rivers from a line somewhat below the thirty-third parallel down to the Persian Gulf. Directly north of Sumer was Uri, which probably consisted of the territory between the Tigris and Euphrates north of the thirty-third parallel, and included the later Akkad and Assyria. East of Sumer and Uri was Shubur-Hamazi, which no doubt included much of western Iran. To the west and southwest of Sumer was Martu, which included the territory between the Euphrates River and the Mediterranean Sea, as well as Arabia. In short, the universe as conceived by the Sumerian poets, extended at least from the Armenian highlands on the north to the Persian Gulf, and from the Iranian highlands on the east to the Mediterranean Sea.

THE FIRST "SICK" SOCIETY

I T HAS LONG BEEN my contention that in spite of the obvious differences, both superficial and profound, between the culture, character, and mentality of the ancient Sumerian and modern man, they are fundamentally analogous, comparable, and reciprocally illuminating. In view of today's pervading concern with the diverse and variegated social ills that mark and mar modern life, it has occurred to me that it might be interesting and useful to try to determine whether or not some of these disturbing problems troubled ancient Sumerian society as well. I therefore turned to the Sumerian literary documents, the only cuneiform writings with which I am more or less on intimate terms, to see if, although composed by visionary poets and emotional bards rather than scholarly sociologists, they might not prove revealing for this comparative inquiry; not directly of course, but inferentially and between the lines, as it were. This chapter will summarize some of the results of this quest for sociological evidence from non-sociological sources and will try to demonstrate that not unlike our own tormented society, the Sumerian society of some 4000 years ago had its deplorable failings and distressing shortcomings: its utopian ideals honored more in the breach than in observance; its "Sunday preaching and Monday practice"; it yearned for peace but was constantly at war; it professed such ideals as justice, equity, and compassion, but abounded in injustice, inequality, and oppression; materialistic and shortsighted, it unbalanced the ecology essential to its economy; it suffered from the "generation gap" between parents and children and between teachers and students; it had its "drop-outs," "cop-outs," hippies and perverts; it had its "unisex" devotees, and perhaps even something like a "mini-maxi" controversy. In any case, for whatever it is worth, here is some of the evidence for the ancient counterparts of the modern woes, beginning with what is generally deemed to be society's most catastrophic affliction: war.

That war and warfare were rampant all over the Ancient Near East is, of course, a well-known melancholy truth, and modern history books are filled with grisly details taken from numerous royal inscriptions, and particularly the annals of the Assyrian kings. These royal inscriptions and annals, however, were written primarily for the purpose of exalting the victors and conquerors and therefore provide little information on war's cataclysmic after-effects on the economic, social, political, and religious life of the conquered and victimized communities. For this kind of information we must turn to the Sumerian literary genre commonly known as "lamentation," which may have had its rudimentary beginnings as early as the second half of the third millennium B.C., but did not become a significant component of the Sumerian literary and liturgical repertoire before the first half of the second millennium. These laments depict copiously and vividly the misery and suffering, the agony and torment of the conquered victims. Thus, in the "Lamentation over the Destruction of Sumer and Ur" we learn that as a consequence of the defeat of the Sumerians by their neighboring enemies, law and order ceased to exist. City, house, and byre were in ruins; rivers and canals were dried up; fields, gardens, orchards, and grazing lands lay untended and uncultivated; family life was utterly disrupted; the people and their king were carried off into captivity and foreigners were settled in their place; temples were defiled and their rites and rituals abolished; communications on land and water broke down; panic, massacre, and famine ravaged the land.

War, as is well known, is a major cause of inflation in our own time, and this was true of ancient Sumer as well. From a composition generally known as the "Curse of Agade" we learn that following the ravaging of Sumer by the invading Gutian hordes, prices rose so high that a shekel of silver could buy but half a *sila* of oil, half a *sila* of grain, half a *mina* of wool, and only one *ban* of fish, that is, prices were anywhere from twenty to two hundred times above normal.

With the bitter fruit of war all about them, the people of Sumer yearned for peace and security, as can be gathered from the impressive, though no doubt exaggerated claims of ruler after ruler. Thus, about 2300 B.C., Lugalzaggesi boasts that after he had become master of all the lands, east, west, north, and south, the people "slept (peacefully) in the meadow" throughout his reign, and he prays to Enlil to see to it that "the lands (continue) to sleep (peacefully) in the meadows," and that "all mankind thrive like plants and herbs." Some two centuries later, on the day that Gudea brought Ningirsu into the restored and purified Eninnu, in words reminiscent of the prophet Isaiah, he professes that

> The beasts, the creatures of the steppe, together kneel,
> The lion, the leopard (?), the dragon of the steppe, together in sweet sleep kneel.

Less than a century later, Shulgi, one of the truly great rulers of the ancient world, asserts:

> On that (?) day, in my inscriptions,
> That no city was destroyed by me,
>   no walls were breached by me,
> That like a frail reed no land was crushed by me,
> The singer will put to song.

A glowing picture of the much longed for peace, security, and stability is provided by the poet who composed the "Lamentation over the Destruction of Nippur," who alleges that after Nippur and Sumer had been delivered by Ishme-Dagan from their enemies, there came

> A day when man abuses not man, the son fears his father,
> A day when humility pervades the land, the noble is honored by the lowly,
> A day when the younger brother defers to the older brother,
> A day when the young sit (attentive) to the words of the learned,
> A day when there is no strife (?) between the weak and strong, when kindness prevails,
> A day when (any) chosen (?) road can be traveled, the weeds (having been) ripped out,
> A day when man can travel where he wills, when (even) in the steppe (?) his ... will not be harmed,

A day when all suffering will be gone from the land, light will
pervade it,
A day when black darkness will be expelled from the land, [and]
all living creatures will rejoice.

What peace and prosperity meant to a city can also be gauged
from the aforementioned composition, the "Curse of Agade,"
which begins with a graphic description of the happy city before
its king, Naram-Sin, committed the unforgivable sacrilege that
brought about its destruction and desolation. According to the poet,
it was then a secure habitation richly supplied with food and drink;
its courtyards were joyous and its festive places were beautiful and
attractive; its people lived in harmony; its homes were filled with
gold and silver; its silos bulged with grain; "its old women were
endowed with (wise) counsel, its old men were endowed with elo-
quence, its young men were endowed with prowess (literally,
strength of weapons), its little children were endowed with joyous
hearts"; music and song filled it inside and out; its quays were
abustle with the loading and unloading of the docking boats.

So deep was the longing for peace among the Sumerians that
they built a special gate in their holy city Nippur, known as the
"Gate of Peace." Just when and why it was first conceived and
constructed, is unknown at present, but according to the poet who
composed the "Curse of Agade," one of Naram-Sin's defiant and
desecrating acts was breaking down the Gate of Peace with a pickaxe, and as a consequence "peace was estranged from the lands." If
nothing else, therefore, this Nippur Gate of Peace served as a symbol of peace, and its breaching was a signal for the outbreak of war
and strife.

The causes of the wars, both civil and foreign, that finally overwhelmed the Sumerians and brought about the end of their preeminence, were, as in the case of the wars of our own days, varied
and complex: economic, the need to obtain the resources not available in the land; political, the pressing demand for security from
attack by its inimical neighbors; psychological, the drive for power
and prestige, preeminence and renown, retaliation and revenge.
These psychological incentives played an inordinately large role in
Sumerian society which, not unlike some of the more "advanced"
of our modern societies, put excessive stress on rivalry and superiority, ambition and accomplishment, competition and success. Su-

merian society, like, for example, present-day American society,
was, to use a current expression, intensely "achievement-oriented,"
and as a consequence, was polarized into poor and rich, weak and
strong, impotent and powerful, oppressed and oppressor. Take for
example the poetic prologue of the Ur-Nammu Law Code which in
part reads:

> Then did Ur-Nammu, the mighty warrior, king of Ur, king of Sumer
> and Akkad, by the might of Nanna, lord of the city, and in accord-
> ance with the true word of Utu, establish equity in the land, banish
> abuse, violence, and strife . . . He fashioned the bronze *sila*-measure,
> standardized the one-*mina* weight, and standardized the stone weight
> of a shekel of silver in relation (?) to one *mina* . . . The orphan was
> not delivered up to the rich man, the widow was not delivered up to
> the powerful man, the man of one shekel was not delivered up to the
> man of one *mina*.

To judge from these high-minded claims, it is obvious that Sumerian society in the days of Ur-Nammu, and no doubt long before
his days, suffered from injustice, inequity, poverty, and oppression.

Whether or not Ur-Nammu made a serious effort to achieve the
humanitarian ideals professed in his prologue, it is hardly likely that
he had much success. In any case, the kingly claims of guaranteeing
justice and equity in the land became a literary stereotype of the
royal hymns. This was usually no more than a brief general statement that he respected justice, loved truth, and hated evil, but the
poet would sometimes expand on this humanitarian theme, and one
of the lengthier versions of the royal utopian dispensations is found
in a self-laudatory hymn to Ishme-Dagan who boasts that

> Utu placed justice and truth in my mouth—
> To give just verdicts and decisions to the people,
> To make truth prevail,
> To sustain the righteous, destroy the evil,
> To see to it that brother speaks the truth to brother, that the
>   father is respected,
> That the older sister in not contradicted, that the mother is feared,
> That the weak are not delivered up to the strong, that the frail
>   are protected,
> That the powerful should not work their will, that man should
>   not strive against man,
> That evil and violence be wiped out, justice flourish—
> Utu, the son born of Ningal, set as my allotted portion.

Later in the same hymn, Ishme-Dagan further elaborates on his impressive achievements in the area of social justice in these words:

> Evil and violence I curbed (?),
> Truth I established in Sumer.
> I am a shepherd who loves justice,
> I am one who was born in Sumer, a citizen of Nippur, . . . ,
> I am a judge who tolerates not inequity (?),
> Who gives nothing but just decisions,
> (So that) the powerful acts not high and mighty,
> The strong oppresses (?) not the weak;
> The noble mistreats not the freeman, . . . ,
> The poor dares to talk back to the rich, ...
> For all times, bribed verdicts, twisted words, I banished (?),
> I wiped out the unseemly, the abusive, . . . ,
> I put to right that which has been perverted, falsehood, and mischief.
> The wronged, the widow, the orphan—
> I respond to their cry "O Utu, O Nanna," . . . ,
> I put an end to the cutthroats that harry (?) the steppe (?),
> Firmly do I sustain the just, ...

To judge from these passages, Sumerian society suffered from such evils as violence and abuse, injustice and inequity, oppression and wrongdoing and that, in many respects, it was a sick society can also be gathered from a hymn to Enlil, which portrays his city Nippur as the holiest of all cities, the guardian of man's loftiest moral and spiritual values. According to the poet

> It grants not long days to the braggart,
> Allows no evil word to be uttered against judgment,
> Hypocrisy (?), distortion,
> Abuse, malice, unseemliness,
> Insolence (?), enmity, oppression,
> Envy, (?), force, libelous speech,
> Arrogance, violation, agreement, breach of contract,
>   abuse (?) of a verdict (?),
> (All these evils) the city does not tolerate.

Even if we credit our poet's noble words and grant him that Nippur, as Sumer's most hallowed city, actually was morally pure and ethically spotless, it is not unreasonable to infer that the other and less holy cities of Sumer, as well as Sumerian society as a whole, did tolerate the vices and evils itemized by the author. It is not sur-

prising, therefore, to find the Sumerian theologians, in the hope of
at least minimizing these distressing social flaws and failings, threatening the wrongdoers with dire divine punishment. Thus a hymn
to the goddess Nanshe, who, for some unknown reason, had been
assigned the role of the guardian of social justice and ethical behavior and who is described by the poet as one who

> Knows the orphan, knows the widow,
> Knows the oppression of man over man, is mother to the orphan,
> Nanshe cares for the widow,
> Finds counsel for the wretched (?),
> The queen brings the refugee to (her) lap,
> Looks after the weak . . . .

we learn that the goddess holds court every New Year's Day
for the purpose of judging mankind. With Nidaba, the "noble
scribe" who holds the "precious tablets" on her knee and the
"golden stylus" in her hand, and with her husband Haiia, the "man
of tablets" acting as examiner, she searches the heart of man for
such vices as boastfulness, greed, violation of contract, falsification
of weights and measures, acts of oppression by the mighty and
powerful, improper and unseemly family behavior. If found guilty,
and no doubt many a Sumerian was guilty of one or another of
these social offenses, Nanshe's vizier, Hendursag, saw to it that they
did not go unpunished.

Turning to another aspect of the social malaise, one relating to
Sumer's economic deterioration, we find that not unlike modern
industrial society, Sumerian agricultural society, materialistic and
shortsighted, tampered with nature's delicate ecological balance and
gradually undermined it. Eager and impatient for ever-richer har-
vests from their fields and farms, they overirrigated and thus
"salted" the soil into sterility and unproductiveness, an unfortunate
predicament that was further accelerated by the recurring pollution
and silting of the life-giving canals.

Another baneful economic plague of both modern and Sumerian
society, is the cheating merchant. In the Nanshe hymn mentioned
above, he is described as one who

> Substitutes the small weight for the large weight,
> Substitutes the small measure for the large measure.

Ur-Nammu, to judge from the prologue to the Law Code cited above, evidently tried to thwart the merchants' iniquitous practices by standardizing weights and measures throughout the land. Even so, he was far from successful, as is clear from the complaint of one lady customer who grumbled:

> The merchant—how he has reduced prices!
> How he has reduced the oil and barley.

This merchant had presumably reduced prices to attract customers, and then reduced the weight of the merchandise on the sly to make up for the price cuts.

In the spheres of family life and education, the "generation gap," the cankerous blight of modern society, infected and embittered Sumerian life as well. There seemed to be constant squabbling and bickering between parents and children, between the older and younger members of the family, between teachers and students. No wonder that the Sumerians longed for the blessed utopian day when their society would be free from discord and strife between the generations. We learn, for example, that when Gudea was chosen to be *ensi* of Lagash, one of his noteworthy social reforms was to see to it that the "mother did not strike the son." Again when he found it imperative to purify his city morally and spiritually in order to make it a fit place for his newly restored temple, the Eninnu, he made sure that "the mother scolded not the son, that the son spoke not disrespectfully to his mother." Similarly, Shulgi claims that during his reign "the mother speaks kindly to the son, the son answers truthfully to his father." The halcyon era ushered in by Ishme-Dagan, the savior of Nippur and Sumer, was noted for such commendable family conduct as the son fearing the father, and the younger brother showing deference to the older brother. In his self-laudatory hymn mentioned earlier, Ishme-Dagan claims that during his reign "brother speaks the truth to brother," "the father is respected," "the older sister is not contradicted," "the mother is feared." Among the reprobates that Nanshe, Sumer's social conscience, as it were, uncovered in the land, are: "the mother who spoke violently to the son, the son who spoke hatefully to his mother, the younger brother who defied (?) his older brother, who talked back to the father."

A graphic depiction of the "generation gap" between father and son is provided by the father-son dialogue-essay prepared by an anonymous Sumerian schoolman, treated in detail in Chapter 3. Beginning with a passage that vividly reveals the lack of meaningful communication between the two, it continues with an harangue by the father, replete with stereotypical parental injunctions that only serve to expose the wide chasm between them. The father complains bitterly of his son's incessant griping and base ingratitude which, he claims, is driving him to an early grave; what especially rankles him is his son's refusal to follow his profession and become a scribe. And so the father continues with his angry reproofs and bitter reproaches, although he has a change of heart toward the end of the composition, and rather unexpectedly closes his harsh tirade with a blessing for his son rather than with a curse, as might perhaps have been anticipated from the rueful Sumerian proverb:

A perverse son—his mother should not have given birth to him,
His god should not have fashioned him.

That Sumerian society suffered from a student-teacher rift as well as a "generation grap" can be surmised from the words of one bored student who, in reporting on his school activities, says resignedly:

Here is the monthly record of my attendance in school:
My vacation days each month are three,
My recurrent (?) monthly holidays are three,
(That leaves) twenty-four days each month
That I must stay in school—(and) long days they are.

Not only were the school days long and boring, but the discipline was harsh and oppressive, and one student complained of being thrashed so often by his teachers and monitors that he grew to hate school. To be sure, he found a practical, though rather unethical solution to his problem by having his father virtually bribe the teacher with gifts and bonuses. But the more activist-type students could become defiant and even violent, as is evident from these threatening words uttered perhaps by one of the monitors in charge of the more obstreperous students:

Why do you behave thus!
Why do you push, curse, hurl insults!

Why do you cause commotion in the school! . . . !
Why do you humiliate him who is your *sheshgal*
Who knows much more about the scribal art than you—
Disobey him, curse, and hurl insults!
The *ummia*, the all-knowing,
Has frowned at your perversity (saying), "Do what you will
    to them.
If I really did what I wanted to you,
To you who behave thus and disobey your *sheshgal*
I would give you sixty lashes with the cane . . . ,
Would put copper chains on your feet,
Lock you up in a room (?) and not let you out of school for
    two months.

Whatever the future of these vocal, defiant, contentious students may have turned out to be, it is clear that school was hardly a happy, comfortable place for the less ambitious and more easygoing students, and certainly not for those who were not intellectually gifted and study-oriented, and who, like many of their modern counterparts, were unable to finish a sentence, take dictation, do arithmetic, geometry, or write a good hand. Not a few of these must have become that society's "dropouts," having left home to wander about in the streets to follow the restful shade in summer and the warm sunshine in winter. They were undoubtedly filthy and did not hesitate to carry a lyre although quite unmusical. What is more, the Sumerian city, as we learn from the Gudea inscriptions, had its share of "unclean," perverts and depraved persons, who had to be expelled on special hallowed occasions as, for example, during the days when the city's main temple was restored, consecrated, and sanctified. There were even "unisex" cultists who practiced transvestism, that is men wore women's clothes and *vice versa;* interestingly enough they were devotees of Inanna, the goddess of sexual love, the passion that is all the rage of many of today's young. Even the "maxi-mini" controversy may not have been unknown, if we stick to the literal translation of a rather ambiguous proverb in which one woman says to another:

"You (can keep on) wearing the large garments,
(But) I will cut down (even) my loin-cloth."

In conclusion let me stress that this chapter concerned with pointing out some of the more distressing similarities between modern society and that of ancient Sumer, as evidenced by the literary documents, is neither comprehensive nor exhaustive; it only skims ever so lightly over the surface of the available material. With the continuing acceleration of the restoration of the Sumerian literary documents, and the deepening understanding of their contents, especially of such "wisdom" compositions as dialogues, disputations, proverbs, and precepts, many more parallels will come to light and will help to enrich comparative sociological research from a source which is very old and yet quite "new."

As noted in this chapter, the Sumerian lamentations provide the major source material of the catastropic effects of war and the yearning for peace that pervaded the land and its people. At present there are available well-nigh complete texts of three such documents: (1) "Lamentation over the Destruction of Ur," which I published more than thirty years ago as *Assyriological Study* No. 12 of the Oriental Institute of the University of Chicago; (2) "Lamentation over the Destruction of Sumer and Ur," a translation of which I published in 1969 in the third edition of *Ancient Near Eastern Texts Relating to the Old Testament*, pages 611-619; (3) "Lamentation over the Destruction of Nippur," now being edited in the University Museum, which is the subject of the next chapter.

THE FIRST LITURGIC LAMENTS

T HE SUMERIAN LAMENTATION is a literary genre
originated and developed by the poets of Sumer and Akkad in melancholy response to the periodic and recurrent ravaging of their
land and its cities and temples. Its incipient germ may be traced as
far back as the days of Urukagina, in the twenty-fourth century
B.C., one of whose archivists has left us a document inscribed with
a remarkably detailed list of the temples and shrines of Lagash
which were burned, looted, and defiled by his fellow Sumerian,
Lugalzaggesi of Umma. To be sure, on the surface it seems nothing
more than a matter-of-fact account of the impious deeds perpe-
trated by Lugalzaggesi against Lagash, compiled for the purpose of
"keeping the record straight," so that the evildoer may receive his
just punishment at the hands of the offended gods. Even so, the
stark itemizing of the shrines destroyed, with its implication of
bitterness and sorrow, its tone of resignation to the divine will, and
its faith in the retribution of the culprit, are all reminiscent to no
little extent of the emotionally more explicit and demonstrative
laments that have come down to us from later times.

Once on its way, the lamentation genre no doubt grew and developed among the Sumerian poets during the distressing days of
the Dynasty of Akkad, when the mighty Sargon and his successors
attacked and conquered such cities as Erech, Ur, Lagash, Umma,
and Adab. But as of today, no lamentation from those days, when
Akkadian power and influence began to prevail in Sumer, have
come down to us. Nor, for that matter, from the Gutian period
that followed, when chaos, anarchy, and famine raged in the land,

when its people were massacred and its cities destroyed, when, therefore, the dirge and lament must have been an important literary form of the poets.

One period in the history of Sumer and Akkad when, it may be surmised, the lamentation certainly did not flourish, or indeed exist at all, was that of the Third Dynasty of Ur. For following the glorious victory over the Gutians by Utuhegal of Erech and the establishment of Ur by Ur-Nammu as the capital of a renascent, powerful Sumer and Akkad, the poets naturally turned to the joyous glorification of its gods and rulers as well as to such compositions as heroic epic tales and divine myths—this was no time for weeping and lamenting, as is evident from the hymns composed for Ur-Nammu's son, Shulgi (see Chapter 31).

Little did Shulgi and his court bards dream that only half a century later, the mournful, plaintive lament would become a major component of the Sumerian literary and liturgical repertoire, a role it would continue to have for well-nigh two millennia. For the tragic destruction of Ur by the Su-people and the Elamites, and the carrying off into captivity of its pathetic ruler, Shulgi's grandson, Ibbi-Sin, left a distressing and harrowing impress on the Sumerian poets, particularly those who studied in the academies of Ur and Nippur which the wise, learned, and mighty Shulgi boasts of establishing. And when in the years following this calamitous catastrophe, some of these bards were called upon to help conduct the temple services and to prepare the liturgies accompanying them, they were moved to compose poems of considerable length, consisting primarily of mournful and sorrowful laments over the bitter fate that afflicted Sumer and its cities, especially Ur and Nippur, though they ended on a note of confidence and hope, of deliverance and restoration.

In the centuries that followed, the lamentation genre was altered and modified with time and place, gradually evolving into a liturgical stereotype used throughout the temples of Babylonia right down to the Seleucid period—it seems to have struck a responsive note in the rather melancholy, jaundiced, and ominous Mesopotamian experience. Just how deeply this mournful literary genre affected the neighboring lands is unknown, no lamentations have as yet been recovered from Hittite, Canaanite, or Hurrian sources.

But there is little doubt that the Biblical Book of Lamentations owes no little of its form and content to its Mesopotamian forerunners, and that the modern orthodox Jew who utters his mournful lament at the "Western Wall" of Solomon's long-destroyed Temple, is carrying on a tradition begun in Sumer some 4,000 years ago where, to cite a line from the "Lamentation over the Destruction of Sumer and Ur": "By its (Ur's) walls as far they extended in circumference, laments were uttered."

"The Lamentation over the Destruction of Nippur," the third of the three documents referred to at the end of the preceding chapter, is a lamentation in its first part only, the second, and larger part, is actually a song of jubilation celebrating the deliverance of Nippur by Ishme-Dagan, who began his reign about half a century after Ibbi-Sin, the last ruler of the Third Dynasty of Ur. It is composed of twelve stanzas, as follows:

The first stanza begins with a passage dominated by the plaintive refrain, "when will it be restored?" "it" referring to one or another of the Nippur shrines. There follows a lament over the destruction and ravages of Nippur: its rites and ritual feasts are no longer celebrated; the city in whose midst the gods issued their instructions for the guidance of mankind and made known their decisions, the city where the gods have established their dwellings and where they partake of their sacred food, the city that refreshed the blackheaded people with its shade—that city, Nippur, has been made desolate, and its people have been dispersed like scattered cows; its gods no longer care for it, and its great estates that were full of hustle and bustle, lie desolate and abandoned. Why, cries the poet, have the multitudinous shrines of Nippur perished! How long will the blackheaded people lie prostrate, eat grass like sheep, suffer in body and spirit! Why do the musicians and bards spend the day in wails and laments, mourning in exile for their destroyed cities and abandoned families, so much so that all reason is lost and understanding confused.

In the second stanza, the poet depicts the city itself bewailing and bemoaning the dreadful misfortunes that have befallen it: the desecration of its rites and rituals; the slaughter and despoliation of its people; the massacre of its young men and women; the bitterness of its temple that walks about like a mother cow separated from its young. No wonder, the poet continues, that the minstrels accustomed to sweet music now turn their songs to a lament that sounds like a nursemaid's lullaby. Because Enlil, the lord of the city, had turned away from it, its temple, the Ekur, once foremost in the land, and had given guidance to the blackheaded people—how the city was destroyed and ravaged!

The third stanza beginning with the plaintive query, "The city—till when will its angered (?) lord not turn to it and utter its 'Enough' (to its suffering)," the poet continues with such anguished plaints as, Why has he forsaken its brickwork and made its cooing doves fly away from their cotes! Why has he turned away from the house accustomed to sweet music! Why did be abandon and reject its *me* as if they were unsanctified, and its rituals as if they had not placated (?) all the lands! Why, indifferent to its fate, did he strike it down as if it were of no account! Why has he banished joy from its brickwork, and filled its heart with lament day and night! Lo, continues the poet, because he treated the city with bitter enmity, because its lord has turned his hand against it like an evil wind, its house has been destroyed, its foundations uprooted, torn up by the pickaxe, and its women and children put to death. The city has fallen into ruins, its possessions have been carried off, its reason gone, its conduct confused, its food and drink carried off. The house, the Ekur, the poet concludes, has been treated with bitter enmity and therefore multiplies in wailing and lamenting, while its sweet-singing minstrels echo its suffering. Enlil has banished its *me*, he no longer "touches its arm," or takes heed of its condition.

But now, in the fourth stanza, comes the first glimmer of hope for Nippur's deliverance and restoration. The stanza consists entirely of a soliloquy uttered by the city itself. As a result of the persistence of her poets, minstrels, and bards in lamenting and bemoaning her bitter fate, her suffering spirit, her anguished heart, the destruction of her shrines, and her "land" as a whole, the lord Enlil, the father of all the "blackheads," took pity on her and ordered her restoration.

The hopeful note of Nippur's deliverance is further developed in the fifth stanza, which consists entirely of an address by the poet to the city. He first makes the joyous announcement of the good news that Enlil has accepted her tears and laments, and then implores her to keep on praying to Enlil for help and support. The stanza concludes with the happy promise that Enlil will show the city mercy and kindness, and transform her anguish to cheer; he will grant joyfully that she hold high her head, and will turn back any inimical deed directed against her.

In the sixth stanza, the poet continues to address the city, depicting her deliverance no longer as a promise for the future, but as an actual reality: Her lord has taken pity on her and blessed her and said, "It is enough," and brought her joyfulness of spirit; he has made the mighty god Ninurta, the son of Enlil, her guardian. And best of all, he has commissioned Ishme-Dagan, his beloved shepherd, to rebuild the mighty Ekur and to restore everything that befits it, reinstituting its rites and rituals which the enemy has suppressed and its *me* that have been dispersed.

In the seventh stanza, the poet continues to comfort Nippur with the glad tidings that Enlil has taken pity on her; that he has caused lamenting to depart from the city and brought in its stead happiness of spirit; that he has commanded its restoration. Moreover, the poet continues, Ninlil, the great mother, has offered a prayer to her husband Enlil, pleading with him to rebuild her house. And so, after the two deities had taken counsel together, Enlil turned the destroyed house into a gracious house; turned back its tears and made joy enter; decreed for it the hum of the pouring of libations; cried: "Enough! Till when! Cease weeping!"; blessed it with a long reign. Enlil, the poet continues, also blessed the *gashua* shrine; both Enlil and Ninlil set up their daises in the Ekur, supplied with food and strong drink, and took counsel to establish firmly the blackheads in their habitations; Enlil returned to Nippur the people who had departed in all directions, "the children from whom their mothers had turned away," "the people who had wandered to wherever they could rest their head."

The theme that it was not Nippur alone, but that all of Sumer and Akkad as well, were delivered by Ishme-Dagan from enemy hands, is elaborated in the eighth stanza which records the restoration of the major cities: Eridu, the seat of wisdom; Ur, the city founded in meadow land; Erech-Kullab, the handiwork of the gods; Zabalam whose "strength had come to an end like the hierodule of

An"; Lagash, An's "great sword"; "Girsu," founded in days of yore; Umma, that had been occupied by the barbarian Tidnumites; Kish, the leading city of Sumer and Akkad; Mardu, the city blessed with fresh water and rich grain. And lastly, there was Isin, Ishme-Dagan's capital, the city whose reign the gods Enlil, Enki, and Ninmah had set to endure for a long time, the city that they had turned over to Ninurta, the mighty hero, and where they had ordained that Ninisinna, "the great daughter of An," "the dream-interpretess of the land," should refresh herself in her lofty temple, and that her son Damu should subdue all the foreign lands.

In the ninth stanza, the poet depicts the days of prosperity and well-being which Enlil has now brought to Nippur and all of Sumer and Akkad, days in which "Nippur raised high its head" and the Ekur prospered; days in which Sumer and Akkad expanded; "houses were built, fields fenced about"; "seed came forth, living creatures were born"; "stalls were built, sheepfolds founded"; "adversity was turned into prosperity" and "justice was proclaimed in the land"; "the ewe gave birth to the lamb, the mother-goat gave birth to the kid"; "the ewe multiplied its lambs, the mother-goat multiplied its kids."

The theme of divine deliverance and restoration is continued and developed in the tenth stanza, although it is primarily Nippur and the Ekur rather than the land as a whole that the poet celebrates, and especially the joyous reestablishment of the food offerings for the tables of the gods, provided in large quantities by Ishme-Dagan in the Ekur, once again pure and holy.

In the eleventh stanza, the poet depicts the utopian days that Enlil has ordained for its people: days when no man will utter an unfriendly word to his fellow man and the son will respect the father; days when humility will prevail, the nobles honored by the lowly, the older brother esteemed by the younger brother; days when the weak will have no complaint against the strong and kindliness will prevail; days when man will travel wherever his heart desires without fear or hindrance; days when bitterness will have departed from the sun-drenched land, when blackness will have been expelled and all breathing creatures will rejoice.

The twelfth and last stanza is devoted almost entirely to Ishme-Dagan's acts of piety. After shedding tears before the merciful

Enlil, Ishme-Dagan put in good order the *me* that had been defiled, sanctified the rites that had been abrogated, as well as the *giguna* which he filled with abundance, comfort, and joy. He then offered prayers, supplications, and orisons to Enlil who, pleased with his piety, humility, and religiosity, ordained for him a happy reign during which the people will live in security. And so, concludes the poet, all the people of Sumer and Akkad will glorify the loftiness of Enlil, "the great mountain," the ruler of heaven and earth.

Ishme-Dagan, the savior of Nippur and Sumer, as well as many of his predecessors and successors, were exalted by the Sumerian poets and bards in royal hymns reminiscent to no little extent of the royal psalms in the Book of Psalms that eulogize and glorify the king as the shepherd of Israel to whom the Lord had said: "You are my son and I am your father." The king is depicted by the psalmists as one endowed with princely gifts from birth and blessed from the womb; he has been given a scepter as a symbol of his power; he wears a gold crown on his head, and is covered with majesty and glory. Just and righteous, he crushes the oppressor and gives succor to the poor and needy; he destroys and annihilates all enemies and brings peace and prosperity to his people; he is blessed with long life, an enduring reign, and long-lived name and fame. All these royal qualities, virtues, and achievements—and a good many more—are attributed, as will be demonstrated in the following chapter, by the Sumerian "psalmists" to the king of Sumer, the faithful shepherd of the land, whom the people envisaged as an ideal, Messianic ruler.

THE FIRST MESSIAHS

BEGINNING WITH UR-NAMMU of Ur (and probably even earlier), and continuing right down to Hammurabi of Babylon and his successors, the Sumerian poets composed a varied assortment of royal hymns that glorify the ruler in hyperbolic diction and extravagant imagery; they tell us very little about the king's true character and authentic historical achievements, but they do reveal the ideal type of ruler, a kind of Sumerian Messiah, whom the people must have envisaged and longed for. In this chapter I have collected some of the more significant relevant statements that help to depict in one way or another the attributes and qualities, the powers and duties, the deeds and achievements of the ruler.

To start with the ideal king's embryonic beginnings, it is of interest to note that the poets who composed the royal hymns conceived of his birth on two levels, the human and the divine, and that it was the latter rather than the former that was close to their heart—hardly ever do they mention the name of the real parents of the king. On the divine level, on the contrary, the hymnal poets rarely fail to mention the ruler's parentage, although the relevant statements are usually rather brief and at times contradictory, or seemingly so. In the case of the kings of the Third Dynasty of Ur, the divine parents are Lugalbanda (a deified hero) and his wife, the goddess Ninsun. In case of the later kings, the parents were usually said to be the great god Enlil and his wife Ninlil, while Hammurabi, on the other hand, boasts of Marduk as his father.

One of the more poetic stylistic features of the royal hymns is the use of imaginative symbolism taken primarily from the animal kingdom, and more rarely from the world of vegetation. Thus in connection with the royal birth, a king may be described as a "true offspring engendered by a bull, speckled of head and body"; "a calf of an all-white cow, thick of neck, raised in a stall"; "a king born of a wild cow, nourished (?) on cream and milk"; "a calf born in a stall of plenty" "a young bull born in a year of plenty, fed on rich milk in halcyon days"; "a fierce-eyed lion born of a dragon"; "a fierce panther (?) fed on rich milk, a thick-horned bull born to a big lion"; "a mighty warrior born to a lion."

The king came into the world blessed from the womb, if we take literally such exulting phrases as "from the womb of my mother Ninsun a sweet blessing went forth for me"; "I am a warrior from the womb, I am a mighty man from birth"; "I am a noble son blessed from the womb"; "I am a king adored, a fecund seed from the womb"; "a prince fit (?) for kingship from the fecund womb." But it must have been during, or following, his coronation, or when he was about to conduct a campaign against the enemy that the poets envisaged him as receiving various divine blessings, most frequently from Enlil of Nippur. Usually this came about through the intervention of another deity. A vivid, concrete example of this procedure as imagined by the poets, is provided by a Shulgi hymn which states that the king "on the day he had been raised to kingship," came before Nanna, the tutelary deity of Ur, with a promise to joyfully restore the *me*. Whereupon the god journeyed to Nippur, entered the Ekur where he was greeted by the assembly of the gods, and addressed Enlil as follows:

> "Father Enlil, lord whose command cannot be turned back,
> Father of the gods who established the *me*,
> You have lifted your face upon my city, you have decreed the
>   fate of Ur,
> Bless the just king whom I have called to my holy heart,
> The king, the shepherd Shulgi, the faithful shepherd full of grace,
> Let him subjugate the foreign land for me."

Enlil, the poet continues, responded favorably to Nanna's plea, and the god returned to Ur with Enlil's blessing and said to Shulgi:

> "Enlil has perfected for you the might of the land,
> Son of Ninsun, king, shepherd Shulgi, may your scepter reach afar.

According to the author of this hymn, Nanna went alone to the

Ekur to obtain the blessing for Shulgi, the king himself stayed in Ur. But there are hymns that depict the intervening deity taking the king along to receive the blessing directly from Enlil's mouth. Thus according to a hymn concerned with Ishme-Dagan, the king is brought to the Ekur by the goddess Bau who asks for his blessing, which Enlil proceeds to pronounce in words that summarize succinctly everything essential for an ideal reign: a throne that gathers all the *me*; an enduring crown; a scepter that exercises firm control over the people; overflow of rivers; fertility of the womb and soil; a name famous and glorious; tribute from the lands near and far; the sending of perennial gifts to the Ekur of Nippur.

Another hymn, one that is even more instructive for the concrete, realistic manner in which the poets envisioned the king's divine benediction, involves the goddess Inanna and her royal husband Ur-Ninurta. This composition begins by stating that Inanna, having made up her mind to see to it that the *me* of kingship be restored and that the "blackheads" be properly guided and governed, has chosen Ur-Ninurta as the shepherd over all the people. Powerful goddess though she was, she nevertheless deems it necessary first to obtain for him the blessings of An and Enlil, both of whom reside in the Ekur of Nippur. She therefore takes the king by the hand, brings him to the Ekur, and implores the two deities for their benediction. An responds first with a series of blessings addressed directly to the king, and Enlil follows with his benediction. After the assembly of the gods in Nippur had said "Amen" to these blessings, Inanna turned over to Ninurta all the "lofty" *me*, and the two of them left the Ekur together for their own domicile where the goddess further eulogizes the king as the blessed of Enlil.

The king, however, did not always have the need of a deity to intervene in his behalf; he could journey all alone to receive blessings from various gods. Shulgi, for example, according to one hymn, traveled by boat first to Erech where, following the performance of the "Sacred Marriage" rite, Inanna blesses and exalts him as the one truly fit for royalty in all its aspects. From Erech he continues his journey to two other cities and is blessed and exalted by their tutelary deities. Finally he arrives in his own city Ur where he presents offerings to Nanna and is further extolled and blessed.

Between the king's birth and his coronation were the days of his childhood and adolescence, and the modern historian is eager for information about the education and upbringing of the king to be. But as of today there is only one hymn that intimates anything at all about the young prince's education, and that only in a very brief passage. However, if taken at its face value, or even if true in part only, its content is most enlightening and culturally speaking, invaluable. In this hymn king Shulgi has this to say about his education:

> During my youth there was the *edubba* (school) where
> On the tablets of Sumer and Akkad I learned the scribal art,
> No youth could write as well as I on clay,
> I was instructed (?) in the learned places of the scribal art,
> I finished to the very end subtraction, addition, arithmetic,
>   accounting,
> Nidaba, the fair *Nanibgal,*
> Has given me generously of wisdom and understanding,
> I am a dextrous scribe whom nothing impedes.

In short, this king, if we may trust the hymn, was himself one of the most literate and erudite personages of his realm.

A few rather vague "human-interest" particulars about the life of a very young prince and motherly love may be gathered from a composition that is not a hymn but a lullaby purported to be uttered by the wife of Shulgi to her ill and restless son (see Chapter 35). In this poem we read of the mother rocking her son to sleep, as it were, with wistful, reassuring chants, and promises of sweet little cheeses and well-watered lettuce, as well as with such blessings as a loving wife, and beloved children attended by a joyous nursemaid, abundance of food, good angels, and a happy reign, once he comes to the throne.

But whatever his education and upbringing, the king of Sumer and Akkad, was the perfect, ideal man: physically powerful and distinguished-looking; intellectually without peer; spiritually, a paragon of piety and probity. Ur-Nammu is described as a "comely lord" invested with grace and a halo of splendor. Shulgi has a comely mouth and a countenance most fair; his "lapis lazuli" beard overlaying his holy chest is a wonder to behold; his majestic appearance qualifies him eminently for dais and throne, and for the precious regalia that cover him from the crown on his head to the sandals on his feet. Lipit-Ishtar has a "lapis lazuli" beard, a fair countenance, a comely mouth that makes bright the heart, a figure full of grace, lips that are the ornament of speech, fingers fair—he is a virile man sweet to gaze at. Ur-Ninurta is a comely, virile man with fair limbs, he is full of grace, an ornament of lordship. Rim-Sin has a graceful forehead, princely (?) limbs, a tall figure.

Even more impressive than his majestic appearance were the king's physical powers, his courage and bravery. Shulgi, for example, is a warrior from the womb, a mighty man from the day he was born; his god Nanna gave him "warriorship" and might in his temple; Enlil gave him a "lofty arm"; he is a mighty king always in the van; he is a mighty warrior born to a lion; he is a king of pre-eminent strength, who exercises firmly his "warriorship," and who glorifies in song his strength and his might.

The importance attributed to the king's physique and courage is evidenced by the rich imagery and symbolism evolved by the hymnal poets: Shulgi is a lion with wide-open mouth; a great wild bull with powerful limbs; a dragon with the face of a lion; he is as strong as an oak (?) planted by the water course; a fertile *mes*-tree bedecked with fruit, sweet to gaze at. Ishme-Dagan is a tall *mes*-tree thick of root and wide of branch; a lofty mountain (?) that cannot be touched; he flashes brightly over the land like electrum (?); he is a cedar shoot planted in a cedar forest; he is luxuriant like the boxwood tree. Lipit-Ishtar holds high his head like a cedar shoot; he is a lion on the prowl that has no rival; an open-mouthed dragon that is the terror of the troops; a wild bull whom none dare attack.

The powerful physique and heroic bravery of the king were naturally of vital importance for victory in the recurrent destructive wars that plagued Sumer and Akkad. Many of the prayers interspersed in the royal hymns are for victory in war, and it is in connection with war that the poets evolved some of their more extravagant imagery: Shulgi is a torrent thundering against the rebellious land; his weapon grinds its teeth like a sharp-toothed beast; his fierce weapon pours out venom like a snake all set for the bite; his arrows fly into the battle like flying bats; his bow pierces like a dragon; he is a warrior in battle who knows no rival, a dragon whose tongue darts out against the enemy; he speeds to subdue the enemy like a lion. Ishme-Dagan is "a warrior of warriors," the wrath of weapons. Lipit-Ishtar is an attacking floodwave in battle; he flashes like lightning. Ur-Ninurta rages like a storm against the enemy; his halo of splendor covers the rebellious land like a heavy cloud.

Related to the king's prowess in war was his skill in the chase. Shulgi boasts that he hunts lions and serpents in the steppe man to man, as it were, without the aid of a net or an enclosure; he simply waits until the beast opens its mouth and hurls the spearhead into it. He claims to be so fast on his feet that he can catch a running gazelle.

The king was endowed with great wisdom and profound understanding as well as with physical prowess and heroic courage. Virtually all the kings in the hymnal repertoire were said to be endowed with wisdom by Enki, the god of wisdom, and with learning by Nidaba, the goddess of writing. The king was also psychologically penetrating and astute: he could give wise and eloquent counsel in the assembly; he could seek and find the wise word; he could discern "the words that were in the heart" to determine the true from the false; he cooled "the hot heart," and "put an end to the burning word." He had a great love for music and song, both of which he knew expertly and practiced diligently. At least this was true of Shulgi—a goodly part of at least two Shulgi hymns depict his devotion to music, both instrumental and vocal, and according to the author of one of these hymns, the king himself had "the power of a poet," and was able to compose songs and psalms.

Spiritually, the achievements of the king concerned two major areas: religion and social behavior. In the sphere of religion, it was the ruler's devotion to the cult that in the main interested the hymnal poets: the king knew how to serve the gods, and saw to it that the temple rites and rituals were properly consummated, that libations were offered daily as well as during the various monthly holidays and New Year day when the king's sacred marriage of Inanna was celebrated. Shulgi also claims that he could himself interpret oracles; carry out perfectly the lustration rites; fill the high priestly offices in accordance with the omens; read the precious words of the gods before going to war by examining the entrails of a white sheep. The hymns on the whole leave the impression that the king cared for the cult in all the more important religious centers of Sumer and Akkad. But it was the Ekur of Nippur that was uppermost in their minds; virtually every king in the repertoire brought gifts, offerings, and sacrifices to Enlil in his temple. As for social behavior, all the kings claimed to be compassionate and humanitarian, devoted to justice, equity, law, and ethical family conduct.

The Oriental monarchs, including those of Sumer and Akkad, are often cited by the modern historian as striking examples of despotic tyrants: cruel, oppressive, ruthless. This is certainly not how the Sumerian poets viewed their rulers; as they saw it, all the king's actions—conducting wars, constructing temples, maintaining the cult, digging and restoring canals, building and repairing highways, promulgating law codes—all had one supreme goal: to make the people happy, prosperous, and secure. This theme is an ever-recurring motif in the hymns: the king is the farmer who fills the granaries and the shepherd who enriches the stalls and the sheepfolds; he is the high protecting wall of the land; the people look up to him as their father, and live securely in his sweet shade. In brief, to quote the oft-repeated summary phrase of the poet: "he makes sweet the flesh of the people." To be sure this was not his sole motive; there was at least one other significant source of inspiration for the ruler's brave, wise, pious, and benevolent deeds: an obsessive, ambitious drive for fame and name. Throughout their hymns, the poets, who obviously had a vested interest in the glorification of the king and the celebration of his achievements, do not tire of reiterating that, as a result of his mighty deeds and unrivaled accomplishments, his "sweet," "noble" name will be honored and exalted in all the lands unto distant days, especially by the "scribes" of the *edubba*, that is by poets and men of letters like themselves.

Speed, as noted above, was an essential attribute of the ideal king, and there is one extant hymn that actually exalts the ruler as a champion long-distance runner. This unusual composition in which the king boasts of his love of the road and his interest in travel—he built the first "motel" in recorded history—is treated in detail in the following chapter.

THE FIRST
LONG-DISTANCE CHAMPION

ONE OF THE MORE renowned kings of Sumer and Akkad was Shulgi, the son of Ur-Nammu, the founder of the Third Dynasty of Ur, whose reign endured for well-nigh half a century. In fact, it is not too much to say that Shulgi was one of the most distinguished and influential monarchs of the ancient world as a whole, one who made his mark as an outstanding military leader, punctilious administrator, energetic builder of monumental temples, and as a cultural Maecenas. He extended Sumer's political power and influence from the Zagros ranges on the east to the Mediterranean Sea on the west. He instituted an effective bookkeeping and accounting system in palace and temple; rearranged the calendar and standardized weights and measures throughout the land. He brought to completion the construction of Sumer's most imposing stage tower, the *ziggurat* of Ur, which his father had left unfinished, and built numerous religious structures in a number of Sumerian cities. Finally, as has become more and more apparent in recent years, Shulgi was a lavish patron of the arts, especially of literature and music—he founded and liberally supported Sumer's two major *edubba*, at Ur and at Nippur. No wonder that the Sumerian poets and men of letters outdid themselves in composing hymns of exaltation and glorification in his honor, and one of the more remarkable of these is a hymn of 101 lines, which the king himself is purported to have uttered, and in which he portrays himself as a champion runner who used his gift of speed for cultic purposes, and as one who made travel pleasant and secure by improving

roads and highways as well as building garden-fringed rest houses—
the ancient counterparts of the modern motels—run by "friendly
folk," where the weary wayfarer could stay and refresh himself.

This rather unusual composition, which is partly narrative in
character, begins with an itemization of Shulgi's virtues and endow-
ments, typical of Sumerian royal hymnography except for the
rather surprising inclusion of his love of the road and passion for
speed.

> I, the king, a warrior from the (mother's) womb am I,
> I, Shulgi, a mighty man from (the day) I was born,
> A fierce-eyed lion born of a dragon am I,
> King of the four corners (of the universe) am I,
> Herdsman, shepherd of the blackheads am I,
> The trustworthy, the god of all the lands am I,
> The son born of Ninsun am I,
> Called to the heart of holy An am I,
> He who was blessed by Enlil am I,
> Shulgi, the beloved of Ninlil am I,
> Truly cherished by Nintu am I,
> Endowed with wisdom by Enki am I,
> The mighty king of Nanna am I,
> The open-mouthed lion of Utu am I,
> Shulgi chosen for the vulva of Inanna am I,
> A princely donkey all set for the road am I,
> A tail-swinging horse on the highway am I,
> A noble donkey of Sumugan eager for the course am I,
> The wise scribe of Nidaba am I.
> Like my heroship, like my might,
> I am accomplished in wisdom,
> I vie (?) with its (wisdom's) true word,
> I love justice,
> I do not love evil,
> I hate the evil word,
> I, Shulgi, a mighty king, supreme, am I.

Shulgi next elaborates on his great interest in travel, claiming that he
saw to it that the roads and highways of the land were always in
good repair, and that he constructed alongside of them rest houses
for the weary traveler:

> Because I am a powerful man rejoicing in his loins,
> I enlarged the footpaths, straightened the highways of the land,
> I made travel secure, built there "big house,"

> Planted gardens alongside of them, established resting-places there,
> Settled there friendly folk,
> (So that) who comes from below, who comes from above,
> Might refresh themselves at the cool of the day,
> The wayfarer who travels the highway at night,
> Might find refuge there as in a well-built city.

He then asserts that, eager to establish his name and fame as a champion runner, he made a journey from Nippur to Ur, a distance of fifteen "double-hours"—roughly about 100 miles, as if it were only one "double-hour":

> That my name be established unto distant days, that it leave not
>   the mouth (of men),
> That my praise be spread wide in the land,
> That I be eulogized in all the lands,
> I, the runner, rose in my strength, all set for the course,
> From Nippur to Ur,
> I resolved to traverse as if it were (but a distance) of one
>   "double-hour."
> Like a lion that wearies not of its virility I arose,
> Put a girdle (?) about my loins,
> Swung my arms like a dove feverishly fleeing a snake,
> Spread wide the knees like an Anzu bird with eyes lifted toward
>   the mountain.

Arriving at Ur amidst the plaudits of the multitudes, he brought immense sacrifices in the Ekishnugal, the far-famed temple of Sin, to the accompaniment of music and song:

> (The inhabitants of) the cities that I had founded in the land,
>   swarmed all about me,
> My blackheaded people, as numerous as ewes, marveled at me.
> Like a mountain kid hurrying to its shelter,
> When Utu shed his broad light on man's habitations,
> I entered the Ekishnugal,
> Filled with abundance the great stall, the house of Sin,
> Slaughtered oxen there, multiplied sheep,
> Made resound there the drum and the timbrel,
> Conducted there the *tigi*-music, the sweet.

After resting, bathing, and dining in his palace, he returned to Nippur in spite of a raging hail storm, and so could celebrate the *eshesh* feasts in both Ur and Nippur on the very same day:

> I, Shulgi, the multiplier of all things, brought bread-offerings
>   there,

Inspiring fear from my royal seat like a lion,
In the lofty palace of Ninegal,
I scoured my knees, bathed in fresh water,
Bent the knees, ate bread,
Like an owl (and) a falcon I arose,
Returned triumphantly to Nippur.

On that day, the storm howled, the tempest swirled,
The North Wind and the South Wind roared violently,
Lightning devoured in heaven alongside the seven winds,
The deafening storm made the earth tremble,
Ishkur thundered throughout the heavenly expanse,
The rains above embraced the waters below,
Its (the storm's) little stones, its big stones,
Lashed at my back.

(But) I, the king, was unafraid, uncowed,
Like a young lion I was set for the spring,
Like a donkey of the steppe I rushed forward,
My heart full of happiness I sped along the course,
Racing like a donkey foal journeying all alone,
(Like) Utu facing homeward,
I traversed the journey of fifteen "double-hours."
My acolytes gazed at me (in wonder),
As in one day I celebrated the *eshesh* feasts in (both) Ur (and
    Nippur).

There in Nippur, he banqueted with the sun-god Utu and his
(Shulgi's) divine spouse, the fertility goddess Inanna.

With virile Utu, my brother and friend,
I drank beer in the palace founded by An,
My minstrels sang for me the seven *tigi*-hymns,
My spouse, the maid Inanna, the queen, the luxuriance of heaven
    and earth,
Seated me by her side at its (the palace's) banquet,
I exalted myself (saying):
"Wheresoever I lift my eyes, thither will you go with me,
Wheresoever my heart moves me, there you will be welcomed."

It was in Nippur, too, that the god An invested him with the royal
insignia, so that he became a mighty king whose power and glory
were exalted in the four corners of the universe.

An set the holy crown upon my head,
Gave me to hold the scepter in the "lapis-lazuli" Ekur,

Raised heaven-high (my) firmly founded throne on the white
dais,
Exalted there the power of my kingship,
(So that) I bent low all the foreign lands, made secure the Land
(Sumer)
(And) the four corners of the universe, the people with heads
bowed call my name,
Chant holy songs,
Pronounce my exaltation (saying):
"He that is the noble power of kingship, the cherished one,
Presented by Sin out of the Ekishnugal,
Heroship, night, and a good life,
Endowed with noble power by Nunamnir,
Shulgi, the destroyer of all the foreign lands, who makes secure
the Land (Sumer),
Who in accordance with the *me* of the universe has no rival,
Shulgi, cherished by the trustworthy son of An (Nanna)!"
Oh, Nidaba, praise!

Hymns, laments, myths, epics, in fact the vast majority of the
Sumerian literary works, are all written in poetic form. The Sumerian poets, however, knew nothing of rhyme and meter; the main
stylistic devices were repetition, parallelism, epithets, and similes,
and it is the latter that will be analyzed and illustrated in the next
chapter.

THE FIRST LITERARY IMAGERY

F

OR OVER THIRTY YEARS now I have been stating in publication after publication that one of the outstanding contributions of this century to the humanities is the recovery, restoration, translation, and interpretation of the Sumerian literary documents, the vast majority of which were composed from about 2100 to 1800 B.C. Since this assertion might sound subjective and self-serving, let me summarize the data in its support.

At present, scattered throughout the museums the world over, there are more than 5,000 tablets and fragments inscribed with Sumerian literary works. Many of these are now available to the scholarly world in one form or another—originals, copies, photographs, and casts—and their contents have been, or are in the process of being painstakingly reconstructed by a number of cuneiformists. As a result it is now known that we have about 20 myths varying in length from just over 100 to close to 1,000 lines (about 5,000 lines in all); 9 epic tales varying in length from just over 100 lines to over 500 lines (about 3,000 lines in all); over one hundred hymns royal and divine varying in length from under 100 to close to 500 lines (about 10,000 lines at least); a score or so of lamentations and lamentation-like texts with about some 3,000 lines; 12 disputations and school essays with about 4,000 lines; a dozen or so collections of proverbs and precepts of some 3,000 lines. All in all, a total of some 28,000 lines!

Not a few of the compositions listed above still have considerable gaps in their text, but to make up for this, there are quite a number of tablets and fragments whose contents are as yet unidentifiable and unplaceable, and these will no doubt add several thousand lines to the total. Moreover we now have a number of literary catalogues compiled by the ancient schoolmen themselves, which list quite a number of compositions of which little or nothing has been recovered to date, although some of which no doubt will turn up in future excavations; these may well increase the total to forty or even fifty thousand lines. There is every reason to conclude, therefore, that quantitatively speaking the Sumerian *belles lettres* surpassed by far such ancient literary compilations as the *Iliad* and *Odyssey*, the *Rigveda*, and the more literary books of the Bible.

As for quality, most scholars, and I am one of them, would agree that the Sumerian literary works are inferior to the Greek and Hebrew classics in sensibility, perception, profundity, and artistry. Literary evaluation and appreciation, however, are matters of taste, and it is my feeling that when, in the course of time, the Sumerian *belles lettres* come to be better understood and lose some of the strangeness that veils them from the mind and heart of the modern reader, they will compare not too unfavorably with the literatures of the ancient Hebrews and Greeks. It is not altogether irrelevant to note that these later and more sophisticated literatures might never have come into being at all, had it not been for the innovative, pioneering Sumerian poets and scribes who prepared the way.

The vast majority of the Sumerian literary works are written in poetic form, characterized primarily by skillful use of repetition and parallelism, as well as by such figures of speech as metaphor and simile. This chapter presents a pioneering attempt at collecting and interpreting the more intelligible similes in more than a score of compositions representing virtually every Sumerian literary genre—myth, epic tale, hymn, lament, and "wisdom." The images evoked in these similes derive from nature, the animal world as well as man and his handiwork. Much of the "footwork" for this chapter was done by my young colleague at the University of Pennsylvania, Barry Eichler, who, in the course of time, had planned to prepare a far more comprehensive and thoroughgoing study of Sumerian imagery, and I take this opportunity to express to him my deep gratitude for his help in the preparation of this chapter, which is but a faint harbinger of better things to come.

The cosmic spheres and entities represented in Sumerian imagery are heaven, earth and sea, and the heavenly bodies, moon, sun, and star. Heaven appealed to the Sumerian poets because of its height. Nippur, Sumer's holy city is "as lofty as heaven"; the ziggurats (temple towers) are repeatedly described "as high as heaven"; the height of the goddess Inanna, according to a *magnificat* glorifying her powers and deeds "is like heaven." Related to heaven's height is its distance from the earth; hence we find one of Sumer's most famous rulers, Ur-Nammu, crying out in the Nether World against the injustice of the gods whom he had served piously during his lifetime but who failed to stand by him in his time of need, that "his good omen is as far away as heaven." Heaven's beauty also impressed the poets. King Shulgi, son of Ur-Nammu, following his victory over the enemy, and the avenging of his capital Ur, builds a boat and decorates it with "stars like heaven"; Nippur is described by one poet as "beautiful within and without like heaven."

Like the height of heaven, the width of the earth lent itself to ready comparison: the goddess Inanna, for example, in the *magnificat* mentioned above, was not only "as high as heaven," but also "as wide as the earth." The earth was also thought as eternally enduring; hence the rituals of the Ekur, Sumer's holiest temple, were "as everlasting as the earth." The sea, on the other hand, seems to have been used sparingly in Sumerian imagery; the only example found in the texts utilized for this study is "as terrifying as the sea."

Height, as might be expected, is also used in the imagery of the moon: mountains, for example, are as high as Nanna (i.e. "the moon") in the upper sky. But it is the beauty of its light that appealed most to the poets: Inanna (i.e. the Venus star) "shines forth like the moonlight"; she (Inanna) is filled with beauty like the "rising moonlight." Light, too, is naturally the most attractive feature of the sun: the king Lipit-Ishtar boasts of "coming forth like the sun, the light of the land"; temples "fill the land with sunlight" and are adorned with "splendid horns like the sun coming forth from its *ganun*." But since, according to the Sumerian theologians, the sun is also the god of justice, kings boast of making "just decisions" like Utu, the sun-god.

In contrast to the light of the moon and the sun, it was the dimness of dusk that served for poetic comparison. Thus, the depth of the downfall of the Ekishnugal, the great temple of the moon-god at Ur, is described in these words:

> It (the Ekishnugal) that had filled the land like sunlight,
> (now) has become as dim as dusk.

However, since dusk is the time of the golden sunset, one poet seems to describe it "as going to its house with blood-filled face." As for the stars, it was their permanence rather than their twinkling that seemed to impress the poets; hence the prayer that Ur "should not come to an end, like a star."

Turning to weather phenomena, it is not surprising to find that the leading place was given to Mesopotamia's major affliction, the storm —the Near-East counterpart to our hurricane and tornado. Angered gods rage about "like the storm"; fierce winds destroy cities "like a flood-storm"; the vengeful Inanna attacks again and again in battle, "like the all-attacking storm"; when the great gods decreed the destruction of Ur during the reign of its last and rather pathetic king, Ibbi-Sin, they sent a deluge that "roared like a great storm over the earth. Who could escape it!"

A weaker relative of the storm is the "torrent" (literally "the gushing forth of high waters). Thus we read that "fierce winds cannot be restrained like torrents"; in order to destroy Ur, the gods sent the cruel Elamites who "trampled it like a torrent"; and if correctly interpreted, we find the oldest counterpart to our English "torrent of words" in the epic tale "Enmerkar and the Lord of Aratta," in the line, "He (Enmerkar) spoke to his herald from where he sat, like a torrent."

The imagery evoked by rain was that of plentitude and copiousness: kings boast of pouring out libations of strong drink "like rain gushing from heaven"; and on a far more somber note, the arrows of the enemy fill the bodies of the people of Ur "like heavy rain." The observation that rain sinks into the earth and does not return to heaven provided the author of the "Lamentation over the Destruction of Ur" with the wishful curse against the storm that had attacked Ur that it "should not return to its place, like rain from heaven." As for water, we find the oldest counterpart of the sad but all too common simile "blood flowed like water," in the boast of Shulgi, that his weapon "made flow the blood of the people like water"; as well as the less apt but no less bitter image that "famine filled the city like water, there was no respite from it."

The obvious and widespread image of flashing lightning has its Sumerian counterparts in such royal boasts as arrows "flash before me like lightning," or "I am one who flashes in battle like lightning." And when the wandering hero Lugalbanda, eager to return to Erech as quickly as possible, asks the grateful Imdugud-bird for his blessing, he pleads: "I would rise like a flame, flash like lightning." The moon-god Sin, distraught because of the suffering of his city, pleads before his father Enlil: "On the anguished heart that you have made tremble like a flame, cast a friendly eye."

In the realm of nature, it was the mountain, high and pure, that played a significant role in Sumerian imagery: cities are made "pure as a mountain"; temples are built in pure places "like a rising mountain"; city walls reach to heaven like a mountain. But there was also the mined mountain whose cuts and gashes evoked thoughts of ruin and destruction; thus the angered Naram-Sin is depicted as forging mighty axes in order "to turn it (the Ekur) into dust like a mountain mined for silver, to cut it to pieces like a mountain of lapis lazuli." Rivers rarely served as images: in the material examined thus far, we find two rather forced and colorless similes: the gates of a city are said to open their mouths "like the Tigris emptying its waters into the sea," and the rivers of one unfortunate city were without water "like rivers cursed by the (water-god) Enki."

Vegetation, as might be expected in a basically agricultural country, is well represented in Sumerian imagery. The tree most popular with the poets was the cedar: Shulgi boasts that he is a "good shade" (for the land) like a cedar; Lipit-Ishtar heaped up incense "like a fragrant cedar forest." The date palm and especially the date palm of Dilmun was highly thought of: Shulgi, according to one poet was cherished by the goddess Ningal "like a date palm of Dilmun." But since virtually every part of the date palm was broken up and utilized in one form or another by the ancients, one poet was moved to lament that "a heavenly throne," as well as the temples' choice oxen and sheep were cut to pieces like date palms. The boxwood impressed the poets with its luxuriance and height; hence the lord Enmerkar wants the craftsmen of Aratta to build him a temple for Enki and make it "luxuriant like the boxwood." The still unidentified *mes*-tree was noted for its fruit, as may be surmised from such similes as "you (Shulgi) are a wondrous sight like a fertile *mes*-tree adorned with fruit; or the *gipar* (part of a temple) is piled high with fruit "like a *mes*-tree." The *ildag*-tree, perhaps a variety of the poplar, must have been remarkable for its strength; hence Shulgi is said to be "as vigorous as a mature *ildag*-tree planted by the water course."

Though the reed of Mesopotamia was put to many practical uses, it evoked a somber, melancholy mood in the poetic imagination. Hence the city Ur in its travail "droops its head like a solitary reed," and when Dumuzi, doomed to die as a surrogate for his angered wife Inanna, dreams of a solitary, drooping reed, it is interpreted as his mother "drooping her head" in melancholy anticipation of his death. Moreover the reed pipe was the musical instrument played on all sad, funereal occasions, and it is no wonder the great Shulgi, who boasts of his love for music and his ability to play any number of musical instruments, asserts that one instrument he did not like to play was the wailing reed pipe that brought nothing but sadness to man's spirit and heart. Reed rushes evoked images of tearing and plucking, as did also the easily plucked crunched leek, in spite of its value as a staple food.

The major source of imagery for the Sumerian poets was the animal kingdom, wild and domestic animals as well as birds and fish. The lion provided such expected stereotypical similes as "the king inspiring terror like a lion," or "springing forward like a lion"; a rather unusual example occurs in a mythical motif which describes angered waters attempting to destroy a boat by "devouring" its bow "like a wolf," and striking at its stern "like a lion." A messenger springing forward to hurry on his mission is like "a wolf pursuing a kid."

The wild ox, or "mountain bull," to use the literal meaning of the compound sign for the word, was a high favorite with the Sumerian poets: the *kiur* of the Ekur of Nippur, for example, raises its shining horns over Sumer "like a wild ox"; Ishme-Dagan boasts of being thick of neck "like a wild ox"; a man secure in his well-being is "like a wild ox," and (though this expressed a metaphor, rather than a simile), the city Ur, in its heyday, was "a great wild ox that steps forth confidently, secure in its own strength"; Shulgi is depicted as "adorned with splendid horns like a virile wild ox, born to a large wild ox." But powerful though he was, there seemed to be Sumerian "cowboys" who had no difficulty in catching and throwing him by means of a nose rope, the ancient equivalent of the modern lariat, to judge from such similes as "He (Gilgamesh) tied a nose rope to him (Huwawa), like a captured wild ox," or "The *Uskumgal*-statues were hurled to the ground by nose ropes like captured wild oxen." It sometimes took a considerable number of hunters to kill a large wild ox, as can be seen from a curse pronounced by the god Ninurta against the *sham*-stone, "Be divided up like a large wild ox killed by a company of men."

Unlike the wild ox, the wild cow is rarely used in the similes. There is but one example in our texts, and that rather ambiguous: a herald who had received a pleasing message for delivery to his king is said to have "turned on his thigh like a wild cow." For the elephant, too, there is only one reasonably intelligible simile, and that relates to his clumsiness: "You are (the kind of man) who climbs on a sinking boat like an elephant." The gazelle, in spite of its speed, was readily trapped and therefore evoked an image of utter defeat: "Like a gazelle caught in a trap, they (the people of Ur) bit the dust"; "I (Shulgi) trapped them (the enemy) like a gazelle in the thicket." It was the mountain kid rather than the gazelle that served as an image of speed; hence Shulgi's boast, "Like a mountain goat hurrying to its shelter . . . I entered the Ekishnugal." The suffering of animals who have drunk contaminated water serves as a simile for the agony of Ur-Namma's queen as a result of his death: "Like the beasts of the steppe brought to a foul well, a 'heavy hand' was placed upon her." Finally, the imagery of the snake relates to such obvious characteristics as crawling, slithering, and spitting forth venom.

Turning to domestic animals, we find the bull (or ox) like his wild ancestor, the wild ox, a high favorite in the imagery of the poets. The bull's bellowing roar served as an image for the voice of rulers, the busy bustle of a temple, the utterance of temple oracles —it is no wonder that the necks of Sumerian lyres are often adorned with the head of a bull. The image of the firm-standing bull appears in such similes as "He (Gilgamesh) stood on the 'great earth' like a bull"; "the hero (Ninurta) whom I lean on like a bull." But firmness can be carried to the point of obstinacy, hence the Sumerian counterpart of our "bullheaded" in the proverb: "You are (a man who) like a bull, does not know how to turn back." If angered, the bull becomes violent, hence the expression "to attack like a bull." The goddess Ningal who had abandoned her unfortunate city Ur is implored by the poet to return "like a bull to your stall, like a sheep to your fold." So too, the fish for whom a house, a kind of ancient aquarium, had been built is urged to enter "like a bull to your stall, like a sheep to your fold."

The ox, not permitted to eat any of the grain he threshes, serves as an image for the frustrated man: "He is a man deceived, like an ox escaping from the threshing floor." Oxen belonging to important bureaucrats were allowed to wander freely through the streets according to the proverb, "You wander about in the street like the ox of a *shabra* (a high official)." The oldest recorded example of "throwing the bull" (in the literal, not figurative, sense) is found in the Sumerian poet's lament that the great gods had made the bitter decision that Ur, "the city of lordship and kingship, built on pure soil, be thrown instantaneously by the nose rope, fastened neck to earth, like a bull." And the pathos of the bull thrown to the ground is revealed in Ningal's bitter words, "Like a fallen bull I cannot rise up from your wall (*your* refers to her destroyed city Ur)."

The cow, ulike the bull failed to inspire the poetic imagination. Of the two intelligible similes found in our texts, one seems to relate to compassion: the goddess Ningal, on witnessing the suffering of her city Ur, is said to prostrate herself on the ground "like a cow for her calf"; the other is in a proverb that characterizes a man given to illusions in these words: "Like a barren cow you keep on seeking your calf which does not exist."

Ewes were images of fecundity, hence the oft-repeated simile "as numerous as ewes." But they were readily scattered, and the people of Aratta in distress are compared to "scattered ewes." The ewes were often deprived of their lambs, hence the goddess Ningal's bitter lament, "Oh my city, like an innocent ewe your lamb has been torn from you." The eagerness of sheep to return "home" prompted the simile cited earlier in connection with the ox: "Like an ox to your stall, like sheep to your fold," and the more "book-ish" comparison in "When you (the fish urged to enter the house newly built for him) raise the head like a sheep to the sheepfold, the shepherd Dumuzi will rejoice with you."

The image of the heavily-laden donkey, the beast of burden of the ancient world, prompted the rather obvious simile: "The Elamites and Subarians (Sumer's inimical neighbors) carried (to Agade) all sorts of goods like sack-laden donkeys." The characteristic stubbornness of the donkey seems to be the source of the rather strange-sounding proverb: "Into a plague-stricken city he has to be driven like a rebellious (?) donkey." It is probably the stupidity of the donkey that is alluded to in a proverb of no little cultural significance that seems to say, "I will not marry a wife who is (only) three years old, like a donkey." The Sumerian poets also knew of wild donkeys, "donkeys of the steppe," and carefully-bred "noble donkeys," all of which evoked images primarily of speed on journeys made by heralds or by travel-minded kings, such as Shulgi, the oldest known counterpart to the modern speed maniac.

The dog, his character, and way of life evoked images which, if correctly interpreted, are of no little cultural and psychological significance: a woman suffering in silence is "like a dog imprisoned in a cage"; the blood-thirsty goddess Inanna devours dead bodies "like a dog"; a man who stands up for his rights is one "who hates to grovel as if he were a dog"; there is also the chap who whelps like "a 'noble' dog beaten by a stick," and the man who has to be admonished not to let himself be mauled by a noble dog "like a bone"; and there is finally the man who acts high-handedly like the "bitch of the scribe."

Birds and their imagery may be divided into two groups. The large birds of prey naturally invoked images of fearless flight: people swoop down on a banquet "like eagles"; Shulgi boasts of rising (in flight) like a falcon; the soul flies from Dumuzi's body, "like a falcon flying against another bird." As for the smaller birds, it is perhaps not without significance for Sumerian culture and character that they did not inspire images of "sweet song," but of terror and mourning: the goddess Ningal flees her destroyed city Ur, "like a flying bird"; pathetic Ibbi-Sin led away captive by the Elamites "will not return to his city like a sparrow that has fled its house"; the high priestess Enheduanna bemoans her fate, saying, "I was forced to flee the cote like a sparrow"; a husband lamenting the death of his wife moans "like a dove in its hole," thrashes about "like a dove in terror"; Shulgi boasts of swinging his arms "like a dove hysterically fleeing a snake."

Bats evoke a similar imagery: "The Anunna, the great gods" flee before Inanna "like fluttering bats to the clefts," the *barbar*-arrows are said to fly in battle "like flying bats." A rare example of an image for tenderness is provided by the as yet unidentified *gam-gam*-bird in the simile: "They (the friends of the sick hero Lugal-banda) gave him food to eat and water to drink like a *gamgam*-fledgling sitting in his nest."

From the insect world, the locust is repeatedly used as an image of devouring and destruction: the possessions of Ur are devoured as by a "heavy swarm of locusts." Shulgi boasts of making the enemy "eat bitter dust like an all-covering locust," and of cutting down the enemy with throw sticks (?) and slingshots "like a locust." Flies, on the contrary, though assuredly a pest and nuisance in Sumer, provide but one simile in our texts, and that rather bland and uninformative: the two sexless creatures especially fashioned by Enki, the god of wisdom, and sent down to the Nether World to flatter its queen Ereshkigal and thus gain access to the "water of life" under her charge, are said to "fly about the door (of Eresh-kigal's palace) like flies." The ant, not unlike the sparrow, dove, and bat, served as an image for terrified men as well as gods seeking refuge and who are described as scurrying into crevices "like ants."

Fish invoked the tragic image of death: the life of the people of Ur is carried off like "fish caught by the hand" or "like fish writh-ing for lack (?) of water"; the little children (of Ur) lying in their mother's lap "were carried off by the waters like fish."

The imagery of inanimate objects, primarily man's artifacts and handiwork, is limited in number and rather poor in quality, but it does help to illuminate certain aspects of Sumerian culture. The "city" appears in one rather interesting simile that records the building of man's first road house or "motel": "He (the night traveler) will find refuge there (in the rest house especially built by Shulgi) like a well built city." In two other similes, however, it is the ruined city that is depicted: Ur is a ruin "like a city torn up by the pickaxe," and the impious Naram-Sin plans to raze the Ekur to the ground "like a city ravaged by Ishkur." High walls and large doors are said to "lock" the approaches of Sumer or the neighboring highland. The gates of the cities were closed at night; hence the simile, "May the door be closed on it (the destructive storm) like the gates of the night." Stalls, sheepfolds, and garden huts serve as comparisons for destroyed cities because of the ease with which they cave in and fall apart. Copper is depicted as piled up on the city quay "like heaps of grain." Molten copper and tin serve as an image for blood flowing in devastated Ur. Stones are said to be crushed "like flour," cut up "like sacks," and plucked "like rushes."

Milk, strange as it may seem, provides an image for the emptying of a city or land in such similes as "Gaesh is poured out like milk by the enemy" or "Ningirsu emptied out Sumer like milk." As for fat, dead bodies melt away "like fat in the sun." Ghee, on the contrary, is used as an image for the ease with which goddesses give birth to their progeny. Honey naturally implied sweetness: words are "sweet" and the lover is a "honey man."

Thirty shekels, for some unknown reason, is an image of contempt and disregard: "Like a runner contemptuous (?) of his body's strength he treated the *giguna* (of the Ekur) like thirty shekels." Gilgamesh is said to handle his armor weighing fifty minas as lightly as thirty shekels. The broken pot and the potsherd, the joy and delight of today's archaeologist, were images of shattering and abandonment. The parched oven is an image for the desiccated plain and steppe. Garments and linen are used for such comparisons as "Your (Ninurta's) awe-inspiring *melam* covered Enlil's shrine like a garment"; "It (the storm) covered Ur like a garment, enveloped it like linen"; He (Gilgamesh) clothed himself with "the word of heroism like a garment, enveloped himself with it like linen." The clinging rag served as an image of Namtar, the demon of death: "Namtar is a biting dog; he clings like a rag." The storm-tossed boat is an image for the distraught wife of Ur-Nammu who "was set adrift in a tempestuous storm like a boat, her anchor was of no avail." A man of vacillating character is one who "bobs up and down in the water like a boat." The boat provided a cumulative series of tersely worded comparisons in one of the most extended similes as yet known from Sumerian literature which reads (the Imdugud-bird is speaking to the hero of Lugalbanda who is eager to return to his city Kullab):

> Come my Lugalbanda,
> Like a boat (laden with) metal,
>   like a boat (laden with) grain,
> Like a boat (laden with) *balbale*-apples,
> Like a boat (laden with) well-shaded (?) cucumbers,
> Like a boat, a place of luxuriant harvest,
> Go head high to the brickwork of Kullab.

The gods and their attributes appear but rarely in the similes. In addition to the sun-god Utu, the moon-god Nanna, and the god of dusk, Usan, cited above in connection with cosmic imagery, we find two similes pertaining to the thundering storm-god Ishkur: when Inanna thunders "like Ishkur, all vegetation comes to an end"; sundry musical instruments are said to be played "like Ishkur." There is also one relating to the warrior-god Ninurta: heroes are depicted as wearing helmets and "lion"-garments to battle "like Ninurta, the son of Enlil."

The mythological creatures and monsters that occur in similes are the Mushhush (raging serpent). Shulgi boasts of releasing his bow, "ready to pierce like a Mushhush; the Imdugud-bird: Shulgi runs as swiftly "as the Imdugud-bird whose face is lifted toward the highland"; the Gudanna (Bull of Heaven): (the people of) Kish are put to death like the Gudanna; the Gudmah (Giant Bull): the house of Erech was ground to dust like the Gudmah; and above all the venon-spitting Ushumgal (Dragon): Inanna fills the (inimical) land with venom "like an Ushumgal"; weapons pour venom into the enemy "like an Ushumgal prepared to bite"; weapons devour corpses "like an Ushumgal"; Enmerkar's herald is said to travel as swiftly "as an Ushumgal seeking his prey in the steppe."

We come at last to man and the imagery which he invoked and which sheds some light on certain aspects of Sumerian character and culture. There was, of course, the kindly, protective father and mother: Ishme-Dagan, for example, compares himself to a "good father and watchful mother," and as one to whom "all the lands direct their eyes "like the father who begot them." The crying child is naturally an image of tragic suffering. A Sumerian "Job" says bitterly, "Suffering overwhelms me like a weeping child"; desolated Ur goes about looking for its goddess Ningal "like a child (wandering) in the devasted streets"; and rather strangely, "the fish in its muttering is like a crying child."

The well-to-do farmer is the very image of a happy man, if we may judge from Enkidu's report to Gilgamesh about "life" in the Nether World, in which he states that the man who had four sons on earth is "as happy as the man who yokes four asses," and that the man who had six sons is "as happy as a ploughman." From the same report we learn that success came readily to a fluent scribe, for the man who had five sons could go straight to (Ereshkigal's) palace "like a goodly scribe whose arm was open." The shepherd appears in such similes as "Let him (the Lord of Aratta) follow behind them like their shepherd" and "May he (the king) multiply the sheepfolds like a trustworthy shepherd." As for rich and poor, we find the lord contrasted with the slave in the tersely worded proverb: "Build like lord, live like a slave; build like a slave, live like a lord." The sad plight of the poor prompted such similes as "Your (desolate) house stretches (its) hands to you (Mother Ningal) like a man who has lost all," and the command to the goddess Ninshubur lamenting the death of her mistress: "Like a pauper in a single garment dress for me."

Sumer had its share of drunkards, gluttons, bandits, and foulmouthed prostitutes. Hence such similes as "Your *lahama*-statues that stand in the *dubla* (temple terrace) lie prostrate like huge fighting men drunk with wine"; "Your land holds its mouth, like a man who has overeaten." "He (Naram-Sin) erected large ladders against the house (the Ekur) like a bandit who plunders a city." "Its (the bird's) mouth hurled invectives like a prostitute."

That the Sumerians were eager for fame and glory, admiration and applause, is well known from their heroic epic tales and boastful royal hymns. Still, it is not uninteresting to read that Gilgamesh longs to "become as one who sits to be wondered on the knee" of his mother Ninsun; or that Naram-Sin is as contemptuous of the Ekur "as a runner is contemptuous (?) of his strength" (that is, presumably in his eagerness to win a race); or that heroes in single combat fight to the bitter end, if we may judge from the simile, "Its cattle (the cattle of the devastated Ekishnugal) were hurled down in front of it like hero smiting hero"; or that the goddess Inanna goes forth to battle "like a hero hastening to his weapon." And it is not to heroes alone that deities are compared. The eagerness and zeal of Inanna to build up the prosperity of Agade is imaged in the simile, "Like a youth newly building (his) house, like a maid setting up (her) private chamber . . . Inanna permitted herself no sleep." The sun-god Utu shows mercy to Gilgamesh like a man of mercy." The "storm" overtakes the goddess Bau "like a mortal." Even the brickwork of a desolate temple is said to cry out "like a human being, 'where are you'," to the goddess who had forsaken it.

So much for this survey of Sumerian similes and their underlying imagery. As is clear from this chapter and from the royal hymns cited in Chapter 30, imagery and symbolism were characteristic features of Sumerian thought and vision. It is not surprising to find therefore that some of the most imaginative symbolism centered about the Sacred Marriage, a fertility rite intended to insure the fruitfulness of the soil and the fecundity of the womb. The following chapter, based largely on my *The Sacred Marriage Rite* (Bloomington: University of Indiana Press, 1969), is devoted primarily to this rite which celebrated the marriage of the king to Inanna, the goddess of love and desire, the courting and wooing that preceded it, the ritual procedures of the ceremony itself, the repertoire of ecstatic, rapturous love lyrics that accompanied it which are reminiscent of the Biblical Song of Songs, the melancholy tale of death and resurrection echoed ever so faintly in the Christ story.

THE FIRST SEX SYMBOLISM

A S IS TRUE OF ALL MANKIND, love among the Sumerians was an emotion that varied in character and intensity. There was the passionate, sensuous love between the sexes, usually culminating in marriage; there was the love between husband and wife, between parents and children, between the various members of the family; between friends and intimates. But it is love between the gods that is of primary interest to the Sumerian mythographers and poets. For as they believed and imagined, it was the sexual union of the gods that was responsible for life on earth, for the prosperity and well-being of mankind, and especially of Sumer and its people. Fortunately for the modern historian, the Sumerian poets were no prudes: a penis was a penis, a vulva was a vulva, and when the twain met, they did not hesitate to say so. And while, in case of some of the myths, the earthly, human consequences of the divine erotic acts are cloaked in a symbolism that still remains obscure to the modern scholar, there are others in which they are stated in reasonably clear language. Here, for example, is a mythological passage depicting the birth of vegetation, the plants and herbs, the trees and reeds essential to life on earth:

> Smooth, big Earth made herself resplendent, beautified her body joyously,
> Wide Earth bedecked her body with precious metal and lapis lazuli
> Adorned herself with diorite, chalcedony, and shiny carnelian,
> Heaven arrayed himself in a wig of verdure, stood up in princeship,
> Holy Earth, the virgin, beautified herself for Holy Heaven,

> Heaven, the lofty god, planted his knees on Wide Earth,
> Poured the semen of the heroes Tree and Reed into her womb,
> Sweet Earth, the fecund cow, was impregnated with the rich
>   semen of Heaven,
> Joyfully did Earth tend to the giving birth of the plants of life,
> Luxuriantly did Earth bear the rich produce, did she exude wine
>   and honey.

While vegetation, according to these image-filled poetic lines, was conceived as the offspring of Father Heaven and Mother Earth, the two personified seasons, Summer and Winter, were the children of the air-god Enlil and the Great Mountains which he impregnated with his sperm. Or as the poet puts it:

> Enlil, like a big bull, set his foot on the earth,
> To make the good day thrive in abundance,
> To make the fair night flourish in luxuriance,
> To make grow tall the plants, to spread wide the grains, ... ,
> To make Summer restrain the heaven,
> To make Winter hold back the water of overflow at the quay,
> Enlil, the king of all the lands, set his mind.
> He thrust his penis into the Great Mountains, gave a share to the
>   Highland,
> (The semen of) Summer and Winter, the fecundating overflow of
>   the land, he poured into their womb,
> Wheresoever Enlil would thrust his penis, he roared like a wild
>   bull,
> There Mountain spent the day, rested happily at night,
> Delivered herself of Summer and Winter like rich cream,
> Fed them, like big wild bulls, the clean grass on the mountain
>   terraces,
> Made them grow fat in the mountain meadows.

One of the more graphic depictions of a divine sexual act and its fruitful consequences for Sumer and its people concerns the Euphrates and Tigris, the two rivers that made life possible in that hot, arid land. According to one poet, it was the wise water-god Enki who filled them with the life-giving waters by pouring his semen into them like a rampant wild bull mating with a wild cow. Or, as the poet paints the scene:

> After Father Enki had lifted (his eye) over the Euphrates,
> He stood up proudly like a rampant bull,
> Lifts his penis, ejaculates,

Fills the Tigris with sparkling water.
The wild cow mooing for its young in the pastures, the scorpion
   (-infested) stall,
The Tigris surrendered to him as (to) a rampant bull.
He lifted the penis, brought the bridal gift,
Brought joy to the Tigris like a big wild bull, made it tend to its
   birth giving,
The water he brought, it is sparkling water,
The grain he brought, it is checkered grain, the people eat it.

But it was in connection with Inanna, the Sumerian goddess of
love and procreation, that the mythographers and poets evolved
some of their most erotic imagery and symbolism. For it was the
Sumerian religious credo that the ritual marriage between the king
of Sumer and this fertility goddess, full of sexual allure, was essential for the fertility of the soil and the fecundity of the womb and
that it brought about the prosperity of the land and the well-being
of its people. The first Sumerian ruler who celebrated this rite, was
the shepherd-king Dumuzi (the Biblical Tammuz) who reigned in
Erech, one of Sumer's great urban centers, early in the third millennium B.C.; at least this was the tradition current in Sumer in later
years. Here, for example, is a poetic myth depicting the selection of
Dumuzi by the goddess as her bridegroom, the actual mating of
the sacred couple, the cohabitation that made vegetation flourish all
about them; the divine spouse's plea for milk from her shepherd-
husband, and her promise forever to preserve the palace, the "house
of life." The poem begins with a soliloquy by the goddess an-
nouncing her choice of Dumuzi for "the godship of the land"—the
king himself became divine by marrying the goddess—in accordance with her parents' wishes.

   "I cast my eye over all the people
   Called Dumuzi to the godship of the land,
   Dumuzi, the beloved of Enlil,
   My mother holds him ever dear,
   My father exalts him."

Then, continues the poet, she bathes, scours herself with soap,
dresses in her special "garments of power," and has Dumuzi brought
to her prayer- and song-filled house and shrine to sit happily by her
side. His presence fills her with such passion and desire that then

and there she composes a song for her vulva in which she compares it to a horn, to "the boat of heaven," to the new crescent moon, to fallow land, to a high field, to a hillock, and ends by exclaiming:

"As for me, my vulva,
For me, the piled-high hillock,
Me, the maid—who will plow it for me?
My vulva, the watered ground—for me,
Me, the Queen, who will station his ox there?"

To which comes the answer:

"Oh, Lordly Lady, the king will plow it for you,
The king, Dumuzi, will plow it for you."

And joyfully the goddess responds:

"Plow my vulva, man of my heart!"

After bathing her holy lap, the couple cohabit, and vegetation flourishes all about them; or as the poet says:

At the king's lap stood the rising cedar,
Plants rose high by his side,
Grains rose high by his side,
. . . . gardens flourished luxuriantly by his side.

And our poet continues:

In the house of life, the house of the king,
His spouse dwelt with him in joy,
In the house of life, the house of the king,
Inanna dwelt with him in joy.

Once happily settled in the king Dumuzi's house, the goddess utters a plea and makes a promise. The plea is for milk and cheese from Dumuzi's sheepfold:

"Make yellow the milk for me, my bridegroom, make yellow the milk for me,
My bridegroom, I will drink fresh (?) milk with you,
Wild bull, Dumuzi, make yellow the milk for me,
My bridegroom, I will drink fresh (?) milk with you,
The milk of the goat, make flow in the sheepfold for me,
With . . . . cheese fill my holy churn . . . ,
Lord Dumuzi, I will drink fresh milk with you."

And her promise is to preserve her spouse's "holy stall" which
seems to be a symbolic designation of the king's palace:

> "My husband, the goodly storehouse, the holy stall,
> I, Inanna, will preserve for you,
> I will watch over your 'house of life.'
> The radiant wonder-place of the land,
> The house where the fate of all the lands is decreed,
> Where people and (all) living things are guided,
> I, Inanna, will preserve for you,
> I will watch over your 'house of life,'
> The 'house of life,' the storehouse of long life,
> I, Inanna will preserve for you."

From this tender, passionate poem, one might well get the impression that Dumuzi was Inanna's enthusiastic, and only choice for
her husband-to-be, and that she could hardly wait to have him at
her side to plow her vulva. Yet there is a version of the premarital
courtship that tells an entirely different story: Inanna actually at
first rejects Dumuzi, the shepherd, for his rival Enkimdu, the
farmer, and it took no little argument and persuasion on the part of
her brother, the sun-god Utu, as well as a long and rather aggressive
speech by Dumuzi himself to induce her to change her mind. This
mythological episode, symbolizing the struggle between the peasant
and the shepherd for fertility and fecundity, is told in two playlet-
like compositions which are closely related, one beginning where
the other ends. The first of the two consists almost entirely of a
question-and-answer tête-à-tête between Utu and the goddess
which concerns the making of a coverlet for her nuptial bed. The
dialogue runs in part as follows:

> "Lordly Queen, the cultivated flax, the luxurient,
> Inanna, the cultivated flax, the luxuriant, ... ,
> I will hoe for you, will give the plant to you,
> Sister mine, I will bring you the cultivated flax,
> Inanna, I will bring you the cultivated flax."

> "Brother, after you have brought me the cultivated flax,
> Who will comb it for me? Who will comb it for me?
> That flax, who will comb it for me?"

> "Sister mine, I will bring it to you combed,
> Inanna, I will bring it to you combed."

"Brother, after you have brought it to me combed,
Who will spin it for me? Who will spin it for me?
That flax, who will spin it for me?"
"Sister mine, I will bring it to you spun,
Inanna, I will bring it to you spun."

And so the poet continues with this question-and-answer dialogue
for the braiding, warping, weaving, and dying of the coverlet, and
it is only then, at the very end of the poem, that we learn the purpose of the colloquy, as Inanna puts forth the question that is really
on her mind:

"Brother, after you have brought it to me dyed,
Who will bed with me? Who will bed with me?"

To which Utu replies unhesitatingly that it is Dumuzi, or to use
two of his epithets, Ushumgalanna (The Dragon of An) and Kuli-
Enlil (The Friend of Enlil), who will be her husband and bed with
her.

"With you he will bed, he will bed,
With you your husband will bed,
With you Ushumgalanna will bed,
With you Kuli-Enlil will bed,
With you he who came forth from the fertile womb will bed,
With you the seed begotten of a king will bed."

But Inanna demurs, gently but firmly:

"Nay, the man of my heart is he—
The man of my heart is he—
Who has won my heart is he—
Who hoes not, (yet) the granaries are heaped high,
The grain is brought regularly into the storehouse,
The farmer, he whose grain fills all the granaries."

Here the poem ends. But, continues the sequel, Utu will not take
"no" for an answer. He insists that Inanna marry the shepherd, not
the farmer.

"Sister mine, marry the shepherd,
Maid Inanna, why are you unwilling?
His cream is good, his milk is good,
The shepherd, whatsoever he touches is bright.
Inanna, marry the shepherd,

You who are bedecked with jewels and brilliants,
Why are you unwilling?
His good cream he will eat with you, he the king protector,
Why are you unwilling?"

But Inanna is adamant:

"I—the shepherd I will not marry,
I will not wear his coarse garments,
I will not accept his course wool,
I, the maid, the farmer I will marry,
The farmer who grows many plants,
The farmer who grows much grain."

This so infuriates Dumuzi that he speaks out vehemently in his own defense with the repeated claim that he has much more to offer than the farmer:

"The farmer more than I, the farmer more than I,
The farmer, what has he more than I?
If he give me his black flour,
I give him, the farmer, my black ewe,
If he give me his white flour,
I give him, the farmer, my white ewe,
If he pour me his prime beer,
I pour him, the farmer, my yellow milk" . . . .

And so on and so on. Dumuzi continues in this vein to show his superiority over the farmer, ending as he began, with the words:

"More than I, the farmer, what has he more than I?"

This outburst seems to have had its intended effect, since Inanna must have had a change of heart. For the poet next tells us that

He rejoiced, he rejoiced,
On the "breast" of the river he rejoiced,
On the river bank, the shepherd, on the river bank rejoiced.

But then, who should come up to the river bank? None other than Enkimdu, the farmer, which puts Dumuzi once again in a fighting mood. Happily, however, the farmer is a meek fellow who craves peace and friendship. He refuses to quarrel with the shepherd and even offers him pasturing ground and water for his sheep. And so the story has a happy ending: Dumuzi invites the farmer to his wedding, and the gratified Enkimdu promises to bring suitable gifts for the bride from the produce of his fields.

Dumuzi has thus seemingly convinced his bride-to-be of the primacy of his wealth and possessions. But, according to another recently edited poem, the goddess also has some misgivings about his pedigree which, she claims, is quite inferior to her own, and it is only after Dumuzi "cooled her down" by demonstrating that his pedigree is as good as hers, that she consents to have him for lover and husband. According to two other versions of the courtship, Inanna first seeks parental approval before bedding with her lover Dumuzi, but there is also one poem that depicts the goddess as deceiving her mother, and she "gets her man" by spending the night making love with Dumuzi under the light of the moon, while her mother thinks she is out with a girl friend in the public square. This is the theme of one of the more ardent and tender love lyrics, which begins with Inanna as the Venus-goddess soliloquizing:

> "Last night as I, the Queen, was shining bright,
> Last night, as I, the Queen of Heaven, was shining bright,
> Was shining bright, was dancing about,
> Was uttering a chant at the brightening of the oncoming light,
> He met me, he met me,
> The lord Kuli-Anna (epithet of Dumuzi) met me,
> The lord put his hand into my hand,
> Ushumgalanna embraced me."

To be sure, she claims that she tried to free herself from his embrace, since she did not know what to tell her mother, or, as the poet has her plead with her lover:

> "Come now, wild bull, set me free, I must go home,
> Kuli-Enlil, set me free, I must go home,
> What can I say to deceive my mother,
> What can I say to deceive my mother Ningal!"

But her lover had an answer that Inanna, noted for deceitfulness, was only too happy to hear from his lips:

> "Let me inform you, let me inform you,
> Inanna, most deceitful of women, let me inform you,
> Say my girl friend took me with her to the public square,
> There she entertained me with music and dancing,
> Her chant the sweet she sang for me,
> In sweet rejoicing I whiled away the time there.

Thus deceitfully stand up to your mother,
While we by the moonlight indulge our passion,
I will prepare for you a bed pure, sweet, and noble,
Will while away the sweet time with you in plenty and joy.

But Dumuzi evidently so relished the savor of Inanna's love that he must have promised to make her his rightful spouse. For the poem ends with the goddess singing exultingly and ecstatically:

"I have come to our mother's gate,
I, in joy I walk,
I have come to Ningal's gate,
I, in joy I walk.
To my mother he will say the word,
He will sprinkle cypress oil on the ground,
To my mother Ningal he will say the word,
He will sprinkle cypress oil on the ground,
He whose dwelling is fragrant,
Whose word brings deep joy.
My lord is seemly for the holy lap,
Ama-ushumgalanna (epithet of Dumuzi), the son-in-law of Sin,
The lord Dumuzi is seemly for the holy lap,
Ama-ushumgalanna, the son-in-law of Sin."

While the celebration of the Dumuzi-Inanna "Sacred Marriage" probably began as a local rite in Erech where Dumuzi was king and Inanna was the tutelary deity, it was transformed in the course of the centuries into a joyous national event in which the king of Sumer, and later, of Sumer and Akkad, took Dumuzi's place as his mystically conceived avatar or incarnation. As yet there is no way of knowing just when this took place, that is, who was the first ruler to celebrate the rite as a reincarnated Dumuzi; probably it took place some time during the third quarter of the third millennium when the Sumerians were becoming ever more nationally minded. In any case, as of today, it is only with Shulgi of Ur, who reigned at the very end of the third millennium, that we begin to get some descriptive details of this nationally oriented version of the rite. There is a Shulgi hymn whose text is now being pieced together, one which may be designated "The Blessing of Shulgi," and which begins with a depiction of the king's journey from his capital Ur to Inanna's city, Erech. There, according to the poet, he left his boat at the quay of Kullab and, loaded down with sacrificial animals, he proceeded to Inanna's shrine, the Eanna. Once there, he dressed himself in a ritual garment, covered his head with a crown-like wig, and so impressed the goddess with his wonder-inspiring presence that she spontaneously broke into a passionate song:

"When for the wild bull, for the lord, I shall have bathed,
When for the shepherd Dumuzi I shall have bathed,
When with ointment (?) my sides I shall have adorned,
When with amber my mouth I shall have coated,
When with coal my eyes I shall have painted,
When in his fair hands my loins shall have been shaped,
When the lord lying by holy Inanna, the shepherd Dumuzi,
With milk and cream the lap shall have smoothed, . . . ,
When on my vulva his hand he shall have laid, . . . ,
When like his black boat he shall have . . it,
When like his "narrow" boat he shall have . . it,
When on the bed he shall have caressed me,
Then shall I caress my lord, a sweet fate I will decree for him,
I will caress Shulgi, the faithful shepherd, a sweet fate I will decree
    for him,
I will caress his loins, the shepherdship of the land
I will decree as his fate."

And this, according to our poet, is the sweet fate the goddess decreed for her beloved:

"In battle I am your leader, in combat I am your armor-bearer,
In the assembly I am your advocate,
On the campaign I am your inspiration.
You, the chosen shepherd of the holy shrine (?),
You, the king, the faithful provider of Eanna,
You, the luminary of An's great shrine,
In all ways you are fit—
To hold high your head on the lofty dais, you are fit,
To sit on the lapis lazuli throne, you are fit,
To cover your head with the crown, you are fit,
To wear long garments on your body, you are fit,
To gird yourself in the garment of kingship, you are fit,
To carry the mace and the weapon, you are fit, . . . ,
To guide straight the long bow and the arrow, you are fit,
To fasten the throw stick and the sling at the side, you are fit,
For the holy scepter in your hand, you are fit,
For the holy sandals on your feet, you are fit,

You, the sprinter, to race on the road, you are fit,
To prance on my holy bosom like a lapis lazuli calf, you are fit,
May your beloved heart be long of days.

Thus has An determined for you, may it not be altered,
Enlil, the decreer of fate—may it not be changed,
Inanna holds you dear, you are the beloved of Ningal (Inanna's
    mother)."

Ever since the days of Shulgi, virtually every king of Sumer and
Akkad, boasts of being the beloved husband of Inanna, as indeed
did Shulgi's father, Ur-Nammu. And at least in one case, namely
that of Iddin-Dagan, a king who reigned about a century after
Shulgi, we learn from a hymn to the goddess, that he too, celebrated the Sacred Marriage Rite as an avatar of Dumuzi, under the
name of Ama-ushumgalanna. The revelant passage that describes in
some detail what actually took place during the wedding ceremony,
reads as follows:

In the palace, the house that guides the land, the "clamp" of all
    the foreign lands,
In the hall of "judgment by ordeal," where gather the people, the
    blackheads,
He (the king) erected a dais for the "Queen of the Palace"
    (Inanna).
The king, as a god, lived with her in its midst
To watch over the life of all the lands,
To verify the true first day (of the month),
To carry out to perfection the *me* on the "day of sleeping" (of
    the moon-god, that is, the last day of the month).
On the New Year, the day of ordinance,
A sleeping place was set up for my Queen;
They (the people) purify rushes with fragrant cedar,
Set them up for my Queen as their bed,
Over it they spread a coverlet,
A coverlet that rejoices the heart, makes sweet the bed.

My Queen is bathed at the holy lap,
Is bathed at the lap of the king,
Is bathed at the lap of Iddin-Dagan,
The holy Inanna is scrubbed with soap,
Fragrant cedar oil is sprinkled on the ground.
The king goes head high to the holy lap,
Goes head high to the lap of Inanna,
Ama-ushumgalanna beds with her,

Fondles lovingly her holy lap,
She murmurs soothingly,
"Oh Iddin-Dagan, you are indeed my beloved."

Then, presumably the following day, a rich banquet is prepared in
the large reception hall of the palace and this is what takes place:

While holy sacrifices were heaped up, while lustrations were
  performed,
While incense was heaped up, while cypress was burned (?),
While bread offerings were arranged, while vessels were arranged,
He entered with her in the lofty palace,
He embraced his holy wife,
Led her forth like the light of day to the throne on the great dais,
Installed himself at her side like the king Utu (the sun-god),
Directed abundance, luxuriance, and plenty before her,
Prepared a goodly feast for her,
Conducted the "blackheads" before her.
With the drum (?) whose speech is louder than the South Wind,
The sweet-voiced *algar-lyre* (?), the ornament of the palace,
The harp that soothes the spirit of man,
The singers utter songs that rejoice the heart.

The king put a hand to the food and drink,
Ama-ushumgalanna put a hand to the food and drink,
The palace is festive, the king is joyous.
By the people sated with plenty,
Ama-ushumgalanna stands in lasting joy,
May his days be long on the fruitful throne.

Some twelve years ago, in 1959 to be exact, there were published
two "Sacred Marriage" tablets which had been lying about in the
cupboards of the British Museum for well-nigh a century, and
these, too, provided a number of interesting, if rather enigmatic,
particulars concerning the celebration of the rite. One of these texts
tells us that after a "fruitful" bed had been set up in the goddess's
shrine, Eanna, ritual priests designated as "linen-wearers," announce
her presence to Dumuzi before whom food and drink had been
placed, and in riddle-like phrases invite him to approach Inanna.
Following a brief blessing of Dumuzi by the goddess, the composition closes with a plea to Inanna, probably uttered by Dumuzi, to
give him her breast, "her field," that pours out rich vegetation.

The second British Museum text parallels to some extent the
Shulgi and Iddin-Dagan versions of the Sacred Marriage Rite, but

the details vary greatly. The poet-priest begins with an address to the goddess, informing her that Gibil, the fire-god, had purified her "fruitful bed bedecked with lapis lazuli," and that the king himself —his name is not mentioned in the text—had erected an altar for her and carried out her purification rites. Following a plea to the goddess to bless the king during the night of love, the poet sings ecstatically of the king's craving for the nuptial bed, and of his preparing a coverlet for it, so that she might "make sweet the heart-rejoicing bed." With the bed prepared and the goddess ready to receive the bridegroom, the poet introduces Ninshubur, Inanna's faithful vizier, who leads the king to the bride's lap with the plea that she bless him with everything essential for a happy, memorable reign, i.e. firm political control over Sumer and its neighboring lands, productivity of the soil and fertility of the womb, prosperity and abundance for all the people.

So much for the several divergent and at times contradictory Sacred Marriage texts; clearly the poets and priests seem to have been as fancy-free in inventing and embellishing the ritual procedures for the nuptial ceremony as they were in depicting the premarital courting and wooing of the holy couple. But we do know that the Sacred Marriage ceremony was a jubilant, rapturous event, celebrated with joyous music and ecstatic love songs. Not a few of these have become known over the years, and many more are no doubt buried in the ruins of Sumer. These Sumerian erotic songs celebrating the marriage of a shepherd-king to the goddess whose Sumerian name was Inanna, and whose Semitic name was Ishtar, may well be the forerunners of the Song of Songs, a loosely organized collection of sensuous love songs whose presence in the Old Testament, cheek by jowl with the inspiring Books of Moses, the Psalms, and the Books of the Prophets, has puzzled and perplexed many a Biblical scholar, ancient and modern. For, as is now evident, the resemblances in style, theme, motif, and occasionally even in phraseology, are quite numerous and varied.

In both the Song of Songs and the Sumerian Sacred Marriage Songs, for example, the lover is designated as both king and shepherd, and the beloved is not only his "bride," but also his "sister." Both the Biblical and Sumerian songs consist largely of monologues and dialogues spoken by the lovers, interspersed here and there with chorus-like refrains. Both make use of polished, ornate, rhetorical figures of speech that bespeak the well-stocked repertoire of the professional court poet. And both dwell on such themes as the reveling of the lovers in garden, orchard, or field; or the maid bringing the lover to her mother's house—no doubt numerous others will be identified in the course of time. It, therefore, seems not unreasonable to surmise that the Song of Songs, or at least a good part of it, is a modified form of an ancient Hebrew liturgy celebrating the marriage of a Hebrew king—a Solomon for example—with a goddess of fertility, a Sacred Marriage rite that had been part of a fertility cult that the early nomadic Hebrews took over from their urbanized Canaanite neighbors, who in turn had borrowed from the Tammuz-Ishtar cult of the Semitic Akkadians, and which was itself but a modified version of the Dumuzi-Inanna cult of the Sumerians. Nor is this as surprising as it might seem at first glance. As has often been noted by Biblical scholars, traces of the fertility cult are found in several books of the Bible, and though the prophets condemned it severely, it was never completely eradicated. There are reflections of it as late as Michnaic times, that is, roughly the time of the canonization of the Old Testament. This hypothesis, moreover, would help to explain the acceptance of the book by the Rabbis as part of the Holy Scriptures. For even after Jahweism had purged its contents by obliterating almost all traces of its fertility cult elements, the Song of Songs still carried a hallowed aura of religious tradition that smoothed the way for its admittance into the sacred canon, especially since the name of King Solomon had in some way become attached to it.

One reasonably clear example of the resemblance in theme, style, and diction between the Biblical and Sumerian songs are the first four verses of the Song of Songs, in which the beloved pleads with the king, presumably Solomon, whom the "maidens love," and who "has brought me into his chambers," "to kiss me with the kisses of your mouth, for your love is better than wine," a plea that is followed by the maidens singing: "We will exalt and rejoice in you, we will extol your lover more than wine"—these verses have their counterpart and prototypes in the ecstatic words of a beloved bride of the king Shu-Sin (about 2000 B.C.) who sang:

Bridegroom, dear to my heart,
Goodly is your pleasure, honey-sweet;
Lion, dear to my heart,
Goodly is your pleasure, honey-sweet.

You have captivated me, I stand trembling before you,
Bridegroom, I would be carried off by you to the bedchamber;
You have captivated me, I stand trembling before you,
Lion, I would be carried off by you to the bedchamber.

Bridegroom, let me give you of my caresses,
My precious sweet, I would be laved (?) by honey,
In the bedchamber, honey-filled,
Let us enjoy your goodly beauty;
Lion, let me give you of my caresses,
My precious sweet, I would be laved (?) by honey.

Bridegroom, you have taken your pleasure of me,
Tell my mother, she will give you delicacies (?),
Tell my father, he will give you gifts.

Your spirit—I know where to cheer your spirit,
Bridegroom, sleep in our house till dawn,
Your heart—I know where to gladden your heart,
Lion, sleep in our house till dawn.

You, because you love me,
Lion, give me, pray, of your caresses;
The lord, my god, the lord my good genie,
My Shu-Sin who gladdens the heart of Enlil,
Give me pray of your caresses.

Your place sweet as honey, pray lay a hand on it,
Like a *gishban*-garment, bring your hand over it,
Like a *gishban-sikin* garment, cup your hand over it.

As the last lines of this rapturous lyric indicate, this was no common maiden unburdening herself of her love for an ordinary sweetheart. This was a devotee of the goddess of love—the ancient poet actually designates it as a *balbale* of Inanna—singing of blissful union with her bridegroom, the king Shu-Sin who "gladdens the heart of Enlil," a sexual mating that would bring the favors of the god to the land and its people. Shu-Sin, not unlike the Solomon of a much later day, seemed to have been a high favorite with the "ladies of the harem," the hierodules and devotees that made up the cult personnel of Inanna-Ishtar. It is not surprising to learn that the excavators

of ancient Erech, where Inanna had her most revered temple, dug
up a necklace of semiprecious stones, one of which was inscribed
with the words: "Kubatum, the *lukur*-priestess of Shu-Sin,"—*lukur*
being a Sumerian word designating an Inanna devotee who may
have played the role of the goddess in the Sacred Marriage Rite.

Shu-Sin, in fact, appears to have made it a habit to present precious gifts to Inanna's worshipers, especially if they cheered him
with sweet song, for we find one of them chanting:

> Because I uttered it, because I uttered it, the lord gave me a gift,
> Because I uttered the *allari*-song, the lord gave me a gift,
> A pendant of gold, a seal of lapis lazuli, the lord gave me a gift,
> A ring of gold, a ring of silver, the lord gave me a gift. . . .

And after extolling Shu-Sin as a great king, she continues:

> My god, sweet is the drink of the wine-maid,
> Like her drink sweet is her vulva, sweet is her drink,
> Like her lips sweet is her vulva, sweet is her drink,
> Sweet is her mixed drink, her drink.

Shu-Sin is also the lover in another lyric chanted by a devotee
who may perhaps have been chosen for a night of love with the
king, and who had therefore prepared a very special hairdo to make
herself attractive in his eyes, for we find her singing:

> "Lettuce is my hair, well watered,
> *Gakkul*-lettuce is my hair, well watered,
> Combed (?) smooth are its tangled coils (?),
> My nursemaid has heaped them high.
> Of my hair luxuriant . . . ,
> She has piled thick its small locks,
> She puts to right my 'allure,'
> The 'allure'—my hair that is lettuce, the fairest of plants.
> The brother has brought me into his life-giving gaze,
> Shu-Sin has chosen me. . . ."

Following a break of about seven lines, we find the hierodule's companions singing in chorus:

> "You are our lord, you are our lord,
> Silver and lapis lazuli, you are our lord,
> Our farmer who makes stand high the grain, you are our lord."

But it is the hierodule who "solos" the last lines:

"For him who is the honey of my eyes, who is the passion of my
heart,
May the day of life come forth—for my Shu-Sin."

Lettuce seems to have been a favorite plant of the Sumerians—
not only was the lofty hairdo of the beloved likened to it, the lover,
too, is "lettuce well watered." He is also a well-stocked garden,
grain in the furrow, and a fruit-laden apple tree, according to the
exuberant chant of the ecstatic beloved:

"He has sprouted, he has burgeoned, he is lettuce well watered,
My well-stocked-garden of the . . . steppe, my 'favorite of his
mother,'
My grain luxuriating in the furrow—he is lettuce well watered,
My apple tree that bears fruit up to its crown—he is lettuce well
watered."

But most of all she loves him because he is a "honey-man," dripping
with sweetness.

"The honey-man, the honey-man sweetened me ever,
My lord, the honey-man of the gods, my 'favorite of his mother,'
Whose hand is honey, whose foot is honey, sweetens me ever,
My sweetener of the . . . navel (?), my 'favorite of his mother,'
My . . . of fairest thighs—he is lettuce well-watered."

Among the several other extant love songs, there is one that ends
with the beloved singing:

"Life is your coming,
Abundance is your coming into the house,
Lying by your side is my greatest joy. . . ."

According to another love lyric, the parents of the beloved open
the door for their "son-in-law" when the day has passed, and night
has come, and "moonlight has entered the house." We then find the
goddess pleading with her bridegroom, to her "brother of fairest
face," who is deeply impressed by his extraordinary "mane," to
"press it close to our bosom." After the sacred couple has united in
bliss, the goddess blesses her lover, the king, with these cheering
words:

"May you be a reign that brings forth happy days,
May you be a feast that brightens the countenance,
May you be bronze that brightens the hands,
Beloved of Enlil, may the heart of your god find comfort in you.

> Come in the night, stay in the night,
> Come with the sun, stay with the sun,
> May your god prepare the way for you,
> May the basket carriers and axe carriers level it smooth for you."

A favorite motif of the Song of Songs is the "going down" of the lovers to garden, orchard, and field, and this also is the theme of several of the Sacred Marriage love lyrics. One of these is a composition that purports to be a dialogue between King Shulgi and his "fair sister" Inanna. It opens with the goddess complaining of a scarcity of vegetation: no one is bringing the date clusters due her and there is no grain in the silos. So Shulgi invites her to his fields and asks her to "fructify (?)" it. The goddess thereupon commands a farmer to plow Shulgi's fields, and the king next invites her to his garden and orchard, presumably for the same purpose.

Closer in content and mood to the Biblical book is a passage in an Inanna composition inscribed on an as yet unpublished tablet in the British Museum in which the goddess sings:

> He made me enter, he made me enter,
> My brother made me enter his garden,
> Dumuzi made me enter his garden,
> He made me approach with him a high grove,
> Made me stand with him by a high bed.
> Steadily I kneel by an apple tree,
> My brother comes chanting,
> The lord Dumuzi comes up to me,
> Comes up to me out of the reddish oak leaves,
> Comes up to me out of the midday heat,
> I pour out before him legumes from my womb,
> I bring into being legumes before him, I pour out legumes
>   before him,
> I bring into being grains before him, I pour out grains before him.

In a like vein, there is a passage in a fragmentary poem which has the goddess chanting that after her lover had placed "his hand in mine," "his foot by mine," had pressed her lips to his mouth, and had taken his pleasure of her, he brought her into his garden where there were "standing trees," and "lying trees," and where she seems to heap up the fruit of the palm tree and the apple tree for her lover, whom she addresses repeatedly as "my precious sweet."

But there can be too much of a good thing, even if it is love, at least according to one *balbale* of Inanna, where the beloved seems to reproach her lover for being all too eager to leave the "fragrant honey-bed," and return to the palace. Only the last half of this poem is preserved, and there we find the goddess sadly relating:

"My beloved met me,
Took his pleasure of me, rejoiced as one with me,
The brother brought me into his house,
Laid me down on a fragrant honey-bed,
My precious sweet, lying by my heart,
One by one "tongue-making," one by one,
My brother of fairest face did so fifty times, ... ,
My precious sweet is sated (saying):
"Set me free, my sister, set me free,
Come, my beloved sister, I would go to the palace . . . ."

"For love is strong as death, jealousy as cruel as the grave," broods the poet of the Song of Songs in one of his more melancholy moods. In some ways this echoes the bitter end of the Dumuzi-Inanna romance that began in joyous bliss and ended in tragic death. The grim, inexorable fate that awaited her lover was foreseen and foretold by the goddess in a poem that links love and death by an inseparable bond. It starts with the lover seemingly quite unaware of his inevitable doom, singing joyously of the delight of his beloved's eyes, mouth, lips, and tasty luxuriance. But the beloved's response is somber and sorrowful. Because he had dared love the goddess, sacred and tabu to mortals, he has been doomed to die, or, to cite the relevant lines:

Oh my beloved, my man of the heart,
You—I have brought about an evil fate for you,
    my brother of face most fair,
My brother, I have brought about an evil fate for you,
    my brother of face most fair,
Your right hand you placed on my vulva,
Your left hand stroked my head,
You have touched your mouth to mine,
You have pressed my lips to your head,
That is why you have been decreed an evil fate.

What the goddess did not disclose to her foredoomed lover and husband, in this melancholy poem, however, is that it would be she herself who would send him to his death, but that fortunately for mankind he would be resurrected every half year. This we learn from one of the more complex and imaginative Sumerian myths commonly known as "Inanna's Descent to the Nether World," which, very briefly sketched, tells the following tale: Inanna has descended to the Nether World probably to satisfy her ambition to become queen of the regions below, as well as of the heavens above. There she is put to death by Ereshkigal, the legitimate queen of the World of the Dead. After three days and nights, she is brought back to life with the help of Enki, the god of wisdom, and is ready to reascend to earth. But it was an unbroken rule of the Nether World that no one who had entered its gates could return to the living world unless he or she produced a substitute to take his or her place, and Inanna, great goddess though she was, was no exception. She was, however, permitted to reascend to the earth, accompanied by a number of heartless demons known as *galla*, who had instructions to bring her back to the World of the Dead if she failed to provide someone to take her place. After wandering for a time on earth accompanied by the ghastly *galla* who kept harassing her with their persistent demand for her substitute, she arrives in Kullab, the sacred district of her own city Erech. There, to her dismay, she finds her husband Dumuzi sitting proudly on a lofty dais by a big apple tree, evidently enjoying his role of sole ruler of Erech, instead of bewailing his wife's absence and welcoming her return in all humility, as had been done by several gods. Enraged, Inanna looked upon him with the "eye of death," pronounced upon him the "word of wrath," uttered against him the "cry of guilt," and turned him over to the impatient *galla* to carry him off to the Nether World. And even though the sun-god Utu, at Dumuzi's tearful plea, turns him into a snake so that he might evade the cruel *galla*, there is no escape: they catch up with him at his sheepfold, bind and torture him, and carry him off to the "Land of No Return."

Just what happens then is uncertain because of the breaks in the text, but the following is a reasonable guess. The disappearance of Dumuzi from his sheepfold in the steppe must have so distressed his loving sister Geshtinanna that she no doubt pleaded tearfully with Inanna to let her take her brother's place in the Nether World. Moved by this sisterly self-sacrifice, the two goddesses went searching for Dumuzi in the steppe but could not find him. Whereupon a clever "holy fly" appeared on the scene and offered to provide them with the information they desired if properly rewarded. Inanna rewards him by decreeing that he could make his home in beer house and tavern where the "sons of the wise" gather, and he tells them that Dumuzi is now in the Nether World. There they find Dumuzi weeping, and Inanna then makes the Solomonic decision that Dumuzi stay in the Nether World half the year and that his sister take his place the other half.

The death of Dumuzi and his tragic, tortured descent to the Nether World moved the Sumerian mythographers to compose poems full of bitterness and grief. The pursuit of Dumuzi by the *galla* became a favorite motif with them and they felt free to elaborate on the details as their fancy dictated. It was not in myth and song only that the death of Dumuzi was commemorated; special days of mourning were set aside in the cities of Sumer, in the course of which solemn rites and rituals centering about his demise were performed. Nor was Dumuzi of Erech the only one doomed to death in the Nether World, the same fate overtook a number of deities of various cities throughout Sumer and Akkad.

From Mesopotamia the theme of the death of Dumuzi and his resurrection spread to Palestine, where we find the women of Jerusalem bewailing Tammuz at the very gates of the Jerusalem Temple. It is not at all improbable that the myth of Dumuzi's death and resurrection left its mark on the Christ story in spite of the profound disparities between the two accounts. Several motifs in the Christ story which may go back to Sumerian prototypes have been known for some time: the resurrection of a deity after three days and three nights in the world below; the fact that "thirty shekels," the sum received by Judas for betraying his master, is a Sumerian term for contempt and disdain; such epithets as "shepherd," "anointed," and perhaps even "carpenter"; the fact that one of the gods with whom Dumuzi came to be identified was Damu, the physician, to whom was entrusted the art of healing by exorcising demons. To all those motifs can now be added the torturing of Dumuzi by the merciless *galla*, reminiscent of the agony of Christ: Dumuzi was bound and pinioned, forced to undress and run naked, beaten and scourged. Above all, Dumuzi, not unlike Christ, played the role of vicarious substitute for mankind—had he not taken the place of Inanna, the goddess of procreation and fertility, in the Nether World, all life on earth would have come to an end. Admittedly, the spiritual differences are more significant by far than the resemblances—Dumuzi was no self-sacrificing Messiah preaching the kingdom of God on earth. But the Christ story did not originate and evolve in a cultural vacuum; it must have had its forerunners and prototypes, and one of the most venerable and influential of these was no doubt the mournful tale of the shepherd-king Dumuzi and his melancholy fate, a myth that was current throughout the Near East for over two millennia.

The tragic death of Dumuzi (or of any of the deities identified with Dumuzi) impelled and inspired the Sumerian poets and bards to compose dirges and laments revolving around the bereaved mother who bewails her grievous loss. One of the more poignant of these is inscribed on a hitherto unpublished tablet in the British Museum whose contents I have edited for a *Festschrift* dedicated to the eminent Biblical scholar, Harry Orlinsky, which will appear in the near future. As the translation presented in the following chapter demonstrates, this motherly lament may well be characterized as a prototype of Rachel weeping for her children "because they are not" (Jeremiah 31:15 and Matthew 2:18) as well as of Mary weeping for her dead son Jesus.

THE FIRST MATER DOLOROSA

T HE SUMERIANS, UNLIKE the Egyptians, for example, tended to take a melancholy and jaundiced view of life. At least this is true of the Sumerian thinkers and men of letters who lived about 2000 B.C. They lived in the aftermath of the devastation of the land and destruction of the capital Ur by the Elamites and Su-peoples (Sumer's neighbors to the east), as well as in the aftermath of the captivity of the pathetic Ibbi-Sin, the last king of the Third Dynasty of Ur, which had ushered in a political and cultural renaissance full of hope and promise. It was in the wake of this tragic event that the Sumerian poets and bards created and developed the image of the "weeping goddess" in their dirges and laments. In the extant texts she appears in numerous guises. She is, for example, Ningal, the queen-goddess of Ur, who bewails the destruction of her city and temple, the desecration and suppression of her cult, the suffering of her ravaged and dispersed people. Or the "weeping goddess" is none other than the multi-faceted Inanna mourning her spouse Dumuzi who had been carried off to the Nether World—a tragic fate that served as a metaphor for the death of the king and the destruction of the Sumerian cities and temples. Or she was conceived as Dumuzi's sister Geshtinanna who loved him more dearly than her own life, and who secured his freedom from the Nether World every half year by offering to become his surrogate. Often she is depicted as the mother-goddess, under such names as Ninhursag, Ninisinna, and Lisin, who wanders about weeping and searching for her disappeared son. One of these laments is inscribed on Tablet No. 98396 of the British Museum.

According to the ancient scribe's subscript, it was uttered by Ninhursag, one of the several forerunners of the *mater dolorosa* of Judaeo-Christian tradition.

The contents of this Ninhursag lament may be divided into three parts. In the first (lines 1–13), the poet sets the stage for his melancholy theme: the comely, attractive son of Ninhursag had disappeared, and the goddess, like a ewe whose lamb had been cut adrift, like a mother-goat whose kid had been cut adrift, went about questioning and searching as she approached a *kur*, a mountain, which she traversed from its base to its summit. Carrying diverse rushes and reeds in front of her, the goddess, designated as the "mother of the lad," and the "mother of the lord," sets up a lament among the reed thickets.

Here begins the second part of the lament (lines 14–25), which consists of a plaintive soliloquy by the goddess which is largely obscure. As I tentatively interpret the passage, it begins with an affirmation by the goddess that once her "man," presumably her son, had been found, she would present him with "something like a heavenly star," perhaps a meteor. She then seems to turn directly to her son, as if he had actually been found, and tells him that she feared this ominous "something like a heavenly star," and paid homage to it. But the truth was that her son had not been found, and so the goddess continues to lament that she did not know where he was, and that she had kept searching for him everywhere as best she knew how. However, it seems that the dreaded "something like a heavenly star" had turned noon to dusk and was setting the earth atremble like "a forest fragrant with cedars" and this presumably interfered with her search.

In the third part (lines 26–31), some individual, probably the poet himself, reveals the bitter truth to the weeping goddess who is portrayed metaphorically as a cow lowing to her lost, unresponding calf: there is no point to her searching and weeping—her son is in Arali (the Nether World) and the officials in charge will not give him back to her.

Here now is a literal translation of this Ninhursag lament:

1. The cow for her calf! The cow for the calf!
   The cow for the inquired about calf!
   The cow—its calf had disappeared.

As for the birth-giving mother—her comely one had disappeared,
The delightful one had been carried off by the waters.
As for the birth-giving mother—inquiring, searching, she
   approached the foot of the *kur*,
By inquiring, searching, she approached the foot of the *kur*,
Like a ewe whose lamb had been cut adrift, she would not be
   restrained,
Like a mother-goat whose kid had been cut adrift, she would not
be restrained.

10. She approached the foot of the *kur*, she approached the summit
      of the *kur*,
    She—in front of her she carries the *numun*-rushes, she carries the
      shumun-rushes,
    The mother of the lad carries the *shushua*-reeds,
    The mother of the lord sheds bitter tears among the reed
      thickets—
    "As for me, my man who will have been found for me,
    My man whose whereabouts will have been found for me,
    To that man I will give 'something like a heavenly star.'
    Lad! Your 'something like a heavenly star,' something ominous,
    Your 'something like a heavenly star' that has been brought
      to you,
    I—I feared it, I paid homage to it,

20. I learned not the whereabouts of my calf.
    I inspected my post,
    I kept searching everywhere in accordance with my
      understanding,
    It turned noon into dusk against me—something ominous,
    As for me—it acted treacherously toward me—it is true!—it is
      true!
    Me, the birth-giving mother—it sets the earth atremble against me
      like a forest fragrant with cedars."
    "Birth-giving mother, do not low to the calf—set your face!
    Cow, (do not low) to the calf, to the unanswering (calf)—set
      your face!
    The *ensi* will not give him to you,
    The lord, the killer, will not give him to you.

30. Cow, set your face toward the bank of the river!
    Set your face toward the wild ox of Arali at the edge of the
      steppe!"

   The love of the mother for her son as it is set forth in this dirge
is also manifested in another, altogether different type of composi-

tion, namely a lullaby introduced by the exclamatory phrases *u-a a-u-a* in imitation of the sing-song sound made by a mother or nursemaid rocking a child to sleep. The contents of this document, inscribed on a fairly well-preserved tablet in the University Museum, were edited by me in 1969 in a volume dedicated to the eminent Italian humanist, Edoardo Volterra.

THE FIRST LULLABY

THIS UNIQUE COMPOSITION, the only one of its kind thus far known from the Ancient Near East, probably consists entirely of a chant purported to be uttered by the wife of Shulgi, who seems to have been anxious and troubled by the ill health of one of her sons. As is true of lullabies in general, most of the mother's chant is addressed directly to the child, but in several of the preserved passages she soliloquizes about her son in the third person, and in one passage she addresses Sleep personified.

The contents of this composition whose translation and interpretation are difficult and to a considerable degree uncertain, may nevertheless be sketched in the following way: the poem begins with a rather wistful and wishful soliloquy in which the mother seems to reassure herself in the *ururu*-chant (perhaps a chant of joy) that her son will grow big and sturdy.

> *U-a a-u-a* (pronounced oo-a a-oo-a)
> In my *ururu*-chant—may he grow big
> In my *ururu*-chant—may he grow large,
> Like the *irina*-tree may he grow stout of root,
> Like the *shakir*-plant may he grow broad of crown.

She then seems to try to buoy up her son's spirit with the promise of oncoming sleep.

> The lord (perhaps Sleep) . . . . ,
> Among its burgeoning apple trees, by the river arrayed,
> He (Sleep?) will spread his hand over him who is . . ,
> He will lift his hand over him who is lying down,
> My son, sleep is about to overtake you,
> Sleep is about to settle over you.

Having mentioned sleep, the mother now addresses it directly, urging it to close her son's wakeful eyes and not let his babbling tongue shut out his sleep.

> Come Sleep, come Sleep,
> Come to where my son is,
> Hurry (?) Sleep to where my son is,
> Put to sleep his restless eyes,
> Put your hand on his painted eyes,
> And as for his babbling tongue,
> Let not the babbling tongue shut out his sleep.

She now turns again to her ailing son and promises that while Sleep will fill his lap with emmer, she will provide him with sweet little cheeses to heal him, the son of Shulgi, as well as well-watered lettuce from her garden:

> He (Sleep) will fill your lap with emmer,
> I—I will make sweet for you the little cheeses,
> Those little cheeses that are the healer of man,
> The healer of man, Oh son of the lord,
> Oh son of the lord Shulgi!
> My garden is lettuce well watered,
> It is *gakkul*-lettuce well cultivated (?),
> Let the lord eat that lettuce.

She now sees herself, again in her *ururu*-chant, as providing her son with a loving wife and a beloved son who will be cared for by a joyous nursemaid.

> In my *ururu*-song—I will give him a wife,
> I will give him a wife, I will give him a son,
> The nursemaid, joyous of heart, will converse with him,
> The nursemaid, joyous of heart, will suckle him.
>
> I—I will take a wife for my son,
> She will bear him a son so sweet,
> The wife will lie on his burning lap,
> The son will lie in his outstretched arms,
> The wife will be happy with him,
> The son will be happy with him,
> The young wife will rejoice in his lap,
> The son will grow big on his sweet knee.

But now anxiety about the illness of her son begins to dominate her mood, and in her next soliloquy, addressed directly to her son, she seems to see him in her troubled fancy as dead, mourned by professional keeners, and crawled over by insects:

> You are in pain,
> I am troubled by it,
> I am struck dumb, I gaze at the stars,
> The new moon shines white on my face:
> Your bones will be arrayed on the wall,
> The "man of the wall," will shed tears for you,
> The keeners will pluck the lyres for you,
> The gekko will gash the cheek for you,
> The fly will pluck the beard for you,
> The lizard will bite (?) its tongue for you.
> Who makes sprout woe, will make it sprout all about you,
> Who spreads about woe, will spread it all about you.

Following a fragmentary passage in which sleep is mentioned once again, we find the mother blessing her son with a wife and son, abundance of grain, a good angel, and a happy, joyous reign.

> May the wife be your support,
> May the son be your lot,
> May the winnowed barley be your bride,
> May Ashnan, the *kusu*-goddess be your ally,
> May you have an eloquent guardian angel,
> May you achieve a reign of happy days,
> May feasts make bright your forehead.

The remainder of the poem is very fragmentary and obscure, but toward the end the mother seems to turn once again to her son, the future king, and admonishes him to stand by the cities of Ur and Erech, to seize and pinion the enemy, a dog who unless cowed, will tear him to pieces.

The consuming love of a mother for her son, depicted in the preceding two chapters, has its counterpart in the loving admiration of a son for his mother, as is attested in a rather unusual composition that purports to be a message by a doting, affectionate son named Ludingirra to his mother. He portrays his mother in extravagant, poetic, similes and metaphors as the ideal woman: beautiful, radiant, diligent, productive, gracious, joyous, sweet-smelling. The text of this poem was first pieced together and later superbly translated (1964) by Miguel Civil, one of my former assistants in the

University Museum. In 1967, Jean Nougayrol, a Sorbonne professor, published a large tablet of a fragment excavated in Ugarit which originally contained the entire text of the document in Sumerian together with translations into Akkadian and Hittite. Nougayrol's careful, thorough study added considerably to the understanding of this text. In 1970, while studying several hundred still unpublished Sumerian literary tablets in the Istanbul Museum of the Ancient Orient, Muazzez Cig, the curator of its tablet collection, and I came across a well-preserved duplicate that added a number of significant variants. The improved rendering and interpretation thus made possible, will be presented in the following chapter.

HER FIRST LITERARY PORTRAIT

THIS UNUSUAL COMPOSITION that provides us with a remarkable literary portrait of the ideal Sumerian mother, consists entirely of a flowery, ornate address by an individual named Ludingirra to a "royal" courier, whom he is dispatching to his mother in Nippur. The first eight lines are introductory—Ludingirra tells the courier that he has traveled a long way from Nippur where his mother lives, and that she is very much worried about his welfare, and that he is therefore sending him to deliver a "letter of greeting" to her:

> Royal courier, ever on the road,
> I would send you to Nippur, deliver this message.
> I have traveled a long way,
> My mother is troubled (?), unable to sleep.
> She, in whose chamber there is never an angry word,
> Keeps asking all travelers after my welfare.
> Put my letters of greeting into her hand,
> (Into the hand of) my rejoicing mother who will have adorned
>   herself for you.

Since the mother was a stranger to the courier, Ludingirra gives him five signs as a guide to identifying her. Actually, none of these signs is specific or precise enough to serve its purpose; their introduction in the composition is a literary device utilized by the author to enable him to portray the mother of his dreams, as it were. The first sign concerns primarily her extraordinary accomplishments as wife and daughter-in-law, though several lines are rather obscure.

> If you know not my mother, let me give you her signs (of
>   identification):
> Her name is Shat-Ishtar (?) . . . . ,
> A figure that is radiant . . . . ,
> A goddess fair, a daughter-in-law delightful (?),
> Blessed is she from the days of her youth,
> By her energy she has managed well the house of her
>   father-in-law.
> She who serves the god of her husband,
> Who knows to tend "the place of (the goddess) Inanna,"
> Does not put to nought the words of the king.
> Vigiliant, she multiplied possessions,
> She who is beloved, cherished, full of life,
> Lambs, good cream, honey, "flowing" butter "of the heart."

The second sign depicts the mother's outstanding beauty in extravagant, hyperbolic metaphors.

> Let me give you my mother's second sign:
> My mother is a bright light of the horizon, a mountain deer,
> The morning star shining bright . . . . ,
> Precious carnelian, Marhashi topaz,
> A jewel of a princess, full of allure,
> Carnelian jewels, joy-creating,
> A ring of tin, a bracelet of iron,
> A staff of gold and bright silver,
> A perfect ivory figurine, full of charm,
> An angel of alabaster, set on a lapis lazuli pedestal.

Fertility of field and garden is the source of Ludingirra's metaphorical portrayal of his mother in the third sign.

> Let me give you my mother's third sign:
> My mother is rain in its season, water for the prime seed,
> A rich harvest, very fine (?) barley,
> A garden of plenty, full of delight,
> A well-watered fir tree, adorned with fir cones,
> Fruit of the New Year, the yield of the first month,
> A canal carrying the fertilizing waters to the irrigation ditches,
> A very sweet Dilmun date, a prime date much sought after.

In the fourth sign, Ludingirra seems to draw his images primarily from festal occasions.

> Let me give you my mother's fourth sign:
> My mother is a feast, an offering full of rejoicing,

> A New Year offering awesome to behold,
> A dancing place made for much joy,
> A procreation of princes, a chant of abundance,
> A lover, a loving heart, whose joy is inexhaustible,
> Good news for a captive returned to his mother.

Fragrance is the theme of the brief fifth sign:

> Let me give you my mother's fifth sign:
> My mother is a chariot of pine, a litter of boxwood,
> A goodly garment (?) perfumed with oil,
> A phial of ostrich shell, the inside filled with prime oil,
> A delightful garland (?), luxuriantly fitted out.

Finally Ludingirra concludes his letter with these words:

> "Ludingirra, your beloved son gives you greetings."

The same Ludingirra who had dedicated the ardent love song to his mother while she was still vigorous and alive, also composed loving tributes to both his father and wife upon their deaths, in the form of two funeral songs—the first known such examples of the elegy genre. The following chapter will sketch the contents of these two elegies inscribed on a tablet in the Pushkin Museum, as well as those of an altogether different type of elegy inscribed on a tablet in the British Museum—a funeral chant of an unnamed maiden for her *gir*, "courier," perhaps referring to the king who had fallen in battle in a distant land.

THE FIRST ELEGIES

I<small>N THE FALL OF</small> 1957, I received an invitation from the Academy of Sciences of the U.S.S.R. for a two months' stay to study as its guest the archaeological collections in Leningrad and Moscow. In exchange, the University Museum of the University of Pennsylvania invited the well-known Russian anthropologist, George Debbetz of the Moscow Institute of Ethnology and Anthropology, to spend two months as its guest in order to pursue his researches in physical anthropology. This professorial exchange— the first such exchange involving the U.S.S.R. and the United States —was negotiated by F. G. Rainey, then Director of the University Museum, in the course of a brief visit to the Soviet Union in the Spring of 1957.

Three weeks of my Soviet stay were passed in Moscow, and primarily in the Pushkin Museum which has a cuneiform tablet collection of about two thousand pieces. During a preliminary examination of this collection I noted a fairly well-preserved four-column tablet inscribed with a Sumerian literary text. On closer study, this text was seen to consist of two separate poems, each containing a funeral dirge as its outstanding feature. Since the funeral song, or elegy, was a literary genre not hitherto found among the numerous Sumerian literary compositions, I was naturally quite eager to make a careful study of this Pushkin Museum tablet and make its contents available to the scholarly world. With the cooperation of the Pushkin Museum authorities, I therefore devoted a good part of my three weeks in Moscow to the preparation of a careful transcription of the Sumerian text. As for the detailed scholarly edition, I soon realized that this would take several months of concentrated effort, and would therefore have to be prepared at leisure in Philadelphia. The Pushkin Museum put at my disposal an excellent set of photographs of the tablet, and in due time my edition of its contents was completed and published by the Oriental Literature Publishing House in Moscow together with an Introduction and translation into Russian by the eminent Soviet historian W. W. Struve.

The tablet, which was probably inscribed in the ancient city of Nippur in the first half of the second millennium B.C.—it might have been first composed about 2000 B.C.—was divided by the scribe into four columns. It contains two compositions of unequal length separated by a ruled line. The first and longer of the two consists of 112 lines of text, while the second has only 66 lines. Following the text of the two compositions, and separated from it by a double line, is a three-line colophon giving the title of each of the compositions, as well as the number of lines which they contain individually and together. Both of the compositions consist in large part of funeral dirges uttered by a single individual, Ludingirra. In the first he laments the death of his father, Nanna, who had died from wounds received in some kind of physical struggle. In the second dirge, the same Ludingirra bewails the death of his good and beloved wife, Nawirtum, who seems to have died of natural causes.

In both compositions, the dirges are preceded by prologues which serve, as it were, to set the scene. The prologue to the first dirge consists of 20 lines, and is therefore relatively brief compared to the rest of the composition. The prologue to the second dirge, on the other hand, consists of 47 lines, and is therefore about two and one half times as long as the remainder of the poem. Stylistically, both compositions make use of a highly poetic diction characterized by various types of repetition, parallelism, choral refrain, simile, and metaphor. The deeds and virtues of the deceased, as well as the grief and suffering of those left behind, are sung in inflated and grandiloquent phrases—an understandable feature of funeral orations the world over and at all times.

Unfortunately quite a number of the lines in both dirges are fragmentary, and the rendering of many of the extant lines is rather uncertain; the interested reader will find a literal translation of the entire text of the tablet, replete with breaks and question marks, in *The Sumerians* (pages 211–17). As for their importance and significance, it goes without saying that they have considerable intrinsic merit as literary efforts. They attempt to convey in imaginative poetic form the deep human passions and emotions generated by the tragic loss, through inevitable death, of the closest and dearest kin. From the point of view of the history of world literature, they are the first precious example of the elegiac genre—they precede by many centuries the Davidic dirges for Saul and Jonathan and the Homeric laments for Hector, which close the Iliad on so said a note, and they should therefore prove of value for purposes of comparative study. The first of the two poems is also of some importance since it sheds light on Sumerian cosmology, for we learn from one of its passages that the Sumerian sages held the view that the sun after setting continues its journey through the Nether World at night, and that the moon-god spends his "day of sleep" —that is the last day of the month—in the Nether World. Moreover, the two poems, and particularly the first, illuminate to some extent the Sumerian ideas about "life" in the world below. Thus, for example, we learn that there was a judgment of the dead and that, as might have been expected, it was the sun-god Utu—the judge par excellence of mankind—who made the decisions, although the moon-god Nanna, too, seemed to decree the fate of the dead on the day he visited the Nether World.

For an elegy of an altogether different kind we turn to the British Museum Tablet No. 24975, a nearly perfectly preserved document, inscribed with a poetic composition which is a funeral chant for a *gir*, an intimate of an unnamed "maid" and beloved by her. Most of the text of the composition can be transliterated with reasonable certainty, and much of it can be translated with a fair degree of accuracy. Nevertheless, its intent and purpose are difficult to fathom, and its real meaning remains rather doubtful. Primarily this is due to the key word, *gir*, a noun usually rendered as "courier," designating an individual whose status, function, and precise relationship to the maid remain enigmatic throughout the composition despite the fact that he is described in considerable realistic and metaphorical detail.

The composition may be described as a playlet featuring two protagonists: the unnamed maid and her friend or mentor, also unnamed. It begins with an address by the latter consisting of 19 lines in which he, or she, first exhorts the maid to prepare herself for the *gir*'s imminent arrival, and then proceeds to depict him as one who has traveled far afield to distant places; as an ill-fated, tearful, suffering individual whose stricken body is floating helplessly on the voracious flood waters. The death of the *gir* and the return of his corpse via mountain and river to the home of the maid, whence he had presumably begun his disastrous journey, are described in enigmatic, metaphorical language—he is depicted as a swallow who has disappeared; as a dragonfly adrift on the river; as mist drifting over the mountain ranges; as grass floating on the river; as an ibex traversing mountains.

The response of the maid constitutes the entire remainder of the composition which consists of two sections. In the first, lines 20–37, she itemizes all the great things she will provide for her *gir*, presumably as cult offerings for his ghost: cakes, fruits of the field, roasted barley, dates, beer, grapes on the vine, apples and figs, honey and wine, hot and cold water, a rein and whip, a clean garment, fine oil, a chair, footstool and bed, cream and milk. The second section, lines 38–49, begins with the maid's melancholy portrayal of the dead *gir* upon his arrival: he cannot walk, see, or speak. She then continues with a description of the funerary ritual she performed immediately upon the dead *gir*'s arrival, and concludes with the bitter realization that her smitten *gir* lay dead, and that his spirit which had only just arrived with his body had—now that it had been liberated from the corpse by the funerary rite—departed from her house.

Here now is a literal translation of the elegy:

1. "Your *gir* is approaching, prepare yourself,
   Maid, your *gir* is approaching, prepare yourself,
   Your dear *gir* is approaching, prepare yourself.
   Ah, the *gir*! Ah, the *gir*!
   Your *gir*, he of the far-away place,
   Your *gir* of distant fields, of alien roads,

Your swallow that will not come out unto distant days,
Your dragonfly of the rising waters, adrift on the river,
Your mist drifting over the mountain ranges,
10. Your river-crossing grass floating on the river,
Your ibex traversing the mountains,
Your . . . . ,
Your . . . . ,
Your *gir*, he of evil omen,
Your *gir* of weeping eyes,
Your *gir*, he of grievous heart,
Your *gir*, whose bones were devoured by the high flood,
Your floating *gir*, whose head was tossed about by the high flood,
Your *gir* who has been struck on his broad chest."

20. "After my *gir* has come, I will do great things for him:
I will offer him cakes and . . ,
I will provide for him the fruits of the field,
I will provide for him roasted barley and dates,
I will provide for him bitter-sweet beer,
I will provide for him grapes on the vine,
I will provide for him apples of the wide earth,
I will provide for him figs of the wide earth,
I will provide for him the . . of the fig tree,
I will provide for him dates on the cluster,
30. I will provide for him the orchard's honey (and) wine.
After my *gir* has come, I will do great things for him:
I will provide for him hot water (and) cold water,
I will provide for him rein and whip,
I will provide for him a clean garment and fine oil,
I will provide for him a chair (and) a footstool,
I will provide for him a verdant bed,
I will provide for him cream and milk of stall and fold."

"My *gir*—he has come, he walks not; he has come, he walks not,
He has eyes—he cannot see me,
40. He has a mouth—he cannot converse with me.
My *gir* has come—approach! He has indeed come—approach!
I have cast down bread, wiped him clean with it,
From a drinking-cup that has not been contaminated,
From a bowl that has not been defiled,
I poured water—the ground where the water was poured, drank
it up.
With my fine oil I anointed the wall for him,
In my new cloth I clothed the chair.

The spirit has entered, the spirit has departed,
My *gir* was struck down in the mountain, in the heart of the
mountain, (and now) he lies (dead)."

Princes and kings, lords and heroes, gods and goddesses—these are
the usual protagonists of the Sumerian literary repertoire. There is,
however, one type of composition, the "disputation" which tells us
no little about the way of life of ordinary people. One of these,
"The Disputation Between the Pickaxe and the Plow," has been recently pieced together and translated, and as will be demonstrated
in the next chapter, from it we glean the rather surprising information that Sumerian society had an unexpectedly high regard for the
laborer and his welfare, and that it deemed the lowly but diligent
pickaxe superior to the aristocratic but rather lazy plow.

CHAPTER 38—*The Pickaxe and the Plow*

LABOR'S FIRST VICTORY

THE SUMERIAN DISPUTATION, the prototype and predecessor of the *tenson* genre popular in Europe in Late Antiquity and the Middle Ages, was a high favorite with the Sumerian men of letters—their polemical, argumentative content was in harmony with the rather ambitious and aggressive character of the Sumerian behavioral pattern. In 1956, when *History Begins at Sumer* was first published, seven disputations involving two contrasting entities were known, but only three of these had been studied with care, since the available texts were full of breaks and gaps. In more recent years, however, scores of tablets and fragments have been identified and become available for study, and Miguel Civil, one of the leading Sumerologists of the younger generation, began working on the restoration and translation of the texts while still my assistant at the University Museum—in due course all of them will be edited and published by him.

One of the more interesting features of these disputations is the determination of the victor which is not revealed by the author until the very end of the composition, for it no doubt corresponded to the relative value attributed to the contrasting pair—it is Winter over Summer, Grain over Cattle, Bird over Fish, Tree over Reed, Copper over Silver. In the debate between "The Pickaxe and the Plow," the document treated in this chapter on the basis of the edition prepared by Civil as a dissertation for the Collège de France, it is the Pickaxe who is the victor over the Plow.

The composition begins with a rather droll description of the Pickaxe as an instrument that one would hardly expect to stand its ground against any opponent:

> Lo, the Pickaxe, the Pickaxe, the string-tied,
> The Pickaxe of poplar with a tooth of the ash tree,
>
> The Pickaxe of tamarisk with a tooth of "seawood,"
> The Pickaxe with two teeth, four teeth,
> The Pickaxe, poor fellow, always losing his loincloth,
> The Pickaxe challenged the Plow.

The burden of the challenge is that it, the Pickaxe, can perform quite a number of tasks that the Plow is unable to perform.

> "I enlarge—what is it that you enlarge?
> I expand—what is it that you expand?
> When water rushes out, I dam it up,
> You don't fill the baskets with earth,
> You don't mix clay, you don't make bricks,
> You don't lay foundations, you don't build houses,
> You don't reinforce the base of old walls,
> You don't make straight the roofs of honest men,
> You don't make straight the boulevards.
> Plow, I enlarge—what is it that you enlarge?
> I expand—what is it that you expand?"

This challenge angers the proud Plow which depicts itself as the creation by the hand of the great god Enlil, and as the farmer of mankind, the favorite of the king and nobles, whose harvested grain adorns the steppe, the sustenance of man and beast. Or in the Plow's own words:

> "I, the Plow, fashioned by a great arm, put together by a great
>   hand,
> I am the noble field registrar of Father Enlil,
> I am the faithful farmer of mankind.
> When my feast is celebrated in the field during the month of
>   Shunumun,
> The king slaughters oxen for me, multiplies sheep for me,
> Pours beer in the stone vases.
> The king brings the gathered waters,
> Drums and tambourines crash,
> And I .... for the king.
> The king takes hold of my handles,
> Harnesses the oxen to the yokes,
> All the great nobles walk by my side,
> All the lands are full of admiration,
> The people look on with joy.

The furrows I set up, adorn the steppe,
By the ears of grain that I place in the fields,
The teeming beasts of Sumugan kneel,
By my ripened grain, ready for harvesting,
The sickle blades, the mighty, vie with each other.
After . . . . the grain had been harvested,
It is a shepherd's churn at rest.
My stacks scattered over the fields,
Are the sheep of Dumuzi at rest.
My mounds spread over the steppe,
Are green hills full of allure.
Stacks and mounds (of grain) I pile up for Enlil,
Emmer, wheat I heap up for him,
I fill the storehouses . . . .
The orphan, the widow, the destitute,
Take the reed baskets,
Glean my scattered ears.
My straw (strewn) over the fields,
I let people haul away,
(While) the teeming beasts of Sumugan come forth alongside.

(Yet you) Pickaxe, measly hole digger, measly tooth gouger,
(You) Pickaxe who works and wallows in mud,
Pickaxe who puts your head in the field,
Pickaxe and brickmold who spend your days in unclean mud,
Who . . . . is unfit for the princely hand,
Whose head adorns the slave's hand,
You dare hurl bitter insults at me!
You dare compare yourself to me!
Away with you to the steppe, I have seen (enough of) you,
Who insult me (saying), 'Plow, dig, dig holes.' "

In answer to the Plow, the Pickaxe holds forth with a long harangue that begins with a description of his services to mankind in
such essential activities as irrigation, drainage, and the preparation
of the ground for plowing.

"Plow . . . . ,
I come ahead of you in the place of Enlil,
I make ditches, I make canals,
I fill the meadows with water.
When the water floods the canebrake,
My little baskets carry it off.
When the river is breached, when the canal is breached,
When the water rushes on like a river in high flood,

And turns everything to marshland,
I, the Pickaxe, set up dykes around it,
Neither the Southwind, nor the Northwind, can break them,
(So) the fowler collects the eggs (undisturbed),
The fisherman catches the fish,
The people take up the traps,
My abundance fills all the lands.
After draining off the water from the meadows,
After the wet earth is all set to be worked,
I precede you, Plow, into the field,
Clear for you (its) floor and the sides of the dykes,
Heap up for you the weeds of the field,
Gather together for you the stumps and roots in the field."

The trouble is, continues the Pickaxe, that the Plow is a clumsy
bungler, and needs constant repairing. It takes six oxen and four
men to operate it, and its parts keep on breaking:

"(You) who work the field, trampling everything under foot,
Your oxen are six, your men are four, you are the eleventh.
All the skilled workers run away from the field,
(Yet) you compare yourself to me!
When you, far behind me, go out into the field,
You look with ecstatic eye upon your one furrow.
When you put your head down to work,
(And) become entangled in roots and thorns,
Your tooth breaks, your tooth is restored,
(But) you cannot hold on to it,
Your farmer (in disgust) calls you by the name 'That Plow Is
    Caput.'
Then carpenters are hired for you, people scurry all about you,
The harness makers scrape a rough hide,
Bring up winding pegs,
Work hard with levers,
(Until) a foul piece of leather is put on your head."

Moreover the Plow only works a small part of the year, as the
Pickaxe points out.

"You, whose accomplishments are meager (but) whose ways are
    proud,
My working time is twelve months,
(But) the time you are present (for work) is four months,
(While) the time you disappear is eight months,
You are absent twice the time you are present.

Following an eight-line passage of rather obscure meaning, the Pickaxe goes on with a narcissistic glorification of its achievements, beginning with some of the tasks mentioned earlier in the harangue.

> "I, the Pickaxe, live in the city,
> No one is more honored than me.
> I am a servant who follows his master,
> I build the house for its owner,
> I enlarge the stall, widen the sheepfold,
> Mix the clay, make the bricks,
> Lay the foundations, build the houses,
> Reinforce the base of the walls,
> Make airtight the roofs of honest men,
> I, the Pickaxe, make straight the boulevards."

The Pickaxe next depicts its contributions to the welfare and earning capacity of the working class, particularly of the construction workers, the boatmen, and the gardeners.

> "Having circled the city, built solid walls about it,
> I brought into being there the temples of the gods,
> Adorned them with red clay, yellow clay, multicolored clay.
> I built the royal city,
> Where dwell the overseers (and) supervisors.
> With me who restored its (the city's) weakened clay, who
>   buttressed its fragile clay,
> They (the workers) refresh themselves in well-built houses.
> By the edge of the fire lit by the Pickaxe they loll about,
> (But) you (Plow) do not come to their party.
> They eat and drink, are paid their wages,
> (Thus) I make it possible for the worker to support his wife
>   (and) children.
> I construct the oven for the boatman, heat up pitch for him,
> Build for him boat (and) bark,
> (Thus) I make it possible for the boatman to support his wife
>   (and) children.
> I plant the garden for (its) owner,
> Having circled the garden, enclosed it with walls after they (the
>   parties) came to an agreement,
> The people take hold of me, the Pickaxe.
> After I had dug its wells, set up its poles,
> (And) constructed the bucket bar, I straighten out the trenches,
> It is I who fill the trenches with water.
> After the apple trees had blossomed (and) the fruit had appeared,
> Its fruit is fit to adorn the temples of the gods,

(Thus) I make it possible for the gardener to support his wife
(and) children."

Finally, the Pickaxe is so concerned about the well-being of the
road workers and field hands that it builds a special tower where
they can refresh themselves and fill their water skins from the well
it dug.

"Having worked at the river by the side of the Plow, having
    straightened there its roads,
(And) built a tower on its banks,
The men who spent the day in the fields,
The worker who passed the night in the fields,
In the tower that I had raised up,
These folks revived themselves like in a well-built city,
In the water skins they had fashioned, I pour water for them,
I place 'life' in them,
(Yet) you, Plow, insult me (saying): 'Dig, Dig, ditches,
(When) I in the waterless steppe,
Have dug up its sweet water,
He who is thirsty is revived by the side of my trenches."

After the Pickaxe finished its side of the argument, the Plow was
not given a chance to rebut. Instead, the author concluded the disputation with the verdict of the great god Enlil who ruled in favor
of the Pickaxe. Enlil, according to one Sumerian myth, had himself
created the Pickaxe for the use of man and proclaimed the Pickaxe
the victor over the Plow.

In the animal world, the Sumerians had a deep, tender, affection
for the fish, the helpless creature that often evoked tragic images
in the minds of the poets, especially those who composed lamentation liturgies. Thus in a poem that may well be designated "The
Home of the Fish," the anonymous author depicts the construction
of a home for the fish, a kind of well-furnished and abundantly provided aquarium, where all sorts of fish could live in undisturbed
peace, safe from preying birds and predator sharks. This text was
edited and published by Miguel Civil in the British archaeological
journal *Iraq*, vol. XXIII (1961): 154–178, and the analysis and
translation of the document presented in the following chapter is
based almost entirely on Civil's work.

THE FIRST AQUARIUM

Fishing and the fishing industry were a major source of Sumer's food supply, especially in the earlier millennia of its history. Close to a hundred different types of fish are mentioned in the Sumerian economic and lexical texts, of which some thirty-odd can now be tentatively identified according to the Finnish Orientalist, Armas Salonen, whose valuable book, *Die Fischerei in Alten Mesopotamien,* was published in 1970 (Helsinki: Finnish Academy of Science). In the extant text of the "Home of the Fish," sixteen fish are named and described in terse, pithy phraseology, and of these a half dozen or so can be roughly identified.

The entire text of our "aquarium" composition consists of an address purported to be uttered by some individual who for one reason or another was an ardent lover of fish. It begins with a reassuring announcement that the speaker has built a house for the fish, large, spacious, and unapproachable, and provided it with fine food and drink, especially beer and sweet cookies.

My Fish, a house . . . .
My Fish I have built a house for you, I have built a granary for you,
In the house an extra court, an extended sheepfold, I have built for you,
Its center I have covered with incense, I have dug (?) a well of jubilation, a place that rejoices the heart,
No one can approach your closely threaded (?) house, I have bedecked (?) it with plants,
In the house there is food, food of top quality,
In the house there is drink, drink of well-being,

In your house, no flies swarm (?) about the liquor bar,
In your entrance (?) no complainer sets an inimical foot
At its threshold and bolt where flour is sprinkled, I have set up
    the censer,
The house smells sweet like a forest of sweet-smelling cedar,
By the house I have placed beer, I have placed fine-quality beer,
I have placed there honey-beer and sweet cookies as . . . .

The speaker now urges the Fish to let all his friends, acquaintances, companions, relatives, in fact anyone who so wishes, come
into his house.

Let your acquaintances come,
Let your dear ones come,
Let your father and grandfather come,
Let your son of the elder brother and son of your younger
    brother come,
Let your little ones and your big ones come,
Let your wife and your children come,
Let your friends and your companions come,
Let your brother-in-law and your father-in-law come,
Let your crowd (whoever says) I, too, would enter, come,
Let none of your neighbors be left out.

But it is his *Fish*, his "beloved son," that the speaker is primarily
concerned with, and so he addresses him saying,

"Enter my beloved son,
Enter my goodly son,
Day is passing, night is coming,
Enter by the light of the moon.
When the day will have passed, the night will have come,
Having entered, you will be at rest there, I have fitted out a place
    for you there,
In its midst I have arranged a 'seat' for you,
My Fish, when lying no one will disturb you,
When sitting, no one will start a quarrel with you.
Enter my beloved son,
Enter my goodly son.
Like (in?) a brackish canal you will not 'know' agitation (?),
Like (in?) river silt you will not 'know' disturbance,
Like (in?) flowing water do not spread, do not (yet) spread your
    bed,
Although the moonlight has entered, do not (yet) spread your
    bed,

I would come with you that I might gaze in wonder,
Like a . . I would come with you that I might gaze in wonder,
Like a dog I would come with you to your sniffing place that I
    might gaze in wonder,
Like a . . I would come to where you 'stand,' that I might gaze
    in wonder.

Lo! Like an ox to your stall, like a sheep to your fold!
When you enter like an ox to your stall,
My Fish, Ashimbabbar (the god of the New Moon) will rejoice
    with you.
When you enter like a sheep to your fold,
My Fish, Dumuzi will rejoice with you."

Following a lacuna of about fifteen lines we find the speaker saying, "My Fish, may all kinds of fish enter with you," a statement
that introduces an itemized listing of some sixteen different fish,
each described with a brief, pithy, riddle-like comment; those that
can be identified with some degree of certainty are the barbel, large
and small, the carp, the sturgeon, the catfish, and the eel. The
speaker now makes an urgent plea to the Fish to come quickly to
his newly built home, for the day has passed and danger is lurking
all about him from the fish-eating birds and the sharks, concluding
with these words:

My Fish, the day has passed, come to me,
The day (?) has passed, come to me,
The queen of the fishermen, the goddess Nanshe, will rejoice
    with you.

CORRIGENDA AND ADDENDA
TO THE SECOND EDITION

Chapter 1. The statement that "Not a single woman is listed as a scribe in the documents," (see p. 3), is not quite correct—there are several rare cases where a female scribe is mentioned. Moreover the daughter of Sargon the Great who lived about 2300 B.C., Enheduanna by name, seems to have been a literary figure of note, cf. now W. W. Hallo and J. J. A. van Dijk, *The Exaltation of Inanna* (New Haven: Yale University Press, 1968). Nevertheless, to judge from the available school essays, women played no role in the schools of Sumer and Akkad, and those women who were literate must have had private tutoring of some sort. On page 6, the statement "He must have had some vacation in the school year, but on this we have no information," can now be modified. According to a tablet excavated at Ur and published by C. J. Gadd and S. N. Kramer in *Ur Excavation Texts VI* (London, 1963), the student had six free days each month (see Chapter 28, page 267).

Chapter 2. In 1952 I copied several additional pieces that belong to the document treated in this chapter, and these have now been published in my *Sumerian Literary Tablets and Fragments* in the Archaeological Museum of Istanbul, II (Ankara, 1976)—these fill in some of the gaps in the text, but do not significantly change the translation or the analysis of this chapter.

Chapter 3. A definitive edition of this document has now been published by my successor in the University Museum, Ake Sjöberg (cf. *Journal of Cuneiform Studies*, vol. XXV (1973): 105–169).

Chapter 4. About a dozen pieces belonging to "Enmerkar and the Lord of Aratta" have been identified since the first publication of *History Begins at Sumer*, and these have made possible a considerable improvement in the restoration of the text of the composition.

The resulting study appeared in 1973 as a dissertation prepared by Sol Cohen, then a graduate student in the Department of Oriental Studies of the University of Pennsylvania. By and large, the plot structure and translation presented in this chapter are still valid, but Cohen's dissertation corrects and amends them in a number of details.

Chapter 5. A translation of the entire poem "Gilgamesh and Agga of Kish" is now available in my *The Sumerians: Their History, Culture, and Character* (Chicago: The University of Chicago Press, 1963), pages 186–190; see also my "Sumerian Epic Literature" in the *Proceedings of the Academia Nazionale dei Lincei* (1970), pages 825–837.

Chapters 6 and 7. No changes.

Chapter 8. Oliver Gurney of Oxford and I published two additional pieces from the excavations at Ur that we identified as belonging to the Ur-Nammu Law Code—see "Two Fragments of Sumerian Laws" in *Assyriological Studies*, vol. 16 (Chicago, 1965), pages 13–19. In 1969, J. J. Finkelstein, an acknowledged authority on cuneiform law, published a revised and improved translation of the extant text of the Ur-Nammu Law Code in the *Supplement to Ancient Near Eastern Texts Relating to the Old Testament*, James Pritchard, Editor (Princeton: Princeton University Press, 1969).

Chapter 9. In 1959, Thorkild Jacobsen published a detailed study of the homicide document treated in this chapter in *Analecta Biblica et Orientalia*, vol. 12 (Rome: Pontificio Instituto Biblico, 1959), pages 130–150, which the reader interested in law will find useful and illuminating. By and large his translation and interpretation agree with those presented in this chapter, except for the end—it is his conclusion that the wife was also punished by death, since according to his interpretation the Nippur assembly found her even more guilty than the actual murderers to whom she had given the information leading to her husband's death. But this interpretation is based on a number of restorations of the text, and is not overly convincing.

Chapter 10. A much improved translation of this medical text, replete with linguistic difficulties because of its technical phraseology will be found in *The Sumerians*, pages 93–98; it is based on a penetrating study by Miguel Civil, published in 1960, in the *Revue d'Assyriologie* LIV, 59–72.

Chapter 11. A considerably fuller paraphrase of the "Farmer's Almanac" will now be found in *The Sumerians*, pages 105–109; a more detailed treatment will now be found in *Agricultura Mesopotamica*, published by the eminent Finnish cuneiformist Armas Salonen in *Annales Academiae Scientiarum Fennicae*, vol. 149 (Helsinki, 1968), pages 202–212. A definitive edition of the document is still lacking.

Chapter 12. Since the publication of this chapter I have identified, studied, and published six additional pieces inscribed with parts of "Inanna and Shukalletuda" (note that *Shukalletuda* is preferable to "Shukallituda" as the reading of the name) and these add considerably to the first and last parts of the myth which were missing in the Istanbul text described in the chapter. It is now clear that the poem begins with a scene depicting Inanna abandoning heaven and earth and descending to the Nether World, although how this relates to the rest of the poem is altogether obscure, since the text is very fragmentary at this point. There follows a folkloristic account of the planting of a garden by a raven at the command of his master, and it is only then that Shukalletuda is introduced in the plot. Moreover, though the very end of the poem is still missing, we now know the fate of Shukalletuda. Following Inanna's journey to Eridu and her plea to Enki (see page 72), the latter turns over Shukalletuda, who seems to have taken refuge in the Abzu of Eridu, to Inanna, and she puts him to death, but consoles him with the promise that his name will not be forgotten, for it will be uttered in sweet song by the minstrel in the royal palace, and by the shepherd in the byre as he swings his churn. A definitive edition of the poem is now in the process of preparation by Sol Cohen, my former student, now professor of Assyriology at Dropsie University.

Chapter 13. The contents of this chapter remain valid virtually in their entirety—for additional details, see my *Sumerian Mythology*, Third edition (The University of Pennsylvania Press, 1972), pages vii–xviii. Note, too, the following important bibliographical details: The poem "Gilgamesh, Enkidu and the Nether World" (pages 82–83) was edited in 1969 by my former student, Aaron Shaffer, now an Associate Professor of Assyriology in the Hebrew University, as a dissertation in the Department of Oriental Studies of the University of Pennsylvania—a translation of the poem will be found in *The Sumerians,* pages 197–205. The myth "Enlil and Ninlil" (pages 85–88) has now been edited by Hermann Behrens and published as *No. 8* of *Studia Pohl: Series Major* (Rome: Biblical Institute Press, 1978)—this myth has a still unpublished variant version according to Miguel Civil, *Journal of Near Eastern Studies,* vol. 25: 200–205). The Enlil hymn treated on pages 91–94 has been edited in 1969 by D. R. Reisman as part of his dissertation for the Department of Oriental Studies in the University of Pennsylvania—a translation of the document will now be found in the third edition of the *Ancient Near Eastern Texts Related to the Old Testament,* pages 573–576. A translation of the greater part of "Enki and the World Order," can now be found in *The Sumerians* (pages 171–183)—an edition of the text was prepared in 1970 by Carlos Benito as part of a dissertation for the Department of Oriental Studies in the University of Pennsylvania. The "anthropological" myth cataloguing the list of *me* treated on pages 99–103, has been edited by Gertrud Farber Flügge and published as *No. 10* of *Studia Pohl* (Rome: Biblical Institute Press, 1973). Note also that the most recent summation of the Sumerian cosmogenic and cosmological views will be found in Chapter 2 of my *From the Poetry of Sumer* (Berkeley: University of California Press, 1979).

    Chapter 14. The "Enki-Ninmah" creation myth treated on pages 108–110 has now been edited with the help of several new duplicating fragments by Carlos Benito in the dissertation noted above—unfortunately a good deal of the myth, especially its denouement, remains obscure. There were mythological versions of the creation of man other than that depicted in the "Enki-Ninmah" myth. Thus to judge from the Flood poem (see especially page 151), all four great gods of Sumer—An, Enlil, Enki, Ninhursag—seem to have participated in the creation of man. Also to be noted is Thorkild Jacobsen's inference (see his *Toward the Image of Tammuz* [Cambridge, Mass.: Harvard University Press, 1970], pages 111–114) that there was a version of the creation of man according to which the earth produced mankind in primeval days, so that the first men grew up from the earth like plants, and it was Enlil who broke through the hard earth with his especially created pickaxe in order that the first beings who developed below could "sprout forth." His evidence is based on the first twenty-four lines of the poem which describe the fashioning and dedication of the pickaxe (see page 83 for the first five lines), a passage that is full of ambiguities and obscurities that have still not been satisfactorily cleared up.

Chapter 15. For a somewhat fuller translation of the "Job" poem, see now *The Sumerians*, pages 125–129—a definitive edition of the document is now in the process of preparation by my former student Jacob Klein, now an Associate Professor of Assyriology at Israel's Bar Illan University.

Chapter 16. The beginning of the last proverb on page 123, "A restless woman" should be corrected to "A thriftless woman."

Chapter 17. No changes.

Chapter 18. For a detailed sketch of the contents of one of the seven disputations mentioned on page 137, see now Chapter 38. "The Wooing of Inanna" poem treated on pages 140–142, is the fuller version of the second of the two related compositions whose contents were sketched in Chapter 33, page 308, in connection with the Sacred Marriage Rite.

Chapter 19. For a new fragmentary duplicate of the Dilmun myth "Enki and Ninhursag," see the Introduction to Gadd and Kramer, *Ur Excavations Texts* VI (1963): *sub* No. 1 (London: The British Museum and Philadelphia: The University Museum).

Chapter 20. Although it is still true that no duplicates of the Flood tablet treated in this chapter have been uncovered to date, there are several new texts available that speak of the Flood and its destructive aftermath in their introductory lines, so that it seems not unjustified to surmise that the poets of Sumer knew of an actual catastrophic deluge that had done immense damage to the land and its people—see now "My Reflections on the Mesopotamian Flood" in *Expedition*, vol. 9 (Philadelphia: University Museum, 1967).

Chapter 21. The text of the myth "Inanna's Descent to the Nether World" is now available almost in its entirety—only some twenty lines toward the end of the composition are still fragmentary; see now my "Sumerian Literature and the British Museum" in *Proceedings of the American Philosophical Society*, vol. 124 (1980): 299–310. The end of the myth as sketched on page 322 is based on this most recent study. For the translation of the myth as a whole, see *The Sacred Marriage Rite* (Bloomington and London: Indiana University Press, 1969), pages 108–121, but note that the end of the myth as sketched on pages 119–121 is no longer valid.

Chapter 22. The end of "Gilgamesh and the Land of the Living" which was missing at the time this chapter was published is now available; for a new translation of the composition see now *The Sumerians*, pages 190–197 (cf. also note 16 of "Sumerian Epic Literature," the paper cited in the comment to Chapter 5). A definitive edition of the myth "The Deeds and Exploits of the God Ninurta" is due to be published by the eminent Dutch cuneiformist J. J. A. Van Dijk.

Chapter 23. The statement on page 195 that the text of "Gilgamesh, Enkidu and the Nether World" is still unpublished is no longer true, cf. the comment to Chapter 13.

Chapter 24. For a brief revised sketch of "Enmerkar and Ensukushsiranna (note that the second of the two names can also be read Ensuhkeshdanna), the epic treated on pages 204–207, see page 825 of "Sumerian Epic Literature" (Rome: Accademia Nazionale dei Lincei, 1970) (cited in the comment to Chapter 5). A definitive edition of the text has just been published by my former student, Adele Berlin, in *Occasional Publications of the Babylonian Fund*, vol. 2 (Philadelphia: University Museum, 1979). The epic tale "Lugalbanda and Mt. Hurum" should have been entitled "Lugalbanda, the Wandering Hero" (see "Sumerian Epic Literature," page 829; there is no Mt. Hurum in the tale).

Chapter 25. For the two love songs treated in this chapter see also pages 317–318. Note that the statement "The only other Sumerian love song" which implies that there were only two available love songs is incorrect; for a list of all those now available, see my "The Dumuzi-Inanna Sacred Marriage Rite" in the *Actes de la XVIIᵉ rencontre assyriologique internationale* (1969), pages 135–141.

Chapter 26. Since the publication of this chapter quite a number of new literary catalogues have been identified and published; for bibliographical details see note 3 of my "Three Old Babylonian *balag-* Catalogues from the British Museum," to appear in the forthcoming *Diakonoff Festschrift*.

Chapter 27. A tablet in Oxford's Ashmolean Museum, copied by Oliver Gurney, has now provided us with a complete text of the

"Golden Age" passage cited on pages 222–223. See my "The Babel of Tongues: A Sumerian Version" in the *Journal of the American Oriental Society*, vol. 88 (1968): 108–111. It reads as follows:

Once upon a time, there was no snake, there was no scorpion,
There was no hyena, there was no lion,
There was no wild dog, no wolf,
There was no fear, no terror,
Man had no rival.
In those days, the land of Shubur-Hamazi,
Sumer of clashing tongues, the great land of the *me* of
    princeship,
Uri, the land having all that is appropriate,
The land Martu, resting in security,
The whole universe, the people well-cared for,
To Enlil in one tongue gave speech.
(But) then, the lord defiant, the prince defiant, the king defiant,
Enki, the lord defiant, the prince defiant, the king defiant,
The lord defiant, the prince defiant, the king defiant,
Enki, the lord of abundance, whose commands are
    trustworthy,
The lord of wisdom who scans the land,
The leader of the gods,
The lord of Eridu, endowed with wisdom,
Changed the speech in their mouths, put contention into it,
Into the speech of man that had been one.

Epilogue. A translation of the complete text of the "Curse of Agade: The Ekur Avenged," can be found in *Ancient Near Eastern Texts Relating to the Old Testament*, Third ed., pages 646–651.

GLOSSARY

Abisimti: Mother of Shu-Sin, king of Ur.

Abu: One of the deities fashioned by Ninhursag to heal one of Enki's sick organs.

Abzu: Sea, abyss; home of the water-god Enki.

Adab: An important city of Sumer, midway between Lagash and Nippur.

Agade: A city in northern Sumer founded by Sargon the Great, who made it his capital. For a short time it was the richest and most powerful city in the ancient world. According to Sumerian tradition, it was destroyed and laid waste during the reign of Naram-Sin, Sargon's grandson, and remained a city forever cursed. Following the reign of Sargon and his dynasty, the land known as Sumer was called "Sumer and Akkad"—Akkad being a variant pronunciation of Agade.

Agga: A ruler of the first dynasty of Kish, one the main protagonists in the epic "Gilgamesh and Agga."

Akkad: See Agade.

Akkadians: The Semitic inhabitants of Mesopotamia. The word is derived from the place name Akkad (so written in the Book of Genesis). Akkadian is the name of the Semitic language used by the people, the two main dialects of which are Assyrian and Babylonian.

ala: A musical instrument, probably the tambourine.

algar: A musical instrument, probably a type of lyre.

allari: A type of love song.

Ama-ushumgalanna: A byname of Dumuzi; literally it seems to mean "Mother-Dragon of Heaven." At times the name is written as Ushumgalanna.

An: The Sumerian heaven-god; the word means "heaven." In Akkadian the name is Anu.

Anshan: An Elamite city-state in southwestern Iran.

Antasurra: A district north of Lagash.

Anu: See An.

Anunna (also Anunnaki): A general name for a group of gods who were probably originally "heaven-gods"; some of them, however, must have fallen from grace and were carried off to the Nether World.

Anzu: Anzu is now known to be the real pronunciation of the name of the mythological bird known in the earlier literature as the Imdugud bird.

Arali: One of the names of the Nether World.

Aratta: An as yet unidentified city in Iran, noted for its wealth of metal and stone; it may have been conquered and subjugated by Erech early in the third millennium B.C.

Asag: A vicious demon whom the god Ninurta slew in the *kur*. See *kur*.

Ashnan: Grain-goddess, sister of Lahar. See Lahar.

Ashurbanipal: The last great king of Assyria who reigned during the seventh century B.C. His library at Nineveh was uncovered in the middle of the nineteenth century and most of its tablet collection is now in the British Museum.

Azimua (also Ninazimua): A deity fashioned by Ninhursag to heal Enki's ailing arm.

Babylon: A city in northern Sumer which became the capital of the land early in the second millennium B.C.—hence the name Babylonia for the land first known as Sumer and later as Sumer and Akkad.

Badtibira: A city in southern Sumer, the legendary seat of one of Sumer's antediluvian dynasties. Its tutelary deity was Dumuzi whose temple was known as Emush and Emushkalamma.

balbale: A type of Sumerian song sometimes characterized by a dialogue between deities.

ban: A measure of capacity, about a gallon and a fifth.

Bilalama: A ruler of Eshnunna who may be the promulgator of the Law Code excavated at Harmal near Baghdad—Eshnuna is a city-state in northern Sumer that flourished in the first half of the second millennium B.C.

Blackheads (or Blackheaded people): An epithet of the Sumerians; its origin is obscure.

Dilmun: A still unidentified land, conceived by the Sumerians as a kind of Paradise.

Dimgal-abzu: A temple near the southern boundary of Lagash.

dubban-reeds: Hedge-sized reeds.

Duku: Creation chamber of the gods.

Dumuzi (Biblical Tammuz): The shepherd-king of Erech who came to be known as the first ruler to wed the goddess Inanna in a Sacred Marriage ceremony.

Dynasty of Akkad: Dynasty founded by Sargon the Great.

Eanna: Inanna's temple in Erech; its literal meaning is "House of An."

Eannatum: A ruler of Lagash who for a brief period reigned over all Sumer.

edubba: "Tablet House," the designation of the Sumerian school or academy.

Ekishnugal: The temple of the moon-god Nanna-Sin at Ur.

Ekur: Enlil's temple in Nippur, Sumer's holiest shrine; its literal meaning is "Mountain House."

Elam: The land to the east of Sumer and often in conflict with it.

Emesh: "Summer," one of the protagonists in the "Disputation Between Summer and Winter."

Emush (also Emushkalamma): Dumuzi's temple in Badtibira. See Badtibira.

en: "High priest" or "high priestess." The *en* was the spiritual head of the temple; his residence was the *gipar*, the shrine where the Sacred Marriage Rite may have taken place.

Enakalli: An ensi of Umma who made a treaty with Eannatum of Lagash. See *ensi*.

Enannatum: The brother of Eannatum.

Enheduanna: The daughter of Sargon the Great whom he appointed to be high priestess of Ur and who may have composed a number of literary works.

Eninnu: Ningirsu's temple in Lagash, rebuilt and restored by Gudea.

Enki: The god of wisdom and of the sea and rivers, his main seat of worship was the "Sea-House" in Eridu.

Enkidu: The faithful servant and companion of the hero Gilgamesh.

Enkimdu: The "farmer," rival of the "shepherd" Dumuzi for the hand of Inanna.

Enlil: The leading deity of the Sumerian pantheon; the literal meaning of the name is "Lord Air"; his main seat of worship was Nippur with its temple the Ekur.

Enmebaraggesi: One of the last rulers of the first dynasty of Kish and the father of Agga.

Enmerkar: One of the heroic rulers of the first dynasty of Kish, celebrated for his conquest of Aratta.

ensi: The Sumerian title for the ruler of a city, who, at times, was as powerful as the king. In Akkadian this word became *ishakku*.

Enshag: The tutelary deity of Dilmun.

Ensuhkeshdanna (or Ensukushsiranna): A Lord of Aratta who challenged Enmerkar for first place in Inanna's affections, and lost.

Entemena: Son of Enannatum and nephew of Eannatum.

Enten: "Winter," one of the protagonists in the "Disputation Between Summer and Winter."

Erech(or Uruk): One of Sumer's leading cities; the capital of Sumer during its Heroic Age.

Ereshkigal: "Queen of the Great Below"; the goddess in charge of the Nether World.

Eridu: The city in southern Sumer whose tutelary deity was Enki.

eshesh: A religious feast about which little is known at present.

gakkul: A special kind of lettuce.

galla: The cruel little demons of the Nether World.

gamgam: A bird as yet unidentified.

Gana-ugigga: Scene of a battle between Enannatum and Ur-Lumma.

ganun: The sleeping chamber of the sun-god Utu.

Ganzir: A byname of the Nether World.

Geshtinanna: Dumuzi's self-sacrificing sister.

giguna: A grove-like shrine found in Sumer's more important temples. It is also the name of Inanna's temple at Zabalam.

Gilgamesh: A ruler of the first dynasty of Erech who came to be celebrated as Sumer's outstanding heroic figure.

gipar: The part of the temple in which the *en* had his or her residence.

gir: Perhaps "courier"; his death was mourned by an unnamed "maid."

Girsu: One of the quarters of the city-state of Lagash.

gishban; gishban-sikin: Types of garments.

Gudea: The devout *ensi* of Lagash who rebuilt the Eninnu. See *ensi*.

Guedinna: The northernmost territory belonging to Lagash which the Ummaites tried to make their own.

gug: An unidentified animal.

Gugalanna: "Great Bull of Heaven," the husband of Ereshkigal.

gur: A measure of capacity equaling 144 *sila*. See *sila*.

Guti (or Gutians): A barbarous mountain people to the east that overwhelmed Sumer toward the end of the second millennium B.C.

Haiia: Husband of he goddess Nidaba.

Hamazi: See Shubur-Hamazi.

Hammurabi: The ruler of Babylon, famous for his Law Code.

Harmal: A relatively small site east of Baghdad which yielded many tablets, including the Eshnunna Law Code.

hashur: A type of cedar tree.

Hendursag: The vizier of the goddess Nanshe. See Nanshe.

huluppu: An as yet unidentified tree.

Hursag: "Highland," the mountainous region to the east of Sumer, so named by the god Ninurta.

Huwawa: The monster who guarded the cedars of the Land of the Living; he was slain by Gilgamesh and Enkidu.

Ibbi-Sin: The last ruler of the Third Dynasty of Ur, who was carried off into captivity by the Elamites.

Idal: A misread name to be eliminated.

Iddin-Dagan: The third ruler of the Dynasty of Isin, which followed the Third Dynasty of Ur; one of the documents from his reign is quite significant for the Sacred Marriage Rite.

Idnun: A canal in southern Sumer.

Il: An *ensi* of Umma.

ildag: An as yet unidentified tree.

Imdugud: See Anzu.

Inanna: The goddess of love, fertility, and procreation who was the tutelary deity of Erech and the principal protagonist of the Sacred Marriage Rite; literally her name means "Queen of Heaven." Her Semitic name was Ishtar.

irina: An as yet unidentified tree.

ishakku: See *ensi*.

ishib: A purification priest.

Ishkur: The deity in charge of rain.

Ishme-Dagan: Son of Iddin-Dagan, who was the savior of Nippur.

Ishtar: See Inanna.

Isimud: Enki's vizier.

Isin: The city that became the capital of Sumer after the fall of the Third Dynasty of Ur.

itirda: A kind of milk.

Kabta: A minor deity in charge of the brickmold.

kalatur (or *kalaturru*): A sexless devotee of the goddess Inanna; a mythological being created by Enki to help revive Inanna in the Nether World.

Karu: A measure of capacity equaling 3600 *sila*. See *sila*.

Kesh: A twin city of Adab.

Ki: Mother Earth.

Kish: Sumer's first capital after the Flood.

kisim: A kind of milk.

kiur: Part of a temple and particularly of the Ekur in Nippur.

Kubatum: A *lukur* of Shu-Sin; a necklace presented her by the king; excavated in Erech.

Kuli-Enlil: "Friend of Enlil," an epithet of Dumuzi.

Kullab: Twin city of Erech.

kur: Principal meaning "mountain"; the word also designates the cosmic realm below the earth as well as the Nether World.

kurgarra (or *kurgarru*): A sexless devotee of the goddess Inanna, companion to the *kalatur*. See *kalatur*.

kusu: An epithet of the goddess Ashnan, whose meaning is uncertain.

Lagash: A city in southern Sumer, the first Sumerian city to be excavated to a significant extent.

lahama: A type of sea monster.

Lahar: Cattle goddess, the sister of Ashnan.

Larak: One of Sumer's antediluvian capitals; perhaps near Isin.

Larsa: The principal seat of worship of the sun-god Utu; a capital of Sumer in the early second millennium B.C.

Latarak: See Lulal.

lilis: A kettledrum.

Lilith: A female demon.

Lipit-Ishtar: A ruler of the Isin Dynasty whose Law Code has been recovered in large part.

Lisin: A Sumerian *mater dolorosa*.

Ludingirra: Presumed author of the "Ideal Mother" poem, and of two elegies.

Lugalbanda: One of the heroic kings of the First Dynasty of Erech, who was later deified.

Lugalzaggesi: A king of Umma who defeated Urukagina of Lagash and was later vanquished by Sargon the Great.

lukur: A priestess and devotee of Inanna who may have represented the goddess in the Sacred Marriage Rite.

Lulal: A god of Badtibira, the son of Inanna (the name was misread as Latarak).

lumah: An important priest whose functions are still unknown.

Magan: A country whose location is still uncertain; perhaps Egypt.

magur: A type of boat.

magilum: A word of unknown meaning.

mah: A priest whose functions are unknown.

Marduk: The leading deity of the Babylonian pantheon.

Marhashi: A city-state in western Iran.

mashgur: An as yet unidentified tree.

Mashgula: One of Nidaba's shepherds.

mashmash: An exorcist.

me: The divine rules and regulations that keep the universe operating as planned.

melam: Divine awe-inspiring radiance.

Meluhha: A country whose location is still unknown; perhaps Ethiopia.

mes: An as yet unidentified tree.

Mesilim: A ruler of Kish who arbitrated a dispute between Lagash and Umma.

Meslamtaea: Another name for Nergal. See *Nergal*.

mikku: An unidentified object that fell into the Nether World to the dismay of Gilgamesh.

mina: A measure of weight, roughly equal to a pound.

Mushdamma: A minor deity in charge of building and construction.

mushhush: A mythological serpent or dragon.

Namhani: A ruler of Lagash defeated by Ur-Nammu.

Namennaduma: The vizier of Enmerkar.

Nammu: The goddess in charge of the primeval sea; the mother of Enki.

Namtar: "Fate" or "Death"; a Nether World demon.

Nanibgal: An epithet of Nidaba of uncertain meaning.

Nanna: The Sumerian name of the moon-god whose Semitic name is Sin; he was tutelary deity of Ur and the father of Inanna. Nanna was also the name of Ludingirra's father. See *Ludingirra.*

Naram-Sin: Grandson of Sargon the Great, the defiler of the Ekur.

Nanshe (or Nazi): A goddess of Lagash in charge of moral conduct.

Nawirtum: Ludingirra's wife.

Nergal: King of the Nether World.

Neti: Chief gatekeeper of the Nether World.

Nidaba: The goddess in charge of writing and literature.

Ninazimua: See Azimua.

Ninazu: A Nether World deity.

Nineagal: "Queen of the Palace," an epithet often applied to Inanna.

Ningal: The spouse of the moon-god Nanna and the mother of Inanna.

Ningirsu: The son of Enlil and tutelary deity of Lagash.

Ninhursag: "Queen of the Highland"; the Sumerian mother-goddess also known as Nintu, "The Birth-giving Queen," and Ninmah, "The Noble Queen."

Ninisinna: The tutelary deity of Isin, one of Sumer's "weeping goddesses."

Ninkasi: Sumerian goddess of strong drink, fashioned by Ninhursag to heal Enki's ailing mouth.

Ninkilim: Deity in charge of field mice and vermin.

Ninkurra: Dilmun deity engendered by Enki.

Ninlil: Faithful spouse of Enlil. See Nunbirdu.

Ninmah: See Ninhursag.

Ninmu: Dilmun deity engendered by Enki.

Ninmug: Dilmun deity engendered by Enki.

Ninshubur: Inanna's faithful vizier.

Ninsun: The spouse of the deified Lugalbanda, and divine mother of the rulers of the Third Dynasty of Ur.

Ninti: "Lady of the Rib," or "Lady Who Makes Live"; the goddess fashioned by Ninhursag to heal Enki's ailing rib.

Nintu: See Ninhursag.

Nintulla: The goddess fashioned by Ninhursag to heal Enki's ailing jaw.

Ninurta: A son of Enlil in charge of the South Wind; a storm and warrior god also known as the "Farmer of Enlil."

Nippur: Sumer's holiest city, seat of its leading deity, Enlil. Nippur was the home of one of the great academies of Sumer, and most of the literary tablets excavated to date come from its scribal quarter.

Nudimmud: A byname of Enki.

numun (or *shumun*): Rushes carried by the weeping mother searching for her lost son.

Nunnamnir: A byname of Enlil.

Nunbarshegunu: Mother of Ninlil and mother-in-law of Enlil.

Nunbirdu: A canal bounding Nippur on the northwest: scene of the rape of Ninlil.

nunuz-stones: Probably egg-shaped stones.

Nusku: Enlil's faithful vizier.

pala: A queenly garment worn by Inanna.

pukku: An unidentified object which like the *mikku* fell into the Nether World.

Rim-Sin: A ruler of Larsa who put an end to the Dynasty of Isin.

Sagburru: The old crone who outwitted the *mashmash*. See *mashmash*.

sagursag: A devotee of Inanna, probably a castrate.

sanga: A high temple administrator.

Sargon: One of the great rulers of the ancient world; founder of the city of Agade and of the Dynasty of Akkad.

Sataran: A deity who arbitrated complaints.

shabra: A high temple official.

shagan: A type of vessel.

shakkir: An as yet unidentified plant.

Shara: Son of Inanna; tutelary deity of Umma.

sham: An unidentified stone.

Sharur: Ninurta's personified weapon.

Shat-Istar: Ludingirra's idealized mother.

shatammu: An official in the *ensi's* entourage.

shekel: A sixtieth of a *mina*. See *mina*.

shesh: An unidentified type of grain.

sheshgal: "Big Brother"; assistant to the teacher in the *edubba*.

shuba: A semiprecious stone; perhaps also name of highland region in Iran.

Shubur-Hamazi: Lands to the north and northeast of Sumer.

shugurra: A turban-like crown worn by Inanna.

Shukalletuda: The gardener who raped Inanna.

shukur-reeds: Small reeds the size of a lance head.

Shulgi: One of the great kings of the ancient world; a patron of literature and music.

Shulutul: The personal god of the rulers of Lagash.

shumun: See *numun*.

shunumun: Name of a month corresponding roughly to April-May.

Shuruppak: A city in south-central Sumer; home of the Sumerian "Noah."

shushima: A type of reed.

shushua: A type of reed carried by the weeping mother searching for her son.

Shu-Sin: Son of Shulgi; main protagonist in a number of love songs.

sila: A measure of capacity; about one fifth of a gallon.

Sin: The Semitic name of the moon-god Nanna.

Sippar: A city in northern Sumer; the seat of one of Sumer's antediluvian cities.

Subarians: The people that inhabited the land Shubur.

Su-people: An unidentified people who, together with the Elamites, put an end to the Third Dynasty of Ur.

Sumugan: A god in charge of the steppe and its animals.

Tammuz: See Dumuzi.

Third Dynasty of Ur: The dynasty of approximately 2050-1950 B.C., which inspired a Sumerian renaissance.

Tidnum: A Semitic land west of Sumer.

tigi: Sweet songs probably accompanied by a lyre.

ub: A small drum.

Ugarit: A city-state near the Mediterranean coast where tablets written in alphabetic cuneiform were excavated by a French expedition.

Umma: A city-state neighboring Lagash and almost constantly at war with it.

ummia: Sage, savant; head of a Sumerian *edubba*.

Unun: A canal in the vicinity of Erech.

Ur: One of the most important cities of Sumer and three times its capital.

Uredinna: One of Nidaba's shepherds.

Ur-Lumma: An *ensi* of Umma.

Ur-Nammu: Founder of the Third Dynasty of Ur.

Ur-Nanshe: Founder of an ambitious Lagash dynasty.

Ur-Ninurta: The fifth ruler of the Isin dynasty.

Urukagina: A ruler of Lagash; the first social reformer in recorded history.

ururu: A type of chant.

Usaw: God of dusk/twilight.

Ush: An *ishakku* of Umma who violated a treaty between Lagash and Umma.

Ushumgalanna: See Ama-ushumgalanna.

Utanapishtim: The Semitic name of Ziusudra, the Sumerian Flood hero.

Uttu: Goddess of weaving.

Utu: The sun-god who had temples in Larsa and Sippar.

Zabalam: A city immediately north of Umma, where Inanna had a temple.

Zabu: A still unidentified locality in western Iran.

ziggurat: The stage-tower of temples that became a hallmark of Sumerian architecture.

Ziusudra: The Sumerian Flood hero.

APPENDIXES

A CURSE AND A MAP:
NEW GLEANINGS FROM
THE TABLETS OF SUMER

THIS APPENDIX was written largely in the city of Jena, where I spent ten weeks, in the fall of 1955, studying and transliterating the Sumerian literary tablets and fragments in the Hilprecht Sammlung ("Hilprecht Collection") of the Friedrich-Schiller University. These documents, all of which were excavated more than fifty years ago by the University of Pennsylvania (see Introduction), formed part of the private collection of antiquities of Hermann Hilprecht, the first to hold the chair of Clark Research Professor of Assyriology at the University of Pennsylvania—the very chair which I now hold. On Hilprecht's death in 1925, the entire collection was bequeathed to the University of Jena, now officially known as the Friedrich-Schiller University.

The Hilprecht Collection has some 2,500 tablets and fragments, but only 150 of these are inscribed with Sumerian literary works. For fifteen years I had been trying to go to Jena to study these tablets, the existence of which was known from a brief note in one of the German scholarly journals. But first came the Nazis, then the war, and then the "Iron Curtain." With the relaxation of international tensions in 1955, the time seemed ripe for another trial. I was granted permission to work in the Hilprecht Collection for several months, and while there received the fullest cooperation of the Friedrich-Schiller University and its Department of Research. The Assistant Keeper of the Hilprecht Collection, Dr. Inez Bernhardt, who is in charge of the tablets, was most helpful.

Here are some of the more important results of this study:

There are 150 Sumerian literary pieces in the Hilprecht Collection. About one hundred are very small pieces, with only a few broken lines preserved. But the rest are fairly well-preserved tablets, thirteen of which are inscribed with from four to eight columns. It is important to bear in mind, however, that at the present stage of the restoration process of the Sumerian literary works, fragments containing new text, no matter what their size, are more valuable from the scientific point of view than well-preserved tablets with texts already available.

The 150 tablets and fragments represent practically all the known Sumerian literary categories: myths and epic tales, hymns and lamentations, historiographic documents and letters, and wisdom and gnomic compositions, such as proverbs, essays, debates, and "catalogues." Relatively few new compositions are represented. Among the more interesting of the new compositions are a hymn to the god Hendursagga as the vizier of the goddess Nanshe, who supervised man's moral behavior; a love-dialogue between Inanna and Dumuzi; a myth involving the underworld deity Ningishzida and the goddess Ninazimua; an extract of a myth, telling how two brother gods brought down barley to Sumer "which knew no barley" from the mountain where it had been stored by the god Enlil; a pleading letter by one Gudea to his personal deity; and finally two precious "book lists," or catalogues, of the type treated in Chapter 26.

However, the major significance of the Sumerian literary tablets in the Hilprecht Collection lies in the fact that they help to fill innumerable gaps and breaks in compositions already known and pieced together, in large part, in the past two decades from the tablets and fragments found in various museums the world over, particularly in the Istanbul Museum of the Ancient Orient and the University Museum in Philadelphia. The text of almost all these compositions will benefit in some degree. But in the case of several of the documents, the relevant pieces in the Hilprecht Collection are of crucial importance.

One of these important documents is analyzed here to illustrate the significance of the newly studied material. It is a composition of close to 300 lines which may be best titled "The Curse of Agade: The Ekur Avenged." Though more than a score of published and unpublished pieces inscribed with parts of this work had been identified, its real character eluded us, particularly since the second half of the document was still restorable in part only. Because much of its text spoke of the destruction, devastation, and desolation of Agade, it was taken to be a lamentation over the destruction of Agade, although its formal structure differed markedly from such comparable works as "Lamentation over the Destruction of Ur" and "Lamentation over the Destruction of Nippur." The Hilprecht Collection has seven pieces inscribed with parts of this myth, and one of these (H. S. 1514) is a well-preserved four-column tablet inscribed with the last 138 lines. With the help of this additional text, it has become clear that this composition is not a lamentation at all but a historiographic document written in a highly poetic prose. In it a Sumerian writer and sage presents his interpretation of the causes behind a memorable historical event which had proved to be catastrophic for Sumer as a whole, and particularly for the mighty city of Agade.

The century beginning with approximately 2300 B.C.—to use the so-called "low chronology"—witnessed the rise in Mesopotamia of a Semitic conqueror and ruler named Sargon. After vanquishing the Sumerian capital cities of Kish in the north and Erech in the south, Sargon made himself master of practically the entire Near East, including Egypt and Ethiopia. His capital was the city of Agade, in northern Sumer, but its exact location is still uncertain. Under the rule of Sargon and his immediate followers, Agade became the richest and most powerful city in Sumer. Gifts and tribute from all the surrounding lands were brought to it. But less than a century after its phenomenal rise came its precipitate fall. It was attacked and destroyed by the Guti, a barbaric, ruthless horde from the mountains to the east, who then proceeded to ravage Sumer as a whole.

This humiliating and disastrous event must have preyed on the hearts and minds of many thinking Sumerians, and some at least were moved to seek an explanation of the cause behind it. One of those who sought an explanation was the author of our historiographic document. He found what, from his point of view (no doubt most of the Sumerians, and in particular the Nippurites, agreed with him) was the only true answer: Naram-Sin, the fourth ruler of the Agade Dynasty, had sacked Nippur and committed all sorts of desecrating acts against the Ekur, Enlil's great sanctuary. Enlil therefore turned to the Guti and brought them down from their mountainous abode, to destroy Agade and avenge his beloved temple. Moreover, eight of the more important deities of the Sumerian pantheon, in order to soothe the spirit of their ruler Enlil, laid a curse upon Agade that it should forever remain desolate and uninhabited. And this, adds the author at the end of his work, was indeed the case: Agade actually has remained desolate and uninhabited.

Our historiographer begins his work with an introduction contrasting the glory and power of Agade which marked its rise, and the ruin and desolation which engulfed it after its fall. The first several lines of the composition read: "After, with frowning forehead, Enlil had put the people of Kish to death like the Bull of Heaven, and like a lofty ox had crushed the house of Erech into dust; after in due time, Enlil had given to Sargon, the king of Agade, the lordship and kingship from the lands above to the lands below," then (to paraphrase some of the more intelligible passages) did the city of Agade become prosperous and powerful under the tender and constant guidance of its tutelary deity, Inanna. Its buildings were filled with gold, silver, copper, tin, and lapis lazuli; its old men and women gave wise counsel; its young children were full of joy; music and song resounded everywhere; all the surrounding lands lived in peace and security. Naram-Sin, moreover, made glorious its shrines, raised its walls mountain-high, while its gates remained wide open. To it came the nomadic Martu, the people who "know not grain," from the west, bringing choice oxen and sheep; to it came Meluhhaites, "the people of the black land," bringing their exotic ware; to it came the Elamite and Subarean from the east and north carrying loads like "load-carrying asses"; to it came all the princes, chieftains and sheiks of the plain, bringing gifts monthly and on the New Year.

But then came the catastrophe, or as the author puts it: "The gates of Agade, how they lay prostrate; . . . . , the holy Inanna leaves untouched their gifts; the Ulmash (Inanna's temple) is fear-ridden (since) she has gone from the city, left it; like a maid who forsakes her chamber, the holy Inanna has forsaken her Agade shrine; like a warrior with raised weapons she attacked the city in fierce battle, made it turn its breast to the enemy." And so in a very short time, "in not five days, not ten days," lordship and kingship departed from Agade; the gods turned against her, and Agade lay desolate and waste; Naram-Sin sulked by himself, dressed in sackcloth; his chariots and boats lay unused and neglected.

How did this come to be? Our author's version is that Naram-Sin, during the seven years in which his rule was firmly established, had acted contrary to Enlil's word; had permitted his soldiers to attack and ravage the Ekur and its groves; had demolished the buildings of the Ekur with copper axes and hatchets, so that "the house lay prostrate like a dead youth"; indeed, "all the lands lay prostrate." Moreover, at the Gate called "Gate of No Grain-Cutting" he cut grain; "the 'Gate of Peace' he demolished with the pickax"; he desecrated the holy vessels, cut down the Ekur's groves, ground up its gold, silver, and copper vessels into dust; loaded up all the possessions of the destroyed Nippur on boats docked right by Enlil's sanctuary, and carried them off to Agade.

But no sooner had he done this than "counsel left Agade," and "the good sense of Agade turned to folly." Then "Enlil, the raging flood which has no rival, because of his beloved house which has been attacked, what destruction wrought": He lifted his eyes to the mountains and brought down the Guti, "a people which brooks no controls"; "it covered the earth like the locust," so that none could escape its power. Communication, whether by land or sea, became impossible throughout Sumer. "The herald could not proceed on his journey; the sea-rider could not sail his boat . . . . ; brigands dwelt on the roads; the doors of the gates of the land turned to clay; all the surrounding lands were planning evil in their city walls." As a result, dire famine came upon Sumer. "The great fields and meadows produced no grain; the fisheries produced no fish; and the watered gardens produced neither honey nor wine." Because of the famine, prices were inflated sky-high, so that one lamb brought only half a *sila* of oil, or half a *sila* of grain, or half a mina of wool.

With misery, want, death, and desolation thus threatening to overwhelm practically all "mankind fashioned by Enlil," eight of the more important deities of the Sumerian pantheon—namely, Sin, Enki, Inanna, Ninurta, Ishkur, Utu, Nusku and Nidaba—decide that it is high time to soothe Enlil's rage. In a prayer to Enlil they vow that Agade, the city which destroyed Nippur, will itself be destroyed like Nippur. And so these eight deities "turn their faces to the city, pronounce (a curse of) destruction upon Agade":

"City, you who dared assault the Ekur, who (defied) Enlil,
Agade, you who dared assault the Ekur, who (defied) Enlil,
May your groves be heaped up like dust, ...
May your clay (bricks) return to their abyss,
May they become clay (bricks) cursed by Enki,
May your trees return to their forests,
May they become trees cursed by Ninildu.
Your slaughtered oxen—may you slaughter your wives instead,
Your butchered sheep—may you butcher your children instead,
Your poor—may they be forced to drown their precious (?) children, ... ,
Agade, may your palace built with joyful heart, be turned into a depressing ruin . . . . ,
Over the places where your rites and rituals were conducted,
May the fox (who haunts) the ruined mounds, glide his tail . . ,
May your canal-boat towpaths grow nothing but weeds,
May your chariot-roads grow nothing but the 'wailing plant,'
Moreover, on your canal-boat towpaths and landings,
May no human being walk because of the wild-goats, vermin (?), snake, and mountain scorpion,
May your plains where grew the heart-soothing plants,
Grow nothing but the 'reed of tears,'
Agade, instead of your sweet-flowing water, may bitter water flow,

    Who says 'I would dwell in that city' will not find a good
      dwelling place,
    Who says 'I would lie down in Agade' will not find a good
      sleeping place."

And, the historian concludes, that is exactly what happened:

    Its canal-boat towpaths grew nothing but weeds,
    Its chariot-roads grew nothing but the 'wailing plant,'
    Moreover, on its canal-boat towpaths and landings
    No human being walks because of the wild-goats, vermin (?),
      snake, and mountain-scorpion,
    The plains where grew the heart-soothing plants, grew nothing
      but the 'reed of tears,'
    Agade, instead of its sweet-flowing water, there flowed bitter
      water,
    Who said 'I would dwell in that city' found not a good dwelling
      place,
    Who said 'I would lie down in Agade' found not a good sleeping
      place.

Probably the most important document in the Hilprecht Collection is not a Sumerian literary work at all, but a map—by all odds the oldest known city map in history. Inscribed in a fairly well-preserved clay-tablet, now 21 by 18 centimeters in size, it consists of a plan of Nippur, the ancient cultural center of Sumer, showing several of its more important temples and buildings, its "Central Park," its rivers and canals, and particularly its walls and gates. It gives more than a score of detailed measurements, which, after due checking, show that the map was drawn carefully to scale. In short, though this particular cartographer lived perhaps about 1500 B.C.—that is, some 3,500 years ago—he drew up the plan with the care and accuracy required of his modern counterpart.

The writing on the map, which includes primarily the names of buildings, rivers, and gates, is a mixture of Sumerian and Akkadian. In most cases the names are still written with their early Sumerian ideographs, although at the time the map was prepared, Sumerian had long been a "dead" language. Only a few of the words are written in Akkadian, the language of the Semitic people who conquered the Sumerians and made them-

selves the masters in the land in the first quarter of the second
millennium B.C.

The map was oriented not due north-south, but more or less
at a 45-degree angle, thus:

In the center is the name of the city (No. 1), written with
its ancient Sumerian ideograph *EN-LIL-KI,* "the place of Enlil"
—that is, the city where dwelt the air-god Enlil, the leading deity
of the Sumerian pantheon.

The buildings shown on the map are the *Ekur* (No. 2),
"Mountain House," Sumer's most renowned temple; the *Kiur*
(No. 3), a temple adjacent to the *Ekur* which seems to have
played an important role in connection with the Sumerian beliefs
concerning the nether world; the *Anniginna* (No. 4), an unknown enclosure of some sort (the reading of the name itself is
uncertain); and far out on the outskirts of the city, the *Eshmah*
(No. 6), "Lofty Shrine." In the corner formed by the Southeast
and Southwest Walls is Nippur's "Central Park" (No. 5), the
Kirishauru, which means literally "Park of the Center of the
City."

Forming the southwest boundary of the city is the Euphrates
River (No. 7), written in its ancient Sumerian form, *Buranun.*
On the northwest, the city was bounded by the *Nunbirdu* Canal
(No. 8), where, according to the ancient Sumerian myth of the
birth of the moon-god (see Chapter 13), the god Enlil first saw
his future spouse bathing and fell instantly in love with her.
Right through the center of the city flows the *Idshauru* (No. 9),
literally "Midcity Canal," now known as the *Shatt-en-Nil.*

But it is the walls and gates to which the ancient mapmaker

pays particular attention, which makes it seem not improbable that the plan was prepared in connection with the defense of the city against an expected attack. The Southwest Wall is shown breached by three gates: the *Kagal Musukkatim* (No. 10), "Gate of the Sexually Impure" (the reading and meaning of this name were suggested to me verbally by Adam Falkenstein); the *Kagal Mah* (No. 11), "Lofty Gate"; and the *Kagal Gula* (No. 12), "Great Gate."

The Southeast Wall, too, is breached by three gates: the *Kagal Nanna* (No. 13), "Nanna Gate" (Nanna is the Sumerian moon-god); *Kagal Uruk* (No. 14), "Erech Gate" (the Biblical Erech, a city to the southeast of Nippur); and *Kagal Igibiurishe* (No. 15), "Ur-facing Gate" (Ur is the Biblical Ur of the Chaldees). The two last-named gates "gave away," in a sense, the orientation of the map, since Erech and Ur were cities located southeast of Nippur.

The Northwest Wall is breached by only one gate, the *Kagal Nergal* (No. 16), "Nergal Gate." Nergal is the god who was king of the nether world and husband of the goddess Ereshkigal, who plays an important role in the myth "Inanna's Descent to the Nether World" (see Chapter 21).

Finally, there is a moat running parallel to the Northwest Wall (No. 17), and another running parallel to the Southeast Wall (No. 18). Both are labeled *Hiritum*, the Akkadian (not Sumerian) word meaning "moat," by the ancient cartographer.

One of the most interesting features of this map is the detail of the measurements, for, as my assistant, Dr. Edmund Gordon, informed me after careful study, most of them are actually drawn to scale. The measure used was in all probability the Sumerian *gar*, although this is never actually written on the map. The *gar* was composed of 12 cubits and measured approximately 20 feet. Thus the width of the Anniginna (No. 4) measures 30 (written as three "tens") *gar*—that is, about 600 feet. Or, to take the Midcity Canal (No. 9), its width is given as 4 (three units on top and one unit at the bottom)—that is, about 80 feet, which corresponds to the width of the present Shatt-en-Nil. The distance between the *Kagal Musukkatim* (No. 10) and the *Kagal Mah* (No. 11) is given as 16 (*gar*)—that is, about 320 feet,

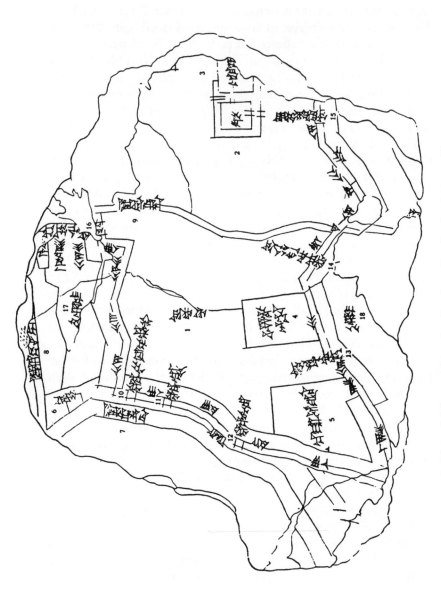

28. Map of Nippur. Copy by Dr. Inez Bernhardt, Assistant-Keeper of the Hilprecht Collection, Friedrich-Schiller University, Jena.

while that between the *Kagal Mah* (No. 11) and the *Kagal Gula* (No. 12), which is practically three times as great, is given correctly as 47 (*gar*), or about 940 feet.

The lay reader can read and test the measurements for himself, if he bears in mind that a vertical wedge may stand for either 60 or 1, and a cornerlike wedge for 10. The two measurements that are off scale to a considerable extent are the 7½ (that is, 7,30 = 7 + 30/60) at the lower right corner of "Central Park" (No. 5); and the 24½ (that is, 24,30 = 24 + 30/60) of the third section of the Northwest Wall. In the latter case it is not improbable that the scribe inadvertently omitted a cornerlike wedge at the beginning, and that the number should have read 34½, which would make it to scale.

The tablet on which this map is inscribed was excavated at Nippur in the fall of 1899 by the University of Pennsylvania. It was found in a terracotta jar, together with a score of other inscribed pieces, which ranged in date from about 2300 to about 600 B.C. This jar, to judge from its contents, was, as the excavators described it, a veritable "little museum." In 1903, Hermann Hilprecht published a very small photograph of the tablet in his *Explorations in Bible Lands* (page 518). But this photograph was largely illegible and practically useless for the translation and interpretation of the document (several scholars have tried their hand at it). Since then the tablet has lain in the Hilprecht Collection uncopied and unpublished all these years. Now at last it has been carefully and painstakingly copied by Dr. Inez Bernhardt, under my guidance, and the resulting study will appear under joint authorship in the *Wissenschaftliche Zeitschrift* of the Friedrich-Schiller University.

Appendix B

THE ORIGIN AND DEVELOPMENT
OF THE CUNEIFORM SYSTEM
OF WRITING AND OTHER
COMMENTS ON THE ILLUSTRATIONS

(*Numbers of halftone plates are in italics*)

THE ORIGIN AND DEVELOPMENT OF THE
CUNEIFORM SYSTEM OF WRITING.

The cuneiform system of writing was probably originated by the Sumerians. The oldest inscriptions unearthed to date—more than one thousand tablets and fragments from about 3000 B.C.—are in all likelihood written in the Sumerian language. Whether it was the Sumerians who invented the script or not, it was certainly they who, in the third millennium B.C., fashioned it into an effective writing tool. Its practical value was gradually recognized by the surrounding peoples, who borrowed it from the Sumerians and adapted it to their own languages. By the second millennium B.C., it was current throughout the Near East.

The cuneiform script began as pictographic writing. Each sign was a picture of one or more concrete objects and represented a word whose meaning was identical with, or closely related to, the object pictured. The defects of a system of this type are twofold: the complicated form of the signs and the fact that the great number of signs required render it too unwieldly for practical use. The Sumerian scribes overcame the first difficulty by gradually simplifying and conventionalizing the form of the signs until their pictographic originals were no longer apparent. As for the second difficulty, they reduced the number of signs and kept them within limits by resorting to various helpful devices. The most significant device was substituting phonetic for ideographic values. The accompanying table was prepared to illustrate this development. It proceeds from top to bottom:

No. 1 is the picture of a star. It represents primarily the Sumerian word *an*, "heaven." The same sign is used to represent the word *dingir*, "god."

No. 2 represents the word *ki*, "earth." It is obviously intended to be a picture of the earth, although the interpretation of the sign is still uncertain.

No. 3 is probably a stylized picture of the upper part of a man's body. It represents the word *lu*, "man."

No. 4 is a picture of the pudendum. It represents the word *sal*, "pudendum." The same sign is used to represent the word *munus*, "woman."

No. 5 is the picture of a mountain. It represents the word *kur*, whose primary meaning is "mountain."

No. 6 illustrates the ingenious device developed early by the inventors of the Sumerian system of writing whereby they were enabled to represent pictorially words for which the ordinary pictographic representation entailed a certain amount of difficulty. The sign for the word *geme*, "slave-girl," is actually a combination of two signs—that for *munus*, "woman," and that for *kur*, "mountain" (signs 4 and 5 on our table). Literally, therefore, this compound sign expresses the idea "mountain-woman." But since the Sumerians obtained their slave-girls largely from the mountainous regions about them, this compound sign adequately represented the Sumerian word for "slave-girl," *geme*.

No. 7 is the picture of a head. It represents the Sumerian word *sag*, "head."

No. 8 is also the picture of a head. The vertical strokes underline the particular part of the head which is intended—that is, the mouth. The sign therefore represents the Sumerian word *ka*, "mouth." The same sign represents the word *dug*, "to speak."

No. 9 is probably the picture of a bowl used primarily as a food container. It represents the word *ninda*, "food."

No. 10 is a compound sign consisting of the signs for mouth and food (Nos. 8 and 9 on our table). It represents the word *ku*, "to eat."

No. 11 is a picture of a water stream. It represents the word *a*, "water." This sign furnishes an excellent illustration of the process by which the Sumerian script gradually lost its unwieldy pictographic character and became a phonetic system of writing. Though the Sumerian word *a* represented by sign No. 11 was used primarily for "water," it also had the meaning "in." This word "in" is a word denoting relationship and stands for a concept which is difficult to express pictographically. To the originators of the Sumerian script came the ingenious idea that, instead of trying to invent a complicated picture-sign to represent the word "in," they could use the sign for *a*, "water," since the words sounded exactly alike. The early Sumerian scribes came to realize that a sign belonging to a given word could be used for another word with an altogether unrelated meaning, if the *sound* of the two words were identical. With the gradual spreading of this practice, the Sumerian script lost its pictographic character and tended more and more to become a purely phonetic script.

No. 12 is a combination of the signs for "mouth" and "water" (Nos. 8 and 11). It represents the word *nag*, "to drink."

No. 13 is a picture of the lower part of the leg and foot in a walking position. It represents the word *du*, "to go," and also the word *gub*, "to stand."

No. 14 is a picture of a bird. It represents the word *mushen*, "bird."

No. 15 is a picture of a fish. It represents the word *ha*, "fish." This sign furnishes another example of the phonetic development of the Sumerian script. The Sumerian word *ha* means not only "fish" but also "may"—that is, the Sumerians had two words *ha*, which were identical in pronunciation but quite unrelated in meaning. And so, early in the development of the script, the Sumerian scribes began to use the sign for *ha*, "fish," to represent also the phonetically sounded *ha*, "may."

No. 16 is a picture of the head and horns of an ox. It represents the word *gud*, "ox."

No. 17 is a picture of the head of a cow. It represents the word *ab*, "cow."

No. 18 is the picture of an ear of barley. It represents the word *she*, "barley."

The signs in the first column are from the earliest known period in the development of Sumerian writing. Not long after the invention of the pictographic script, the Sumerian scribes found it convenient to turn the tablet in such a way that the pictographs lay on their backs. As the writing developed, this practice became standard, and the signs were regularly turned 90 degrees. The second column in the table gives the pictographic signs in this turned position. The next two columns represent the "archaic" script current from approximately 2500 to 2350 B.C.: column III shows the wedgelike signs written on clay, while column IV shows the linear form of the signs as inscribed upon stone or metal. Columns V and VI show the signs current from about 2350 to 2000 B.C. In column VII the signs resemble those current during the first half of the second millennium B.C., the period in which most of the tablets treated in this book were actually written. The more simplified forms depicted in the last column were the signs used by the royal scribes of Assyria in the first millennium B.C.

COMMENTS ON THE ILLUSTRATIONS

1. In Front of the Temple at Tell Harmal. From left to right: a photographer on the staff of the Iraqi Directorate of Antiquities, Taha Baqir, the excavator of Tell Harmal; Selim Levy, then Assistant Director of the Iraq Museum in Baghdad (now in Israel), and the writer.

Tell Harmal: Temple, Palace, and School (?). Tell Harmal is a small mound six miles due east of Baghdad. The site was probably first settled in the middle of the third millennium B.C., but the most important discoveries made here were from the early part of the second millennium B.C. The most noteworthy building was a temple (right center on the photograph) consisting of an entrance vestibule, courtyard, antecella, and cella, all arranged with communicating doors on a single axis, so that the niche in the cella, on which the statue of the deity probably rested, was visible from the street when all doors were open. Among the other buildings were a palace, smaller temples, and what was perhaps a school building, where a number of "textbooks" were excavated, as well as the Semitic Bilalama law code. The smooth brick walls surrounding parts of the excavation as a kind of façade are modern. They were built to help conserve the building, at least for a reasonable time. Otherwise they would be turned into ruins—by wind, rain, and storm—almost immediately after excavation. Harmal was excavated by the Iraqi, who now have a flourishing, capable, and productive Directorate of Antiquities under the dynamic directorship of Dr. Naji al Asil, a man of archaeological vision. Members of its staff like Taha Baqir, Fuad Safar, and Mohammed Ali have become world-famous excavators. Further details on the Harmal excavations can be found in *Sumer,* vols. 2–6.

2. *In front of the Ziggurat at Aqar Quf.* Aqar Quf is the modern Arabic name of the ancient royal city Dur-Kurigalzu situated some twenty miles west of Baghdad. Here King Kurigalzu (about 1400 B.C.) built a ziggurat, a stage-tower, which in spite of over three thousand years of wind-swept Iraqi weather, still towers more than two hundred feet above the surrounding plain. The site was excavated by the Iraqi Directorate of Antiquities between the years 1942-1946, and quite a number of important discoveries were brought to light; for details, cf. my *Iraqi Excavations During the War Years (Bulletin of the University Museum vol. XIII No. 2)*. The photograph shows standing in front of the ziggurat: Dr. Naji al Asil, the Director of Antiquities (center); to his right is Taha Baqir, the excavator of the site, who was my student in the Oriental Institute of the University of Chicago in the early 1930s; to his left is the writer who spent some six weeks in Iraq in 1946 studying the results of the Iraqi excavations during the war years, as Annual Professor of the American Schools of Oriental Studies. (The other two individuals in the photographs are unidentified members of the staff of the Iraqi Directorate of Antiquities.)

3. *Nippur Scribal Quarter—New Excavations.* Expedition photograph of ruins of houses on Tablet Hill, which was carefully excavated and recorded by the joint Oriental Institute–University Museum expedition to Nippur, under the direction of Donald McCown. About one thousand Sumerian literary pieces, mostly fragments, were unearthed in three excavating seasons between 1948 and 1952.

4. *Schooldays: The Teacher's Blessing.* Obverse of a well-preserved four-column tablet in the University Museum inscribed with an essay on the joys and sorrows of school life. The teacher's "blessing" of the student after he had been showered with gifts by his well-to-do father, begins nine lines from the top of the right-hand column. Below the double line on the left column is the "signature" of the writer of the tablet. It reads "Copy of Nabi-Enlil."

5. *Schooldays: The Teacher's Blessing.* This is the reverse of Tablet 4.

6. *Juvenile Delinquency.* Obverse of a small tablet in the University Museum inscribed with an extract of the document which Ake Sjöberg, my successor as curator of the Tablet Collection of the University Museum, has pieced together from some fifty tablets and fragments. The text inscribed on this obverse corresponds to lines 124-134 of the composition that includes the father's bitter rebuke to his son as one who is concerned only with his material well-being to the total neglect of his humanity.

7. *A Sumerian of about 2500* B.C. A limestone statuette 23 centimeters high, excavated by the University of Pennsylvania in a temple at Khafaje. The person represented was probably an important temple or palace official. The poets who composed the Enlil myths illustrated on plate No. *10* may have looked like him.

8. *Dudu: A Sumerian Scribe of (ca.) 2350* B.C. The Sumerian school owed its origin and importance to the very practical need of training the professional scribes and archivists essential for the economic and administrative development of the land. Here is one of these scribes. He lived in

the city of Lagash and practiced his profession about 2350 B.C. To Ningirsu, Lagash's tutelary deity, he dedicated a statue of himself in a position of prayer. The statue is now in the Iraq Museum in Baghdad. For further details on Dudu, see *Sumer*, vol. 5 (pp. 131–35).

9. A Bearded Priest. Statuette excavated at Khafaje by a University of Pennsylvania Expedition. It is now in the University Museum.

10. Enlil Myth of about 2400 B.C. This clay cylinder is inscribed with an Enlil myth written about 2400 B.C., a period from which very few literary texts have as yet been unearthed. The criterion for dating the document is the script. The signs correspond with those in column III of the table in illustration No. 5. This myth is ample proof that Sumerian literary works were being composed and written as early as the last half of the third millennium B.C. The tablet was copied by George Barton and published in 1918 in his *Miscellaneous Babylonian Inscriptions,* but the text still remains obscure.

11. A "Botany-Zoology Textbook." Reverse of a tablet excavated in 1944 by Taha Baqir, of the Iraqi Directorate of Antiquities, at Tell Harmal on the outskirts of Baghdad. It is inscribed with hundreds of names of trees, reeds, wooden objects, and birds. The names of the birds, more than one hundred of them, are listed in the last three columns from the right. They can be readily recognized as birds by the reader once he knows that they all end in the sign which stands for the Sumerian word *mushen,* "bird." Below the middle of the uninscribed left column of the tablet, the ancient scribe Irra-Imitti, who may or may not have been the original author of the "textbook," signed his name—one of the first author's signatures in the history of writing. In accordance with the religious ideas of the day, he took care to include as fellow writers the goddess Nidaba, her husband Haia, and the goddess Geshtinanna—the three patron deities of the scribal art. The signature reads: "Nidaba, Haia, Geshtin-anna, and Irra-Imitti, the son of Nurum-Lisi, the scribe, wrote it (that is, this tablet)."

12. Enmerkar and the Lord of Aratta: The Istanbul Tablet. Obverse of the twelve-column Nippur tablet in the Istanbul Museum of the Ancient Orient, which was published in 1952 in the University Museum monograph "Enmerkar and the Lord of Aratta: A Sumerian Epic Tale of Iraq and Iran." Most of the "breaks" on this tablet were filled in with the help of nineteen other tablets and fragments in Istanbul and Philadelphia. Note in particular the broken-away lower left corner.

13. War and Peace: The "Standard" from Ur. Depicted on this University Museum photograph are two scenes of the type that may have been present in the minds and hearts of the Erech "Congress" as its members were pondering fateful decisions. One scene shows the Sumerian king in his chariot, triumphant in battle over an enemy whose soldiers are shown either led away as captives or trampled to death under the chargers' merciless hooves. The other scene depicts a rich royal banquet, probably in celebration of the victory. Note in particular the lyre-carrying minstrel in the upper right corner of the top register. He is no doubt one of the illiterate minstrels who were the prototypes of the poets who composed the myths and epic tales treated in the present volume. For details on the "standard" from Ur, and on other epoch-making discoveries, see Leonard Woolley's *Ur Excavations: The Royal Cemetery* (1934).

14. Ur-Nanshe, King of Lagash. This ruler, who lived some 150 years before Urukagina, history's first known social reformer, founded the aggressive Lagash dynasty which, in time, developed an oppressive and deeply resented bureaucracy. Ur-Nanshe is shown in this limestone plaque, now in the Louvre, as a man of peace, surrounded by his children and courtiers. In the upper register he is carrying on his head an earth-filled basket for the initiation of building operations; in the lower, he is sitting and drinking at a feast probably celebrating their completion. For full details on the Lagash excavations—the first successful excavations at a Sumerian site—which have been conducted by French archaeologists intermittently since 1877, see the comprehensive and valuable book *Tello*, by the French archaeologist André Parrot.

15. Stele of the Vultures. War scenes depicting Eannatum, Ur-Nanshe's grandson, leading the Lagashites to battle and victory. Eannatum, who preceded Urukagina by about a century, was the great conquering hero of the Lagash dynasty, which came to an inglorious end when defeated by Lugalzaggisi of Umma. In between and all around the figures, wherever space permits, is inscribed the oldest historiographic document as yet known to man: an inscription recording Eannatum's victory over the Ummaites, and the treaty of peace which he forced upon them. Full details of the stele and its inscription are given in Heuzey and Thureau-Dangin's exemplary work *Restitution matérielle de la Stèle des Vautours.* See also Parrot's *Tello.*

16. Aesopica. Reverse of a tablet in the University Museum inscribed with animal proverbs and fables. This tablet is by far the largest of twenty-nine tablets and fragments utilized by Edmund Gordon for his goundbreaking study "Sumerian Animal Proverbs and Fables: Collection Five," published in the *Journal of Cuneiform Studies,* vol. XII (1958): 1-21 and 43-75. The side illustrated in this photograph is inscribed with Nos. 67-125 of the collection that relate to the wolf and the dog.

17. Ur-Nammu's Law Code: The Laws. Reverse of the Istanbul tablet, originally inscribed with some 22 laws, of which only five can be read with some degree of confidence. In the upper portion of the column on the extreme left are the three laws which seem to show that the *lex-talionis* was not practiced in the days of Ur-Nammu, at the close of the third millennium B.C.

18. Ur-Nammu: The First "Moses." Part of a stele excavated by Leonard Woolley in Ur in 1924 and now in the University Museum. In the middle panel Ur-Nammu is shown twice, standing and pouring a libation to the moon-god Nanna (seated on the right), the tutelary deity of Ur, and to the god's wife Ningal (seated on the left). In the bottom panel Ur-Nammu is shown carrying building implements. He is preceded by a deity in a horned miter, and followed by a servant who is lightening the burden on his shoulder by supporting the heavy tools with his hands. In the upper panel, only the lower half of the standing Ur-Nammu is preserved. The words "Ur-Nammu, king of Ur" can be seen engraved on the lower part of his garment. The stele was studied and restored by Leon Legrain, curator emeritus of the Mesopotamian Section of the University Museum. Details are given in his article "The Stele of the Flying Angels" *Museum Journal,* vol. 18 (1927): 75-98.

19. Man's Oldest Prescriptions. Reverse of the "medical" tablet from Nippur in the University Museum. The two marked-off sections are two prescriptions which read as follows:

(1) *gish-hashhur-babbar* (white pear (?) -tree); *e-ri-na u-gish-nanna* (the root (?) of the "moon"-plant); *u-gaz* (pulverize); *kash-e u-tu* (dissolve in beer); *lu al-nag-nag* (let the man drink); and

(2) *numun-nig-nagar-sar* (the seed of the "carpenter"-plant); *shim-mar-kazi* (gum resin of *markazi*); *u-ha-shu-an-um* (thyme); *u-gaz* (pulverize); *kash-e u-tu* (dissolve in beer); *lu al-nag-nag* (let the man drink).

For details, see *Illustrated London News*, February 26, 1955, pp. 370-71.

20. Inanna and Shukalletuda: The Gardener's Mortal Sin. Reverse of a six-column tablet in the Istanbul Museum of the Ancient Orient. The tablet is inscribed with the myth concerning the rape of the goddess Inanna by the gardener Shukalletuda, and noted for a "blood-plague" motif similar to that of the Biblical exodus story. This myth was unknown until 1946, when I copied the tablet in Istanbul. Now a number of fragments in the University Museum and Istanbul can be identified.

21. Separation of Heaven and Earth. Nippur tablet in the University Museum. The tablet is inscribed with the first part of the poem "Gilgamesh, Enkidu, and the Nether World," which contains the cosmological passage quoted on pages 81-82. It was copied by Edward Chiera and published in 1934 in his *Sumerian Epics and Myths* (No. 21). See also page 353.

22. Cultural Anthropology: List of Me's. Reverse of a six-column tablet in the University Museum inscribed with the myth "Inanna and Enki: The Transfer of the Arts of Civilization from Eridu to Erech." The tablet was copied by Arno Poebel and published in 1914 in his *Historical and Grammatical Texts*. Note the missing upper left corner; this was identified and copied by the writer in the Istanbul Museum of the Ancient Orient, and published in 1944 in his *Sumerian Literary Texts from Nippur* (No. 31).

23/24. Creation of Man. These two photographs illustrate the obverse of the same Nippur tablet in the University Museum before and after "joining." The lower piece was copied and published by Stephen Langdon in 1919 in his *Sumerian Liturgies and Psalms* (No. 14). The upper fragment was copied by Edward Chiera and published in 1934 in his *Sumerian Epics and Myths* (No. 116), without his having recognized that it joined the Langdon piece. The third piece was identified by the writer as belonging to the same tablet and actually "joining" the lower piece.

25. Proverbs: The "Fate" Collection. Nine-column Nippur tablet in the University Museum originally inscribed with 126 proverbs of a collection which includes a group on *namtar*, "fate." Other groups in this collection center about the poor man, the scribe, the singer, the fox, the ass, the ox, the dog, the house.

26. Sumerian Original of the Twelfth Tablet of the Babylonian Epic of Gilgamesh. Reverse of a six-column Nippur tablet in the University Museum originally inscribed with the entire Sumerian epic tale "Gilgamesh, Enkidu, and the Nether World." Its approximately three hundred lines of text can now be restored from some twenty-five tablets and fragments, about half of which are still unpublished (but see Corrigenda and Addenda to Chapter 13).

27. Sacred (?) Cows. A mosaic dairy frieze unearthed by Leonard Woolley at Al-Ubaid near Ur, dating from about the twenty-fifth century B.C., reminiscent of Nidaba's holy cow stalls and sheepfolds mentioned in the poem "Enmerkar and Ensukushsiranna."

28. Map of Nippur. Photograph of original tablet. See Appendix A, pp. 369-379.

29. Perverse Students. Reverse of a tablet in the University Museum inscribed with the concluding section of a dispute between two raucous students, replete with insults and taunts hurled by the protagonists against each other, including some directed against members of their family. For several other compositions of this type that reveal student defiance and contention in the schools of Sumer, see my *The Sumerians,* pp. 222-223.

30. Shulgi, the Ideal King. Fragment of a large tablet in the University Museum inscribed with a self-laudatory Shulgi hymn in which he portrays himself as a combination of sage, soldier, sportsman, diviner, diplomat, patron of the arts, and happy provider of all that is good for Sumer and its people. I first sketched the contents of this myth in considerable detail in 1967, in the *Seventy-Fifth Anniversary Volume* of the *Jewish Quarterly Review,* published under the auspices of Dropsie University in Philadelphia. In 1972, the Italian scholar, G. R. Castellino, who had studied some of the Shulgi texts in the University Museum at my suggestion, published an edition of the composition based on some fifty tablets and fragments in a book entitled *Two Shulgi Hymns* (Instituto de Studi del Vicino Oriente, University of Rome). Since then more than twenty new pieces belonging to the hymn have been identified, and a new edition is in the process of preparation by G. Hayyer, a young Dutch scholar, who has spent some months in the University Museum for the completion of this task. But this Shulgi hymn is only one of more than a dozen whose text is now available wholly or in part, and most of these are being edited and prepared for publication by Jacobe Kline, my former student, who is now an Associate Professor at the Bar-Ilan University in Israel.

31. Lyre from Ur of the Chaldees. Reconstruction of an eleven-stringed lyre excavated by Leonard Woolley in the royal cemetery at Ur, now in the University Museum. This lyre is well-nigh identical with that carried by the court minstrel in the banquet scene depicted on the standard of Ur (see comment to plate 13.)

32. Death and Resurrection. Obverse of a tablet excavated by Leonard Woolley at Ur and now in the British Museum. This tablet provides at long last the concluding episode of the myth "Inanna's Descent to the Nether World," which involves Inanna's Solomon-like decision to have Dumuzi stay in the Nether World half the year and to let his sister Geshtinanna take his place the other half (see p. 325 and the Corrigenda and Addenda to Chapter 21).

33. Right edge of tablet 32.

34. U-a a-u-a. Obverse of the "lullaby" tablet excavated at Nippur and now in the University Museum. The first line reads u-a a-u-a in imitation of the sing-song humming of a mother or nursemaid rocking a child to sleep.